DATE DUE

Demco, Inc. 38-293

AGGRESSIVE OFFENDERS' COGNITION

WILEY SERIES IN
FORENSIC CLINICAL PSYCHOLOGY

Edited by

Clive R. Hollin
Clinical Division of Psychiatry, University of Leicester, UK

and

Mary McMurran
School of Community Health Sciences, Division of Psychiatry,
University of Nottingham, UK

For other titles in this series please visit www.wiley.com/go/fcp

AGGRESSIVE OFFENDERS' COGNITION
Theory, Research, and Practice

Edited by

Theresa A. Gannon
University of Kent, UK

Tony Ward
Victoria University of Wellington, NZ

Anthony R. Beech
University of Birmingham, UK

and

Dawn Fisher
Llanarth Court Hospital & University of Birmingham, UK

John Wiley & Sons, Ltd

Copyright © 2007   John Wiley & Sons Ltd, The Atrium, Southern Gate, Chichester,
West Sussex PO19 8SQ, England

Telephone (+44) 1243 779777

Email (for orders and customer service enquiries): cs-books@wiley.co.uk
Visit our Home Page on www.wiley.com

Other Wiley editorial offices

John Wiley & Sons Inc., 111 River Street, Hoboken, NJ 07030, USA

Jossey-Bass, 989 Market Street, San Francisco, CA 94103-1741, USA

Wiley-VCH Verlag GmbH, Boschstr. 12, D-69469 Weinheim, Germany

John Wiley & Sons Australia Ltd, 42 McDougall Street, Milton, Queensland 4064, Australia

John Wiley & Sons (Asia) Pte Ltd, 2 Clementi Loop #02-01, Jin Xing Distripark, Singapore 129809

John Wiley & Sons Canada Ltd, 6045 Freemont Blvd, Mississauga, ONT, L5R 4J3, Canada

Wiley also publishes its books in a variety of electronic formats. Some content that appears in print
may not be available in electronic books.

Anniversary Logo Design: Richard J. Pacifico

Library of Congress Cataloging-in-Publication Data

Aggressive offenders' cognition : theory, research, and practice / edited by Theresa A. Gannon ... [et al.].
        p. cm. – (Wiley series in forensic clinical psychology)
    Includes bibliographical references and index.
    ISBN 978-0-470-03402-6 (cloth : alk. paper) – ISBN 978-0-470-03401-9
(pbk. : alk. paper)
    1. Cognitive therapy.   2. Emotions and cognition.   3. Sex offenders–Counseling of.   4. Sex
offenders–Mental health.   5. Sex offenders–Psychology.   6. Violent offenders–Counseling
of.   7. Violent offenders–Mental health.   8. Violent offenders–Psychology.   9. Criminal
psychology.   I. Gannon, Theresa A.
    RC489.C63A43 2007
    616.89'142–dc22   2007029097

British Library Cataloguing in Publication Data

A catalogue record for this book is available from the British Library

ISBN 978-0-470-03402-6 (ppc) 978-0-470-03401-9 (pbk)

Typeset in 10/12pt Palatino by Thomson Digital, New Delhi, India
Printed and bound in Great Britain by Antony Rowe, Chippenham, Wiltshire.
This book is printed on acid-free paper responsibly manufactured from sustainable forestry in
which at least two trees are planted for each one used for paper production.

To my parents, Fiona and John Gannon for making
my education possible – TAG.

To my mentors: Bill Marshall and Richard Laws – TW.

For my Mother and Father – AB.

To my family – human, canine and equine – DF.

CONTENTS

ABOUT THE EDITORS

Theresa A. Gannon, DPhil, CPsychol, is Lecturer in Forensic Psychology at the University of Kent, United Kingdom, and also works in a practical setting, one day a week, at the Trevor Gibbens Unit Forensic Psychiatry Services, Kent, UK. Her research interests include the examination of cognition in child sexual abusers, rapists and violent offenders using experimental techniques. She is lead investigator on two funded projects investigating the cognition of offenders. One is investigating the existence of offence-supportive schema in women sexual abusers and the other is the development of a pictorial cognitive test for adolescent offenders. Theresa is also interested in public attitudes towards offending populations and models of offender rehabilitation.

Tony Ward, PhD, DipClinPsyc, is Director of the Clinical Psychology Programme at Victoria University of Wellington, New Zealand. His research interests include the offence process in offenders, cognitive distortions and models of rehabilitation. He has published over 200 research articles, chapters and books. These include *Remaking Relapse Prevention,* with D. R Laws and S. M. Hudson (Sage, 2000), *Sourcebook of Treatment Programs for Sexual Offenders,* with W. L. Marshall, Y. A. Fernandez, and S. M. Hudson (Plenum, 1998), and *Theories of Sexual Offending,* with D. L. L. Polaschek and A. R. Beech (WIley, 2005).

Anthony R. Beech, PhD, CPsychol, is a professor of criminological psychology at the University of Birmingham in the United Kingdom, and a Fellow of the British Psychological Society. Over the last 10 years he has been involved in treatment evaluation and the development of systems to look at treatment need and treatment change in sex offenders. He has written widely on these topics and other related subjects.

Dawn Fisher, PhD, is Head of Psychological Services at Llanarth Court Psychiatric Hospital, Raglan, Wales and is a Senior Research Fellow at the University of Birmingham. Her current research interests are risk assessment, sexual offenders' perspectives on treatment, treatment of adult and adolescent sexual offenders and the use of equine assisted psychotherapy. She has published widely in the area of sexual offending.

CONTRIBUTORS

Bruce D. Bartholow

Assistant Professor, Department of Psychological Sciences, University of Missouri, Columbia, Missouri 65211, USA.

Anthony R. Beech

Professor in Criminological Psychology, The International Centre for Forensic and Family Psychology, School of Psychology, University of Birmingham, Edgbaston, Birmingham, B15 2TT, UK.

Claire A. J. Bloxsom

PhD Candidate, Henry Wellcome Building, School of Psychology, University of Leicester, Leicester, LE1 9HN, UK.

Rachael M. Collie

Clinical Psychologist, Department of Psychology, Victoria University of Wellington, PO Box 600, Wellington 6001, New Zealand.

Christopher Dean

Senior Psychologist, Offending Behaviour Programmes Unit, HM Prison Service, Abell House, John Islip Street, London, SW1P 4LH, UK.

Lynne Eccleston

Lecturer in Forensic Psychology, Department of Criminology, The University of Melbourne, Victoria 2010, Australia.

Dawn Fisher

Head of Psychological Services, Llanarth Court Psychiatric Hospital, Raglan, Wales, NP15 2YD, and Senior Research Fellow at the University of Birmingham, Edgbaston, Birmingham, B15 2TT, UK.

Theresa A. Gannon

Lecturer in Forensic Psychology, Department of Psychology, Keynes College, University of Kent, Canterbury, Kent, CT2 7NP, UK.

Elizabeth Gilchrist

Reader in Forensic Psychology, Department of Psychology, Keynes College, University of Kent, Canterbury, Kent, CT2 7NP, UK.

Clive R. Hollin

Professor of Criminological Psychology, Henry Wellcome Building, School of Psychology, University of Leicester, Leicester, LE1 9HN, UK.

Kirsten Keown

Clinical Psychology and PhD Candidate, Department of Psychology, Victoria University of Wellington, PO Box 600, Wellington 6001, New Zealand.

Calvin M. Langton

Research Fellow, Peaks Unit, Rampton Hospital, Retford, Nottinghamshire, DN22 OPD, UK.

Ruth E. Mann

Director, Offending Behaviour Programmes Unit, HM Prison Service, Room 725, Abell House, John Islip Street, London, SW1P 4LH, UK.

Shadd Maruna

Reader in Criminology, Institute of Criminology and Criminal Justice, School of Law, Queen's University Belfast, 28 University Square, Belfast, BT7 7NN, Northern Ireland.

Mary McMurran

Professor of Personality Disorder Research, Section of Forensic Mental Health, Division of Psychiatry, School of Community Health Sciences, University of Nottingham, Duncan Macmillan House, Porchester Road, Nottingham, NG3 6AA, and Consultant Clinical and Forensic Psychologist, Llanarth Court Hospital, Raglan, NP5 2YD, UK.

Rebecca Milner

Senior Psychologist, Offending Behaviour Programmes Unit, HM Prison Service, Abell House, John Islip Street, London, SW1P 4LH, UK.

Sharlene Murdoch

Clinical Psychologist, Department of Psychology, Victoria University of Wellington, PO Box 600, Wellington 6001, New Zealand.

Shruti Navathe

Psychology PhD Candidate, Department of Psychology, Victoria University of Wellington, PO Box 600, Wellington 6001, New Zealand.

Karen Owen

Forensic Psychologist/Manager, Sex Offender Programs, Corrections Victoria, Department of Justice, 19-21 Argyle Place, South Carlton 3053, Melbourne, Australia.

Emma J. Palmer

Reader in Forensic Psychology, Clinical Division of Psychiatry, Department of Health Sciences, University of Leicester, Leicester General Hospital, Gwendolen Road, Leicester, LE5 4PW, UK.

Marc A. Sestir

PhD Candidate, Department of Psychology, University of North Carolina at Chapel Hill, Chapel Hill, NC27599, USA.

Joanne Thakker

Clinical Psychologist and Senior Lecturer in Psychology, University of Waikato, Hamilton, PO Box 3105, New Zealand.

James Vess

Senior Lecturer in Criminal Justice Psychology, Department of Psychology, Victoria University of Wellington, PO Box 600, Wellington 6001, New Zealand.

Tony Ward

Professor of Psychology, Department of Psychology, Victoria University of Wellington, PO Box 600, Wellington 6001, New Zealand.

Jane Wood

Lecturer in Forensic Psychology, Department of Psychology, Keynes College, University of Kent, Canterbury, Kent CT2 7NP, UK.

SERIES EDITORS' PREFACE

ABOUT THE SERIES

At the time of writing it is clear that we live in a time, certainly in the UK and other parts of Europe, if perhaps less so in areas of the world, when there is renewed enthusiasm for constructive approaches to working with offenders to prevent crime. What do we mean by this statement and what basis do we have for making it?

First, by 'constructive approaches to working with offenders' we mean bringing the use of effective methods and techniques of behaviour change into work with offenders. Indeed, this view might pass as a definition of forensic clinical psychology. Thus, our focus is the application of theory and research in order to develop practice aimed at bringing about a change in the offender's functioning. The word *constructive* is important and can be set against approaches to behaviour change that seek to operate by destructive means. Such destructive approaches are typically based on the principles of deterrence and punishment, seeking to suppress the offender's actions through fear and intimidation. A constructive approach, on the other hand, seeks to bring about changes in an offender's functioning that will produce, say, enhanced possibilities of employment, greater levels of self-control, better family functioning, or increased awareness of the pain of victims.

A constructive approach faces the criticism of being a 'soft' response to the damage caused by offenders, neither inflicting pain and punishment nor delivering retribution. This point raises a serious question for those involved in working with offenders. Should advocates of constructive approaches oppose retribution as a goal of the criminal justice system as a process that is incompatible with treatment and rehabilitation? Alternatively, should constructive work with offenders take place within a system given to retribution? We believe that this issue merits serious debate.

However, to return to our starting point, history shows that criminal justice systems are littered with many attempts at constructive work with offenders, not all of which have been successful. In raising the spectre of success, the second part of our opening sentence now merits attention: that is, 'constructive approaches to working with offenders *to prevent crime*'. In order to achieve the goal of preventing crime, interventions must focus on the right targets for behaviour change.

In addressing this crucial point, Andrews and Bonta (1994) have formulated the *need principle*:

> Many offenders, especially high-risk offenders, have a variety of needs. They need places to live and work and/or they need to stop taking drugs. Some have poor self-esteem, chronic headaches or cavities in their teeth. These are all 'needs'. The need principle draws our attention to the distinction between *criminogenic* and *noncriminogenic* needs. Criminogenic needs are a subset of an offender's risk level. They are dynamic attributes of an offender that, when changed, are associated with changes in the probability of recidivism. Non-criminogenic needs are also dynamic and changeable, but these changes are not necessarily associated with the probability of recidivism. (p.176)

Thus, successful work with offenders can be judged in terms of bringing about change in noncriminogenic need *or* in terms of bringing about change in criminogenic need. While the former is important and, indeed, may be a necessary precursor to offence-focused work, it is changing criminogenic need that, we argue, should be the touchstone in working with offenders. While, as noted above, the history of work with offenders is not replete with success, the research base developed since the early 1990s, particularly the meta-analyses (e.g. Lösel, 1995), now strongly supports the position that effective work with offenders to prevent further offending is possible. The parameters of such evidence-based practice have become well established and widely disseminated under the banner of 'What Works' (McGuire, 1995).

It is important to state that we are not advocating that there is only one approach to preventing crime. Clearly there are many approaches, with different theoretical underpinnings, that can be applied to the task of reducing offending. Nonetheless, a tangible momentum has grown in the wake of the 'What Works' movement as academics, practitioners, and policy makers seek to capitalise on the possibilities that this research raises for preventing crime. The task now facing many service agencies lies in translating the research into effective practice.

Our aim in developing this Series in Forensic Clinical Psychology is to produce texts that review research and draw on clinical expertise to advance effective work with offenders. We are both committed to the ideal of evidence-based practice and we will encourage contributors to the Series to follow this approach. Thus, the books published in the Series will not be practice manuals or 'cook books': they will offer readers authoritative and critical information through which forensic clinical practice can develop. We are both enthusiastic about the contribution to effective practice that this Series can make and look forward to continuing to develop it even further in the years to come.

ABOUT THIS BOOK

Following the dissemination of the 'What Works' research a great deal of work with offenders has adopted a cognitive-behavioural approach to practice. This cognitive-behavioural orientation has become increasingly evident in a range of programmes aimed at a wide diversity of offenders and types of offending

(Hollin & Palmer, 2006). A cognitive-behavioural approach to both theory and practice seeks to understand human behaviour, including offending, in terms of a complex interplay between the three elements of environment, cognition, and action (Bandura, 1977; 1986). Understanding the complexities of the relationships between these three elements relies on a research base that elucidates the individual properties of each of the three individual elements.

In this addition to the Series, Theresa Gannon, Tony Ward, Anthony Beech, and Dawn Fisher have focussed on cognition and, even more precisely, cognition in the context of aggressive offenders. They have gathered and edited a collection of contributions, written by researchers and practitioners, that seeks to review extant knowledge, ask new questions, and speak to practice. The scope of the text is wide, ranging from sex offences against children to domestic abuse; from cognitive distortions to moral cognition; and to the treatment of angry aggression. Given such a range of coverage, this book can justifiably claim to present the 'state of the art' with regard to current knowledge of cognition in aggressive offenders. Further, the emphasis on using the research base to inform a rapidly developing area of forensic practice will be welcomed by all those engaged in working with aggressive offenders.

Clive Hollin
Mary McMurran

REFERENCES

Andrews, D. A., & Bonta, J. (1994). *The Psychology of Criminal Conduct*. Cincinnati, OH: Anderson Publishing.

Bandura, A. (1977). *Social Learning Theory*. Englewood Cliffs, NJ: Prentice Hall.

Bandura, A. (1986). *Social Foundations of Thought and Action: A Social-Cognitive Theory*. Englewood Cliffs, NJ: Prentice Hall.

Hollin, C. R., & Palmer, E. J. (Eds.). (2006). *Offending Behaviour Programmes: Development, Application, and Controversies*. Chichester: John Wiley & Sons.

Lösel, F. (1995). Increasing consensus in the evaluation of offender rehabilitation? *Psychology, Crime, & Law, 2*, 19–39.

McGuire, J. (Ed). (1995). *What Works: Reducing Reoffending*. Chichester: John Wiley & Sons.

PREFACE

This edited collection originated in a coffee shop in Wellington, New Zealand, where the first two editors were working and where the latter two later came to visit. It became clear to us all – from working and teaching in the area of offender cognition – that professionals and students were forced to consult numerous piecemeal chapters and papers on the topic, as no single textbook synthesised the material needed into one readily accessible resource. From this realisation we began to approach leading professionals involved in various aspects of aggressive offenders' cognition, about whether they would be interested in writing a chapter for a book devoted to offender cognition. The response that we received was overwhelmingly enthusiastic and we feel privileged to edit a text of special interest to us with such a group of enthusiastic and informed professionals. The strength of this book – we hope – lies in its structure. Each offender population is treated separately, allowing readers to compare and contrast developments, knowledge and practice across sexual offending, general violence and domestic violence. We hope that professionals involved and interested in this area will use this text, not only as a reference but also to further develop an area that is beginning to gain powerful momentum.

ACKNOWLEDGEMENTS

We would like to acknowledge all of the individuals who have made this collection of work possible. First of all, a big thank you to all of the authors who, during their hectic schedules, put so much effort into writing their chapters. We would also like to thank all those at Wiley who gave advice and help with this work from start to finish. In particular, thank you Claire Ruston, Gillian Leslie, Sarah Tilley and Nicole Burnett for dealing with all our queries and little hiccups. A big thank you also goes to the series editors, Clive Hollin and Mary McMurran, for supporting this piece of work. We would also like to thank Sage Publications for permission to reproduce the tables presented in Chapter 2. Finally, we would like to thank Mariamne Rose, at the University of Kent for her help with proof-reading this work. Thanks Mariamne!

INTRODUCTION

Theresa A. Gannon
University of Kent, UK

Tony Ward
Victoria University of Wellington, NZ

Anthony R. Beech
University of Birmingham, UK

Dawn Fisher
Llanarth Court Hospital and University of Birmingham, UK

Studying how the human mind works is always fascinating; perhaps even more so when a person's behaviour is at odds with legal and moral conventions. In fact, even the most lifeless of dinner parties can be reignited by idle talk of the latest high profile offender: "Why did he do it?" "What must he have been thinking?" "He must be really messed up in the head." Yet behind such questions lies an important assumption that plays a pivotal role in the theoretical underpinnings of forensic psychology. Put simply, the majority of theories proposed to explain aggressive offending assert that offenders' thinking at the time of their offence is deviant, abnormal, and offence-supportive.

From an academic perspective, the term "cognition" refers to the basic operations involved in human perception, memory and thinking (Solso, 1998). For example, how do we perceive a written question, interpret its meaning, think about a possible answer to that question and ultimately select and implement a verbal response? (Solso, 1998). All aspects of these operations involve a complex interplay of perceptual (e.g., attention), thinking (e.g., concept formulation) and memory processes (e.g., retention, retrieval). These processes have been investigated by

Aggressive Offenders' Cognition: Theory, Research and Practice. Edited by T. A. Gannon, T. Ward, A. R. Beech and D. Fisher. © 2007 John Wiley & Sons, Ltd.

cognitive psychologists utilising a wide range of methodologies and have resulted in immense payoffs of knowledge production (e.g., Broadbent, 1958; Chomsky, 1968; Loftus, 1979/1996; Posner, 1980). More recently, however, psychology has become interested in understanding these processes when individuals interact with each other.

The term "social-cognition" refers to the study of social or interpersonal relationships using the knowledge and methods derived from basic cognitive psychology. In other words, social cognition aims to explain how people perceive themselves and others, interpret the meaning of interpersonal behaviour, think about the possible answer to a social problem and choose a behavioural response to that social problem.

A cognitive construct of paramount importance for investigating such social-cognitive questions is that of the *schema*. A schema may be conceptualised as a structured framework of knowledge – stored in long-term memory – that contains information and knowledge associated together from prior experience and learning (Fiske & Taylor, 1991; Huesmann, 1998). Thus, a schema relating to a particular concept (e.g., children) will contain information concerning characteristics or core attributes (e.g., naïve, innocent) and about the relationships between such attributes and behaviours (e.g., how this naivety relates to a child's tendency to ask socially unacceptable and sometimes very embarrassing and public questions). Each individual's unique variety of schemas provides her or him with the capacity to describe, interpret and predict that individual's own and other people's behaviour.

When resources and time are plentiful, individuals can and do interpret their own and others' behaviours in a rational and careful manner (i.e., they behave as *naïve scientists*; Fiske & Taylor, 1991). Most often, however, individuals behave as *cognitive misers.* Put simply, individuals perceive their complicated and rather ambiguous world through reliance on pre-existing schemas (Augoustinos & Walker, 1995; Fiske & Taylor, 1991). Thus, when dealing with a situation that is similar to one encountered previously, individuals use their pre-existing schemas (largely unconsciously) to predict how others will behave and how they themselves should behave (Williams *et al.*, 1997). Consequently, everyday social encounters provide rich opportunities for schema rehearsal, which subsequently strengthen the links between associated knowledge units and increase schema accessibility (Anderson & Bushman, 2002). If a particular schema is rehearsed and supported regularly, it is likely to become *chronically accessible.* In other words, it is highly likely that such a schema will be used to interpret and guide social behaviour in the future (Pettit, Polaha & Mize, 2001). Research suggests that schemas – including those that are chronically accessible – are highly affected by situational priming (e.g., Bargh, 1982; Bargh, Lombardi & Higgins, 1988; Tiedens, 2001). This is probably because situational primes such as positive or negative affective states reduce the individual's ability to perceive the world carefully and rationally (Kardes, 1994). A variety of situational primes are likely to affect an individual's ability to process information rationally, including sexual arousal, anger, excitement, alcohol and drug use. Such primes increase individuals' reliance on pre-existing schemas, leading them to attend preferentially to schema-supportive information, ignore or minimise disconfirming evidence and interpret ambiguous social information in

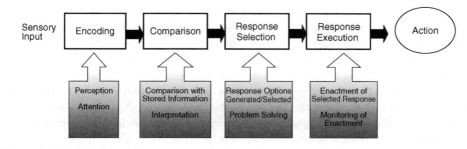

Figure 0.1 Basic information processing stages.
Source: Adapted from Barber, P. J. (1988). *Applied Cognitive Psychology.* London: Methuen & Co.

a schema-supportive manner. Thus, this reliance on schemas can create an entire chain of information-processing events that are schema-supportive.

A related conceptualisation in social-cognition is that of sequential *information-processing models* (see Barber, 1988; Fiske & Taylor, 1991; Welford, 1960). Such models typically attempt to break down and describe the intervening steps that occur between initial stimuli perception and the final response, or behaviour (Fiske & Taylor, 1991). All steps – to some degree – are driven by stored knowledge in the form of schemas. The basic components of information-processing may be conceptualised as stages incorporating *encoding* (i.e., perception and representation of stimuli in memory), *comparison* (i.e., the generated representation is compared to current memory representations), *response selection* (i.e., the search and selection of an appropriate responses) and *response execution* (i.e., the organisation, enactment and cognitive monitoring of responses) as outlined in Figure 0.1.

The advantage of sequential information-processing models is that they can be used by researchers to divide the complex mental operations involved in inter-personal cognition into basic stages that may be tested empirically. For example, Stage 1 is concerned with the basic perceptual processes involved in information processing. Social-cognitive scientists propose that attentional resources are allocated to schema-relevant information. In other words, we attend to schema-consistent information. Thus, Stroop tasks (Stroop, 1935) may be used to test attention at the encoding level as participants should take longer to name the colours of words that are schema-consistent compared with less personally meaningful words due to interference associated with involuntary attention mechanisms. The second stage of the model is concerned with how individuals interpret en-coded social information using existing stored knowledge (i.e., schemas). Since ambiguous information is predicted to be interpreted in schema-supportive ways, simple tasks that probe participants' interpretation of ambiguous social events may provide valuable insight into pre-existing schemas. Methods used to test this stage of the model may involve asking participants to recall a piece of ambiguous text (e.g., Copello & Tata, 1990) in the hope that this recollection will provide some insight into how the ambiguous text was initially interpreted. The third stage of the model relates to the generation of solutions to a social problem or encounter and the decision making involved in selecting a response. Such a stage is often referred to as *social problem solving* (McGuire, 2005) and may be tested by asking individuals to generate options to a hypothetical social event and to isolate a response option that they believe is an appropriate response (see Nezu *et al*, 2003). The final stage of the model refers to the actual enactment of the behavioural option chosen. This stage is harder to test empirically, but involves the individual cognitively monitoring the effects of an enacted behaviour. Thus, behaviour may be adjusted according to fluctuating context and cognitive feedback. Conceptualising information-processing according to the basic model described above allows researchers to theorise and research potential problems within the cognitive system and to note at which point in the system problems are likely to occur.

Of course, we can all experience difficulty – of one form or another – dealing effectively with social encounters due to the powerful effects of our cognitive apparatus. For example, we may misinterpret a partner's silence as a personal slight and respond with sullen behaviour or even verbal confrontation. In other words, everyone is susceptible to making biased and unrealistic social interpretations and behavioural responses; especially when our cognitive system is pressured or overloaded. However, when a person is physically aggressive, a key question concerns whether he or she holds unique and offence-supportive schemas that affect information processing and generate antisocial behaviour. For example, how do offenders view themselves and their social world? Do they hold offence-supportive schemas that lead them to see their social world in an offence-supportive manner? Further, do such schemas result in an inability to communicate effectively or resolve interpersonal conflict via nonaggressive means? It is these questions which ultimately drive social-cognitive psychology applications to forensic populations.

Forensic psychology professionals often note that offenders frequently utter offence-supportive statements when recounting their offence, which appear to indicate the existence of offence-supportive schemas (e.g., "He was staring at me all night – he was asking for it" or "She was taking the piss out of me; she needed to know who's boss"). Such statements and the offence-supportive thinking that they imply are commonly referred to as "cognitive distortions", which serve to justify, minimise and facilitate offending behaviour (Gannon, Polaschek & Ward, 2005; Gibbs, 1993; Murphy, 1990). It is intuitively pleasing – and comforting – to believe that aggressive offenders think differently from law-abiding members of the community. Perhaps this is why the term "cognitive distortion" has been so readily accepted into the research community. This term implies a type of cognitive pathology that separates offenders from us, implying some type of cognitive *abnormality*. But are offenders so different from us?

Thankfully, the explosion of interest in social-cognition has penetrated the forensic psychology world since the mid-1980s, allowing us to develop theory and research methodologies that provide some tantalising – albeit imperfect – insights into aggressive offenders' cognition. Our book describes the fruits of this research on aggressive offenders' cognition since that period. This text is not intended to be exhaustive but the specific lineup of chapters was chosen to provide readers with one text that would give key guidance on cognition in a broad range of areas. We hope that researchers and practitioners who consult the forthcoming chapters will find the information useful for future theory and research generation and for implementing evidence-based practice.

SPECIFIC CONTENT

Part I of the book concerns sexual abusers. In Chapter 1, Joanne Thakker, Tony Ward and Shruti Navathe describe and evaluate the main theoretical perspectives proposed to explain the concept of cognitive distortions in child sexual abusers. These authors also present their own useful conceptualisation of child sexual abusers' schemas or implicit theories in the form of an integrative model. Following on from this, Dawn Fisher and Anthony Beech outline current theoretical literature pertaining to rapists' schemas/implicit theories and describe the results of a unique qualitative study conducted with rapists and sexual murderers. In Chapter 3, Tony Ward, Kirsten Keown and Theresa Gannon put forward a new model, which attempts to clarify the nature of sexual offenders' cognitions through describing them as belief, value and action-related judgments. Within this model, cognitive distortions are viewed as stemming from a number of mechanisms including implicit beliefs, but also impression management strategies. In Chapters 4 and 5, the empirical research investigating sexual offenders' cognition is presented and evaluated. Chapter 4 outlines the available evidence pertaining to child sexual abusers (Theresa Gannon & Jane Wood). Gannon and Wood's review suggests that the evidence supporting generic offence-supportive schemas in child sexual abusers is relatively weak and they conclude the chapter with an interesting question; that is, are researchers misinterpreting the available information in a manner which supports professionals own pre-existing and intuitively plausible beliefs? Chapter 5 (Calvin Langton) systematically reviews empirical findings concerning the cognition of men who rape. To our knowledge, this is the first published review fully synthesising the knowledge of rape-related cognition. We anticipate that this review will prove valuable as a resource for researchers interested in further investigating rapists' cognition and for forensic practitioners who want to ensure their current practice is empirically guided. Moving onto some more practice-focused chapters, Christopher Dean, Ruth Mann, Rebecca Milner and Shadd Maruna, in Chapter 6, provide readers with what we believe is a most engaging and novel chapter. As well as outlining some of the more traditional methods of treating child sexual abusers' cognition, Christopher Dean and his colleagues take on the challenge of considering how forensic practitioners should consider dealing with the vast array of offence-supportive accounts in therapy. In particular, they consider the problem of sifting aetiological cognition from *red herring* accounting behaviours (i.e., normative excuse making). The final chapter of this section – Chapter 7 – is written by Lynne Eccleston and Karen Owen who focus our attentions on the cognitive treatment of rapists. In particular, they evaluate our current tendency to treat rapists alongside child sexual abusers, and report their unique experiences of having developed and run a rapist-only treatment group. Treatment "just for rapists" is seemingly not for the faint hearted, representing a series of unique challenges for forensic practitioners!

Part II of this book examines the cognition of nonsexual, generally violent offenders. The first chapter of this part (Chapter 8) is written by Marc Sestir and Bruce Bartholow and provides a firm grounding for the chapters that follow by evaluating the range of cognitive and social-cognitive explanations of aggression and violence. Leading on from this, Rachael Collie, Jim Vess and Sharlene Murdoch provide an excellent review of current empirical evidence regarding violent offenders' cognition (Chapter 9). Their review highlights the urgent need for further empirical investigation of violent offenders' cognition using many of the cognitive paradigms so often utilised to investigate clinical psychopathology. In Chapter 10, Emma Palmer then presents a very clear overview of the links between moral cognition and aggressive behaviour and describes the range of tools that may be used to measure moral cognition, as well as the types of treatment programmes that incorporate moral cognitive components. In Chapter 11, Clive Hollin and Claire Bloxsom do an excellent job of describing the current model of choice for treating anger and of the interventions available for treating angry and aggressive individuals; an excellent source for those interested in anger management. Following on from this, Mary McMurran gets to grips with reviewing the fascinatingly complex relationship between alcohol and aggression and makes some important observations and recommendations regarding therapy for aggressive offenders whose antisocial actions appear to be alcohol-linked (Chapter 12).

The final chapter of this section is provided by Elizabeth Gilchrist, who describes and integrates knowledge to date concerning domestically violent abusers' cognition. She highlights the strong need for the domestic violence literature to establish some more robust measures of cognition since the research base to date is not at all clear regarding the key cognitive factors underlying domestic violence. It seems, then, that this area is one that may potentially benefit in one way or another from a mini "cognitive revolution".

REFERENCES

Anderson, C. A. & Bushman, B. J. (2002). Human aggression. *Annual Review of Psychology*, **53**, 27–51.

Augoustinos, M. & Walker, I. (1995). *Social Cognition. An Integrated Introduction*. London: Sage.

Barber, P. J. (1988). *Applied Cognitive Psychology*. London: Methuen.

Bargh, J. A. (1982). Attention and automaticity in the processing of self relevant information. *Journal of Personality and Social Psychology*, **43**, 425–36.

Bargh, J. A., Lombardi, W. J. & Higgins, E. T. (1988). Automaticity of chronically accessible constructs in person and situation effects on person perception: it's just a matter of time. *Journal of Personality and Social Psychology*, **55**, 599–605.

Broadbent, D. E. (1958). *Perception and Communication*. London: Pergamon Press.

Chomskey, N. (1968). *Language and Mind*. New York: Harcourt Brace Jovanovich.

Copello, A. G. & Tata, P. R. (1990). Violent behaviour and interpretative bias: An experimental study of the resolution of ambiguity in violent offenders. *British Journal of Clinical Psychology*, **29**, 417–28.

Fiske, S. T. & Taylor, S. E. (1991). *Social Cognition* (2nd edn). New York: McGraw-Hill.

Gannon, T. A., Polaschek, D. L. L. & Ward, T. (2005). Social cognition and sexual offenders. In M. McMurran & J. McGuire (eds), *Social Problem Solving and Offenders* (pp. 223–48). Chichester: Wiley.

Gibbs, J. C. (1993). Moral-cognitive interventions. In A. P. Goldstein & C. R. Huff (eds), *The Gang Intervention Handbook* (pp. 159–85). Champaign, IL: Research Press.

Huesmann, L. R. (1998). The role of social information processing and cognitive schema in the acquisition and maintenance of habitual aggressive behavior. In R. G. Geen &

E. Donnerstein (eds), *Human Aggression: Theories, Research, and Implications for Social Policy* (pp. 73–109). San Diego, CA: Academic Press.

Kardes, F. R. (1994). Consumer judgement and decision processes. In R. S. Wyer Jr. & T. K. Srull (eds), *Handbook of Social Cognition* (pp. vii–xii) (2nd edn). Hillsdale, NJ: Erlbaum.

Loftus, E. (1979/1996). *Eyewitness Testimony.* London: Harvard University Press.

McGuire, J. (2005). Social problem solving: basic concepts, research, and applications. In M. McMurran & J. McGuire (eds), *Social Problem Solving and Offenders* (pp. 3–29). Chichester: Wiley.

Murphy, W. D. (1990). Assessment and modification of cognitive distortions in sex offenders. In W. L. Marshall, D. R. Laws & H. E. Barbaree (eds), *Handbook of Sexual Assault* (pp. 331–42). New York: Plenum Press.

Nezu, C. M., Nezu, A. M., Dudek, J. A., Peacock, M. & Stoll, J. (2003). Social problem-solving correlates of sexual deviancy and aggression among adult child molesters. *Journal of Sexual Aggression,* **11**, 27–36.

Pettit, G. S., Polaha, J. A. & Mize, J. (2001). Perceptual and attributional processes in aggression and conduct problems. In J. Hill & B. Maughhan (eds), *Conduct Disorders in Childhood and Adolescence* (pp. 292–319). Cambridge: Cambridge University Press.

Posner, M. I. (1980). Orienting of attention. *Quarterly Journal of Experimental Psychology,* **32**, 3–25.

Solso, R. L. (1998). *Cognitive Psychology* (5th edn). London: Allyn & Bacon.

Stroop, J. R. (1935). Studies of interference in serial verbal reactions. *Journal of Experimental Psychology,* **18**, 643–62.

Tiedens, L. Z. (2001). The effect of anger on the hostile inferences of aggressive and non-aggressive people: Specific emotions, cognitive processing, and chronic accessibility. *Motivation and Emotion,* **25**, 233–51.

Welford, A. T. (1960). The measurement of sensory-motor performance: Survey and reappraisal of twelve years progress. *Ergonomics,* **3**, 189–230.

Williams, J. M. G., Watts, F. N., MacLeod, C. & Mathews, A. (1997). *Cognitive Psychology and Emotional Disorders* (2nd edn). Chichester: Wiley.

PART I

SEXUAL ABUSERS

Chapter 1

THE COGNITIVE DISTORTIONS AND IMPLICIT THEORIES OF CHILD SEXUAL ABUSERS

JOANNE THAKKER

University of Waikato, NZ

TONY WARD AND SHRUTI NAVATHE

Victoria University of Wellington, NZ

Child sexual abuse is typically judged by society to be a particularly abhorrent crime and those who commit such crimes receive severe – typically prison-based – penalties. However, along with the assigned punishment there is also often an expectation that the offender will engage in some sort of rehabilitation process to reduce risk of reoffending. As in many areas of psychological intervention, treatment in the sexual offending area is an evolving field – a work in progress (Marshall, Anderson & Fernandez, 1999). A large amount of both theoretical and empirical research has been conducted but outcome data suggest that there is room for improvement (Hanson *et al.*, 2002). In order to advance treatment it is advantageous to develop an understanding of the many different factors associated with child sexual abuse – in particular causal factors.

A growing body of research since the mid-1980s has explored the role of cognition in the genesis and maintenance of child sexual abuse. This research indicates that child sexual abusers often harbour beliefs that justify sexual offending and appear to precipitate and maintain offence behaviour (Gannon, Ward & Collie, 2007; Ward & Keenan, 1999). It has been determined that child sexual abusers tend to describe their offending in an offence-supportive manner (Ward, 2000). For example, they may suggest that the sexual interaction with the child was justified because the child appeared to enjoy the experience, that it was harmless because there was no actual penetration involved, or that it is inherently good for human beings of all ages to engage in sexual activity.

This chapter discusses and evaluates the theory developed to explain child sexual abusers' offence-supportive cognitions or beliefs, opening with early

Aggressive Offenders' Cognition: Theory, Research and Practice. Edited by T. A. Gannon, T. Ward, A. R. Beech and D. Fisher.   © 2007 John Wiley & Sons, Ltd.

theoretical conceptualisations. We then look at the major theoretical developments since; that is, schema-based approaches. The discussion concludes with the presentation of a model that summarises the various key ideas and attempts to identify their interrelationships. Note that this model places cognitive factors within the context of all of the other variables that also play a role in child sexual abuse, thereby acknowledging that cognition is just one of many psychological factors associated with this particular problematic behaviour.

COGNITIVE DISTORTIONS

Origins and Early Conceptualisations

The term "cognitive distortions" was first used by Beck (1963) in reference to the intrusive and disruptive thoughts typically associated with depression. It was Beck's view (a view that he has developed extensively since) that the unrealistic thoughts that are frequently exhibited by depressed individuals are fundamental to their clinical condition and so should be further pinpointed for successful therapy.

It appears that the first researchers to utilise the term "cognitive distortions" within the area of sexual offending were Abel, Becker and Cunningham-Rathner (1984). As argued by Abel and colleagues, men typically engage in sexual activity with children because they experience feelings of sexual attraction to prepubescent individuals. In explaining how such maladaptive feelings of sexual arousal develop in men, Abel *et al.* suggest that during their childhoods, boys are typically exposed to a wide range of stimuli that may be associated with deviant sexual interests. However, most boys learn to control such responses and limit them to stimuli that would ordinarily be considered erotic by the majority of people in their society. In other words, the process by which boys' sexual fantasies and sexual responses develop is strongly influenced by societal norms and societal expectations. According to Abel and colleagues, for some unidentified reason, this shaping process does not occur in some men, resulting in the manifestation of deviant arousal.

Abel *et al.* suggest that as the individual develops an awareness of the disparity between his own sexual preferences and societal norms, he creates an internal dialogue between his thoughts and attitudes. This internal dialogue then serves to justify his sexual feelings and allows him to feel at ease with himself. Abel *et al.* refer to these thoughts and attitudes as *cognitive distortions* and propose that there are a number of key distortions that are commonly articulated by child sexual abusers. These are:

- A child who does not physically resist sexual advances really wants to have sex.
- Having sex with a child is a good way for an adult to teach a child about sex.
- Children do not tell others about having sex with a parent because they really enjoy the sexual activity and want it to continue.
- Some time in the future our society will come to realise that sex between a child and an adult is acceptable.

- An adult who only feels a child's body or genitals is not really being sexual with the child so no harm is done.
- When a child asks an adult a question about sex it means that the child wants to see the adult's genitals or have sex with them.
- Relationships with children are enhanced by my having sex with them. (Abbreviated, from Abel, Becker & Cunningham-Rathner, 1984, pp. 98–101.)

The way in which Abel and others explicate the idea of cognitive distortions bears strong similarity to aspects of Freud's psychoanalytic theory (Freud, 1923/1989), although this connection has not been made elsewhere. Freud coined the term "defence mechanism" in his early writing, in reference to psychological techniques that individuals use to protect themselves from unpleasant thoughts and feelings (Cramer, 2000). Sometimes these mechanisms are referred to as "ego defences", reflecting the idea that their purpose is to protect the ego from some perceived psychological threat. Freud focused, in particular, on the tendency for the ego to suppress aggressive and sexual impulses that would pose a threat to the individual's integrity (Baumeister, Dale & Sommer, 1998). The three defences that are most relevant here are "denial," "rationalisation" and "reaction formation." *Denial* refers to total refutation of an idea. *Rationalisation* refers to the creation of beliefs and explanations that (erroneously) justify particular behaviours or events. Finally, reaction *formation* refers to the process of exchanging a negative feeling for a positive one by taking an opposing view. It has been noted that Freud's hypotheses of defence mechanisms are surprisingly well supported by both theoretical and empirical literature (see Baumeister, Dale & Sommer, 1998).

Thus, cognitive distortions appear to function as cognitive defence mechanisms, which allow the child sexual abuser to feel more comfortable with his behaviour and reduce dissonance between his actions and attitudes condemning such activities. While all seven of Abel's cited cognitions may be described as both denial (insofar as they serve to deny wrongdoing), and rationalisation (insofar as they provide a justification for the behaviour), the potential effect of these is reaction formation. For example, rather than thinking that sex between an adult and a child is harmful and having negative feelings about one's inappropriate behaviour, an offender may entertain the idea that sex between an adult and child is good because it strengthens their intimacy. Subsequently, this offender would be more likely to hold positive feelings in association with that sexual interaction.

Placing their theory within a broader theoretical context, Abel *et al.* (1989) suggest that cognitive distortions are consistent with the account of human behaviour provided by Bandura's social learning theory (SLT) (Bandura, 1977). They state that while SLT emphasises the importance of various conditioning processes in the regulation of behaviour it also maintains that cognition plays a fundamental role in these processes, and that conditioning, in turn, influences cognition. Accordingly Abel *et al.* argue that "cognitive distortions are the products of conflict between external reinforcements and internal self-condemnation" (p. 138). The more prominent focus of this article by Abel *et al.* is the development of a scale for measuring the presence of "cognitive distortions" in child sexual abusers (see Chapter 4 of this volume for more details). Labelled the Cognitions Scale or CS, this measure presents a range of offence-supportive cognitions and requires respondents to rate their strength of agreement with each cognition on a Likert scale. Using this measure, Abel *et al.* conclude that, "child molesters do report beliefs and attitudes that are dramatically different from those of non child molesters" (p. 147). Abel *et al.*'s findings also illustrate a positive correlation between the number of cognitions endorsed by child sexual abusers and the number of years they have been engaging in sexual activity with children. As noted below there has been criticism of this measure, however, it has nonetheless been widely used in the assessment of child sexual abusers.

Critique and Elaboration of Early Ideas

Perhaps the most notable confusion evident within Abel's early conceptualisation of cognitive distortions is the lack of clarity concerning whether these "distortions" represent some type of permanent belief structure, or whether they are, in fact, more temporary dissonance-reduction cognitions used to facilitate and justify offending behaviour (Gannon & Polaschek, 2006; Ward, Polaschek & Beech, 2005). As Gannon and Polaschek (2006) note, although the latter explanation appears more likely, Abel *et al.*'s development of a scale to measure attitudes and beliefs appears incongruous with this explanation. In other words, how useful is it to develop a scale that measures beliefs and attitudes when the cognitive construct being targeted is more temporary dissonance reducing cognitions? Similarly, Gannon *et al.* (2007) criticise the ambiguity that arose out of Abel's broad and indistinct definition of cognitive distortions. As noted by Gannon *et al.* the literature that followed Abel's work has been littered with a variety of terms and definitions indicating a lack of consensus in regard to the nature of cognitive distortions and their underlying conceptual foundation. On reflection, then, this early conceptualization of child sexual abusers' cognition shows some evidence of theoretical confusion or a lack of internal coherence (Gannon & Polaschek, 2006).

Mann and Beech (2003) also critique Abel and his colleagues for such incoherence arguing that it is unclear whether cognitive distortions are conscious or unconscious cognitive processes. They propose that according to the original description, individuals could use cognitive distortions in a conscious, intentional manner in order to avoid feeling judged by others, or they could emerge quite spontaneously and automatically as a protective mechanism. Interestingly Abel *et al.* assert that one aspect common to all seven cited cognitions is that the offender does not seek support for them from other members of the general public. Abel *et al.* propose that this act of omission indicates that the offender has at least some understanding of the inappropriateness of his cognitions. Hence, in response to Mann and Beech perhaps Abel would suggest that cognitive distortions emerge in child sexual abusers in at least a semi-conscious manner.

In relation to this discussion, Gannon and Polaschek point out that one of the problems with the CS is that it assumes that offenders' offence-supportive cognitions are always accessible for self-report. In other words, Abel and his colleagues appear to believe that the offender has a continuous and stable awareness of his cognitions that is directly transferable to pen and paper assessment. As stated by Gannon and Polaschek, however, the offender's ability to access offence-supportive cognitions is likely to vary according to key contextual factors clearly absent from questionnaire-testing contexts (e.g., extreme affect and sexual arousal).

Mann and Beech also argue that there is a lack of clarity or coherency regarding the *function* of offence-supportive cognition in the offence process. On one hand such cognition may provide retrospective justifications for past offending, or, it could be construed as preceding offending and therefore playing a *causative* role.

More recently, Drake *et al.* (2001) and Ward (2000) point out that there is no theoretical foundation underlying the presentation of the seven cited cognitive distortions presented by Abel *et al.* (1984). In other words, it seems as though the seven beliefs described by Abel *et al.* (1984) are construed as being independent of each other; a proposal that is simply incongruous with other psychological disciplines (i.e., the developmental or social-cognition literature relating to implicit theories and schemas respectively). A further criticism meted out by Drake *et al.* is that according to Abel *et al.* the seven types of distortions presented are a subset of possible distortions that may be present in child sexual abusers. This begs the questions of: What other distortions may be present? And, on what basis have these seven been chosen?

Feelgood, Cortoni and Thompson (2005) postulate that cognitive distortions are associated with maladaptive coping strategies in sexual offenders. Specifically, they suggest that there is likely to be " ... a mechanism whereby distortions may facilitate and maintain deviant sexual coping by reducing internal inhibitions such as guilt and shame" (p. 166). In this instance "deviant sexual coping" refers to a child sexual abuser's tendency to use sexual interaction with children as a means of dealing with stress and high levels of unpleasant emotion. In this way cognitive distortions may be used by offenders to support their maladaptive coping strategies. Feelgood *et al.* found, in their study of coping strategies across three offender groups (rapists, child sexual abusers and violent offenders) that child sexual abusers tended to use sexual coping more than the other two types of offenders. Feelgood *et al.* propose that deviant sexual practices probably develop during adolescence as a way of managing isolation and rejection from peers. It is hypothesised that feeling lonely and rejected by others may result in men seeing sex as one of the few ways that they can experience pleasure and autonomy in their lives. Subsequently, attitudes and beliefs emerge that support the deviant sexual practices and these, in turn, reinforce the use of deviant sexual practices as a coping strategy. Note, however, that Feelgood and colleagues do not provide any detail in regard to the psychological mechanisms that may be involved in the development of such attitudes and beliefs.

Abel and colleagues' theory of cognitive distortions in child sexual abusers has proven to be fertile; it has precipitated further theoretical and empirical research in the area (see Chapter 4 of this volume) and has strongly influenced the development of treatment approaches that target offence-supportive-cognition (see Marshall, Anderson & Fernandez, 1999). It is also reasonably externally consistent (although we have noted some problems with this consistency) as it is broadly consistent with a social learning model of behaviour that provides some detail of how offence-supportive cognitions develop. However, as argued by a number of other theorists, it lacks coherence and explanatory depth (see Ward, Polaschek & Beech, 2006). For example, Gannon and Polaschek (2006) argue that

Abel and colleagues' explication of cognitive distortion theory was conducted in a "piece meal fashion across many published sources" (p. 4). As stated earlier, there is no rationale provided for the inclusion of the seven particular distortions that they listed and there is no overarching theory to structure their interrelationships. In terms of parsimony, the theory itself is fairly straightforward, however, the omission of a more concrete theoretical foundation adds complexity insofar as the theory brings with it, a degree of uncertainty. Also, the lack of clarity around the issue of the accessibility of distortions in one's consciousness is problematic in this regard. Arguably Abel's approach is limited in terms of scope as it is only able to explain a narrow range of psychological phenomena.

A Schema Model of Offenders' Cognition

In response to some of the weaknesses of Abel's exposition a number of theorists have attempted to provide a more coherent account of cognitive distortions in child sexual abusers. One such account (Mann & Beech, 2003) uses the notion of schemas, which feature prominently in cognitive psychology literature. As explained by Mann and Beech schemas are essentially "structures in memory in which prior knowledge and expectancies are organized" (p. 138) and they "contain attitudes, ideas about the self and the world, specific beliefs, conditional assumptions, and core issues" (p. 140). Schemas are categories consisting of prototypical entities that are created over time in response to the multitude of stimuli individuals come across. They allow for more efficient processing of information by simplifying and classifying the information gained from past experiences. Hence rather than having to sift through a large amount of detail in one's recollections one can simply apply the generalised ideas or schema and use these as a framework for interpreting current experiences.

As explained by Mann and Beech (2003) the notion of a schema may be traced originally to Bartlett (1932) who defined a schema as a general mental representation that is drawn from a specific situation. Later, Beck (1964, 1967) defined schema as a "cognitive structure" used for processing information. Safran (1990) emphasised the significance of schemas in peoples' social interactions. It is Safran's view that schemas are fundamental to human relationships because they provide a template for interpreting and guiding the way in which individuals interact with one another.

Mann and Beech review the literature examining schemas in sexual offenders and, as they point out, it is a small body of work. However, as demonstrated by their discussion, there have been some useful empirical analyses (e.g., Malamuth & Brown, 1994; Malamuth et al., 1991; Mann & Hollin, 2001) and there is a growing body of theoretical research. Mann and Hollin (2001) reported the findings of two empirical studies of schemas in sexual offenders. The first study, which used a qualitative methodology, examined transcripts of rapists describing their offences. This approach was used in order to avoid the problems associated with self-report questionnaires (such as beliefs not being immediately present in offenders' conscious awareness). The methodology involved sorting the offenders' statements into general categories in order to determine the overarching schema and five emerged from the data (see also Chapter 2 of this volume). These were:

- Grievance – these statements suggested that the offender believed he had been wronged in some way and felt justified in behaving aggressively.
- Self as victim – these statements indicated the presence of self-pity and feelings of hopelessness.
- Control – these statements suggested a desire to have command over others in order to feel successful.
- Entitlement – these statements suggested that the offender believed he had a right to satisfy his own needs without any consideration for the wellbeing of others.
- Disrespect for certain women – these statements indicated that the offender believed that some groups of women (such as prostitutes) deserved to be treated poorly and without respect.

Mann and Hollin developed a questionnaire based on these results (called My Life) and factor analysis revealed that there were three underlying factors, which they referred to as Passive Victim, Vengeful Entitlement and Need for Control. In their second study Mann and Hollin included child sexual abusers along with rapists and found that the two most prominent schemas for both rapists and child sexual abusers were "grievance" and "need for respect/control". However, they found that schemas were less prominent in the child sexual abusers' offence narratives than in the narratives of rapists. This finding is consistent with other research suggesting that cognitive distortions may be present and play a causal role in only some sex offences (Mann & Beech, 2003). For example, Ward and Siegert (2002) conclude (in their comprehensive analysis of key theories in the child sexual abuser literature) that there may be a variety of problems or deficits in child sexual abusers. While some may have "distorted sexual scripts" that are related to faulty core schemas, for others the key problem may be in the area of relationship skills or emotional regulation.

Mann and Beech present a "schema-based model of sexual assault", which draws on these empirical findings as well as literature in the areas of social cognition and the theory of cognitive therapy. The model provides a linear representation of the role of schemas in offending in which developmental experiences lead to the emergence of dysfunctional beliefs and then these, coupled with negative (or ambiguous) life events, lead to problems with information processing and faulty interpretations. It is these misinterpretations that along with other factors associated with offending, are believed to lead to the commission of a sexual offence. In summary, the model proposes that cognitive distortions, along with a variety of other factors, play an important role in sexual offending, however, Mann and Beech stress that they are not likely to be the most important causal factors.

Mann and Beech also propose that there are two general types of schemas that are present in sexual offenders, namely, "category schemas" and "belief schemas." These are defined (respectively) as stereotypes about women and children, and assumptions about the self, other people and the world. Category schemas are construed as operating in the same way as ordinary stereotypes; they lead to biased information processing, especially in the case of ambiguous stimuli. Belief schemas are seen as having important connections with emotion, physiology, motivation and behaviour, meaning that they are in a sense entrenched ways of being and interacting with the environment. Mann and Beech suggest that belief schemas may be conceptualised as a "mode" in that they form an interconnected network of ideas that mediates an individual's thoughts, feelings, and behaviours. In this way belief schemas are particularly powerful because their manifestation may trigger certain emotional experiences.

Recent research by Milner and Webster (2005) examined differential schema content in violent offenders, rapists, and child sexual abusers. As in Mann and Hollin's research, they used a qualitative research design in which prominent themes were drawn out of offenders' offence narratives and they also administered the My Life questionnaire. Milner and Webster found a number of important differences between the three offender groups. The most prominent schema for child sexual abusers was "a sense of worthlessness" (p. 434) and this was found to be significantly less evident in violent offenders and rapists (who predominantly exhibited schemas of "grievance/revenge" and "suspicious hostility to women" respectively). In discussing their findings, Milner and Webster relate the apparent importance of a "sense of worthlessness" to literature that has reported the presence of low self-esteem in child sexual abusers. Specifically they suggest that low self-esteem may be the factor that underlies this finding; however, they note that low self-esteem has also been found in other types of offenders.

Milner and Webster point out that their research simply examined the nature of schemas in different groups of offenders and did not seek to determine the role of schemas in the commission of offences. Thus Milner and Webster conclude that the hypothesis that schema play a causal role in sexual offending remains hypothetical. Given society's typical abhorrence of sexual offending and sexual offenders it is of course possible that individuals who commit such crimes and go through the court and prison systems develop low self-esteem and feelings of worthlessness in response to the realization that they have stepped well outside the bounds of social norms.

Another recent study (Richardson, 2005) used the Young Schema Questionnaire (Young & Brown, 1994) to analyse schema in adolescent sexual offenders and they reported a number of interesting findings. Comparison of adolescents who abused younger children with those who offended against adults or peers showed that three schemas were significantly more predominant in the latter group, namely: "entitlement/self-centredness", "insufficient self-control/self-discipline" and "emotional inhibition". The study also found that abusers of younger children were significantly more likely to report that they had previously been victims of sexual abuse. Because of this finding, abusers of young children who themselves had been victims of sexual abuse were compared to abusers of young children without such a history (i.e., a *victim* versus a *nonvictim* group). Richardson found that the victim group scored higher on schemas of "abandonment/instability," and "defectiveness/shame," while the nonvictim group scored higher on the schema of "emotional inhibition" and "entitlement/self-centeredness". This suggests that child sexual abusers' past abuse experiences may be associated with the manifestation of specific schema; specifically feelings of abandonment and insecurity and feelings of shame and inferiority. It also suggests that adolescent abusers of young children are less likely to be self-centred and to have problems with self-control and the regulation of emotion when compared with other sexual offenders.

Critique and Elaboration of the Schema Approach

The schema approach to the understanding of cognitive distortions in child sexual abusers represents advancement over Abel's approach. It provides an overarching framework that organises the distortions and illuminates their interrelationships, and this is an improvement in terms of internal consistency although it should be noted that there remains a lack of clarity in terms of how the schemas may be related to each other and how they emerge in offenders. The schema model provides a parsimonious and straightforward means of structuring the various ideas. This framework also allows for superior external consistency as the theory shows greater compatibility with the general clinical and forensic literature. Additionally, self-reported empirical research appears to have confirmed the presence of some offence-related schemas in child sexual abusers, although it is unclear to what extent they play a causal role. Furthermore, it appears that offence-related schemas are less prominent in child sexual abusers than in rapists and other violent offenders (see Chapter 4 of this volume). Evidence suggests that the schemas that *are* present are somewhat different from those seen in other offenders. In particular, thoughts of worthlessness are prominent (Milner & Webster, 2005; Richardson, 2005).

The schema-based approach has yet to be proven fully fruitful in terms of research; however, it is a relatively new model so requires sufficient time for further theoretical and empirical research. Certainly the approach is testable, as demonstrated by Mann and colleagues, but what is more important is to tease out the exact nature of schema and their role in child sexual offending. With regard to treatment the schema approach is likely to be useful given the widespread use of schema-focused therapy (e.g., Young, 1990). In this sense the schema approach has the advantage of being consistent with an already well established clinical intervention methodology. In terms of scope, the schema model appears to be somewhat limited as it does not seem to account for many of the offence-supportive statements articulated by child sexual abusers. The implicit theories approach – described below – appears a little broader in this regard.

Implicit Theories

Ward and colleagues (Drake *et al.*, 2001; Ward, 2000; Ward & Keenan, 1999) propose that cognitive distortions in child sexual abusers arise out of a number of underlying implicit theories (ITs). Ward (2000, p. 494) points out that the term schema is ambiguous:

> Schema can refer to an abstract concept or category, a behavioural script (information about a frequently occurring event capturing its temporal sequence and actions), a belief (McGinn & Young, 1996), or an explanatory theory. In all its various senses schemata function to facilitate the encoding, storage, and retrieval of information, and constitutes a framework that actively modifies individuals' experience of the world.

Thus Ward stresses the functional role of schemas and uses the term IT to capture the explanatory nature of this sense of the term. As Ward explains, this proposition was based on research in developmental psychology, which suggests that ITs play a crucial role in children's cognitive development. According to this view children function a bit like scientists who routinely develop theories in order to explain and predict events in the world around them. As in science, hypotheses are tested and may be confirmed or disconfirmed depending on the evidence. In order to develop an increasingly accurate interpretation of the world theories are modified over time according to evaluations of their empirical adequacy. Ward and Keenan write: "According to this perspective, children develop a succession of increasingly adequate theories of mind (where "adequate" refers to their goal of explaining and predicting behaviour)" (p. 822).

Implicit theories are viewed as functioning in the same way as scientific theories insofar as they are used to explain empirical phenomena and to make predictions about the future and like scientific theories they are viewed as being interconnected. A scientific theory that is assessed as having good external coherence will be consistent with other theories in the field. Similarly an enduring IT will be a theory that fits with other ITs. Ward proposes that ITs are essentially a number of interconnected beliefs that form a coherent picture of the world: they are comprised of beliefs concerning the nature of the world, the offender, and the victim, and values or desires associated with all three. In other words, they form a complex framework of interrelated ideas. A noteworthy feature of Ward's (2000) theory is the stipulation that ITs contain ideas of varying degrees of abstraction:

> I hypothesize that offenders' maladaptive ITs include general assumptions about the nature of people and the world (e.g., mental states and their relationships to each other and behaviour), middle level beliefs dealing with categories of entities, such as women, children, and finally beliefs attributed to a particular victim. The key beliefs are those at the general and middle level; they persist and constitute the conceptual foundation of offenders' interpretations and explanations of victims' actions and mental states. (p. 499).

Thus, according to Ward, there are elements of stereotyped thinking evident in the middle levels of offenders' ITs. With regard to child sexual abuser-specific ITs, Ward states that they represent "reconstructions" based on analysis of the cognitive distortions that have been described by researchers. In other words they are inferred from the range of distorted beliefs that the literature has identified as being present in child sexual abusers. In explaining his theory Ward first elucidates the ways in which lay knowledge is "theory like." He states that (1) knowledge often refers to the ontology of human psychology; that is, it includes interpretations and understandings of psychological processes, and their instantiation in persons, (2) these interpretations and understandings are used to explain human behaviour, (3) the ideas are interconnected and form a relatively coherent picture, and (4) these ideas have a profound influence on individuals' interpretations of experiences and events.

Ward also points out, however, that there is one important difference between the way in which lay theories are used and the way in which scientists typically use theories. Whereas scientists strive to evaluate evidence from an objective point of view, generally human beings interpret evidence according to their ITs. While ITs may still change over time in response to new evidence, this process is inhibited by the already held theories. To illustrate, in the case of child sexual abusers, when evidence is presented that contradicts the IT, the offender simply modifies his interpretation of the evidence – implicitly – so that it is consistent with his theory. Naturally, such an approach would not be described as good science. However, it is worth mentioning that those who are cynical about the objectivity of science may well argue that this is in fact how most science operates!

Ward proposes that there are five key ITs which are often manifest in child sexual abusers' cognition. These are:

- *Children as sexual beings*. According to this IT, sexuality plays a central role in the lives of all human beings and all people, including children. Children are seen as having knowledge about sexuality and a desire for sexual interaction. They are also assumed to have the capacity to make informed decisions about whether, when, and with whom, to have sex. Moreover this knowledge and desire is seen as arising out of a natural (biologically determined) inclination to be interested and drawn towards sexual behaviours. This latter point is associated with the suggestion that the sexual interaction is harmless because it arises out a natural (and therefore normal) predisposition. This IT is purported to lead to beliefs such as "the child wanted sex" and "touching a child sexually can be a way of showing love and affection."
- *Entitlement*. This IT essentially asserts that some individuals are superior to others and that superior individuals should be afforded superior rights and status. For example, men may be seen as being inherently superior to women and children. Accordingly, a child sexual abuser may believe that because he is an adult male he is justified in using a child to meet his own sexual needs because the child will understand that he or she is subservient. Individuals who adhere to this IT see their own superiority and their own needs as legitimising their behaviour and as being more important than the law. Some examples of beliefs that may arise from this IT are "I deserve a special treat and she will make me feel better" and "I'm the boss in this family".
- *Dangerous world*. According to this IT the world is perilous and dominated by people who are negative, abusive and self-promoting. There are two aspects to this theory. First, there is the idea that given the nature of the world it is important to defend oneself by retaliating and gaining dominion over others. An example of a belief of this nature is "I had to teach her a lesson". Second, there is the idea that adults are inherently untrustworthy and dangerous whereas children, by contrast, are inherently innocent and reliable. This variant is also associated with the idea that the offender is vulnerable and fragile and therefore should turn to children for affection and care. An example of this sort of belief is, "Kids really know how to love you."
- *Uncontrollable*. This IT takes a fatalistic view, asserting that the world is basically uncontrollable and unchangeable. The behaviour of human beings is seen as predetermined and immutable and arising out of biological fundamental factors and early life experiences. A variant of this view is that an individual's behaviour

may be seen as arising out of powerful outside forces such as an *evil* force. Accordingly, a child sexual abuser may believe that he is not responsible for his behaviour because it was precipitated by forces beyond his control. Examples of beliefs emerging from this IT are "Many men sexually assault children at times of stress" and "I did it because I was sexually abused as a child."

- *Nature of harm.* This IT is founded on two general ideas: (1) that there are degrees of harm and if a lesser amount of harm results from an action then the action is justified on the grounds that greater harm was avoided, and (2) sexual activity is inherently good and not likely to result in harm. So, according to this theory, sexual activity is generally harmless and if it does result in harm it is likely to be only a small degree of harm. Examples of this IT are "she is asleep so she will never know what I am doing" and "many children who are sexually assaulted do not experience any major problems."

As mentioned above, these ITs are conceptualised by Ward as influencing the way that experiences are interpreted. For example, when a child clearly states that he or she does not want to engage in sexual activity with the offender, the offender may assume that the child actually wishes to participate but is too shy to articulate his or her desire. Or he may assume that the statement is simply an extraneous piece of data that can be ignored because it does not fit with his view of the world. Thus the Ward theory of cognitive distortions is able to account for the way the *content* of ITs can distort offenders' interpretations of other people and also why they can be used to *manage* social and self-*impressions*. That is, discrepant evidence is frequently dismissed by offenders or its importance underplayed, a process affected by a desire to be consistent and also acceptable in the eyes of the self and others. This is a facet of the theory often insufficiently noted by commentators.

Ward explains that it is possible for the offender to harbour one, two or many of these ITs but that they tend to be clustered into a number of general content areas. For example, an offender who views children as sexual beings may also see himself as being superior to the child and as therefore being in charge. However he would not necessarily see the world as perilous and unpredictable. Ward suggests that different types of child sexual abusers may hold specific ITs or aspects of these theories (i.e. particular cognitive distortions) and that they may be differentiated from one another in terms of these cognitions. For example, one offender may be fixated on seeing the world as inherently malicious and those in it as generally deserving of revenge, while another may be primarily motivated by thoughts of children's sexuality.

Ward points out that the ITs that he describes may also be present in other types of offenders and nonoffenders. For example, there may be other men, besides child sexual abusers, who believe they are superior to others, who see the world as an essentially dangerous place, and who even see children as sexual beings but who do not sexually abuse children. According to Ward, then, ITs may be necessary for child sex offending to occur, but not sufficient. He suggests that there are likely to be a range of others factors that also play an important role, such as deviant sexual preferences, insecure attachment, and a lack of social competency.

The IT approach is founded upon the idea that just a few core beliefs may give rise to a large number of cognitive distortions. Ward proposes, therefore, that it is vital that therapists involved in the treatment of child sexual abusers recognise the underlying ITs that are associated with the offending rather than simply identifying individualised beliefs. Ward likens this process to the approach frequently used in cognitive therapy that focuses on the identification of core beliefs that are then systematically challenged. This sort of therapeutic approach is virtually indistinguishable from Young's schema-focused therapy (mentioned above) which also aims to identify and modify core belief systems.

A self-report study (by Marziano *et al.*, 2005) examined the presence of these five ITs in child sexual abusers and found evidence that each of these theories occurs in this offender group. The study found that *children as sexual beings* was the most commonly articulated theory (28 % total frequency across transcripts), closely followed by *uncontrollability* and then *dangerous world* (26 % and 22 % respectively). The ITs of *nature of harm* and *entitlement* were less frequently evidenced but were still endorsed by some. One particularly interesting finding was that offenders who reported a history of sexual abuse were significantly more likely to evidence the IT *dangerous world*. Moreover, overall, this subgroup of offenders evidenced significantly more offence-supportive beliefs. The authors reason that this may indicate different developmental pathways among child sexual abusers. Specifically, they suggest that particular sorts of experiences early in life may lead to the development of "specific sets of implicit theories" (p. 7). Note that this is consistent with findings in the schema-focused literature; individuals who identified themselves as being victims of abuse tended to exhibit different schemas from nonvictims (Richardson, 2005).

Critique and Elaboration of the Implicit Theory Approach

The ITs approach to understanding the cognitive distortions that are seen in child sexual abusers bears some similarity to the schema model. Indeed, Ward was careful to point out that ITs are simply another way of conceptualising schema: one that has a clear functional role in helping individuals interpret and explain events in their internal and external environments. It organises the various distortions into categories and in doing so attempts to explain their interrelationships. However, in some respects, the ITs approach has greater breadth (or scope) insofar as it appears to cover more of the cognitive distortions that are exhibited by child sexual abusers. Also, as a theory, it is more fully explicated; ITs are explained and conceptualised in relation to general scientific theories, whereas the exact nature of the schema that Mann and colleagues discuss is not fully elucidated. The ITs conceptualization has good internal and external consistency and it presents a parsimonious model of the phenomena. In terms of the fertility of the theory it remains unclear to what extent it has penetrated the treatment arena, but there is evidence that it has been fruitful in terms of research (e.g., Marziano *et al.*, 2005; Mihailides, Devilly & Ward, 2004).

THEORY INTEGRATION

From Abel's early work on cognitive distortions to the more recent research on schema and ITs, it is evident that there is a growing sophistication in the understanding of the beliefs that are associated with child sexual offending. As depicted in Table 1.1, most of Abel's cognitive distortions (six out of seven) are consistent with the IT that views children as sexual beings. The remaining cognitive distortion (that touching a child's genitals does not count as sex and is therefore harmless) falls within the category of ITs that views harm along a continuum. Comparison of the schema-based approach with the ITs approach (as depicted in Table 1.1) shows a reasonable degree of overlap. The schema of *need for control* is consistent with the IT of entitlement, which includes the idea that those individuals who are superior to others have the right to have control over and dominate other people. The *grievance* schema appears to be consistent, at least to some extent, with the IT of *dangerous world*, which includes the idea that people are generally unkind and rejecting and deserving

Table 1.1 Conceptual organisation of implicit theories, schemas and cognitive distortions

Implicit theories	Belief schemas	Abel's cognitive distortions
Children as sexual objects		A child who does not physically resist my sexual advances really wants to have sex with me.
		Having sex with a child is a good way for an adult to teach a child about sex.
		Some time in the future our society will come to realise that sex between a child and an adult is alright.
		Children do not tell others about having sex with a parent because they really enjoy the sexual activity and want it to continue.
		When a child asks an adult a question about sex it means that the child wants to see the adult's sex organs or have sex with the adult.
		My relationship with my daughter or son or other child is enhanced by my having sex with them."
Entitlement	Need for control	
Dangerous world	Grievance	
Nature of harm		An adult who only feels a child's body or feels the child's genitals is not really being sexual with the child so no harm is being done.
Uncontrollable	Abandonment and instability	
	Worthlessness, shame and inferiority	

of retaliation. The schema of *abandonment and instability* is consistent with the IT of *uncontrollability* as it evokes the idea that people have a lack of control over their destinies and are at the mercy of malevolent and unpredictable forces. The remaining schemas of *worthlessness, shame and inferiority*, appear to be quite different to any of Ward's ITs and are therefore inserted together in the last row of the table.

Given the very broad definitions of each of the ITs it appears that the schemas delineated by Mann and other researchers are subsets of the ITs. For example, the schema of *abandonment and instability* refers essentially to a subset of the IT of *uncontrollability*. It may be theorised, then, that schemas are a more narrow set of cognitions that fall within the broader ITs. However, in terms of the definitions that are provided by the authors of the two approaches it appears that they are referring to the same type of psychological construct. Cognitive distortions are more specific beliefs that may be categorised in terms of both schemas and ITs. These interrelationships are depicted in Figure 1.1.

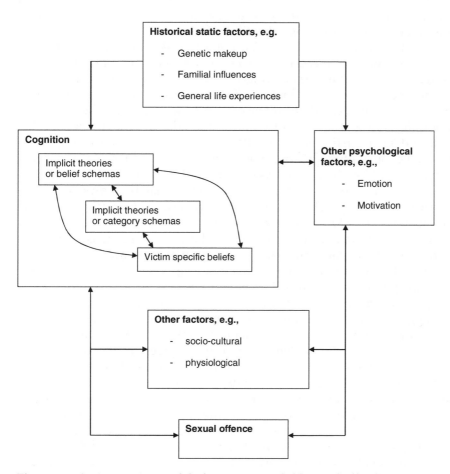

Figure 1.1 An integrative model of cognition in child sexual offending.

This model is not presented as a complete model of the factors involved in child sexual offending, but rather as a possible representation of (1) the interrelationships between the theorised elements of cognition, and (2) the juxtaposition of the various cognitive factors in relation to other psychological factors. ITs contain aspects of both Mann and Beech's beliefs and category constructs by virtue of their multi-level structures and therefore are listed in both the beliefs and category boxes. In our view they are complex cognitive structures that contain multiple strands and therefore are capable of integrating other structural perspectives while also stressing the important functional role of cognitive distortions.

It is possible that the schema of worthlessness, shame and inferiority may be related to another, as yet unidentified, IT. It certainly features prominently in the schema literature. However, regardless of its classification it may be a particularly important set of distortions due to its potential influence on other beliefs. For example, Abel pointed out the way in which distortions may arise as a way of allowing oneself to feel more comfortable when behaving in an antisocial manner. The distortions serve to allow the offender to continue with the behaviour and avoid negative thoughts and emotions. Therefore if thoughts of worthlessness and inferiority arise, they could potentially perpetuate the other cognitive distortions, which would then serve to minimise the discomfort caused by this set of beliefs.

Note that in the model the sexual offence itself is seen to feed back into the cognitions, and the other influential variables. This is an important feedback loop as it highlights the possible perpetuating nature of child sexual offending. Because the presence of specific ITs and cognitive distortions influence the way in which information is processed, the offence itself is likely to be a belief-affirming event. As it is likely to be charged with emotion it may be particularly powerful in this regard. As depicted in the model, emotion is construed as having an important two-way connection with cognition; it is seen as both influencing and being influenced by cognition. This emphasises the multifaceted nature of human experience. While in a theoretical discussion cognition may be analysed in isolation from other important psychological factors, such discussion may inadvertently present a somewhat skewed impression of reality.

To counter this it is advantageous to refer to the work of Lazarus (1991), who discusses the important relationships between cognition, motivation and emotion. Lazarus argues that cognition is both a necessary and sufficient condition for emotion; thus, cognition alone can lead to emotion and that there can be no emotion without cognition. He makes this argument with reference to the notion of appraisal, suggesting that there is always an element of appraisal in the experience of emotion. For example, even the spontaneous intense anxiety that may be experienced in response to the sudden appearance of a spider involves the cognitive processing of the spider. The word and idea of spider are evoked in the processing of the information and the associated emotional experience. It may be argued, then, that more complex emotional responses and experiences will inevitably involve cognition. It is thus essential to consider the important associations between cognition and various other psychological phenomena, especially emotion, which is also likely to play an important role in offending. The point is that the discussion herein may inadvertently give the impression that cognition is being conceptualised as a distinct entity. This is not the case; clearly, psychological variables interact in profound ways and cognition is affected by many other variables. As Lazarus points out there is a particularly close and important connection between cognition and emotion and this has important implications for treatment.

As shown in Figure 1.1, physiological factors are also theorised to interact with cognitive factors in the emergence of child sexual offending. These factors may be proximal (for example, sexual arousal) or distal (for example, genetically determined predisposition). As explained earlier, Abel and colleagues (1984, 1989) discussed the socially derived shaping process that takes place as boys develop sexually throughout their adolescence. It may reasonably be theorised that this shaping process is also influenced by evolutionary pressures, as according to Darwinian theory, sexual behaviour in all animals is influenced by the process of natural selection (see Siegert & Ward, 2003, for a discussion of evolutionary theory and sexual offending). It is not simply societal attitudes that motivate individuals to find the opposite gender attractive. It is likely that an attraction to minors would decrease one's reproductive fitness because one would be less likely to successfully reproduce. Successful reproduction obviously requires sexual activity between opposite sex adults.

Accordingly, it is reasonable to assume that the process by which males limit and shape their sexual arousal is not simply a matter of responding to social norms but also to biological tendencies. Therefore it is advantageous to consider such pressures when considering the role of cognition in child sexual offending. Clearly, from the point of view of evolutionary theory child sexual offending makes no sense, yet these offenders are able to develop beliefs that allow them to make sense of it and even believe that it is inherently good. One way of making sense of this anomaly is to see sexual arousal to young females as an extension of normal arousal. From an evolutionary point of view an optimal female mate is one who has only just emerged from puberty because they have the most time in which to reproduce. This would have been especially important in prehistoric times when the average human life was significantly shorter. Therefore there is perhaps a natural tendency for men to prefer young females and sexual arousal to preadolescent females may be an unexpected maladaptive extension of that tendency.

CONCLUSIONS

Readers may wonder about the present discussion and especially cynical readers may ask whether the terms and ideas discussed are simply in the realm of semantics. In response it may be suggested that yes it is a matter of semantics but that it is nonetheless an important matter. As eloquently argued by Lazarus (1991) there is no emotion without cognition and this, in itself, highlights the important role of thought in behaviour, and therefore, child sexual offending. In order to effectively treat child sexual abusers it is crucial to understand their psychology and evidence suggests that they may hold a specific range of beliefs that are different from other sorts of offenders and from nonoffenders.

Early research simply identified some of these beliefs, however more recent research has moved towards understanding their structure and foundations. The change in focus in the research is analogous to the process of uncovering the various layers of beliefs that are central to cognitive therapy, wherein the client begins by identifying the more readily accessible superficial cognitions and then moves over time to the identification of core beliefs. A similar process has taken place in the sex offender literature insofar as the early work focused on particular, easily identifiable, cognitive distortions and later approaches have attempted to "dig deeper" and identify the more fundamental cognitions from which these particular beliefs emanate.

Further research is needed to more fully explicate the significant cognitions in child sexual offending and to determine more accurately the nature of their role in the offence process. More research is also clearly required in order to understand how cognition interacts with other variables such as emotion and physiology, in the manifestation of this sort of offending. The ultimate goal of such research would be the development of improved treatment approaches that accurately target and treat problematic thoughts.

REFERENCES

Abel, G. G., Becker, J. V. & Cunningham-Rathner, J. (1984). Complications, consent, and cognitions in sex between children and adults. *International Journal of Law and Psychiatry*, **7**, 89–103.

Abel, G. G., Gore, D. K., Holland, D. K *et al.* (1989). The measurement of the cognitive distortions of child molesters. *Annals of Sex Research*, **2**, 135–53.

Bandura, A. (1977). *Social Learning Theory*. New York: General Learning Press.

Bartlett, F. A. (1932). *Remembering: A Study in Experimental and Social Psychology*. New York: Cambridge University Press.

Baumeister, R. F., Dale, K. & Sommer, K. L. (1998). Freudian defense mechanisms and empirical findings in modern social psychology: reaction formation, projection, displacement, undoing, isolation, sublimation and denial. *Journal of Personality*, **66**, 1081–124.

Beck, A. T. (1963). Thinking and depression: 1. Idiosyncratic content and cognitive distortions. *Archives of General Psychiatry*, **9**, 324–33.

Beck, A. T. (1964). Thinking and depression: 2. Theory and therapy. *Archives of General Psychiatry*, **9**, 324–33.

Beck, A. T. (1967). *Depression: Causes and Treatment*. Philadelphia: University of Pennsylvania Press.

Cramer, P. (2000) Defense mechanisms in psychology today. *American Psychologist*, **55**, 637–46.

Drake, C., Ward, T., Nathan, P. & Lee, J. (2001). Challenging cognitive distortions: An implicit theory approach. *Journal of Sexual Aggression*, **7**, 25–40.

Feelgood, S., Cortoni, F. & Thompson, A. (2005). Sexual coping, general coping, and cognitive distortions in incarcerated rapists and child molesters. *Journal of Sexual Aggression*, **11**, 157–70.

Freud, S. (1923/1989). *The Ego and the Id*. New York: W. W. Norton & Company.

Gannon, T. A. & Polaschek, D. L. L. (2006). Cognitive distortions in child molesters: A reexamination of key theories and research. *Clinical Psychology Review*, **26**, 1000–19.

Gannon, T. A., Ward, T. & Collie, R. (2007). Cognitive distortions in child molesters: theoretical and research developments over the past two decades. *Aggression and Violent Behavior*, **12**, 402–16.

Hanson, R. K., Gordon, A., Harris, A. J. R. *et al.* (2002). First report of the collaborative outcome data project on the effectiveness of psychological treatment for sex offenders. *Sexual Abuse: A Journal of Research and Treatment*, **14**, 169–94.

Lazarus, R. S. (1991). Cognition and motivation in emotion. *American Psychologist*, **46**, 352–67.

Malamuth, N. M. & Brown, L. M. (1994). Sexually aggressive men's perceptions of women's communications: Testing three explanations. *Journal of Personality and Social Psychology*, **67**, 699–712.

Malamuth, N. M., Sockloskie, R., Koss, M. P. & Tanaka, J. (1991). The characteristics of aggressors against women: testing a model using a national sample of college students. *Journal of Consulting and Clinical Psychology*, **59**, 670–81.

Mann, R. E. & Beech, A. R. (2003). Cognitive distortions, schemas, and implicit theories. In T. Ward, D. R. Laws & S. M. Hudson (eds), *Sexual deviance: Issues and Controversies* (pp. 135–53). Thousand Oaks, CA: Sage.

Mann, R. E. & Hollin, C. R. (2001). *Schemas: A model for understanding cognition in sexual offending.* Paper presented at the 20th Annual Research and Treatment Conference, Association for the treatment of Sexual Abusers, San Antonio.

Marshall, W. L., Anderson, D. & Fernandez Y. M. (1999). *Cognitive Behavioral Treatment of Sexual Offenders*. Toronto, ON: Wiley.

Marziano, V., Ward., T., Beech, A. R. & Pattison, R. (2005). Identification of five fundamental implicit theories underlying cognitive distortions in child abusers: A preliminary study. *Psychology, Crime and Law*, **12**, 97–105.

McGinn, L. & Young, J. E. (1996). In P. M. Salkovskis (ed.), *Frontiers of Cognitive Therapy* (pp. 182–207). New York: Guilford Press.

Mihailides, S., Devilly, G. J. & Ward, T. (2004). Implicit cognitive distortions and sexual offending. *Sexual Abuse: A Journal of Research and Treatment*, **16**, 333–50.

Milner, R. J. & Webster, S. D. (2005). Identifying schemas in child molester, rapists and violent offenders. *Sexual Abuse: A Journal of Research and Treatment*, **17**, 425–39.

Richardson, G. (2005). Early maladaptive schemas in a sample of British adolescent sexual abusers: Implications for therapy. *Journal of Sexual Aggression*, **11**, 259–76.

Safran, J. D. (1990). Towards a refinement of cognitive therapy in light of interpersonal theory: 1. Theory. *Clinical Psychology Review*, **10**, 87–105.

Siegert, R. & Ward, T. (2003). Back to the future: Evolutionary explanations of rape. In T. Ward, D. R. Laws & S. M. Hudson, (eds), *Sexual Deviance: Issues and Controversies* (pp. 45–64). Thousand Oaks, CA: Sage.

Ward, T. (2000). Sexual offenders' cognitive distortions as implicit theories. *Aggression and Violent Behavior*, **5**, 491–507.

Ward, T. & Keenan, T. (1999). Child molesters' implicit theories. *Journal of Interpersonal Violence*, **14**, 821–38.

Ward, T., Polaschek, D. L. L. & Beech, A.R. (2006). *Theories of Sexual Offending*. New Jersey: Wiley.

Ward, T. & Siegert, R. J. (2002). Toward a comprehensive theory of child sexual abuse: a theory knitting perspective. *Psychology, Crime and Law*, **8**, 319–51.

Young, J. E. (1990). *Cognitive Therapy for Personality Disorders: A Schema-focused Approach.* Sarasota, FL: Professional Resource Press.

Young, J. E. & Brown, G. (1994). Young Schema Questionnaire, 2nd edn. In J. E. Young (ed.), *Cognitive Therapy for Personality Disorders: A A Schema-focused Approach* (revised edition, pp. 63–76). Sarasota, FL: Professional Resource Press.

Chapter 2

THE IMPLICIT THEORIES OF RAPISTS AND SEXUAL MURDERERS

Dawn Fisher
Llanarth Court Hospital and University of Birmingham, UK

Anthony R. Beech
University of Birmingham, UK

The importance of cognition in offending has long been established as central to understanding the motivation of offenders, and as such is central to the assessment and treatment of sex offenders (Beech, Fisher & Thornton, 2003). However, until relatively recently the focus in both assessment and treatment of sex offenders has been on what may be regarded as surface cognitions. That is, articulated thoughts, attitudes and beliefs that seem to support sexual offending. These are generally labelled as "cognitive distortions" (see Chapter 2 of this volume and also Abel *et al.*, 1989) and have become the subject of much debate in recent years as to whether they precede offending in order to give the offender permission to offend and whether, as such, they are causative (Finkelhor, 1984; Ward & Siegert, 2002). Alternatively, do they arise post-offence to make the offender feel better about the offence by justifying, excusing or externalising blame to others, thereby minimising self-blame and guilt and playing a maintenance role in offending (Abel *et al.*, 1989)? It has also been suggested that offence-supportive statements are used by people in general to explain their behaviour, or act as excuses and are as common in general offenders who desist from crime as those who continue to offend (Maruna & Mann, 2006). This raises the question as to whether there is any value in assessing and treating surface cognitions *per se* or whether the focus should be more on the deeper level cognitions: the schemas and implicit theories (Mann & Beech, 2003; Polaschek & Ward, 2002; Ward, 2000).

A further difficulty when working with cognitive distortions is that it has been difficult to measure them in certain groups of sex offenders, namely rapists and sexual murderers. While many studies have reported on the typical cognitive

---

Aggressive Offenders' Cognition: Theory, Research and Practice. Edited by T. A. Gannon, T. Ward, A. R. Beech and D. Fisher. © 2007 John Wiley & Sons, Ltd.

distortions of child sex abusers using self-report questionnaires, similar studies of rapists have generally failed to show that this group hold more distorted views than nonoffenders or nonsexual offenders and, indeed, in many cases, the rapists report less distorted or victim-blaming views than the controls (Beech *et al.*, 2005). This has been suggested as being partly due to the problem of using self–report questionnaires and also the belief that perhaps rapists only access their pro-offending attitudes when in certain mood states (Malamuth, 1981). This has caused problems in the assessment of rapists and sexual murderers as they generally do not show up as having difficulties, regarding their cognitions and attitudes, which are often fairly easily assessed by the use of self-report techniques in child abusers (e.g., Beech, 2001; Fisher, Beech & Browne, 1999). Thus, another type of assessment is required to examine the beliefs and attitudes of this group.

One approach, which has been adopted in more recent years in the assessment and treatment of sex offenders, is to address the underlying cognitions held by sex offenders as a way of understanding their view of the world and their motivation to offend. Ward (2000) describes how cognitive distortions arise in sexual offenders from causal theories about the nature of their victims. In the general literature these underlying cognitions have been labelled as schemas. Schemas have been defined by Beck (1964) as cognitive structures used for assessing, screening and encoding incoming stimuli. Ward suggests that schemas are broad based and, therefore, refer to a number of mental structures such as categories, beliefs, scripts or theories. These systems are also "deep cognitions" (Kwon, 1994), which can only be assessed indirectly via the "cognitive products" to which they give rise. Anderson, Anderson and Deuser (1996) suggest that the degree to which schemas dominate information processing can vary over time. Ward (2000) has attempted to be more specific in definition and prefers to use the term "implicit theory" rather than schema because of the latter's ambiguity and lack of conceptual develop-ment. Implicit theories (ITs) are seen by Ward (2000, p. 494) as being similar to "lay scientific theories" where individuals attempt to "explain, predict, and interpret cognitive phenomena". These theories are termed implicit as they are rarely articulated formally, they are not easily expressed by the individual and the individuals are not usually aware that they view the world in an idiosyncratic way. Ward also notes that:

- A number of ITs identified in sexual offenders (see below) specify the ontological characteristics of people (i.e., the nature of their being in terms of core psycho-logical structures and processes).
- These ontological constructs, and their relationships, are used to explain human actions; and
- implicit theories produce interpretations of evidence about others' behaviours, desires and motivations.

Therefore ITs contain *beliefs* about the world and have reference to offenders' *desires/goals* in that they create a framework which influences the goals that are salient in the interpretation of interpersonal phenomena. Therefore, ITs are complex systems containing integrated sets of cognition and goals/desires.

In this chapter we will review the types of implicit theories found in both rapists and sexual murderers and discuss how they may relate to cognitions at different levels of processing and consciousness. We will also discuss how the identification of implicit theories in rapists and sexual murderers can determine motive (i.e., cognitions, desires/goals) and how consideration of these motivational ITs can lead to a broad typology of these offender groups. Finally, we will discuss the treatment implications of this work.

DEFINING CORE SCHEMAS/IMPLICIT THEORIES IN SEXUAL OFFENDERS

Based on the typical themes found in sex offender questionnaires and clinical observations of statements made by sex offenders, Ward and Keenan (1999) originally identified five implicit ITs in child sex abusers (see Chapter 1, this volume). They regarded these ITs as being "underlying beliefs that underpinned the various cognitive distortions held by child sex abusers". They make the point that the ITs cover a range of beliefs and different ITs will be found in different child abusers. It would not be expected to find all five ITs in every offender. The five ITs identified have been empirically identified by Marziano, Ward, Beech and Pattison (2006) and are as follows:

- *Entitlement* – individuals with this IT regard some people as superior to others and believe that they therefore have a right to impose their desires upon individuals they see as less important.
- *Dangerous world* – this IT centres round the core belief that the world is a dangerous place and that other people are malevolent and therefore likely to be abusive and rejecting. Therefore children are seen as less threatening.
- *Children as sex objects* – children are viewed as sexual beings who have sexual needs and desires and are capable of making plans that will enable them to achieve sexual experiences.
- *Uncontrollable* – individuals holding this IT regard their personality and sexual preferences as unchangeable and believe that they have no control over their expression. They therefore do not take responsibility for their behaviour but regard it as outside of their control, at the mercy of external forces.
- *Nature of harm* – individuals with this IT do not regard sexual activity alone as being sufficient to cause harm to another person. They may even see sexual activity as being beneficial to the child. They view harm as only being caused by serious physical damage and view their own sexual behaviour with a child as benign.

More recently, Polaschek and Ward (2002) applied a similar approach to Ward and Keenan (1999) to look at the presence of ITs in rapists. They took into account the numerous distortions contained in a variety of source material regarding rapists. This included reviewing research sources of attitudinal statements such as the interview-based research by Scully and Marolla (1984, 1985). Using this approach they identified five implicit theories, which Ward (2000) suggests tends to focus on issues of responsibility, hostility towards women, and acceptance of interpersonal violence towards women (Burt, 1983). Each implicit theory was based on a core theme around which clusters of specific distortions could be organised. The following ITs were identified and are described below:

- *Entitlement* – this is the same as the IT found in child sex abusers. In respect of rapists it proposes that men should have their needs, including their sexual needs, met on demand. For example, men might be viewed as more powerful and important than women and therefore have the right to have their sexual needs met when they want and with whom they want. In this implicit theory the desires and beliefs of the offender are paramount and those of the victim ignored or viewed as only of secondary importance.
- *Dangerous world* – again this is the same IT as found in child abusers. The world is seen as a dangerous place and other people are thought likely to behave in an abusive and rejecting manner in order to promote their own interests. Therefore if women are perceived as threats and in need of retribution, they may become victims of sexual abuse. The beliefs and desires of other people are a focus of this implicit theory, particularly those signifying malevolent intentions. Therefore, the content of this theory refers to the desires of other people to dominate or hurt the offender. In addition, the offender views himself as capable of retaliation and asserting his dominance over others.
- *Women as sex objects* – in this IT women are seen to exist in a constant state of sexual reception. They were created to meet the sexual needs of men and women's most significant needs and desires centre around the sexual domain. From these propositions, it follows that women will constantly desire sex, even if it is coerced or violent, and that as sexual entities, women should always be receptive to and available to meet men's sexual needs, when they arise. One implication of this theory is that there is often a discrepancy between what women say and what they actually want. This inconsistency arises because their sexual needs may be unknown to them. Thus women don't deliberately deceive men; instead they simply don't know that they are fundamentally sex objects. They are unaware of the unconscious messages their bodies are emitting.
- *Male sex drive is uncontrollable* – this IT states that men's sexual energy is difficult to manage and that women have a key role in its loss of control. Like child sex abusers, men who rape adult women attribute the causes of their offending to external factors (i.e., external to the self, and personal responsibility). These factors can be located in the victim or in other features of the environment (for example, availability of alcohol). Serious involuntary sexual deprivation is usually attributed to insufficient access to women and therefore it follows that a woman denying reasonable sexual access is one cause of loss of control for men.
- *Women are unknowable/dangerous* – this IT proposes that either because of biology or socialisation, women are inherently different from men and that these differences cannot be understood readily by men. One variant of this theory that is less benign occurs with the addition of the corollary that women are unable or unwilling to communicate honestly with men. Here women are portrayed as inherently deceptive (see Malamuth & Brown, 1994). Supposedly, they know that their own desires and needs are incompatible with those of men and so they do not communicate these desires and needs directly, but instead present them in a disguised manner.

It can be seen that two of the nonsexual ITs identified are broadly similar to those found in child sex abusers: *entitlement* and *dangerous world*. Although with the *dangerous world* IT for child abusers, children may be seen as a less threatening option to abuse, while for rapists the *dangerous world* IT predominantly stipulates that it is necessary to fight back and achieve dominance and control over other people. This involves punishing individuals who appear to inflict harm on the offender and especially to ensure that their own position is strengthened. The *children/women as sex objects* ITs can be broadly seen as measuring the sexualisation of potential victims, women or children, dependent upon offender type. An argument can be made that the *male sex drive is uncontrollable* IT is similar to the *uncontrollable* IT found in child abusers except it is confined to male sex drive. It can also be argued, although speculative at the present time, that the *nature of harm* IT in child abusers and *women are unknowable/dangerous* IT in rapists have similarities in that they both tap into a 'harm' concept: i.e., children not being harmed by child abuse; or women as harmful.

EMPIRICAL STUDIES ASSESSING IMPLICIT THEORIES IN ADULT ABUSERS

A number of empirical studies have examined interview transcripts for the presence or absence of these implicit theories in sex offenders and the findings have generally been supportive. We will now look at these in some detail.

The Identification of Implicit Theories in Rapists

Polaschek and Gannon (2004) examined offence process descriptions from 37 incarcerated rapists, based on interviews and official accounts. They reported that all five ITs were present and that *women are unknowable/dangerous*, and *women as sex objects* and *entitlement* were particularly prevalent. *Women are unknowable/dangerous* was found in 65 % of the rapists' offence accounts, women as sex objects in 70 % and entitlement in 68 %. Surprisingly *male sex drive is uncontrollable* and d*angerous world* only occurred in a minority of offences. They did not find evidence of any new ITs. They reported that a prominent finding was that many rapists described women as being malevolent and unpredictable and as a result suggested that *women as unknowable* should be changed to *women are dangerous* to more accurately describe this IT.

Beech, Ward and Fisher (2006) analysed the interview transcripts from 41 rapists who had participated in the sex offender treatment programme run in prisons in England and Wales. The five ITs proposed by Polaschek and Ward were found to be present, as expected, with the *dangerous world* IT being most prevalent, being found in 79 % of the sample. *Women as sex objects* was the next most common, being found in 51 % of the sample. With regard to the remaining ITs *entitlement* was found in 44 % of the sample, *male sex drive is uncontrollable* 15 % and *women are unknowable/dangerous* in only 9 % of the sample. Evidence for the identification of these types of ITs or schemas in rapists has also been reported by Mann (Mann &

Beech, 2003; Mann & Hollin, 2001). Here, treatment records of 45 rapists were examined and statements they had made to explain their offending were extracted. These explanatory statements of their offence behaviours were then sorted into categories. From this analysis Mann identified five types of schema: *entitlement, control, grievance, self as victim* and *disrespect for certain women* (usually prostitutes).

If the schema definition of Mann and the IT definition of Polaschek and Ward are compared, it can be seen that there is a clear overlap with *entitlement* IT being identified by both Mann and by Polaschek and Ward. The *dangerous world* IT also has a lot of commonalities with the *control* schema identified by Mann. In both, there is a need to be in a position of power or control over others and this involves punishing individuals who appear to inflict harm on the offender. Mann notes that sometimes the offence was described as a competition for control or a response by the offender to someone trying to control or humiliate him. Even though Mann notes that the *disrespect for certain women* was more of a category schema than a belief schema, the kind of statements emerging from this schema were found to be grouped around ideas implying that some women did not deserve the normal standards of respectful behaviour. Hence, this schema may to some extent overlap the *women as sex objects* schema outlined by Polaschek and Ward, especially as Mann notes that prostitutes are often viewed in this way (see above). In the Mann scheme, the *grievance* schema is about the notion of women causing the offender harm. Statements related to this schema include ideas around the notions that women are responsible for hurting the offender (emotionally) and that it is always women's fault when something goes wrong in the offender's life. Hence this schema can be seen as overlapping with Polaschek and Ward's *women are unknowable*, where women are portrayed as inherently deceptive. Mann points out that statements around the *grievance* schema often suggested that revenge or punishment was justifiable when the individual perceived he has "been wronged". The final two ITs/schemas, *male sex drive is uncontrollable* and *self as victim*, seems to have little overlap. However, when they are examined closely it could be argued that both contain the idea that the offender's behaviour is outside of the offender's control. Mann notes that statements around the *self-as-victim* beliefs have a flavour of passive self-pity containing aspects of hopelessness, or helplessness, in the face of the world's demands, such as "bad things always happen to me".

Implicit Theories in Sexual Murderers

Given that child sex abusers and rapists have ITs in common and some that are different, we (Beech, Fisher & Ward, 2005) examined the extent sexual murderers share the same ITs as rapists, as there is now some evidence that sexual murderers against adult women may not be qualitatively different from offenders who have raped but not murdered. For example, Proulx, Beauregard and Nichole (2002) reported no significant differences between sexual murderers and sexual aggressors against women who had not killed in the Canadian penal system on: age and previous charges (sexual, violent or property); personality profile, as measured by the Millon Clinical Multiaxial Inventory (MCMI) (Millon, 1997); and reported level of deviant fantasy and drug consumption. Oliver *et al.* (2007) compared 58 sexual murderers and 112 rapists who were about to undergo treatment in prison for their sexual offending behaviour on background, personality, offence, and victim characteristics and found few differences. Milsom, Beech and Webster (2003) found that sexual murderers reported more similarities, than differences to rapists in self-reported levels of emotional loneliness and fear of social intimacy in adulthood. Proulx (personal communication, April 2003) makes the point that the differences between sexual murderers and aggressors of adult women may reside in the situation where the offence took place rather than in any underlying differences in offence-related thought processes.

Given these similarities, Beech, Fisher and Ward (2005) hypothesised that an examination of sexual murderers' offence descriptions would result in the uncovering of the same types of ITs reported in rapists by Beech et al. (2006). They interviewed 28 sexual murderers following treatment on the English and Welsh Prison Service's Sex Offender Treatment Programme (SOTP) (Mann, 1999; Mann & Thornton, 1998). Because of the unique nature of the study and its relevance to this book, we will now provide some detail about this study.

All of the subjects were serving a mandatory life sentence for murder. The murder was judged to have a sexual element such that they were offered treatment for sexual offending and they had all completed the SOTP. Subjects participated in a semi-structured interview, which focused on their account of the offence and their motivation. Care was taken to use open-ended questioning and avoid leading or closed questions. Typically questions in the first part of the interview included: who they had offended against, whether they knew the victim prior to the offence(s) that they had committed and what had led up the offence. Prompt questions were asked about the offender's motivation, to find out whether the offence was related to sex or anger. Other areas covered in the interview were: the offenders' feelings at the time of the offence toward their victims (if known) and others in their lives; distal and proximal antecedents of their offending, including fantasies around sex and violence; sexual behaviours they had committed in the offence(s), and the *modus operandi* of the killing. Where appropriate, questions were also asked about their previous offences.

An analysis of the interview protocols using the five rapist ITs supported the research hypothesis, that the way the sexual murderers' viewed themselves, the world and their victims could be coded into the five ITs previously identified in rapists. In other words, there were no appreciable differences in the kinds of ITs exhibited by rapists and individuals who had committed a sexual murder. Examples of how each IT was represented in the sexual murderers is described below.

Dangerous World

This IT was found to be the most common in the sample, and was present in 22 (79 %) of the 28 cases. The form this IT took in the sexual murderers' description of their offending behaviour was that of generalised malevolence. That is, the individual concerned viewed other people as being unreliable and having treated them abusively and unjustly. This view resulted in entrenched feelings of resentment and anger and the adoption of retaliation interpersonal strategies. That is, many of the sexual murderers decided to retaliate against the individual(s) who they believed had wronged them or else simply selected someone they could vent their frustrations against. Examples of participants' responses to the question "What do you think the motivation for your offence was?" were as follows:

> I committed the offence because I was not thinking of anybody but myself, I was taking my anger, bitterness, my hatred and my frustration out [on somebody else].

> The pain I was feeling I wanted to transfer it onto to someone else and all that ... because it's stuff that's happened in the past and also stuff that was going on around at the time. It meant quite a lot too, everything just boiling up, boiling it all up, then it all came out at the same time. I was abused as a child by my foster father ... I think it was kind of like, the humiliation part was from then, the abuse was, it was all inside of me and I just wanted it out, I wanted it out.

> We went to a night-club, started to have sex and she refused to have sex with me and because of all the anger and the emotions of the previous events. A break-up previous to that, an assault charge previous to that all got on top of me that night and I took all my frustrations and anger out on X.

Male Sex Drive is Uncontrollable

This IT was the second most common in the sample being found in 20 (71%) of cases. There were three strands to this IT. First, the participants would often report feeling powerless in their lives and unable to control their actions, including their sexual behaviour. Second, the aggressive emotions that resulted in the murder were often described as external to the person; they simply overwhelmed him. Third, individuals described feeling overwhelmed by their sexual fantasies and the associated sexual urges. The sexual element in their offending was viewed as particularly compelling and compulsive in nature. It was as if the sexual fantasies took on a life of their own and it was inevitable that sooner or later they would rape and/or murder a woman. In some instances the fantasies contained explicitly sadistic components that revolved around the infliction of pain and suffering (and death) on the victim. Examples of elements of this IT reported by participants in the study are as follows:

When an offender was asked what he was fantasising about prior to the offence he said:

> All sorts. Rapes, murders ... all kinds of fantasies. Anything that made me feeling good as, I would fantasise about ... It was mostly about having somebody within my power so I could, because I felt powerless, at the time.

Another offender said:

> I lost it. I lost my temper and I lost it all together. I tried to dominate physically, by using physical force and then she went for me, that's where it was ... I've got to get the upper hand here and that's where I lost it and the physical violence started.

A third said:

> Things have built up for a long time … which allowed me in way to chose a deviant set of behaviours as a sexual outlet, peeping and exposing and stuff like that, if I liked someone I'd expose myself to them … On the night I killed X if that had been someone else I would have chosen that person [to rape]. I recognized her so I assumed that she'd recognise me and I panicked.

Entitlement

This IT was the next most common and was identified in just under a half ($n = 12$, 43 %) of cases. There was a sense in this IT that men in the study holding this IT were entitled to take sex if they wanted it because they were males. For example, some men saw themselves as more physically powerful. Others believed that they simply deserved sex because the women had sexually aroused them or had been in some type of relationship with them. Examples of this IT are as follows.

One offender reported that prior to his offence he felt that:

> I was strung along by a prostitute, I got angry because she was stringing me along, playing games, if you know what I mean she wanted more money … I thought well I'm going to have sex with her whatever … I thought she's a prostitute and she's holding out for more money.

Another said:

> I got round there [the victim's house] and I was talking to her and during the course of the evening, it was pretty late, say about half an hour into the conversation. I was telling her about my problems … and I made a pass at her. Which was I kissed her for a couple of seconds. She pushed me away, so because of not being able to handle the rejection … I killed her … but I'm used to getting everything my own way y'know.

Women as Sex Objects

This IT was found to be present in just under a third (n = 9, 32 %) of cases. Men holding this IT reported viewing women as sexual objects or existing merely as recipients of males' sexual attention. They were regarded as conduits of male sexual interest and not viewed as autonomous beings with preferences and interests of their own. This IT functioned as a background one and frequently led to situations where the offenders simply expected sex and if it was not forthcoming would become aggressive. Examples of this IT are as follows.

One participant said that:

> "I took on so much y'know proving myself to be top dog at work, living a life of a lie, with having two girlfriends, lying to them, seeing women as sex objects, having bets with work colleagues over how many you could bed, things like that."

Another said that:

> "I had a tendency to sexualise, I still have a tendency to sexualise women, is that a trait of a sex offender or is that just me being … a Neanderthal type man?"

Women are Unknowable/Women are Dangerous

This IT was the least common being found in less than a fifth (n = 5, 18 %) of cases. Participants holding this IT expressed frustration and confusion and tended to behave in a sexually aggressive way to teach the women a lesson. Thus the key ideas seem to be that women are believed to be responsible for failed relationships and intentionally set out to make life difficult or deliberately create problems for some men. Examples of this IT as are follows:
One man said:

> "So what I had to do then … was to humiliate her enough to satisfy my need if you like, to say OK now you've been hurt as much as I've been hurt, you won't mess me or anybody else about again, and I said to myself she wasn't dead … "

Another said that:

> "She went into a verbal assault on me which I couldn't handle so I said to myself the only way I can get you back for hurting me is to rape you. So [I] dragged her upstairs."

A third participant said that:

> "I used to think it was a case of just rape and it being a sex thing but it wasn't, it was much deeper than that, and I realise I was carrying a lot of bad attitude about women, and the way I've not dealt with rejection at all, it was my fault, I was the one carrying all the crap if you were, because I never coped with it and dealt with it and it all came out on my victim that day."

DERIVING MOTIVATIONS FOR SEXUAL MURDER AND RAPE BY THE RELATIVE PRESENCE/ ABSENCE OF KEY IMPLICIT THEORIES

In the Beech, Fisher and Ward (2005) study of sexual murderers, the pattern of occurrence of the ITs was investigated, as shown in Table 2.1.

By a process of sorting the most common ITs (Dangerous world, present in 79 % of cases and Male sex drive is uncontrollable, 71 %) three main groups of sexual murderers were identified, by the presence or absence of the violence IT *dangerous world* and the sexual IT *male sex drive is uncontrollable*. Group 1 was identified by the presence of both these sexual and violent ITs, Group 2 by the presence of the *dangerous world* IT and the complete absence of the *male sex drive is uncontrollable*. Group 3 were defined by the presence of the *male sex drive is uncontrollable* and the complete absence of the *dangerous world* IT. Table 2.2 shows the offence demographics of these three groups.

Table 2.1   Distribution of implicit theories across the Beech *et al.* (2005) sexual murderer sample

Group 1	Dangerous world	Male sex drive is uncontrollable	Entitlement	Women as sex objects	Women as unknowable
1	X	X	X	X	X
2	X	X	X	X	
3	X	X	X	X	
4	X	X	X	X	
5	X	X	X		
6	X	X	X		
7	X	X	X		
8	X	X			X
9	X	X			
10	X	X			
11	X	X			
12	X	X			
13	X	X			
14	X	X			
Group 2					
15	X		X		X
16	X		X	X	
17	X		X		
18	X				X
19	X			X	
20	X				
21	X				
22	X				
Group 3					
23		X	X	X	
24		X	X		
25		X		X	X
26		X		X	
27		X			
28		X			
TOTAL	22 (79 %)	20 (71 %)	12 (43 %)	9 (32 %)	5 (18 %)

Source: Tables 1 to 4 were originally published in Beech, A., Fisher, D. and Ward, T. (2005). Sexual murderers' implicit theories. *Journal of Interpersonal Violence*, **20**, 1366–89 and Beech, A., Ward, T. and Fisher, D. (2006). The identification of sexual and violent motivations in men who assault women: implications for treatment. *Journal of Interpersonal Violence*, **21**, 1635–53.

It can be seen from Table 2.2 that when these groups were compared on a number of offence demographics clear differences were found between the groups. *Group 1* was motivated by a prior intention to kill, and violent and sadistic thoughts and fantasies. Some men in this group also reported specific thoughts around control and domination. These thought patterns co-occurring with *male sex drive is uncontrollable*, and in half of the group – *entitlement* (where the offender holds that his desires and beliefs are paramount) – led men in this sample to brutal sexual crimes. Their victims tended to be unknown, targeted strangers, or those who

Table 2.2 Offence characteristics of sexual murderers grouped by the presence/absence of *dangerous world/male sex drive is uncontrollable* implicit theories in sexual murderers

Main Implicit Theories	Group 1 (n = 14) (Dangerous world + male sex drive uncontrollable)	Group 2 (n = 8) (dangerous world)	Group 3 (n = 6) (male sex drive uncontrollable)
Reported Motivation	To carry out fantasies	Grievance	Avoid detection
Main reported thoughts/fantasies prior to murder	Intent to murder Rape/murder Sadistic fantasy Control/ domination	Resentment/Anger towards women	Sexual fantasies
Method of killing n (%)	6 (43%) strangulation 5 (36%) stabbed 1 (7%) stabbed/ set on fire 1 (7%) beaten 1 (7%) beaten/killed by train	5 (63%) beaten 1 (12%) drowned 1 (12%) stabbed 1 (12%) suffocated	3 (50%) stabbed 2 (33%) beaten 1 (17%) strangulation
Targeted stranger n (%)	9 (65%)	2 (25%)	1 (17%)
Known n (%)	2 (28%)	4 (50%)	2 (33%)
Age of victim M (SD)	36.79 (6.24)	38.25 (10.33)	29.17 (6.12)
Sexual mutilation n (%)	9 (65%)	1 (13%)	1 (17%)
Sexual interference after death n (%)	5 (36%)	3 (37%)	1 (17%)
History of violence against women n (%)	10 (71%)	2 (25%)	1 (17%)
Previous sexual convictions n (%)	5 (36%)	1 (13%)	2 (33%)
Previous violent convictions n (%)	6 (43%)	1 (13%)	2 (33%)
Previous sexual + violent convictions n (%)	7 (50%)	7 (88%)	4 (67%)

were known and who had been targeted for sexual assault. A high level of sexualised violence was committed in these men's' offences. Sexual mutilation was high, as was sexual interference after death. Mutilation and interference included acts such as exposure of, and bites to, the breast, partial severance of the breast and vaginal mutilation. This behaviour can be considered ritualistic in nature. In at least one case the offender committed necrophilic acts on the victim's body. Strangulation was often used as a method of killing in the group, which was rare in the other two groups. Strangulation can be considered as a method of killing where the perpetrator has complete control over the life of the victim at all times until the victim has died. Members of this group were found to be the most dangerous repeat sexual offenders in that half were rated as high or very high risk of sexual reconviction as measured by Risk Matrix 2000 (Thornton *et al.*, 2003), an actuarial risk assessment commonly employed in the United Kingdom to assess risk.

Group 2 was characterised by grievance towards women. Most men in this group reported that motivation to offend was primarily driven by anger and resentment towards women. The *dangerous world* IT would appear to be the primary underlying IT in terms of how men viewed the world where thoughts about punishment and control are primary motivators. The sexual murder itself was characterised by a high level of expressive violence with multiple attacks on the victim, using different weapons (knives, blunt instruments and hands) and evidence of "overkill" (gouging the victims eyes out, attempted scalping, numerous stabbings or repeated blows such that body parts were partially severed) – for example, one victim had received over 140 different wounds to her body. Sexual mutilation of the victim's body was low in this group although a third of the group had sexually interfered with the body after death. This behaviour took the form of further humiliating acts on the victim such as inserting knives or other objects into the vagina. Members of this group were the most likely to have known their victim prior to the offence.

Group 3 were found to have murdered in order to keep the victim quiet during the offence, or in order to avoid detection by making sure that the victim was not around to subsequently identify the perpetrator. Some men in this group admitted that they were prepared to murder their victim before they had committed their sexual offence. Here the primary IT found in this group was *male sex drive is uncontrollable*, hence there was generally little evidence of a history of overt hostility towards women or overkill in this group, as seen in Group 2. The *male sex drive is uncontrollable* IT acts as a motivator to commit a sexual offence whatever the cost to the victim.

Beech *et al.* (2006) also used this system to investigate motivations in rapists and again identified three groups by the relative presence/absence of the violence IT: *dangerous world* and the sexual ITs: *women as sex objects* or *male sex drive is uncontrollable*. Table 2.3 shows the groups of these ITs.

It can be seen from Table 2.3 that in Group 1 there was the presence of both *Dangerous world* and the sexual ITs: *women as sex objects or male sex drive is uncontrollable*. Group 2 were characterised by the presence of *dangerous world* and the absence of any sexual ITs. These were seen as being primarily violently motivated to offend. Group 3 were characterised by the presence of *women as sex objects* and the complete absence of *dangerous world*, nearly three-quarters (73%) of this group also reported the *entitlement* IT (i.e., that these men felt their needs, especially their sexual needs should be met on demand) and hence were seen as being sexually motivated. Table 2.4 shows the offence demographics of the three rapist groups.

It can be seen from Table 2.4 that comparison of the offence demographics between the groups found that all of Group 1 (the sexually sadistic group) had previous convictions for sexual/violent or both sexual and violent offences compared to just over half of Groups 2 and 3 combined. Individuals in Group 2 (violently motivated rapists) were highly likely to have offended against a known victim (typically a partner/ex-partner), have previous convictions for sexual violence/nonsexual violence or both sexual and nonsexual violence compared to the sexually motivated rapists (Group 3). Members of Group 3 were more likely to

Table 2.3 Distribution of iplicit theories across the Beech *et al.* (2006) rapist sample

	Dangerous world	Women as sex objects	Entitlement	Male sex drive is uncontrollable	Women are dangerous
Group 1					
1	X			X	X
2	X			X	
3	X			X	
4	X			X	
5	X	X			
6	X	X			
7	X	X			
8	X	X			
9	X	X			
10	X	X	X		
11	X	X			
Group 2					
12	X		X		X
13	X		X		
14	X		X		
15	X		X		
16	X				
17	X				X
18	X				
19	X				
20	X				
21	X				
22	X				
23	X				
Group 3					
24		X	X	X	
25		X	X		
26		X	X		
27		X	X		
28		X	X		
29		X	X		
30		X	X		
31		X	X		
32		X	X		
33		X	X		
34		X	X		
35		X			
36		X			
37		X			
38		X			
39					
Unclassified					
40			X	X	
41			X		
TOTAL	25 (61 %)	22 (54 %)	18 (44 %)	6 (15 %)	3 (9 %)

Table 2.4   Offence characteristics of rapists grouped by the presence/absence of dangerous world/women as sexual objects implicit theories

	Group 1 (n = 11)	Group 1 (n = 13)	Group 2 (n = 15)
Main implicit theories	Dangerous world plus Male sex drive uncontrollable/ Women as sex objects	Dangerous world	Women as sex objects
Reported motivations	Desire for paraphilic activities Desire to sexually humiliate women; Power and domination	Anger Revenge Inadequacy	Carry out sexual thoughts/ fantasies Desire for sex
Main reported thoughts/ fantasies prior to murder	Sadistic fantasy	Resentment/ Anger towards women	Sexual fantasies
Targeted stranger n (%)	8 (73 %)	5 (38 %)	10 (67 %)
Victim known n (%)	3 (27 %)	8 (61 %)	5 (33 %)
Age of victim n (%) (SD)	33.50 (16.39)	33.04 (14.60)	22.10 (4.80)
Previous sexual convictions only n (%)	3 (27 %)	4 (31 %)	1 (7 %)
Previous violent convictions only n (%)	4 (36 %)	4 (31 %)	2 (13 %)
Previous sexual plus violent convictions n (%)	4 (36 %)	2 (15 %)	2 (13 %)
Previous all sexual/ violent convictions n (%)	11 (100 %)	10 (77 %)	5 (33 %)

have offended against strangers, and to have offended against younger victims compared to Groups 1 and 2.

CONVERGENT UTILITY OF THE IDENTIFIED GROUPS OF SEXUAL MURDERERS AND RAPISTS

The urge to rape has been described as being driven by anger/hostility, sexual or sadistic motives (for example Groth, Burgess & Holstrom, 1977; Knight & Prentky, 1990; Malamuth & Brown, 1994). In particular, the most well known system for the classification of rapists is probably the Massachusetts Treatment Centre: Revision 3 (MTC: R3) system developed by Knight and Prentky. Here, five main types of rapists have been described, grouped around three motivational types identified: sexual motivation, anger motivation and sadistic motivation. There are two types of *sexually motivated rapists* identified in the system. The first is *the opportunistic rapist*, where the offender has a number of pro-offending attitudes, including the belief that there is nothing wrong with having coercive sex with women. The sexual assault committed by this type of rapist is an impulsive, predatory act, controlled more by situational circumstances than by explicit sexual fantasy or anger. The second type is the *nonsadistic sexual rapist* where there will be a high level of sexual fantasy that precedes the offence(s). These fantasies will reflect sexual arousal and distorted attitudes about women and sex. Typically, there may be comparatively low levels of interpersonal aggression in this type of offender, with the offender using instrumental force to ensure compliance from the victim.

There are two types of *anger-motivated rapists* identified in the Knight and Prentky system. For the *vindictive rapist*, women are the central and exclusive focus of these men's anger. The sexual assault is marked by behaviours that are physically damaging and intended to degrade and humiliate their victim(s). There is no evidence that anger is eroticised or that they are preoccupied with sexual fantasies. The system notes that the violence of the vindictive rapist may be so severe that it results in murder. *The pervasively angry rapist* is hypothesised to be motivated by undifferentiated anger in all aspects of his life. Such offenders are equally likely to express their unmanageable aggression towards men and women. These men will have long histories of anti-social behaviour where rape is another expression of their anger and hostility.

There is one further type referred to as the *sadistic sexual rapist*. Here, there is a fusion of sex and aggression. Knight and Prentky note clinically that there is a frequent occurrence of erotic and destructive thoughts and fantasies, i.e. anger is eroticised.

Hence it is not surprising that these motivational types were identified here. Perhaps what is more surprising was that these types were also clearly identified in sexual murderers. However, examination of the sexual murder literature would again suggest commonalities in both profiling and clinical work in that the sexual murderers in Group 1 appear to contain what might be considered the prototypical, usually serial, sexual murderer where the killing is the primary sexual motive. Myers *et al.* (1999) have described such an offence as a fusion of sexual assault and killing and where an overt (penile penetration), or symbolic sexual assault (such as insertion of a foreign object into one of the victim's orifices) is present. Ressler, Burgess and Douglas (1988) note that in such a sexual homicide, exposure of sexual parts of the victim's body, insertion of objects, sexual positioning of the body, as well as evidence of sexual activity indicate a sexual element to the murder has taken place. Hazelwood and Douglas (1980) note that murder may play an instrumental role in either the commission of a sexual assault, to avoid detection, i.e., by avoiding identification by the victim or to keep the victim quiet. This type of sexual murderer appears to been have been identified in Group 3. Revitch (1980) notes that murder with a sexual component may be motivated by an angry outburst or in response to rejection of a proposed or actual sexual advance. This type of sexual murderer appears to have been identified in Group 2.

These groups, identified purely on the basis of identified ITs, also seem to relate to clinical descriptions of sexual murderers, involved in treatment, reported by Clarke and Carter (2000). Clarke and Carter identified three main types of sexual murderers. Although there are a number of differences in the offence demographics of the men identified in this study, there are a number of commonalities to warrant mentioning. In Clarke and Carter's clinical descriptions, the *sexually motivated murderer* is characterised by a primary sexual motivation to kill, in which there are sophisticated and detailed masturbatory fantasies to killing, where the victim is usually unknown and has been specifically targeted, and the method of killing is sexually stimulating. Hence this description is similar to the profile of Group 1 men. *The sexually triggered/aggressive control* sexual murderer is characterised by Clarke and Carter as having a primary motivation to offend sexually, where the killing is instrumental, but intentional, e.g., to keep the victim quiet during the offence or to avoid detection. The Clarke and Carter type shows striking similarities with Group 3 in the current research. The *sexually triggered/aggressive dyscontrol* sexual murderer, in the Clarke and Carter system, is described as having no prior intention to kill or sexually offend. The offender explains the killing as having resulted from something the victim said or did in a sexual context, triggering a substantial sense of grievance held for some time against an intimate party. Extreme violence or humiliation against the victim takes place in the offence, suggesting loss of control and perspective. Sexual intercourse may or may not take place, but violence against the victim has sexual characteristics, e.g., mutilation of the genital area. This type of sexual offender, identified clinically by Clarke and Carter, shows striking similarities with offenders contained in Group 2 in the current research.

TREATMENT NEEDS OF THREE IDENTIFIED RAPE AND SEXUAL MURDER GROUPS

We believe that these results have significant implications for treatment as it suggests that sexual murderers are not qualitatively different from rapists in terms of the underlying schemas they have about the world. Therefore, it would appear that schema focused treatment, such as that employed by the UK Prison Service in England and Wales, would be just as beneficial with this type of sexual offender as it has been with other high risk sexual offenders as reported by Thornton and Shingler (2001). Specific treatment should be guided by the particular type of IT present in each individual. In fact, as Proulx, Beauregard and Nichole (2002) note, the essential difference between the types of offenders examined here may not be whether they are rapists or sexual murderers but whether their offences were sadistically or non sadistically motivated.

However, in terms of the groupings identified we would suggest the following:

• *Group 1* offenders, i.e., those who have both the *dangerous world* IT and the sexual ITs *male sex drive is uncontrollable/women as sex objects* running at the same time, are very dangerous offenders. They need a high level of treatment intervention in order to reduce the possibility of committing further serious sadistic sexual crimes. There clearly needs to be behavioural work to modify deviant sexual arousal to their violent/sadistic fantasies. However, the identified synergism of the two specific strands of how the offender views the world should be addressed and disentangled in targeted schema-focused therapy. We would suggest that caution should be exercised in carrying out any forms of treatment, where victim empathy training is involved, as this work involves making offenders aware of the distress caused to their victims. Sexual offenders with a sadistic motivation to their offending could be problematic on standard treatment programmes where a major component of therapy is making offenders aware of the distress caused to their victims. Here, it could be argued that sadistic offenders are all too well aware of the impact their offending has had upon their victim as this was one of the main aims of the offence. However, there arises the problem of defining the concept of sadism. As Marshall (2001) notes, it may be better for those with "sadistic" motivations to be treated separately to other sexual offenders for this block of treatment or perhaps for the whole treatment programme. However, schema-focused treatment may also have a lot to offer to this type of sexual offender. At the present time it is probably fair to say that we are not aware of any particularly successful cognitive-behavioural/schema focused work for sadistically motivated offenders and hence behavioural options, including aversive conditioning, may offer the most effective approach to treatment with this group.

- For *Group 2*, where the *dangerous world* IT is operating without any sexual ITs, problems appear to underpin grievance and hostile thoughts about women rather than any deviant thoughts/fantasies that are specifically sexual in origin. Here, the data would suggest that offence-focused work may be better targeted towards anger and hostility problems, as well as schema-focused work around these men's longstanding grievance schemas about women. Here, a more general schema focused treatment (as described by Young, Klosko & Weishaar, 2003), such as employed on the Extended Programme in the Prison Service in England and Wales (Mann, 1999) may be beneficial with this type of sexual offender, as it has been with high-risk sexual child abusers (Thornton & Shingler, 2001). In such schema-focused work, offenders are encouraged to identify their habitual patterns of thinking (implicit theories) by reviewing their life histories and developmental experiences. When these are identified they are then related to other difficulties in their lives, such as relationship difficulties and poor emotional regulation, as well as to their offending behaviour. Anger management training would also seem to be necessary with this group.

- For *Group 3* where the sexual ITs: *male sex drive is uncontrollable/ women as sex objects* is operating, there is a willingness to undertake sexual assaults to satisfy their sexual urges and a general failure to control such deviant sexual thoughts and behaviours. These men might be considered as individuals driven by urges to commit sexual offences. Therefore, cognitive-behavioural techniques typically employed with sexual offenders (Beech & Fisher, 2002; Marshall, Anderson & Fernandez, 1999) may be useful with this group. Here, any offence/schema focused work should be clearly related to getting the offender to control his actions so that he does not regard any sexual or offence-related thoughts as being unstoppable and translating to a sexual assault.

CONCLUSIONS

The findings in both our research (Beech, Fisher & Ward, 2005; Beech, Ward & Fisher, 2006) and that of Mann and Hollin (2001) and Milner and Webster (2005) suggest that it is possible to identify an offender's underlying motivations without the offender explicitly acknowledging these. This is invaluable given the difficulty of assessing these offenders using standard psychometrics and interview where they are frequently defensive and denying. The research further suggests that the identification of ITs prior to the commencement of treatment could indicate treatment paths for offenders who are less than honest and open about their reasons for offending.

Given the difficulty of accessing deep-level schemas and obtaining honest responding in sex offenders noted in this chapter, approaches other than direct psychometric questionnaires need to be used. Qualitative approaches where offenders are encouraged to give a free narrative about their offending can be valuable in identifying the types of implicit theories held by the offender. The specific types of implicit theory and deep level schemas held by the individual have treatment implications. Different categories of schemas indicate specific treatment needs. Identifying the primary schemas and implicit theories can therefore be extremely useful in identifying the treatment needs of individuals and could save placing offenders in unsuitable programmes. The use of schema-based therapy is starting to be applied to sex offenders and will hopefully be subject to empirical study into its' efficacy in the future.

As for assessment and treatment implications, it is possible that there are a number of different levels of cognition in sex offenders. At the deep, probably unconscious level are general schemas such as those early maladaptive schemas described by Young (1990). Based on his work with personality-disordered clients, Young (1990) identified a number of early maladaptive schemas that he and colleagues later described as "self-defeating emotional and cognitive patterns that begin early in our development and repeat throughout life" (Young et al., 2003, p. 7). He has identified 18 distinct schemas that can then be grouped into five general categories, referred to as schema domains (see Young et al., 2003). It is likely that the distorted type of thinking described by Ward as an "implicit theory" largely arises from these early maladaptive schemas. Taking the ITs of *dangerous world* and *women are unknowable/dangerous* it can easily be seen that they could stem from the underlying schema of "mistrust/abuse" described by Young. *Male sex drive is uncontrollable/uncontrollable* fits well with the Young schema named "insufficient self-control/self-discipline" and *entitlement* could stem from Young's "entitlement/grandiosity" schema. *Women/children as sex objects* is more difficult to place accurately but is likely to stem from "entitlement/grandiosity" where other people are seen as less worthy and perhaps there to be used. Individuals with this schema may be more inclined to objectify others and see them as being there to meet their needs. These give rise to more specific categories of implicit theories and surface level cognitive distortions seen in many sex offenders. Therefore, we would suggest that it is necessary to look in more detail at the aetiology of problematic ITs in different groups of sexual offenders as happens in the English and Welsh Prison Service

Extended Treatment Programme (Mann, 1999), where schema focused work is an important part of this programme. The focus on deeper level schemas as targets of treatment, rather than on the surface cognitive distortions, is a relatively recent development in treating sex offenders. It is to be hoped that over the next few years evidence as to the efficacy and benefits of using this approach will become apparent through more research in this important area.

REFERENCES

Abel, G. G., Gore, D. K., Holland, C. L. *et al.* (1989). The measurement of the cognitive distortions of child molesters. *Annals of Sex Research*, **2**, 135–53.

Anderson, C. A., Anderson, K. B. & Deuser, W. E. (1996). Examining an affective aggression framework: weapon and temperature effects on aggressive thoughts, affect, and attitudes. *Personality and Social Psychology Bulletin*, **22**, 366–76.

Beck, A. T. (1964). Thinking and depression. II. Theory and therapy. *Archives of General Psychiatry*, **10**, 561–71.

Beech, A. R. (2001). Case material and interview. In C. Hollin (ed.) *Handbook of Offender Assessment and Treatment* (pp. 123–38). Chichester: Wiley.

Beech, A. R. & Fisher, D. (2002). The rehabilitation of child sex offenders. *Australian Psychologist*, **37**, 206–14.

Beech, A., Fisher, D. & Thornton, D. (2003). Risk assessment of sex offenders. *Professional Psychology: Research and Practice*, **34**, 339–52.

Beech, A., Fisher, D. & Ward, T. (2005). Implicit theories in sexual murderers. *Journal of Interpersonal Violence*, **20**, 1366–89.

Beech, A., Oliver, C., Fisher, D. & Beckett, R. C. (2006). *STEP 4: The Sex Offender Treatment Programme in Prison: Addressing the Needs of Rapists and Sexual Murderers*. Birmingham: University of Birmingham. Available electronically from: www.hmprisonservice.gov. uk/assets/documents/100013DBStep_4_SOTP_report_2005.pdf

Beech, A. R., Ward, T. & Fisher, D. (2006). The identification of sexual and violent motivations in men who assault women: Implications for treatment. *Journal of Interpersonal Violence*, **21**, 1635–53.

Burt, M. R. (1983). Justifying personal violence: A comparison of rapists and the general public. *Victimology: An International Journal*, 8, 131–50.

Clarke, J. & Carter, A. J. (2000). Relapse prevention with sexual murderers. In D. R. Laws, S. M. Hudson & T. Ward (Eds.), *Remaking Relapse Prevention with Sex Offenders* (pp. 389–401). London: Sage.

Finkelhor, D. (1984). *Child Sexual Abuse*. New York: The Free Press.

Fisher, D., Beech, A. R. & Browne, K. (1998). Comparison of sex offenders to nonoffenders on selected psychological measures. *International Journal of Offender Therapy and Comparative Criminology*, **43**, 473–91.

Groth, A. N., Burgess, A. W. & Holstrom, L. L. (1977). Rape: Power, anger, and sexuality. *American Journal of Psychiatry*, **134**, 1239–43.

Hazelwood, R. & Douglas, J. (1980). The lust murderer. *FBI Law Enforcement Journal*, **49**, 1–8.

Knight, R. A. & Prentky, R. A. (1990). Classifying sexual offenders: The development and corroboration of taxonomic models. In W. L. Marshall, D. R. Laws & H. E. Barbaree (Eds.), *Handbook of Sexual Assault: Issues, Theories and Treatment of the Offender* (pp. 23–53). New York: Plenum.

Kwon, S. M. (1994). The roles of two levels of cognitions in the development, maintenance, and treatment of depression. *Clinical Psychology Review*, **14**, 331–58.

Malamuth, N. M. (1981). Rape proclivity among males. *Journal of Social Issues*, **37**, 138–57.

Malamuth, N. M. & Brown, L. M. (1994). Sexually aggressive men's perceptions of women's communications: Testing three explanations. *Journal of Personality and Social Psychology*, **67**, 699–712.

Mann, R. (1999). The sex offender treatment programme HM Prison Service England and Wales. In S. Hofling, D. Drewes & I. Epple-Waigel (eds), *Auftrag pravention: Offensive gegen sexuellen kindesmibbrauch* (pp. 346–52). Munich: Atwerb-Verlag KG Publikation.

Mann, R. & Beech. A.R. (2003). Cognitive distortions, schemas and implicit theories. In T. Ward, D. R. Laws & S.M. Hudson (eds), *Sexual Deviance: Issues and Controversies* (pp. 135–53). London: Sage.

Mann, R. & Hollin, C. R. (2001, November). *Schemas: A model for Understanding Cognition in Sexual Offending.* Paper presented at the 20th Annual Research & Treatment Conference, Association for the Treatment of Sexual Abusers, San Antonio, Texas, USA.

Mann, R. & Thornton, D. (1998). The evolution of a multi-site sexual offender treatment program. In W. L. Marshall, Y. M. Fernandez, S. M. Hudson & T. Ward (eds), *Sourcebook of Treatment Programs for Sexual Offenders* (pp. 47–57). New York: Plenum Press.

Marshall, W. L. (2001). Adult sexual offenders against women. In C. R. Hollin (ed.), *Handbook of Offender Assessment and Treatment* (pp. 1–23). Chichester: Wiley.

Marshall, W. L., Anderson, D. & Fernandez, Y. (1999). *Cognitive-behavioural Treatment of Sexual Offenders.* Chichester: Wiley.

Maruna, S. & Mann, R. (2006). Fundamental Attribution Errors? Re-thinking Cognitive Distortions. *Legal and Criminological Psychology,* **11**, 155–77.

Marziano, V., Ward, T., Beech, A. & Pattison, P. (2006). Identification of five fundamental implicit theories underlying cognitive distortions in child abusers: A preliminary study. *Psychology, Crime & Law,* **12**, 97–105.

Millon, T. (1997). *Millon Clinical Multiaxial Inventory-III Manual* (2nd edn). Minneapolis, MN: National Computer Systems.

Milner, R. J. & Webster, S. D. (2005). Identifying schemas in child molesters, rapists, and violent offenders. *Sexual Abuse: A Journal of Research and Treatment,* **17**, 425–39.

Milsom, J., Beech, A. R. & Webster, S. (2003). Emotional loneliness in sexual murderers: A qualitative analysis. *Sexual Abuse: A Journal of Research and Treatment,* **15**, 285–96.

Myers, W. C., Burgess, A. W., Burgess, A. G. & Douglas, J. E. (1988). Serial murder and sexual homicide. In V. Van Hasselt & M. Hersen (eds), *Handbook of Psychological Approaches with violent offenders: Contemporary strategies and issues* (pp. 153–72). New York: Kluwer Academic/Plenum Publishers.

Oliver, C. J., Beech, A. R., Fisher, D. & Beckett, R. C. (2007). A comparison of rapists and sexual murderers on selected psychological measures. *International Journal of Offender Therapy and Comparative Criminology,* **51**, 298–312.

Polaschek, D. L. L. & Gannon, T. A. (2004). The implicit theories of rapists: what convicted offenders tell us. *Sexual Abuse: A Journal of Research and Treatment,* **16**, 4, 299–314.

Polaschek, D. L. L. & Ward, T. (2002). The implicit theories of potential rapists. What our questionnaires tell us. *Aggression and Violent Behavior,* **7**, 385–406.

Proulx, J., Beauregard, É. & Nichole, A. (October, 2002). *Developmental, Personality and Situational Factors in Rapists and Sexual Murderers of Women.* Paper presented at the 21st Annual Conference of the Association for the Behavioral Treatment of Sexual Abusers, Montreal, Canada.

Ressler, R. K., Burgess, A. W. & Douglas, J. (1988). *Sexual Homicide: Patterns and Motives.* New York: Lexington Books.

Revitch, E. (1980). Gynocide and unprovoked attacks on women. *Corrective and Social Psychiatry,* **26**, 6 –11.

Scully, D. & Marolla, J. (1984). Convicted rapists' vocabulary of motive: Excuses and justifications. *Social Problems,* **31**, 530–44.

Scully, D. & Marolla, J. (1985). "Riding the bull at Gilley's": Convicted rapists describe the rewards of rape. *Social Problems,* **32**, 251–63.

Thornton, D., Mann, R., Webster, S. *et al.* (2003). Distinguishing and combining risks for sexual and violent recidivism. In R. Prentky, E. Janus, M. Seto & A. W. Burgess (eds), *Understanding and Managing Sexually Coercive Behavior. Annals of the New York Academy of Sciences,* **989**, 225–35.

Thornton, D. & Shingler, J. (November, 2001). *Impact of schema level work on sexual offenders' cognitive distortions.* Paper presented at the 20th Annual Research & Treatment Conference, Association for the Treatment of Sexual Abusers, San Antonio, Texas.

Ward, T. (2000). Sexual offenders' cognitive distortions as implicit theories. *Aggression and Violent Behavior*, **5**, 491–507.

Ward, T. & Keenan, T. (1999). Child molesters' implicit theories. *Journal of Interpersonal Violence*, **14**, 821–38.

Ward, T. & Siegert, R. J. (2002). Toward and comprehensive theory of child sexual abuse: A theory knitting perspective. *Psychology, Crime & Law*, **9**, 319–51.

Young, J. E. (1990). *Cognitive Therapy for Personality Disorders*. Sarasota, FL: Professional Resources Press.

Young, J. E., Klosko, J. S. & Weishaar, M. E. (2003). *Schema Therapy: A Practitioner's Guide*. New York: Guilford Press.

Chapter 3

COGNITIVE DISTORTIONS AS BELIEF, VALUE, AND ACTION JUDGMENTS

Tony Ward and Kirsten Keown
Victoria University of Wellington, NZ

Theresa A. Gannon
University of Kent, UK

Sexual offenders who are questioned about their abusive behaviour often make statements that seem to justify, excuse, or minimise their crimes (see Abel, Becker & Cunningham-Rathner, 1984; Polaschek & Gannon, 2004; Pollock & Hashmall, 1991; Salter, 1988). For example, child sexual abusers have made claims such as "If a child doesn't resist my advances they want sexual contact with me" and "sex is good for children" (Abel *et al.*, 1989; Ward, 2000; Ward *et al.*, 1997). Similarly, rapists often claim that "women like to be dominated and controlled" or "nice women do not get raped" (Beech, Ward & Fisher, 2006; Briere, Malamuth & Check, 1985; Bumby, 1996; Polaschek & Gannon, 2004; Polaschek & Ward, 2002).

These types of offence-related statements have typically been referred to as "cognitive distortions" (e.g., Abel *et al.*, 1984; Hartley, 1998; Saradjian & Nobus, 2003; Ward, 2000), although definitional and conceptual issues surrounding the term have created confusion in the sexual offending literature (Mann & Beech, 2003; Maruna & Mann, 2006). The general consensus appears to be that sexual offenders' cognitive distortions reflect thoughts about children, women, the world, and themselves that facilitate and maintain sexual offending (Gannon, Ward & Polaschek, 2004; Marshall, Anderson & Fernandez, 1999; Ward *et al.*, 1997). However, research has not yet clarified whether cognitive distortions represent some type of belief structure, self-deception that may or may not have been implicated in the offence, or simply post offence justifications and excuses used to deflect public criticism (Gannon & Polaschek, 2005; Marshall, Fernandez & Anderson, 1999 & Mann, 2006). In this chapter, we aim to set out a preliminary framework for understanding the mechanisms underlying cognitive distortions.

Aggressive Offenders' Cognition: Theory, Research and Practice. Edited by T. A. Gannon, T. Ward, A. R. Beech and D. Fisher.   © 2007 John Wiley & Sons, Ltd.

Throughout our discussion we will use the term *cognitive distortion* to refer to the general, offence-endorsing statements that sexual offenders commonly make.

To formulate a clear and coherent model of cognitive distortions we have drawn from the literature on rationality, which focuses on three related types of judgments: *beliefs* (i.e., statements about the nature of self and the world that an individual purports to be true; Nisbett & Ross, 1980), *values* (i.e., experiences or attributes an individual considers worthwhile and by which the individual is motivated) and *actions* (see Baron, 2000; Hammond, 1996; Kekes, 1989; Rescher, 1992, 1993). The basic premise is that all humans make judgments about (a) what they *believe* events in the social world mean, (b) the goals they *value*, and (c) the meaning behind others' and one's own *actions*. These acts of reasoning interact in complex ways. For example, an individual's beliefs can shape their actions and their motivating values. In turn, the judgments a person makes about their actions and the value of certain goals can inform the beliefs that they hold. In this paper, we present the judgment model of cognitive distortions (JMCD), in which a judgment-based framework is applied to the study of offenders' cognition. The JMCD reveals how beliefs and their associated values serve as the basis for sexual offending actions, and how all offence-endorsing statements reflect different combinations of these beliefs, values, and actions (see Baron, 2000; Hammond, 1996 for discussion of these concepts). We believe that this approach allows us to better conceptualise sexual offenders' cognitive distortions and to account for the fact that such distortions sometimes appear to reflect distorted beliefs, and at other times appear simply to be post-hoc statements that offenders make to protect their self image. In addition, our approach allows for a broader perspective on cognitive distortions, enveloping not only the individual's unique cognitive system, but also the fundamental values associated with the wider environment.

In setting out our model, we will proceed as follows. First, we review the literature on cognitive distortions in sexual offenders, highlighting an almost exclusive focus on *faulty beliefs* as the mechanism generating cognitive distortions. Second, we outline the main components of the JMCD, illustrating how it can incorporate and explain such issues. Third, we demonstrate how the JMCD can account for the content and function of cognitive distortions. Finally, we explore the JMCD's clinical and research implications.

THE ORIGINS OF SEXUAL OFFENDERS' COGNITIVE DISTORTIONS

The term "cognitive distortion" was first coined by Beck (1967) to describe the automatic, systematic errors in thinking that he observed in depressed patients. In the early 1980s Abel and colleagues applied the term to sexual offenders, using it to describe the offence-endorsing statements commonly articulated by child sexual abusers (e.g., it was educational for the child or would not cause long-term harm – Abel *et al.*, 1984).

Because the mechanisms underlying sexual offenders' offence-endorsing statements were poorly understood, Abel *et al.* (1984) did not provide a precise definition of cognitive distortions. Although the term was used interchangeably with "belief", in a later paper Abel *et al.* (1989) used the term "cognitive distortion" to refer to rationalisations, excuses, and justifications. Unfortunately, conceptual and definitional issues surrounding the term have never been resolved and the literature continues to be plagued by its imprecise and inconsistent usage (see Mann & Beech, 2003; Maruna & Mann, 2006). Take, for instance, a definition supplied by Bumby (1996) which highlights the ongoing confusion about whether cognitive distortions arise from faulty beliefs structures or other sources (e.g., self-deceptive excuses and justifications, or more general impression management):

> Cognitive distortions related to sexual offending are learned assumptions, sets of beliefs, and self-statements about deviant sexual behaviours such as child molestation ... which serve to deny, justify, minimise, and rationalise an offender's actions. (Bumby, 1996, p. 38)

Note that this definition is also unclear about whether cognitive distortions are uttered by offenders in order to deflect *their own* negative thoughts and feelings about themselves, or whether they are attempts to deflect criticism and dislike *from others*. This is yet another indistinct element that has not been fleshed out by researchers and clinicians.

The ill-defined nature of cognitive distortions has not prevented researchers from compiling lists of child sexual abusers' and rapists' offence-endorsing statements (e.g., Hartley, 1998; Neidigh & Krop, 1992; Polaschek & Gannon, 2004; Saradjian & Nobus, 2003; Scully, 1988; Scully & Marolla, 1984; Ward *et al.*, 1995). In a recent attempt to clarify the origins of these statements, Ward (Ward, 2000; Ward & Keenan, 1999) proposed that "implicit theories", or schemas, generate sexual offenders' cognitive distortions (see Chapter 1 of this volume). Implicit theories are hypothesised networks of interrelated beliefs that sexual offenders use to make sense of their social world and make inferences about the behaviour and mental states of their victims. As is the case with all schemas, the content of these implicit theories guide the information that is attended to, perceived, and interpreted. Thus, the underlying content of implicit theories leads sexual offenders to attend to and interpret the social world in offence-congruent ways.

In formulating their work on implicit theories, Ward and Keenan (1999) initially reviewed cognitive distortion measures and interview studies from the child sexual offending literature. They proposed that five implicit theories can generate the offence-endorsing cognitions typically articulated by child sexual abusers (see Chapter 1 of this volume). Using similar methods, Polaschek and Ward (2002) identified five implicit theories that account for rapists' offence-endorsing cognitions (see Chapter 2 of this volume). We will briefly outline these implicit theories later in the chapter when we discuss our concept of *thematic networks*.

While Ward and colleagues' work on implicit theories represents a step towards understanding the structure of sexual offenders' distorted beliefs and associated information-processing errors, the complexity of cognitive distortions has yet to be theoretically addressed. Two issues in particular need to be tackled. First, if cognitive distortions are conceptualised as implicit theories (or core false beliefs), an explanation is needed as to how the beliefs (particularly those that are nonsexual in nature) are transmitted into sexual offending *actions*. We believe that a solution to this issue is to acknowledge that *values* are often the motors of human action (Emmons, 1999; Kekes, 1989). The second major issue is that recent empirical evidence has emerged that calls into question the view that cognitive distortions necessarily involve implicit theories or core beliefs (e.g., Neidigh & Krop, 1992; Gannon, 2006; Gannon & Polaschek, 2005; Gannon, Wright, Beech, & Williams, 2006; Keown, Gannon & Ward, 2007; Keown *et al.*, 2007). Gannon and colleagues, for instance, conducted a series of cognitive-experimental studies that minimised child sexual abusers' opportunities to respond in a socially desirable manner (see Chapter 4 of this volume). Findings suggested that a proportion of Gannon's child sexual abuser sample did not hold core false beliefs (Gannon, 2006; Gannon & Polaschek, 2005; Gannon, Wright, Beech, & Williams, 2006), despite the fact that those same abusers articulated distorted statements while discussing their crimes with the experimenters. An earlier study by Neidigh and Krop (1992) found that child sexual abusers recorded almost twice as many cognitive distortions when writing about the "thoughts, ideas or beliefs" (p. 210) that contributed to their offending behaviour than when completing a conventional self-report measure of cognitive distortions (the Pedophile Cognition Scale) (Abel *et al.*, 1984). These differences may occur because some sexual offenders, when asked to *explain* their actions, feel some pressure to produce justifications and denial to deflect criticism. The JMCD attempts to address this possibility (which has been largely overlooked by the research literature – see Maruna & Mann, 2006), and account for differences between such *post hoc* cognitive distortions and those that stem from faulty beliefs and value-based judgments. In short, our model aims to address some of the theoretical gaps present in current understanding of cognitive distortions.

THE JUDGMENT MODEL OF COGNITIVE DISTORTIONS IN SEXUAL OFFENDERS

The JMCD (see Figure 3.1) proposes that cognitive distortions are statements that involve sexual offenders' judgments. The term "judgment" highlights the fact that cognitive distortions express offenders' evaluations of aspects of their world. According to the JMCD, cognitive distortions arise from offenders' judgments about (a) what is true (i.e., *belief-based judgments*); (b) what is worthwhile or desirable (i.e., *value-based judgments*); and (c) how one should explain one's offending (i.e., *action-based judgments*).

Beliefs serve as cognitive maps that represent important aspects of the world whereas values serve to produce goals that can guide individuals to achieve desired outcomes. Actions are often performed in the service of beliefs and values (although, as we later discuss, actions can also occur when people engage in singular moments of sloppy thinking). Beliefs, values, and actions interact to help humans navigate their way in the world and overcome such challenges as mate selection, conflict resolution, human needs (or goods) promotion, and the creation of social alliances. For example, judgments about values are appraisals about what is true, of significance, or worth doing (Baron, 2000; Hammond, 1996). These appraisals may become automatic and are not necessarily conscious judgments.

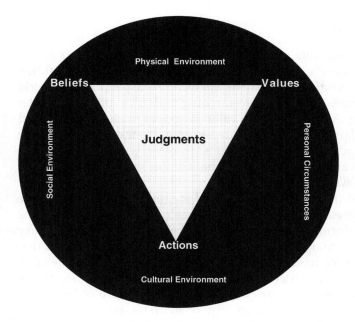

Figure 3.1 The judgment model of cognitive distortions.

We will now provide a more in-depth discussion of the three types of judgments (relating to beliefs, values and actions) that the JMCD is concerned with.

Beliefs

As noted, empirical and theoretical literature has primarily focused on sexual offenders' offence-supportive beliefs as the drivers of cognitive distortions and associated offending. Here, we shall refer to such beliefs as *false beliefs* because they are beliefs for which there is thought to be little or no supporting evidence (see Baron, 2000). As discussed in Chapters 1 and 2, theorists have hypothesised that sexual offenders' false beliefs are held in the form of implicit theories, or schemas, which are most likely acquired during childhood when abusive family environments and poor modelling provide distorted interpersonal experiences. We think it is fair to say that since Abel *et al.*'s early work on cognitive distortions *most* sexual offenders have been considered to hold pervasive false beliefs (see Gannon & Polaschek, 2005). However, as noted earlier (and in Chapter 4), preliminary evidence appears to indicate that the picture is more complicated than first thought and that not all child sexual abusers hold core false beliefs (Bickley & Beech, 2002; Gannon, 2006; Gannon & Polaschek, 2005; Gannon, Wright, Beech, & Williams, 2006; Keown *et al.*, 2007; Keown, Gannon & Ward, 2007). This fact fits comfortably with the underlying assumptions of the JMCD. For example, the JMCD posits that cognitive distortions may be driven by context-dependent temporary conclusions that have been formed on the basis of faulty reasoning (see the section *Interaction Between Beliefs, Values and Actions* for further discussion of this concept).

Values

In addition to beliefs, judgments about what is *valuable* are evident in sexual offenders' offence descriptions. Value judgments assert that specific qualities, which are evaluated as positive or negative, characterise aspects of the world or people. These judgments reveal the overarching ends that people consider good and worth seeking. An example of a value judgment made by some child sexual abusers is the claim that children are sexually desirable because they are more trustworthy and accepting than adults. In other words, intimate and loving relationships are valued, although the pursuit of this value with children is dysfunctional and offensive.

In order to understand the types of value-based judgments that offenders are likely to make, it is necessary to consider the types of qualities that humans generally value. This information can be found in the literature on primary human needs or *goods*. Primary human goods are essentially the benefits that individuals seek out (see Ward & Stewart, 2003; Kekes, 1989). In other words, primary human goods are the experiences that people value. According to the literature on primary human goods, the qualities that people value and typically need to flourish include knowledge, creativity, relatedness, good health, and autonomy. However, the extent to which an individual requires each of these goods will depend upon their unique preferences, abilities, and circumstances (Ward & Stewart, 2003).

People use goals to achieve primary human goods. In other words, goals are the "game plan" that people set out in order to achieve something that they value. For instance, the primary human good of relatedness (which can involve intimate relationships, friendships, or sexual intimacy) is pursued via specific goals, such as seeking a particular friendship in a certain context.

We believe that sexual offenders seek the kinds of primary goods that all humans seek to achieve life satisfaction (Deci & Ryan, 2000; Ward & Stewart, 2003). However, the attainment of these valued goods requires a set of capabilities, opportunities, and resources that offenders frequently lack. Being unable to achieve goals in a prosocial and personally satisfying manner leads sexual offenders to meet their aims via more harmful and illegal methods. In other words, offenders make distorted judgments about what behaviours will best lead them to the attainment of the values they seek. Note that we are *not* saying that values are relevant to sexual offenders' cognitive distortions because sexual offenders *value the wrong things*. Rather, we are saying that values are relevant because sexual offenders make bad judgments about how to obtain valued goods, or because they place too much emphasis on pursuing some values at the expense of others.

It is our opinion that the types of values that sexual offenders are overly focused on and the types of ill-formed goals they use to achieve valued goods will vary according to context and offender type. For example, some rapists may be too concerned with the value "autonomy" and may be more likely to implement destructive goals aimed at achieving power and control than other offenders. Likewise, some child sexual abusers may assign too much weight to the value of relatedness and may be more likely to implement harmful goals aimed at achieving sexual intimacy.

Actions

Judgments about *actions* have received scant attention in the cognitive distortion literature. Nevertheless, we consider them to be an important strand in individuals' discussions of their sexual offending.

It is our contention that judgments about actions may lead some sexual offenders to utter offence-endorsing statements despite the fact that they do not hold false beliefs. This is because action-based judgments often reflect socially desirable responding, (i.e., a tendency to portray oneself in an unrealistically favourable light – Paulhus, 1984). Paulhus reported that socially desirable responding comprises two major factors: self-deception and impression management. Self-deception refers to the tendency to deny one's socially unfavourable qualities to oneself, and hence to present unwittingly a distorted, more desirable picture of one's behaviours and beliefs when answering questionnaires. Impression management refers to the tendency to deliberately inflate the social desirability of one's behaviours and beliefs when answering questionnaires. Self-deception and impression management can drive the judgments that offenders utter when discussing their actions. *Minimisation* and *denial*, for instance, are designed to alter how offenders' actions are judged by both themselves and others; they either deny that those actions occurred at all, or they reformulate their actions (e.g., claiming that they did not commit rape and instead participated in a mutually agreed upon sexual encounter). Similarly, *justifications* may be used by sexual offenders to defend their motives and goals and to deflect self-criticisms and criticisms from others (Gannon & Polaschek, 2006). If an offender engages in – and seeks evidential support for – this type of post-offence reasoning often enough it may alter his belief structures. Hence, the JMCD accounts for fluctuations in the origins of offence-endorsing statements *within* individuals.

Because of the sexual offending literature's focus on *beliefs* as the drivers of cognitive distortions we currently lack knowledge about sexual offender's action-related judgments. For example, we cannot identify groups of sexual offenders most likely to utter cognitive distortions of this type. Nor can we say to what extent action-related judgments enter into the discourse of offenders who act on the basis of false beliefs and associated value judgments. This issue needs to be addressed in future research (see also Chapter 6 of this volume).

Interaction Between Beliefs, Values, and Actions

In the JMCD, judgments based on beliefs, values and actions are hypothesised to interact as offenders navigate problems posed by the environment. When individuals hold misleading beliefs they tend to make consistent mistakes in the importance they assign to certain values, or in the choice of goals and subsequent actions they implement to achieve those values. Even when accurate beliefs are held, individuals can make bad judgments in certain contexts because they do not consider wider available evidence, which leads them to reach temporary false beliefs or conclusions. For example, a man could come to the *false conclusion* that a female co-worker is sexually interested in him because she invites him out for coffee (although other workmates know that she often invites colleagues out for coffee). Contextual factors such as alcohol consumption and the presence of sexual primes in the environment could encourage this type of sloppy thinking. The false conclusion that is reached might lead the offender to make a bad judgment about the type of behaviour he should engage in when sharing coffee with his workmate in order to achieve the activated value of intimacy. In other words, context-driven sloppy thinking may trigger bad judgments on the offender's part about which values it is appropriate to pursue and what actions are best implemented in the service of those values. This may set off a train of events that ultimately lead the offender to sexually assault his co-worker even though, as noted earlier, the offender may not necessarily hold core faulty beliefs. Of course, it should be noted here that holding false core beliefs may lead to more pervasive interpretations of this type.

Just as actions are shaped by belief- and value-based judgments, belief and value formation can be affected by action-based judgments. This can occur in a *direct* manner, where an individual evaluates the effectiveness of actions in achieving important goals (Carver & Scheier, 1990). To illustrate, consider the above-mentioned example of a man whose sloppy thinking leads him to sexually assault his colleague. If he later feels guilt about the assault he may try to reduce that guilt by internally justifying his actions (e.g., "if she hadn't put herself in that situation I would never have touched her") and/or by actively trying to recall signs of sexual interest on his colleague's part. Long-term repetition of these justifications and selective recollections may lead to the development of offence-supportive *beliefs* (e.g.; "women want sex more than they let on"). Likewise, when reflecting on his actions the offender may perceive that the assault gave him a sense of control over the situation. He may thus decide that it was a good way to deal with unpleasant feelings of rejection. This action-based judgment may then heighten the importance that he assigns to the *value* of control/mastery. Alternatively, the process may occur *indirectly*, when the consequences of actions produce changes in the individual's environment that alter his or her belief- and value-based judgments. For example, the actions of a man who lacks social skills may create an environment in which women constantly reject him. Operating in this environment may lead him to the belief-based judgment that adult women are unattainable, and the value-based judgment that seeking intimacy from children is a preferable goal to seeking it from adults.

To summarise, the JMCD contends that cognitive distortions are offence-endorsing statements that reflect different combinations of judgments offenders make according to their beliefs, values, and actions. In other words, cognitive distortions are statements about what the offender considers true, what he sees as worthwhile or desirable, and what he thinks is the best way to act. Cognitive distortions may also reveal the influence of broad social and cultural factors, (e.g., when an individual attempts to justify his offending by claiming he was drunk at the time).

Having argued that cognitive distortions reflect judgments about beliefs, values, and actions, we will now turn to an investigation of the content of these three categories. We have observed that certain themes run through the cognitive distortions that sexual offenders utter. That is, the judgments that sexual offenders' make (based on their beliefs, values, and actions) tend to cluster together in categories that we call *thematic networks*. We will now explore this idea more fully.

THEMATIC NETWORKS: BELIEFS, VALUES, AND ACTIONS

As outlined in Chapters 1 and 2, research on sexual offenders' cognitive distortions suggests that at least seven themes pervade the offence descriptions of rapists and child sexual abusers. Three of these themes (*uncontrollability, dangerous world, entitlement*) are common to rapists and child sexual abusers. Two other themes (*children as sexual beings, nature of harm*) have been identified in child sexual abusers but not rapists, while a further two (*women are unknowable, women as sex objects*) have been identified in rapists but not child sexual abusers.

Investigations of sexual offender discourse have focused almost solely on the belief content associated with each of these themes but we believe they may also encompass associated values and actions. We use the term "thematic network" because the term *network* intimates interacting factors (i.e., judgments about beliefs, values, and actions), and thereby encourages the reader to envisage offence-endorsing statements as stemming from almost any combination of factors within the network.

In the following discussion we provide specific examples of the false belief content that may drive the distorted statements associated with each thematic network. We will also explore the value- and action-based judgments that may produce the distorted statements categorised under each thematic network. Readers who consult Chapter 6 of this volume will notice that there are some important connections that may be made between the JMCD and Dean *et al.*'s discussion of differing cognition categories. For example, the belief component of the JMCD may be conceptualised as general beliefs supportive of sexual offending that are commonly measured using questionnaires. However, statements made regarding the judgment part of the JMCD may be conceptualised as attributions of external responsibility (e.g., blaming drink, mood disorders, or other people who could have seen or stopped the abuse). As Dean *et al.* note, these latter statements are probably protective cognitions used to alleviate shame and stigma. Such cognitions are unlikely to play an aetiological role in sexual offending and so it may be unwise for treatment providers to waste valuable therapy time attempting to restructure such normative cognitions.

In the descriptions that follow, as well as making connections with Chapter 6, readers should bear in mind that our list of thematic networks may not be exhaustive.

THEMATIC NETWORKS COMMON TO RAPISTS AND CHILD SEXUAL ABUSERS

Uncontrollability

False Beliefs

The belief content of this thematic network leads offenders to view themselves as having little control over their lives. They believe that they are unable to alter the internal and external forces that shape their day-to-day existence and that they cannot control their own actions or outcomes in relation to factors such as sexual desire, drugs, alcohol, stress, and others' dominating behaviour (e.g., Neidigh & Krop, 1992; Pollock & Hashmall, 1991).

Values

The value that is linked with this thematic network is that of autonomy; the ability to self-regulate one's thoughts, feelings, and behaviour in order to achieve important goals.

Actions

Sexual offenders are likely to make statements under this main theme when they are trying to convince themselves or others that they cannot be blamed for their actions. They perceive that they have done something harmful but rather than allowing themselves to be labelled as "bad" they judge (or ask others to judge) that they had no choice in the matter. Sometimes an action-based judgment reflecting this thematic network will also represent an attempt by the offender to rationalise his behaviour when he doesn't understand his own motives. For instance, a child sexual abuser may reason "I think child abuse is wrong, yet I touched my own child. . . something (external) must have forced me into it."

Dangerous World

False Beliefs

Beliefs that may be associated with this thematic network involve the idea that humans are hostile, aggressive, rejecting, and likely to inflict suffering on each other. The offender believes himself to be at risk from other people's malevolent intentions and disregard. He judges that the best response to this state of affairs is to either seek relationships with children (who are viewed as accepting and "safe"), or to attack others (including children) as punishment or to pre-empt them hurting him.

Values

The key value judgments linked to these types of beliefs concern safety, trust, and justice. With respect to safety, the offender is very concerned with self-protection and closely monitors the degree of risk posed by the environment. With respect to trust, the offender is strongly driven to find trustworthy individuals who offer protection and pose no threat.

Actions

Under this thematic network, the statements that sexual offenders make about their actions involve the assertion that their actions were an appropriate response to a perceived threat or wrongdoing. They may judge (or ask that others judge) their offending to be the infliction of deserved punishment.

Entitlement

False Beliefs

The core beliefs associated with this thematic network lead offenders to consider themselves superior to others because of their social role or personal qualities. They believe that their superiority grants them the right to put their needs ahead of other's and when they feel this superiority is challenged they are hypothesised to feel irritation and sometimes anger.

Values

The values of status and autonomy are linked to *entitlement* beliefs. Here the offender measures a person's value and importance according to their position within a hierarchy of specific qualities. The value of autonomy is involved in the claim that others are not entitled to doubt the offender's special rights.

Actions

Action-related statements linked to this thematic network are often based on the judgment that victims were disrespectful and so "deserved what they got". Offenders' judgments about their abusive actions may lead them to make statements such as, "My actions were justified given that I am the child's father and head of my household."

IMPLICIT THEORIES IDENTIFIED IN CHILD SEXUAL ABUSERS

Children as Sexual Beings

False Beliefs

Beliefs that may be associated with this thematic network concern children's sexual interests and ability to make informed decisions about sex. Children are seen to actively seek sex, and the expression of their sexual desires is viewed as legitimate.

Values

Value judgments associated with this thematic network hold that sex is always beneficial and takes precedence over other values or human primary goods. Another related value is autonomy; in this case the value judgment is made that children should be given agency to make their own decisions about sex.

Actions

Child sexual abusers' statements relating to this thematic network are likely to reflect the judgment that children are free and informed agents who can decide for themselves whether or not they want sex. They judge (or ask others to judge) that their actions were justified because their child victims actively wanted sexual contact.

Nature of Harm

False Beliefs

Beliefs that may appear within this thematic network deny that sexual activity with children is harmful, or as harmful as other behaviours (e.g., physical assault; Ward & Keenan, 1999).

Values

The value judgment that sex is beneficial and cannot on its own cause harm is apparent in this thematic network.

Actions

Here offenders are likely to judge (or ask others to judge) that their actions were acceptable because they caused the victim(s) no harm. Offenders may also make statements that portray their actions as differing in nature or frequency than as described by authorities or the victim (e.g., "I only touched her and did not have sex with her").

IMPLICIT THEORIES IDENTIFIED IN RAPISTS

Women are Unknowable/Dangerous

False Beliefs

Beliefs evident in this thematic network hold that women are combative in nature and have a tendency to maliciously deceive and frustrate men (Polaschek & Ward, 2002).

Values

The values of knowledge, integrity and relatedness are linked with this thematic network. The role of the value of knowledge is reflected in offenders' claim that women are obtuse and difficult to understand. The value of integrity is involved because individuals with integrity speak and behave in ways that express what they stand for, so by being deceptive women are displaying a lack of integrity and respect. The value of relatedness (which concerns the importance of intimacy and social interactions) is involved because perceived female deception prevents this good from being realised.

Actions

Statements about actions associated with this thematic network are likely to reflect the judgment that the offence was not an offence at all. In other words, the offender will claim (to himself or others) that his victims are lying and that the sexual abuse was consensual. In denying or justifying his actions, the offender may demonstrate a suspicion of women and ignorance of their wants and needs.

Women as Sex Objects

False Beliefs

False beliefs that may be associated with this thematic network involve claims about women's desires, sexual receptiveness, and self-knowledge. In this case, offenders believe that a desire for sex is the prime driver of women's daily activities (Polaschek & Ward, 2002). This leads the offender to misconstrue many of the things females say and do as indicators of sexual receptivity. Another related belief that is linked to this thematic network sees women as "gatekeepers" of male access to sexual gratification. As gatekeepers, women deprive men of adequate sexual outlets whenever they decline sex (Polaschek & Ward, 2002).

Values

The value of knowledge, pleasure, status, and naturalism are linked to these beliefs. The offender considers women to be unaware of their own motives and so he judges that males should use their superior knowledge and status to show females what they really want. The offender's belief that sex is a primary and "natural" drive may also lead him to judge sexual satisfaction as a necessarily positive and beneficial experience.

Actions

Here the offender judges (or invites others to judge) his actions as appropriate because any expressed reluctance on the part of the female was simply a ruse that masked what she really wanted. Statements relating to this thematic network may also reflect an attempt by the offender to cast his actions in a positive light by claiming that they were aimed at unleashing a female's presumed sexual urges.

IMPLICATIONS OF THE JMCD

In the above section we noted that sexual offenders' offence-endorsing statements can be broadly categorised under seven thematic nets. The key message of our model is that when an offender makes such a statement it is important to identify the *mechanism* underlying their claim. In other words, one must ask whether the distorted statement stems from a *belief-based judgment* or a *value-based judgment* (both of which would actually facilitate the offender's sexual crimes), or whether it is a *post-hoc judgment about actions* that has been uttered in an attempt to reduce self-criticism or the opprobrium of others. The type of mechanism driving an offender's statements will affect the type of treatment that is administered. For instance, if the offender genuinely *believes* that their sexual crime was acceptable, therapy should focus primarily on restructuring relevant faulty cognitions.

Alternatively, if the driving mechanism is a reduced understanding of the best way to achieve valued goods, for example, then therapy should focus on building skills and resources that enable those goods to be achieved via legitimate goals. Importantly, however, distorted core beliefs and core values are likely to go hand in hand, and so both may need to be targeted by the treatment professional. On the other hand, if distorted statements are merely an offender's way of reducing feelings of guilt, say, about an incident that occurred under offence-facilitating circumstances (e.g., becoming intoxicated while feeling lonely), a facilitator's time may be best spend ensuring that the offender is equipped to manage or avoid such circumstances in the future.

In our view the literature's narrow focus on enduring false beliefs as the drivers of cognitive distortions has discouraged therapists from exploring other important drivers of sexual offenders' behaviour. While it is often important to address faulty core beliefs in therapy, belief modification is not always necessary or sufficient. In fact, it is our view that values are frequently the key mechanism underlying sexual offending. Values represent the overarching goods that motivate people in their personal strivings, and they can engage, antagonise, and frustrate individuals to the point that they use antisocial acts to achieve their goals (Emmons, 1999; Deci & Ryan, 2000; Ward & Stewart, 2003). Ignoring the full range of mechanisms that can drive sexual offences may be damaging for clients – whose therapist has missed an essential element of their experience – and may lead therapists to target schemas in individuals whose beliefs have little relevance to their offending.

Research Implications

The JMCD provides a framework for a number of potentially valuable research projects. For instance, it would be instructive to investigate ways of discovering whether the distorted statements offenders make are driven by judgments based on beliefs, values, actions, or some combination of these factors. At present it is generally assumed that cognitive distortions reflect false core beliefs, so techniques for exploring the mechanisms underlying distorted statements are underdeveloped. If we are to truly understand what a cognitive distortion represents when a sexual offender utters it, future research needs to help to uncover and develop such techniques.

We have embarked on a research programme that aims to clarify some of these issues. For example, we have recently conducted two studies that used an experimental approach to investigate faulty interpretations made by child sexual abusers as a consequence of their (presumed) faulty core beliefs (see Keown et al., 2007; Keown, Gannon & Ward, 2007). In one study a memory recall task was used to examine child sexual abusers' *online* interpretations of the social world and children (Keown et al., 2007), whereas the other study used a lexical decision task for the same purpose (Keown Gannon & Ward, 2007). Evidence for false beliefs in child sexual abusers was not detected in either study. These results underscore the importance of investigating the full range of judgments that may underlie cognitive distortions, rather than focusing solely on belief-based drivers. For instance, future studies could explore the relationship between human goods and sexual offending, noting the kinds of values individuals pursue when engaging in sexual crimes.

Clinical Implications

Although the clinical implications of the JMCD are numerous, we have space to share only a handful of major possibilities. One of these possibilities stems from the recommended attention to value judgments, as this is a powerful way of motivating offenders and securing their involvement in the difficult process of self-change. Acknowledging the fact that offenders are being asked to give up something of value underscores the rationality of any ambivalence they experience and can make it easier to motivate them to change (McMurran, 2002; Miller & Rollnick, 2002). Therapists can reassure offenders that their core values are legitimate, even though the goals and actions they are implementing as a means of obtaining them are problematic. Stressing that they share needs and interests with the rest of humanity can lessen the sense of stigma and aid construction of a prosocial or "redemptive" script in sexual offenders (Maruna, 2001). Additionally, the recognition that cherished goods or values are taken seriously and the emphasis on changing strategies (not personal identity) is likely to lessen resistance in the offender (Emmons, 1999; Nussbaum, 2000; Ward & Stewart, 2003).

A second clinical implication rests on the idea that cognitive distortions may simply be things that offenders say to avoid their own or other's criticism. In these instances, the offender is trying to judge (or ask others to judge) that his actions do not make him a bad person. This situation offers a treatment opportunity to help the offender recognise that he made a bad decision in a particular circumstance. Therapy can then focus on helping the offender avoid that circumstance again, or helping the offender to think more carefully on occasion so that sloppy reasoning does not guide future actions. Focusing attention on offenders' *future* actions rather than their past offences breaks the cycle of blame and recrimination they are caught up in. This should discourage offenders from trying to "repackage" their past sexual assaults as acceptable acts. This, in turn, should prevent their excuses, justifications, and minimisations from feeding more long-term false beliefs and distorted value judgments.

A third implication rests on the representation of cognitive distortions as multifaceted phenomena containing value, belief, and action components. Linking cognitive restructuring to the process of identifying offenders' values and commitments builds a bridge to subsequent parts of treatment. It frames a therapy process in which the aim is to provide offenders with important internal (i.e., capabilities) and external (i.e., opportunities, resources, supports) provisions for obtaining values in prosocial, personally satisfying ways. This process of identity building can procure a stronger commitment to living an offence-free life (Maruna, 2001).

CONCLUSIONS

This chapter has introduced the JMCD, a new model of cognitive distortions. According to the JMCD, sexual offenders' offence-endorsing statements (i.e., cognitive distortions) may arise from three mechanisms: judgments based on beliefs, judgments based on values, and judgments based on actions. The model is designed to account for all types of cognitive distortions, whether they are founded on false core beliefs and values or not. Within the model, cognitive distortions are sensitive to contextual, social, and cultural conditions, meaning that the relevance of sexual offenders' beliefs and values must be considered in light of the problems that each offender addresses in his or her unique environment.

We contend that the emphasis on values that has been built into the JMCD offers a significant contribution to the study of cognitive distortions. Ultimately, values drive offenders' goals, influence their thoughts and actions, and play a large role in the shaping of their lives. In light of this, we believe that the current lack of focus on sexual offenders' values requires immediate attention. While it will be a challenge for clinicians and researchers alike to reconceptualise the factors that motivate sexual offenders, the potential rewards make it a challenge worth embracing.

REFERENCES

Abel, G. G., Becker, J. V. & Cunningham-Rathner, J. (1984). Complications, consent and cognitions in sex between children and adults. *International Journal of Law and Psychiatry*, **7**, 189–203.

Abel, G. G., Becker, J. V., Cunningham-Rathner, J. *et al.* (1984). *Treatment Manual: The Treatment of Child Abusers*. Tuscaloosa, AL: Emory University Clinic.

Abel, G. G., Gore, D. K., Holland, C. L. *et al.* (1989). The measurement of the cognitive distortions of child abusers. *Annals of Sex Research*, **2**, 135–53.

Baron, J. (2000). *Thinking and Deciding* (3rd ed). Cambridge: Cambridge University Press.

Beck, A. T. (1967). *Depression: Clinical, Experimental and Theoretical Aspects*. London: Staples Press.

Beech, A., Ward, T. & Fisher, D. (2006). The identification of sexual and violent motivations in men who assault women: implications for treatment. *Journal of Interpersonal Violence*, **21**, 1625–53.

Bickley, J. & Beech, A. R. (2002). An investigation of the Ward and Hudson Pathways model of the sexual offence process with child abusers. *Journal of Interpersonal Violence*, **17**, 371–93.

Briere, J., Malamuth, N. & Check, J. V. P. (1985). Sexuality and rape-supportive beliefs. *International Journal of Women's Studies*, **8**, 398–403.

Bumby. K. M. (1996). Assessing the cognitive distortions of child abusers and rapists: Development and validation of the MOLEST and RAPE scales. *Sexual Abuse: A Journal of Research and Treatment*, **8**, 37–54.

Carver, C. S. & Scheier, M. F. (1990). Principles of self-regulation: Action and emotion. In E. T. Higgins & R. M. Sorrentino (eds), *Handbook of Motivation and Social Behavior* (pp. 3–52). New York: Guilford.

Deci, E. L. & Ryan, R. M. (2000). The "what" and "why" of goal pursuits: Human needs and the self-determination of behavior. *Psychological Inquiry*, **11**, 227–68.

Emmons, R. A. (1999). *The Psychology of Ultimate Concerns*. New York: Guilford.

Gannon, T. A. (2006). Increasing honest responding on cognitive distortions in child molesters: The bogus pipeline procedure. *Journal of Interpersonal Violence*, **21**, 358–75.

Gannon, T. A. & Polaschek, D. L. L. (2005). Do child abusers deliberately fake good on cognitive distortion questionnaires? An information processing-based investigation. *Sexual Abuse: A Journal of Research and Treatment*, **17**, 183–200.

Gannon, T. A., Ward, T. & Polaschek, D. L. L. (2004). Child sexual offenders. In M. Connolly (ed.), *Violence in Society: New Zealand Perspectives* (pp. 31–48). Christchurch: Te Awatea Press.

Gannon, T. A., Wright, D. B., Beech, A. R. & Williams, S. (2006). Do child molesters hold distorted beliefs? What does their memory recall tell us? *Journal of Sexual Aggression*, **12**, 5–18.

Hammond, K. R. (1996). *Human Judgment and Social Policy*. New York: Oxford University Press.

Hartley, C. C. (1998). How incest offenders overcome internal inhibitions through the use of cognitions and cognitive distortions. *Journal of Interpersonal Violence*, **13**, 25–39.

Kekes, J. (1989). *Moral Tradition and Individuality*. Princeton, New Jersey: Princeton University Press.

Keown, K., Gannon, T. A. & Ward, T. (2007). *What Were They Thinking? An Exploration of Child Sexual Offenders' Beliefs Using a Lexical Decision Task*. Manuscript submitted for publication.

Keown, K., Gannon, T. A., Ward, T. & Polaschek, D. (2007). *The Effects of Visual Priming on Information Processing in Child Sexual Offenders*. Manuscript submitted for publication.

Mann, R. & Beech. A.R. (2003). Cognitive distortions, schemas and implicit theories. In T. Ward, D. R. Laws & S.M. Hudson (eds), *Sexual Deviance: Issues and Controversies* (pp. 135–53). London: Sage.

Marshall, W. L., Anderson, D. & Fernandez, Y. M. (1999). *Cognitive Behavioural Treatment of Sexual Offenders*. Chichester: Wiley.

Maruna, S. (2001). *Making Good: How Ex-convicts Reform and Rebuild their Lives*. Washington, DC: American Psychological Association.

Maruna, S. & Mann, R.E. (2006). A fundamental attribution error? Rethinking cognitive distortions. *Legal and Criminological Psychology*, **11**, 155–77.

McMurran, M. (2002). Motivation to change: selection criterion or treatment need? In M. McMurran (ed.), *Motivating Offenders to Change: A Guide to Enhancing Engagement in Therapy* (pp. 1–14). Chichester: Wiley.

Miller, W.R. & Rollnick, S. (2002). *Motivational Interviewing: Preparing People for Change* (2nd ed.). New York: Guilford.

Neidigh, L. & Krop, H. (1992). Cognitive distortions among child sexual offenders. *Journal of Sex Education and Therapy*, **18**, 208–15.

Nisbett, R. E. & Ross, L. (1980). *Human Inference: Strategies and Shortcomings of Social Judgment*. Englewood Cliffs, NJ: Prentice-Hall.

Nussbaum, M. C. (2000). *Women and Human Development: The Capabilities Approach*. New York: Cambridge University Press.

Paulhus, D. L. (1984). Two-component models of socially desirable responding. *Journal of Personality and Social Psychology*, **46**, 598–609.

Polaschek, D. L. L. & Gannon, T. A. (2004). The implicit theories of rapists: What convicted offenders tell us. *Sexual Abuse: A Journal of Research and Treatment*, **16**, 299–315.

Polaschek, D. L. L. & Ward, T. (2002). The implicit theories of potential rapists: What our questionnaires tell us. *Aggression and Violent Behavior*, **7**, 385–406.

Pollock, N. L. & Hashmall, J. M. (1991).The excuses of child abusers. *Behavioral Sciences and the Law*, **9**, 53–9.

Rescher, N. (1992). *A System of Pragmatic Idealism. Vol I: Human Knowledge in Idealistic Perspective*. Princeton, NJ: Princeton University Press.

Rescher, N. (1993). *A System of Pragmatic Idealism. Vol II: The Validity of Values*. Princeton, NJ: Princeton University Press.

Salter, A. C. (1988). *Treating Child Sex Offenders and their Victims: A Practical Guide*. Newbury Park: Sage

Saradjian, A. & Nobus, D. (2003). Cognitive distortions of religious professionals who sexually abuse children. *Journal of Interpersonal Violence*, **18**, 905–23.

Scully, D. (1988). Convicted rapists' perceptions of self and victim: Role taking and emotions. *Gender and Society*, **2**, 200–13.

Scully, D. & Marolla, J. A. (1984). Convicted rapists' vocabularies of motive: Excuses and justifications. *Social Problems*, **32**, 530–44.

Ward, T. (2000). Sexual offenders' cognitive distortions as implicit theories. *Aggression and Violent Behavior*, **5**, 491–507.

Ward, T., Hudson, S. M., Johnston, L. & Marshall, W. L. (1997). Cognitive distortions in sex offenders: sn integrative review. *Clinical Psychology Review*, **17**, 479–507.

Ward, T. & Keenan, T. (1999). Child abusers implicit theories. *Journal of Interpersonal Violence*, **14**, 821–38.

Ward, T., Louden, K., Hudson, S. M. & Marshall, W. L. (1995). A description of the offense chain for child abusers. *Journal of Interpersonal Violence*, **10**, 452–72.

Ward, T. & Stewart, C. A. (2003). The treatment of sex offenders: Risk management and good lives. *Professional Psychology: Research and Practice*, **34**, 353–60.

Chapter 4

CHILD SEXUAL ABUSE-RELATED COGNITION: CURRENT RESEARCH

THERESA A. GANNON AND JANE WOOD

University of Kent, UK

A common question asked by members of the general public who hear of child molestation is *"Why* did they do it?" or "How *could* they do it?" A number of comprehensive theories have been proposed to explain why men sexually molest children (Finkelhor, 1984; Hall & Hirschman, 1992; Marshall & Barbaree, 1990; Ward & Beech, 2006; Ward & Siegert, 2002) and within each of these, cognition is always recognised as a core aetiological component that should be targeted for successful rehabilitation (Marshall, Anderson & Fernandez, 1999; Ward, 2003). Thus, *cognition* or the way in which a person thinks, perceives, understands, and reasons is believed to be inextricably intertwined with how a person interacts with, and behaves, in their social world (hence the term *social cognition*). Using this account, then, child sexual abusers are believed to experience their social world somewhat differently to nonoffending men, and it is this social-cognitive experience which is believed to contribute, in part, to men's sexually offensive behaviour against children. A great amount of research appears to support this hypothesis. For example, child sexual abusers often describe their child victim as having initiated or enjoyed the sexual contact (Abel, Becker & Cunnningham-Rathner, 1984; Neidigh & Krop, 1992) and men who abuse their own daughters will sometimes argue that it was their "right" or "entitlement" to behave in this way towards subordinate family members (Gilgun & Conner, 1989; Phelan, 1995). It is perhaps not surprising then, to find that the majority of respected treatment programmes for child sexual abusers are preoccupied with the task of altering child sexual abusers' perceptions of their social world (Beech & Mann, 2002; Marshall, Anderson & Fernandez, 1999).

In this chapter, we will use the term cognition to refer to the *structure of mental knowledge* and the associated *thoughts, perceptions, understanding* and *reasoning* used by men who sexually molest children. In particular, we ask the following questions. How do child sexual abusers perceive themselves and their surrounding social

---

Aggressive Offenders' Cognition: Theory, Research and Practice. Edited by T. A. Gannon, T. Ward, A. R. Beech and D. Fisher. © 2007 John Wiley & Sons, Ltd.

world? Do they view social situations in a manner likely to facilitate child molestation? How should treatment programmes for child sexual abusers proceed in light of current research evidence? The chapter is structured as follows. First, we briefly introduce the major principles underlying the social cognitive perspective. Second, we examine the available research evidence regarding child sexual abusers' social-cognition, highlighting the major pattern of results. Finally, we tie together the major findings and make suggestions as to how future research and treatment efforts should proceed in this specialist area.

THE SOCIAL COGNITIVE PERSPECTIVE

As we have already alluded, *social cognition* is the term used to describe the cognitive processes associated with social interactions (Adolph, 1999; Augoustinos & Walker, 1995). In essence, scientists working under the social-cognitive paradigm use knowledge and methods associated with cognitive psychology to study social behaviour (Augoustinos & Walker, 1995; Fiske & Taylor, 1991). A core component of the social-cognitive approach is recognition of the differences between individuals' world views (Fiske & Taylor, 1991). Put another way, each individual is hypothesised to experience the world, their own behaviour, and the behaviour of others, in wholly different ways. These perceptions are complex, and are subject to the ongoing influence of each observer's goals, as well as their fluctuating emotional states (Fiske & Taylor, 1991).

Knowledge Content and Structure

According to the social-cognitive perspective, human behaviour differs between individuals as a result of each individual's unique knowledge content, and the organisation of this content in long term memory (i.e., knowledge *content* and *structure* respectively – Fiske & Taylor, 1991; Hollon & Kriss, 1984; Kendall, 1992). Individuals accumulate knowledge through life experience and by the time adulthood is reached they have developed strong networks of associated information in the form of *schemas* (Anderson & Bushman, 2002). These schemas are used – largely unconsciously – to make the complex social world a somewhat more predictable place. To illustrate, an individual faced with a social interaction that resembles a previous one, may unconsciously refer back to their knowledge of this previous event so as to predict what usually occurs and how one should behave (Fiske & Taylor, 1991). It should be noted here, however, that using previously stored information to predict and understand social information means that people make predictions as to what is *likely* to be true rather than what is *objectively* true (Gannon & Polaschek, 2006).

Social Information Processing

Individuals do not always rely on their pre-existing schemas to make sense of surrounding social information. For example, when the cognitive system is fuelled by plentiful time and reserves, motivated individuals are likely to take the effort to make meticulous and logical decisions (i.e., a *naïve scientist* style; Fiske & Taylor, 1991). It is far more typical, however, for people to take a *cognitive miser* approach to social information processing due to time pressure, and limited cognitive resources (Augoustinos & Walker, 1995; Fiske & Taylor, 1991). Such an approach is typified by an automatic and unconscious overreliance on pre-existing information in order to explain and understand social information quickly and effortlessly (Kunda, 1999). In other words, a complex world is made relatively uncomplicated and valuable energy is conserved through relying on pre existing information to predict, understand, and navigate likely occurrences in complex social situations. Typically, pre-existing schemas function to guide individuals' attention to, and encoding of, schema-congruent information; schemas also function to generate predictions about the mechanisms lying behind ambiguous social occurrences (Bartlett, 1932; Dodge, 1980; Dodge & Frame, 1982). Thus, schemas shape the individual's experience of the social world in a self-fulfilling manner, ensuring that the schema is strengthened and rehearsed each time it is further activated (Gannon, Polaschek & Ward, 2005). It is hypothesised that frequent schema activation increases schema *accessibility*, resulting in schemas that are *chronically accessible* and highly likely to shape social information processing (Pettit, Polaha & Mize, 2001).

It is important to note, however, that even chronically accessible schemas are subject to motivational and affective primes (Bargh, 1982; Tiedens, 2001). This is likely to be a result of the fact that primes minimise an individual's motivation and cognitive resources for careful and logical social information processing (Pettit, Polaha & Mize, 2001). For example, both positive and negative emotional states appear to further increase the likelihood that individuals will act as cognitive misers (Bodenhausen, Kramer & Süsser, 1994; Kunda, 1999; Tiedens, 2001). In addition to emotion, researchers hypothesise that factors such as alcohol and drug use, and sexual arousal lead individuals to take information processing short-cuts (Pettit, Polaha & Mize, 2001). Such a hypothesis is especially relevant for child sexual abusers, whose offences are often associated with these factors.

Generally, individuals are not believed to hold deeply sophisticated insight into their own cognition (Nisbett & Wilson, 1977), making the task of understanding social cognition a complex and demanding one. Typically, researchers deduce information concerning individuals' cognitive content and structure based upon individuals' self-reported thoughts, decisions, beliefs and reasoning; since these are hypothesised to result from the system of cognitive content, structure, and processing working in unison (Hollon & Kriss, 1984). This self-reported cognition, commonly termed *cognitive products*, may well provide researchers with valuable information regarding social perception, but it should be borne in mind that the quality of cognitive products are highly variable since they are susceptible to social desirability bias, as well as individual differences in introspection skills (Gannon & Polaschek, 2006).

CHILD SEXUAL ABUSERS' COGNITION: RESEARCH EVIDENCE

Examining research on child sexual abusers' cognition from a social-cognitive framework provides a clear structure for assessing current research contributions in this area. Such a framework enables swift identification of areas that are being under researched, or that are in need of further investigation, and provides valuable information concerning where future research and treatment efforts should be concentrated. Thus, in the following section we examine the cognitive research tapping each of the three subdivisions of the social-cognitive system: cognitive content and structure, socio-cognitive processing, and cognitive products. It should be noted that the studies that we are about to describe have not generally been designed in line with this particular social-cognitive framework, and so placement of each study within each subdivision is, to some extent, a subjective process. We begin our review by examining the literature tapping child sexual abusers' cognitive products, since this is the best developed aspect of the social-cognitive literature. Descriptions of less extensively researched aspects of child sexual abusers' cognition (i.e., research investigating social-cognitive processing and cognitive structure and content) will then follow.

Cognitive Products

Abel, Becker and Cunningham-Rathner (1984) are credited with the first attempt at making inferences about the content of child sexual abusers' cognition through examining child sexual abusers' cognitive products (see Chapter 1 of this volume). From interactions with child sexual abusers in clinical practice, Abel *et al.* argued that child sexual abusers develop a set of atypical beliefs – or *cognitive distortions* – about the appropriateness of adult sexual interactions with children that help minimise the emotional distress associated with their sexually abusive behaviour, thus facilitating the likelihood of further re-offending. Abel *et al.* noted that child sexual abusers typically described their child victim as being a willing sexual partner (e.g., because the child did not actively resist the assault or tell anyone about the assault). Child sexual abusers also appeared to believe that molestation was acceptable for a variety of reasons (e.g., it was educational, would not cause long-term damage and would eventually be accepted by society). Other researchers then followed Abel's general method, compiling lists of child sexual abusers' offence-supportive cognitive products (see Neidigh & Krop, 1992; Pollock & Hashmall, 1991). As others have noted elsewhere, however, such lists are of limited value for research or treatment since it is almost impossible to pinpoint the exact mechanisms generating such statements (Gannon & Polaschek, 2006; Maruna & Mann, 2006). Put another way, such lists of offence-supportive statements may simply reflect normative impression management strategies employed by all individuals called to account for socially unacceptable behaviours (Maruna & Mann, 2006).

Despite this potential problem, offence-supportive statements inform many of the items used on questionnaire assessments of child sexual abusers' cognition (see Abel *et al.*, 1989). The resulting questionnaires are typically distributed amongst child sexual abuser and differing nonchild sexual abuser comparison groups, the hypothesis being that if cognition plays an aetiological role in child molestation, child sexual abusers should display differential (and offence-supportive) endorsement of the cognitive items.

The results of questionnaire assessments have been surprisingly mixed, although they are often interpreted as indicating an inability to accurately perceive core offence-relevant information (see Marshall *et al.*, 2003 for an example). The 29-item Cognition Scale (CS) (Abel *et al.*, 1989) is the oldest, and perhaps best known self-report measure of child sexual abusers' offence-supportive cognition. Yet within the first published report of the measure, Abel *et al.* found that, although the CS statistically discriminated child sexual abusers from community control comparisons, it did not discriminate child sexual abusers from paraphilics. A similar finding has been reported by Tierney and McCabe (2001) who were also unable to detect statistically significant differences between child sexual abusers and other sexual offenders. In fact, in their study, child sexual abusers could not be statistically discriminated from offenders who had *not* sexually offended. Other studies using the CS, however, have had more success in statistically discriminating child sexual abusers from other sexual offenders *as well as* nonsexual offending comparison groups (Hayashino, Wurtele & Klebe, 1995; Stermac & Segal, 1989). It is not exactly clear why some studies using the CS have been able to demonstrate full discriminative ability while others have not. Presumably, such discrepancies may be an artefact of the differing samples used. The failure of the CS to show full discriminative ability when comparing child sexual abusers to other offenders could also suggest an overlap between the cognitive constructs characterising child sexual abusers and those characterising other general offenders.

More recently, Bumby (1996) developed a similar, yet more elaborate and lengthy measurement of child sexual abusers' cognition in the form of the 38-item MOLEST scale. To date, researchers have been able to discriminate reliably between child sexual abusers, other sexual offenders, and nonoffender comparison men on this measure (see Arkowitz & Vess, 2003; Bumby, 1996; Feelgood, Cortoni & Thompson, 2005; Marshall, *et al.*, 2003). For example, in the first study describing the development of this measure, Bumby found that child sexual abusers – in statistical terms – were significantly more likely to endorse items supporting child molestation than rapists, and other nonsexual offenders. Feelgood, Cortoni and Thompson (2005) found similar results when they gave the MOLEST to groups of child sexual abusers, rapists and violent offenders. However, Feelgood *et al.* pointed out that child sexual abusers' answers tended to cluster into the *slightly disagree* response option.

Is such a finding unusual? A close examination of even the most successful questionnaire findings shows – quite systematically – that child sexual abusers, on average, very rarely *qualitatively* differ from comparison groups on their responses (Feelgood, Cortoni & Thompson, 2005; Gannon & Polaschek, 2006). In other words, when researchers report statistically significant differences between child sexual abusers' responses and those of comparison groups it appears that child sexual abusers are simply slightly less vehement in their disagreements than comparison men (see Arkowitz & Vess, 2003; Bumby, 1996; Feelgood, Cortoni & Thompson, 2005). This raises questions, then, about the aetiological significance of even the most successful questionnaire studies.

A number of other questionnaire assessments of child sexual abusers' cognition are available to researchers, although these measures are not commonly used. The Hanson Sex Attitude Questionnaire is a 47- item questionnaire containing six subscales designed to measure the offence-supportive cognition of men who sexual abuse children within their family. During the development and validation of this questionnaire, Hanson, Gizzarelli and Scott (1994) reported that child sexual abusers made significantly higher endorsements on scales measuring the concepts of sexual entitlement, children as sexual beings, and sexual harm than batterer and community comparison groups. However, like the other studies mentioned earlier, the child sexual abusers' average responses did not appear to be particularly high.

The *Multiphasic Sex Inventory* is a broad measure designed to assist clinicians in their overall assessment and diagnosis of sexual offenders' treatment needs. Two subscales are devoted to the measurement of sexual offenders' cognition: the Cognitive Distortions and Immaturity Scale (CDIS) and the Justifications Scale (JS). The former measures offenders' offence accountability, and the latter measures offenders' justifications for their offending (Nichols & Molinder, 1984). The problem with these scales, however, is that they cannot be used to compare sexual offender samples with nonsexual offending comparison groups since items assume that respondents have sexually offended (see Vanhouche & Vertommen, 1999).

Finally, the Child Molester Scale (McGrath, Cann & Konopasky, 1998) is a 22-item measure of child sexual abusers' cognition that has demonstrated limited evidence of discriminant validity to date. To illustrate, during the initial testing of this scale, McGrath, Cann and Konopasky (1998) were able to statistically discriminate child sexual abusers (who completed the measure within an assessment battery prior to parole) from a university male comparison group, but not from offender comparisons. A later study conducted by Tierney and McCabe (2001) raised further doubts about the clinical usefulness of the Child Molester Scale. In this study, the researchers found that child sexual abusers could not be statistically differentiated from sexual offenders against adults, or offender and community comparisons.

There are many reasons why research investigating child sexual abusers' cognitions appear to show conflicting findings. Differing questionnaire quality, participant groups, and research settings are all likely to play a significant role in what appears to be a conglomeration of questionnaire findings. Often, for cognitive distortion questionnaires, researchers cite impression management as representing a key factor in fluctuating questionnaire endorsement, especially when offence-belief endorsements are almost nonexistent in child sexual abuser samples (Kolton, Boer & Boer, 2001; Langevin, 1991). For example, Langevin (1991) reported that a mere 7.2 % of child sexual abusers' responses on the Cognition Scale (CS) (Abel *et al.*, 1989) were *neutral, agree* or *strongly agree* judgments. In other words, the overwhelming majority of child sexual abusers' responses (about 93 %) were *disagreements* with the offence-supportive items. Although no comparison groups were used in this study, and no social desirability scales were used, Langevin argued that such low endorsements on the CS were most likely the product of social desirability bias. Having found similarly disappointing results using a modified version of the CS, Kolton *et al.* argued that only offenders who respond with *strongly disagree* to offence-supportive beliefs should be deemed distortion free. In other words, the responses of *disagree, unsure, agree* and *strongly agree* should all be interpreted as being offence-supportive.

If child sexual abusers do impression manage on self-report measures, then this may explain why they very rarely *agree* with offence-supportive cognitions. So what is the empirical evidence to back the claim that child sexual abusers deliberately conceal their offence-supportive beliefs? Apart from the obvious inclusion of social desirability scales, which could be manipulated by sophisticated "fakers", there is very little research directly investigating the claim that child sexual abusers hide their offence-supportive beliefs on questionnaire measures. McGrath, Cann and Konopasky (1998) compared the social circumstances of child sexual abusers who were asked to complete the 22-item Child Molester Scale described earlier. Perhaps unsurprisingly, those child sexual abusers guaranteed anonymity made significantly higher endorsements of offence-supportive beliefs than child sexual abusers completing the same measure for the purpose of an impending parole hearing. Thus, the context of the assessment is important for researchers and practitioners to consider, when making judgments about child sexual abusers' cognitions.

To our knowledge, there are only two other studies that have attempted to establish whether child sexual abusers intentionally hide their offence-supportive cognitions from assessors (see Gannon, 2006; Gannon, Keown & Polaschek, 2007). In both studies, child sexual abusers were asked to complete a self-report measure of offence-supportive beliefs at two time-points, separated by either a 1 week (Gannon, 2006) or 4–6 week (Gannon, Keown & Polaschek, 2007) time interval. At Time 1, all child sexual abusers completed the self-report measure under standard conditions. In other words, there was nothing to stop child sexual abusers from hiding and mini-mising their offence-supportive cognitions. At Time 2, however, the same child sexual abusers were randomly allocated into either the *control condition* (where they completed the measure again under identical conditions to Time 1) or the *experimental condition*. Those child sexual abusers allocated to the experimental condition – like the controls – were again asked to complete the self-report measure of cognition. This time, however, the child sexual abusers were attached to a fake polygraph machine, and informed that the machine would detect any dishonest responses. Gannon hypothesised that if child sexual abusers were intentionally faking good then their responses would become more offence-supportive when they believed their answers were being screened by a polygraph.

The results of the first study showed that child sexual abusers did *not* make more offence-supportive answers when they were attached to the fake polygraph compared to (a) their own responses at Time 1 (which, unsurprisingly tended to be *disagreements* with the items), or (b) child sexual abusers' responses in the con-trol condition. Put another way, there was no evidence to suggest that these child sexual abusers had been hiding their beliefs when they had initially disagreed with the items at Time 1. In the second study, however, Gannon *et al.* found – as originally hypothesised – a significant effect of the fake polygraph on reported offence-supportive beliefs. In other words, child sexual abusers connected to the fake polygraph made more endorsements than (a) their previous endorsements under standard conditions (which had largely fallen between the *disagree* and *unsure* response options) and (b) child sexual abusers' responses in the control condition. Interestingly, however, child sexual abusers within the fake polygraph condition never qualitatively shifted their responses to begin *agreeing* with offence-supportive items.

There are many potential interpretations of the discrepancy between these results since the second study made several methodological improvements upon the first (i.e., the fake polygraph's veracity was further improved, as was the measure of offence-supportive cognition). However, one alteration of particular note revolves around the samples recruited for each study. In the first study, many of the men recruited had offended primarily within their own family and/or had received treatment for their sexual offending. Men who offend only against children within their own family are hypothesised to hold less entrenched networks of offence-supportive information since they typically have fewer victims and offence situations with which to strengthen and reinforce deviant beliefs (Ward, 2000). Similarly, child sexual abusers who have received treatment are likely to have been involved in work designed to reduce the effect of offence-supportive beliefs on information processing. Consequently, it is feasible that many of the child sexual abusers sampled in this study would have had no reason to cover up their beliefs at Time 1. In study two, however, only *untreated* child sexual abusers who had offended outside of the family, or both inside and outside of the family were recruited, increasing the chances that these men would both hold and hide offence-supportive cognitions.

Before concluding our discussion of child sexual abusers' cognitive products, it is worth noting that many measures designed to examine child sexual abusers' ability to cognitively empathise with sexual abuse victims contain items strongly resembling a good deal of the content presented within offence-supportive belief questionnaires – see Beckett and Fisher's (1994) Victim Empathy Distortion Scale; Fernandez *et al.*'s (1999) Child Molester Empathy Measure (part A); or McGrath, Cann and Konopasky's (1998) Empat-A scale. Not surprisingly, then, research studies have shown that higher endorsements of offence-supportive beliefs are associated with an inability to empathise with child sexual abuse victims (Hayler, Pardie & Rivera, 2002; Marshall, Hamilton & Fernandez, 2001; McGrath, Cann & Konopasky, 1998; Tierney & McCabe, 2001). A simple explanation for this well established finding, is that child sexual abusers' cognitive empathy deficits represent specific, offence-supportive beliefs concerning victim harm (Marshall, Anderson & Fernandez, 1999; Marshall, Hamilton & Fernandez, 2001; Serran, 2002). Alternatively, it could be that failing to acknowledge victim harm is simply a defence mechanism used (either consciously or unconsciously) to minimise the discomfort associated with committing acts at odds with the general social mores.

In this section, we have evaluated the literature investigating child sexual abusers' *cognitive products*. That is, the judgments, thoughts, decisions, and beliefs directly measured from asking child sexual abusers via interview or questionnaire. Our review has shown that the questionnaire research does not always consistently differentiate child sexual abusers from comparison groups, and that child sexual abusers rarely agree with the questionnaire items so often used both pre and post treatment. Yet child sexual abusers appear to articulate a plethora of offence-supportive beliefs when talking about their own offending behaviour (see Abel, Becker & Cunningham-Rathner, 1984; Saradjian & Nobus, 2003; Marziano *et al.*, 2006). So, why is there such a discrepancy between the findings of interview and questionnaire studies? We believe that there could be three main logical explanations for this discrepancy (see also Gannon & Polaschek, 2006). First, it is possible that when offenders recount their offences, they relive certain contextual cues that prime their offence-supportive beliefs, making them chronically accessible. If this hypothesis is correct, then in the absence of priming (i.e., when asked to complete a questionnaire) researchers are unlikely to detect cognitive content used in sexual offending situations. Second, regardless of priming, it could be the case that child sexual abusers – like all of us – are unable to access implicit schemas completely when asked officially to do so via questionnaire. However, when asked to recount their offences, they unconsciously provide material that reflects how they perceived offence-relevant information around the time of their offence. Finally, we believe it likely that child sexual abusers' narrative descriptions of their crimes are filled with post-offence impression-management strategies (i.e., justifications and excuses) that strongly resemble belief content but have been elicited to bolster self-esteem and avoid social disapproval. If this hypothesis is correct then many theoretical developments concerning offence-supportive beliefs may have been seriously mislead by such normative accounting behaviours (e.g., Abel, Becker & Cunningham-Rathner, 1984; Ward, 2000; Ward & Keenan, 1999; Ward, Gannon & Keown, 2006).

Social-Cognitive Processing

If child sexual abusers hold generalised offence-supportive beliefs, then evidence for such a hypothesis should be found using the guiding tenets of social-information processing theory described earlier. In other words, child sexual abusers should show evidence of *processing* social information in a manner which strengthens their existing offence-supportive beliefs. This could include *attending* preferentially to belief-supportive information, *minimising* attention on belief-incongruent information, and *reinterpreting* ambiguous material in a belief-supportive manner. The interested reader will perhaps be disappointed to discover that the examination of information processing in child sexual abusers has largely been neglected. This is in contrast to cognitive work with mainstream clinical pathologies where the majority of work relates to processing paradigms, with very little work examining cognitive content – see Wenzel and Rubin, 2005. It is not exactly clear why this is so although we suspect it may have something to do with the methodological difficulties inherent in conducting complex cognitive paradigms with aging sexual offender populations.

So, what information do we have about whether child sexual abusers process social-information in a manner likely to facilitate child molestation? A popularly cited but aged study conducted by Hudson *et al.* (1993) examined the emotional recognition component of child sexual abusers' social perception skills. In this study, Hudson *et al.* compared child sexual abusers and community controls on their ability to identify children and adults' emotional expressions via simple line drawings. The findings showed that, in comparison to the community controls, child sexual abusers *were* deficient in their ability to recognise facial affect. However, this processing deficit was not child specific; diluting conclusions specific to child molesting per se.

Some recent unpublished research by Oliver, Watson, Gannon and Beech (2007) set out to further investigate Hudson *et al.*'s (1993) findings using a sexual priming procedure; and pictures of adult facial affect depicting either fear or surprise. Unlike Hudson *et al.*, however, Oliver, Watson, Gannon and Beech were unable to find statistically significant deficits in child sexual abusers' ability to recognise fearful facial affect when their responses were compared to forensic hospital workers. Interestingly, however, when child sexual abusers were sexually primed with sentences (e.g., "she strokes your cock") they appeared to become more adept and faster at recognising fear relative to surprise. The mechanism driving this puzzling result is unclear and is not easily explained by any underlying methodological weakness.

Stermac and Segal (1989) conducted a popularly cited investigation into child sexual abusers' social processing. They asked child sexual abusers, other sexual offenders and community persons to read 12 vignettes describing sexual contact between an adult and a child. The described sexual contact was manipulated from touching to genital contact with ejaculation. The child's response was also manipulated so that it depicted either a positive response (i.e., smiling), a neutral response (i.e., no response), or a negative response (i.e., crying and resisting). Using a five-point Likert scale, respondents were asked to rate the child's responsibility and thoughts for each of the described interactions. Interestingly, child sexual abusers – in comparison to controls – described the child as experiencing more rewards in relation to the abuse (in the form of increased enjoyment and decreased harm) and reported somewhat more child responsibility for the abuse (i.e., increased child desire and responsibility). It was only when the vignettes depicted an overall negative response from the child (in the form of crying and resisting) that child sexual abusers' attributions of harm and blame softened, resembling the attributions made by the control groups. Similar minimisations of victim harm have also been reported by Beckett *et al.* (1994) using vignette methodology. Hanson and Scott (1995), however, were unable to detect discriminatory perspective taking deficits amongst child sexual abusers who were asked to make judgments regarding children's affect from a series of abuse-relevant vignettes. It is hard to exactly pinpoint the mechanism(s) underlying this null result since they are numerous. It is interesting to note, however, that Hanson and Scott found child sexual abusers did appear to hold deficits on *rape-specific* vignettes developed to highlight perspective taking difficulties towards women.

Two more recent vignette studies have attempted to test the fallibility of child sexual abusers' abuse-related perceptions. Gannon and colleagues (see Gannon *et al.*, 2006; Gannon & Williams, 2007) asked child sexual abusers to read a lengthy one-page vignette describing an interaction between a child and adult that culminated with explicit child sexual abuse. A number of ambiguous themes were planted within the vignette that were designed to be easily interpreted using implicit theories (see Chapter 1 of this volume). For example, the child in the vignette is described as initiating hand-holding with the male adult; a description that could easily be interpreted as offence-supportive (i.e., a provocative come-on) or as nonoffence-supportive (i.e., an innocent childhood gesture). Unlike previous vignette studies, Gannon *et al.* attempted to test participants' *automatic* interpretations of the vignette by asking them – in a surprise memory task – to recall everything they could about the vignette. Surprisingly, Gannon *et al.* found that while child sexual abusers and nonsexual offender controls reinterpreted many of the ambiguous themes in a benign manner neither group reinterpreted the ambiguous themes in an *offence-supportive* manner. Put another way, while child sexual abusers' free recall showed a number of benign memory distortions, it did not suggest that they had used offence-supportive schemata to first interpret the vignette.

It is possible that child sexual abusers in this study were able to see through the nature of the surprise recall task, and adjusted their "recall" accordingly, or that their offence-supportive schemata were not primed adequately. However, it is also possible that offence-supportive schemata or implicit theories do not play a strong aetiological role in sexual offending, making it impossible for them to be detected in social information processing tasks.

A follow up study by Keown, Gannon and Ward (in press) further investigated this interesting finding. In this study, Keown *et al.* adapted a robust experimental cognitive processing procedure – the lexical decision task – to test for differences between the schemata of child sexual abusers and nonsexual offending comparison groups. Child sexual abusers, nonsexual offenders, and community comparisons were shown – via computer – word *stems* (e.g., "Sometimes, after doing sexual things children feel … ") designed to tap each of the implicit theories proposed by Ward and Keenan (1999). Immediately after each word stem, participants were presented with a word to complete the sentence which was either offence-supportive (e.g., "nice"), nonoffence-supportive (e.g., "sick"), or a nonword matched on word length (e.g., "hing"). The participants' task was simply to indicate, using a key press, whether the word completion was real or ficticious. Previous research shows that participants make accelerated decisions when words complete the sentence in a schema-consistent manner (see Baldwin *et al.*, 1993). Surprisingly, however, relative to the comparison groups, child sexual abusers in Keown *et al.*'s study did not respond faster to implicit theory-consistent words relative to implicit theory-inconsistent words overall. The mechanisms behind this null result remain open to further investigation. It could be the case, for example, that specific priming procedures like those used in the Oliver *et al.* study are required to elicit detectable "distortions" in cognitive-experimental testing conditions.

In the research so far evaluated, we have examined child sexual abusers' initial perceptions, interpretations, and social information encoding. Yet researchers have hypothesised that there are likely to be other processing stages that lie between preliminary perceptions and behavioural responses (Crick & Dodge, 1994; McFall, 1990). For example, McFall (1990) hypothesises that individuals not only have to perceive, interpret, and understand social information accurately but they must also choose an effective response to this perception (*decision skills*) and then execute and monitor a behaviour based on this response (*enactment skills*). Unfortunately, the volume of research conducted with child sexual abusers on these latter two stages is almost nonexistent. However, some research has indicated that child sexual abusers tend to be characterised by maladaptive problem-solving styles such as viewing problem solving in a negative and threatening fashion, problem solving avoidance, and impulsive or careless problem solving (Nezu *et al.*, 2005).

In terms of the very last processing step – enactment skills – there is also little research available. However, some research by Ward and his colleagues appears relevant (see Ward *et al.*, 1995; Ward, Hudson & Keenan, 1998). Ward and his colleagues have examined child sexual abusers' offence behaviours and discovered that these behaviours tend to be enacted differently depending upon the molesters' goals and attendant monitoring skills. In short, avoidance child sexual abusers – who wish to avoid assaulting a child – typically expend a great deal of energy attempting to cognitively monitor and control their offensive urges. However, because their cognitive system is placed under immense pressure, behavioural control and monitoring can become disrupted resulting in an individual who relinquishes all self-regulatory attempts, and thus sexually offends (Gannon *et al.*, 2005). Other child sexual abusers, however, have been found to be dominated by approach goals, in which they desire sex with children and actively monitor, plan, and seek out offending situations. Thus, this research illustrates that child sexual abusers show a great deal of variety in their offence enactment, and cognitive monitoring and adjustment of offence-related behaviours.

In summary, research on child sexual abusers' social-cognitive processing is still very much in its infancy, and so it may be some time before concrete conclusions can be drawn. At present however, it appears that researchers need to further concentrate their research efforts on further developing automatic processing paradigms that include priming procedures. There also appear to be some significant gaps in the stages of processing that occur following initial interpretation and perception of social stimuli, that is, research examining response decision and enactment skills.

Cognitive Content and Structure

In recent years, an increasing number of studies have been designed in an attempt to provide insight into the content and configuration of child sexual abusers' cognition. While these studies examine the information-processing speed of participants, this is largely in the aim of providing information on cognitive structure and configuration, and so we have chosen to describe these studies under this subheading. In recent years, a number of studies have emerged that use Greenwald's Implicit Association Test methodology (IAT) (Greenwald, McGhee & Schwartz, 1998) to examine whether child sexual abusers – relative to offender and non-offender comparison groups – hold more frequent, or stronger associations between words chosen to reflect the implicit theories proposed by Ward (Ward, 2000; Ward & Keenan, 1999). Mihailides, Devilly and Ward (2004) hypothesised that child sexual abusers – relative to comparison groups – would respond more quickly to the task of placing offence-supportive word pairings (e.g., children and sex words) together as child sexual abusers are hypothesised to hold stronger and more elaborate networks of this information in long term memory (Ward & Keenan, 1999). Mihailides, Devilly and Ward (2004) only tested three of the five proposed implicit theories – children as sexual beings, entitlement, and uncontrollability. The results showed that child sexual abusers displayed accelerated response times to both offender and nonoffender comparisons for both the children as sexual beings and uncontrollability implicit theories. In other words, child sexual abusers appeared to find it relatively easy to place offence-supportive word pairings together, as this was presumably facilitated by their offence-supportive cognitive architecture. Weaker support was shown for the entitlement implicit theory since child sexual abusers' response times were only statistically differentiable from nonoffenders.

This latter finding could simply further illustrate the generality of entitlement as an antisocial cognitive characteristic.

Other successful findings using IAT measures are emerging, but these tend to focus only on the concepts of children and sex (Brown, Gray & Snowden, 2007; Gray *et al.*, 2005). For example, Gray *et al.* confirmed that child sexual abusers showed a stronger likelihood of associating children and sex words compared with offender comparisons. The *receiver operating characteristics curve* (ROC) was also used to assess the predictive ability of IAT scores. The ROC defines predictive ability using the area under the curve (AUC), which expresses no predictive ability as an AUC of 0.5, and perfect predictive ability as an AUC of 1. Using these statistical procedures, Gray *et al.* report that IAT scores showed very respectable predictive validity (AUC = 0.73) for predicting CM group status.

In their most recent study using the IAT, Brown, Gray and Snowden (2007) further strengthened previous IAT findings through demonstrating the IAT's ability to discriminate between men who abuse prepubescent children, and those who abuse older children. In short, only the former abuser types showed the IAT effect, whereas the latter performed similarly to nonabuser comparisons. However, studies focusing only on children and sex concepts were designed to more explicitly tap sexual preferences and so conclusions regarding belief structures may be a little premature at this time. In other words, associating sex with children may not necessarily indicate a complex belief system that leads child sexual abusers to misinterpret children's behaviour as sexual.

Recently, Kamphuis *et al.* (2005) adapted the lexical decision methodology to investigate whether child sexual abusers associate power and sex concepts in long term memory. Three word types – presented in Dutch – were shown to child sexual abusers, violent offenders, and undergraduate male participants: *sexual* (e.g., attractive, seduction), *power* (e.g., touch, dominant), and *neutral* (e.g., store, balance). First, these words were *subliminally* presented to participants, at a time period short enough to ensure only subconscious processing (i.e., the subliminal prime). Following this, participants were presented with these types of words again or a nonword at a time period long enough for conscious awareness. The participants' task was to decide – as quickly as possible – whether the letter string was a word or nonword. As hypothesised, when child sexual abusers were presented with sexual subliminal primes, they showed accelerated response times to power words relative to the control groups, and to their own responses following the neutral subliminal primes. In other words, these results suggest that when child sexual abusers' sexual concepts are unconsciously activated, so too are power and dominance representations within their memory structures. There was also a tendency for child sexual abusers to show accelerated response times to sexual words following the presentation of the power subliminal primes. Thus these findings suggest that the feelings of dominance and superiority likely to be relevant to cognitions of entitlement (see Chapter 1 of this volume) are inextricably linked with – and may possibly activate – sexual thoughts and concepts. It is encouraging to see this work being conducted with child sexual abusers as such subliminal priming techniques have typically been reserved for work with analogue samples of students (see Bargh *et al.*, 1995; Bargh & Raymond, 1995).

In summary, the research investigating the structure and content of child sexual abusers' cognition has just begun to gain momentum, but shows great promise for both research and clinical investigations of child sexual abusers' cognition. We believe that a substantial improvement to future investigations might be to pair these types of paradigms with those investigating the role of offence-supportive cognitions in social information processing. In other words, does the offence-supportive content identified actively distort social information processing?

TREATMENT IMPLICATIONS

Treatment interventions with any type of offender should be carefully constructed using empirically validated theories and methodologically sound research (i.e., empirically driven practice; McGuire & Hatcher, 2001). Further, intervention packages should be periodically reviewed, to ensure that they reflect the very latest knowledge available. Our evaluation of the research literature investigating child sexual abusers' cognition has shown – surprisingly – a complete lack of consensus in the research findings to date. Yet treatment providers have been attempting to restructure child sexual abusers "faulty" cognitions for almost two decades, and practitioners continue to emphasise this core element in treatment designed to reduce future risk of offending (see Drake *et al.*, 2001; Marshall *et al.*, 1999; Ward, 2003). Our perusal of the available research literature has not been able to demonstrate unequivocally that most child sexual abusers offend sexually because they hold offence-supportive schemas that bias their social information processing. In other words, we do not *yet* hold clear and unambiguous information supporting the aetiological role of offence-supportive beliefs in child sexual offending. In fact contemporary meta-analyses of available recidivism studies have not been able to link such concepts as offence minimisation or lack of victim empathy with future recidivism (see Hanson & Morton-Bourgon, 2005). We believe that many of the deeply entrenched assumptions that both researchers and practitioners hold about child sexual abusers' cognition are in need of more open-minded investigation. As Maruna and Mannn (2006) have rightly pointed out, for example, many child sexual abusers may provide post offence excuses and justifications for their offences that are actually normative social practices rather than clear indications of faulty cognitive structures and increased risk of reoffending. In other words, the offence-supportive statements so often heard in therapy may reflect offenders' relatively normative need to protect himself against potentially devastating blows to self-image and esteem. Maruna and Mann (2006) point out that internalising complete accountability for socially disapproved acts is likely to be associated with stress, anxiety, low self-esteem, depression – and perhaps most importantly – an inability and lack of motivation to formulate a new, nonoffending identity. Yet our current treatment programs do not allow for such excuse making; and instead remain preoccupied with targeting distortions yet to be empirically validated in the research literature. In summary then, perhaps we as researchers and therapists should reflect upon why *we* find child sexual abusers' post offence syntax so distasteful to us, and how this may well have affected our shaping of a whole research field.

CONCLUSIONS AND FUTURE DIRECTIONS

In this chapter, we have reviewed and evaluated the current literature investigating child sexual abusers' offence-supportive cognitions. In particular, we have made note of the inconsistency inherent in the research to date, and of some of the large gaps apparent in the literature. One issue, which needs to be firmly addressed within the research literature, concerns the interpretations made from results of self-reported offence-supportive beliefs, most notably those from interview type studies. It is relatively easy to conduct such studies and find a "significant" result, yet not so easy to determine where the offence-supportive statements actually stem from. Such results provide little guiding information for treatment providers as to how best to conceptualise offenders' offence-supportive statements or how such statements should be tackled. Thus, care should be taken when designing such studies, to ensure the interpretability of results is optimal. Manipulating the context in which offenders provide their narratives, or pairing such studies with paradigms more amenable to belief detection might be one way of achieving this. For quantitative-type paradigms, an important issue concerns the difficulty many researchers have in publishing null results; even though these results may be the product of fairly rigorous methodology (e.g., questionnaire or cognitive-experimental studies). We are not suggesting for one moment that journal editors should accept all manner of null studies whether or not they are well designed. However, accepting relatively robust studies that have revealed no evidence of offence-supportive beliefs is vital if knowledge is to progress in this important arena.

It is clear to us, for example, that in comparison to research in the rape and aggression subfields (see Chapters 5 and 9 of this volume), clear examples of research supporting the existence of offence-supportive beliefs in child sexual abusers are less prevalent. This may simply be explained by the fact that the child molestation field is less frequented by analogue student samples who are more amenable to cognitive-experimental laboratory tasks. Clearly then, researchers interested in child molestation could begin to pay more attention to this research possibility, and recruit student men who indicate some propensity or interest in children and sex for such studies in addition to groups of apprehended child sexual abusers.

A further problem inherent in this research field, is the lack of theoretically driven research. It may seem unfair that we are taking researchers (including ourselves) to task over this issue since schema-based accounts of cognitive distortions were presented within this research field only relatively recently (e.g., Beech & Mann, 2002; Ward, 2000; Ward & Keenan, 1999). It should be noted, however, that many recent researchers testing the cognitive correlates of child molesting still do so with no explicit reference to dominant cognitive theory relating to child molestation (e.g., Saradjian & Nobus, 2003; Gray et al., 2005). In addition, a significant problem with current questionnaire research revolves around the selection of items used in these measures. To date, the selection of questionnaire items has been based – necessarily – upon clinical intuition. This means that many questionnaires used for current research and interventions do not yet measure each of the hypothesised implicit schemas outlined by Ward and

Keenan (1999) adequately. If Ward and Keenan's theory is correct, and child sexual abusers do hold heterogeneous patterns of offence-supportive schemas, then our current atheoretical measures are not adequately equipped to detect such differences. In other words, current questionnaire measures were not designed to test Ward and Keenan's implicit schemas. Clearly, theory support or refutation in this field would be greater accelerated through a concentrated and united effort from child molestation researchers to provide research that is theoretically comparable. Until this time, it is well worth asking ourselves whether it is child sexual abusers who hold the biased information processing tendencies, or whether we – as research investigators and practitioners – hold the ultimate information processing bias.

REFERENCES

Abel, G. G., Becker, J. V. & Cunningham-Rathner, J. (1984). Complications, consent and cognitions in sex between children and adults. *International Journal of Law and Psychiatry*, **7**, 189–3.

Abel, G. G., Gore, D. K., Holland, C. L. *et al.* (1989). The measurement of the cognitive distortions of child molesters. *Annals of Sex Research*, **2**, 135–53.

Adolph, R. (1999). Social cognition and the human brain. *Trends in Cognitive Science*, **3**, 469–79.

Anderson, C. A. & Bushman, B. J. (2002). Human Aggression. *Annual Review of Psychology*, **53**, 27–51.

Arkowitz, S. & Vess, J. (2003). An evaluation of the Bumby RAPE and MOLEST scales as measures of cognitive distortions with civilly committed sexual offenders. *Sexual Abuse: A Journal of Research and Treatment*, **15**, 237–49.

Augoustinos, M. & Walker, I. (1995). *Social Cognition. An Integrated Introduction*. London: Sage.

Baldwin, M. W., Fehr, B., Keedian, E. *et al.* (1993). An exploration of the relational schemata underlying attachment styles: Self-report and lexical decision approaches. *Personality and Social Psychology Bulletin*, **19**, 746–53.

Bargh, J. A. (1982). Attention and automaticity in the processing of self relevant information. *Journal of Personality and Social Psychology*, **43**, 425–36.

Bargh, J. A. & Raymond, P. (1995). The naive misuse of power: Nonconscious sources of sexual harassment. *Journal of Social Issues*, **26**, 168–85.

Bargh, J. A., Raymond, P., Pryor, J. B. & Strack, F. (1995). Attractiveness of the underling: an automatic power-sex association and its consequences for sexual harassment and aggression. *Journal of Personality and Social Psychology*, **68**, 768–81.

Bartlett, F. C. (1932). *Remembering: A Study in Experimental and Social Psychology*. London: Cambridge University Press.

Beckett, R. C., Beech, A. R., Fisher, D. & Fordham, A. S. (1994). *Community-based Treatment for Sex Offenders: An Evaluation of Seven Treatment Programmes*. London: Home Office.

Beckett, R. C. & Fisher, D. (1994). *Assessing victim empathy: A new measure*. Paper presented at the 13th Annual Conference of the Association for the Treatment of Sexual Abusers, San Francisco, November.

Beech, A. R. & Mann, R. (2002). Recent developments in the assessment and treatment of sexual offenders. In J. McGuire (ed.), *Offender Rehabilitation and Treatment: Effective Programmes and Policies to Reduce Re-offending* (pp. 259–88). Chichester: Wiley.

Bodenhausen, G. V., Kramer, G. P., & Süsser, K. (1994). Happiness and stereotypic thinking thinking in social judgement. *Journal of Personality and Social Psychology*, **66**, 621–32.

Brown, A. S., Gray, N. S. & Snowden, R. J. (2007). *Implicit Measurement of Sexual Preferences in Child Sex Abusers: Role of Victim Type and Denial*. Manuscript under review.

Bumby, K. M. (1996). Assessing the cognitive distortions of child molesters and rapists: Developments and validation of the MOLEST and RAPE scales. *Sexual Abuse: A Journal of Research and Treatment*, **8**, 37–54.

Crick, N. R. & Dodge, K. A. (1994). A review and reformulation of social information-processing mechanisms in children's social adjustment. *Psychological Bulletin*, **115**, 74–101.

Dodge, K. A. (1980). Social cognition and children's aggressive behavior. *Child Development*, **51**, 162–70.

Dodge, K. A. & Frame, C. L. (1982). Social cognitive biases and deficits in aggressive boys. *Child Development*, **33**, 620–35.

Drake, C., Ward, T., Nathan, P. & Lee, J. (2001). Challenging the cognitive distortions of child molesters: An implicit theory approach. *Journal of Sexual Aggression*, **7**, 25–40.

Feelgood, S., Cortoni, F. & Thompson, A. (2005). Sexual coping, general coping and cognitive distortions in incarcerated rapists and child molesters. *Journal of Sexual Aggression*, **11**, 157–70.

Fernandez, Y. M., Marshall, W. L., Lightbody, S. & O'Sullivan, C. (1999). The child molester empathy measure: Description and examination of its reliability and validity. *Sexual Abuse: A Journal of Research and Treatment*, **11**, 17–31.

Finkelhor, D. (1984). *Child Sexual Abuse: New Theory and Research*. New York: Free Press.

Fiske, S. T. & Taylor, S. E. (1991). *Social Cognition* (2nd edn). New York: McGraw-Hill.

Gannon, T. A. (2006). Increasing honest responding on cognitive distortions in child molesters: the bogus pipeline procedure. *Journal of Interpersonal Violence*, **21**, 1–18.

Gannon, T. A., Keown, K. & Polaschek, D. L. L. (2007). Increasing honest responding on cognitive distortions in child molesters: the bogus pipeline revisited. *Sexual Abuse: A Journal of Research and Treatment*, **19**, 5–22.

Gannon, T. A. & Polaschek, D. L. L. (2006). Cognitive distortions in child molesters: a re-examination of key theories and research. *Clinical Psychology Review*, **26**, 1000–19.

Gannon, T. A., Polaschek, D. L. L. & Ward, T. (2005). Social cognition and sexual offenders. In M. McMurran & J. McGuire (Eds.), *Social problem solving and offenders* (pp. 223–48). Chichester: Wiley.

Gannon, T. A. & Williams, S. E. (2007). *Investigating the Belief Systems of Extrafamilial Child Molesters*. Unpublished manuscript.

Gannon, T. A., Wright, D. B., Beech, A. R. & Williams (2006). Do child molesters hold distorted beliefs? What does their memory recall tell us? *Journal of Sexual Aggression*, **12**, 5–18.

Gilgun, J. F. & Connor, T. M. (1989). How perpetrators view child sexual abuse. *Social Work*, **34**, 249–51.

Gray, N. S., Brown, A. S., MacCulloch et al. (2005). An implicit test of the association between children and sex in pedophiles. *Journal of Abnormal Psychology*, **114**, 304–8.

Greenwald, A. G., McGhee, J. L. & Schwartz, J. L. (1998). Measuring individual difference in implicit cognition: the Implicit Association Test. *Journal of Personality and Social Psychology*, **74**, 1464–80.

Hall, G. C. N. & Hirschman, R. (1992). Sexual aggression against children: a conceptual perspective of etiology. *Criminal Justice and Behaviour*, **19**, 8–23.

Hanson, R. K., Gizzarelli, R. & Scott, H. (1994). The attitudes of incest offenders: Sexual entitlement and acceptance of sex with children. *Criminal Justice and Behavior*, **21**, 187–202.

Hanson, R. K. & Morton-Bourgon, K. E. (2005). The characteristics of persistent sexual offenders: A metaanalysis of recidivism studies. *Journal of Consulting and Clinical Psychology*, **73**, 1154–63.

Hanson, R. K. & Scott, H. (1995). Assessing the perspective-taking among sexual offenders, nonsexual criminals, and nonoffenders. *Sexual Abuse: A Journal of Research and Treatment*, **7**, 259–77.

Hayashino, D. S., Wurtele, S. K. & Klebe, K. J. (1995). Child molesters: An examination of cognitive factors. *Journal of Interpersonal Violence*, **10**, 106–16.

Hayler, B., Pardie, L. & Rivera, B. (2002). *An impact evaluation of specialized sex offender probation programs in Coles, Vermilion, and Madison counties*. Chicago, Illinois: Illinois Criminal Justice Information Authority.

Hollon, S. D. & Kriss, M. R. (1984). Cognitive factors in clinical research and practice. *Clinical Psychology Review*, **4**, 35–76.

Hudson, S. M., Marshall W. L., Wales D. *et al.* (1993). Emotional recognition skills of sex offenders. *Annals of Sex Research*, **6**, 199–211.

Kamphuis, J. H., De Ruiter, C., Janssen, B. & Spiering, M. (2005). Preliminary evidence for an automatic link between sex and power among men who molest children. *Journal of Interpersonal Violence*, **20**, 1351–65.

Kendall, P. C. (1992). Healthy thinking. *Behavior Therapy*, **23**, 1–12.

Keown, K., Gannon. T. A. & Ward, T. (in press) *What Were They Thinking? An Exploration of Child Sexual Offenders' Beliefs Using the Lexical Decision Task*. Manuscript under review.

Kolton, D. J. C., Boer, A. & Boer, D. P. (2001). A revision of the Abel and Becker Cognition Scale for intellectually disabled sexual offenders. *Sexual Abuse: A Journal of Research and Treatment*, **13**, 217–19.

Kunda, Z. (1999). *Social Cognition: Making Sense of People* (2nd edn). Cambridge: The MIT Press.

Langevin, R. (1991). A note on the problem of response set in measuring cognitive distortions. *Annals of Sex Research*, *4*, 287–92.

Marshall, W. L., Anderson, D. & Fernandez, Y. M. (1999). *Cognitive Behavioural Treatment of Sexual Offenders*. Chichester: Wiley.

Marshall, W. L. & Barbaree, H. E. (1990). An integrated theory of sexual offending. In W. L. Marshall, D. R. Laws & H. E. Barbaree (eds), *Handbook of Sexual Assault: Issues, Theories and Treatment of the Offender* (pp. 363–85). New York: Plenum.

Marshall, W. L., Hamilton, K. & Fernandez, Y. (2001). Empathy deficits and cognitive distortions in child molesters. *Sexual Abuse: Journal of Research & Treatment*, **13**, 123–30.

Marshall, W. L., Marshall, L. E., Sachdav, S. & Kruger, R. (2003). Distorted attitudes and perceptions, and their relationship with self esteem and coping in child molesters. *Sexual Abuse: A Journal of Research and Treatment*, **15**, 171–81.

Maruna, S. & Mann, R. E. (2006). A fundamental attribution error? Rethinking cognitive distortions. *Legal and Criminological Psychology*, **11**, 155–77.

Marziano, V., Ward., T., Beech, A. R. & Pattison, R. (2006). Identification of five fundamental implicit theories underlying cognitive distortions in child abusers: A preliminary study. *Psychology, Crime and Law*, **12**, 97–105.

McFall, R. M. (1990). The enhancement of social skills: An information processing analysis In W. L. Marshall, D. R. Laws & H. E. Barbaree (eds), *Handbook of Sexual Assault: Issues, Theories, and Treatment of the Offender* (pp. 311–30). New York: Plenum.

McGrath, M. L., Cann, S. & Konopasky, R. J. (1998). New measures of defensiveness, empathy, and cognitive distortions for sexual offenders against children. *Sexual Abuse: A Journal of Research and Treatment*, **10**, 25–36.

McGuire, J. & Hatcher, R. (2001). Offence focused problem solving: Preliminary evaluation of a cognitive skills program. *Criminal Justice and Behaviour*, **28**, 564–87.

Mihailides, S., Devilly, G. J. & Ward, T. (2004). Implicit cognitive distortions and sexual offending. *Sexual Abuse: A Journal of Research and Treatment*, **16**, 333–50.

Neidigh, L. & Krop, H. (1992). Cognitive distortions among child sexual offenders. *Journal of Sex Education and Therapy*, **18**, 208–15.

Nezu, C. M., Nezu, A. M., Dudek, J. A. *et al.* (2003). Social problem-solving correlates of sexual deviancy and aggression among adult child molesters. *Journal of Sexual Aggression*, **11**, 27–36.

Nichols, H. R. & Molinder, I. (1984). *Multiphasic Sex Inventory manual*. Available from the authors, 437 Bowes Drive, Tacoma, WA, 98466.

Nisbett, R. E. & Wilson, T. D. (1977). Telling more than we can know: verbal reports on mental processes. *Psychological Review*, **84**, 231–59.

Oliver, C., Watson, D., Gannon, T. A. & Beech, A. R. (2007). *The Effect of Sexual Priming Cues on Emotional Recognition in Child Sexual Abusers*. Manuscript under review.

Pettit, G. S., Polaha, J. A. & Mize, J. (2001). Perseptual and attributional processes in aggression and conduct problems. In J. Hill & B. Maughan (eds), *Conduct Disorders in Childhood and Adolescence* (pp. 292–319). Cambridge: Cambridge University Press.

Phelan, P. (1995). Incest and its meaning: the perspectives of fathers and daughters. *Child Abuse and Neglect*, **19**, 7–24.

Pollock, N. L. & Hashmall, J. M. (1991). The excuses of child molesters. *Behavioral Sciences and the Law*, **9**, 53–9.

Saradjian, A. & Nobus, D. (2003). Cognitive distortions of religious professionals who sexually abuse children. *Journal of Interpersonal Violence*, **18**, 905–23.

Serran, G. (2002). The measurement of empathy. In Fernandez, Y. (ed.) *In Their Shoes: Examining the Issue of Empathy and its Place in the Treatment of Offenders* (pp. 16–35). Oklahoma City, Oklahoma: Wood 'N' Barnes Publishing & Distribution.

Stermac, L. & Segal, Z. (1989). Adult sexual contact with children: an examination of cognitive factors. *Behavior Therapy*, **20**, 573–84.

Tiedens, L. Z. (2001). The effect of anger on the hostile inferences of aggressive and non-aggressive people: specific emotions, cognitive processing, and chronic accessibility. *Motivation and Emotion*, **25**, 233–51.

Tierney, D. W. & McCabe, M. P. (2001). An evaluation of self-report measures of cognitive distortions and empathy among Australian sex offenders. *Archives of Sexual Behavior*, **30**, 495–519.

Vanhouche, W. & Vertommen, H., (1999). Assessing cognitive distortions in sex offenders: a review of commonly used versus recently developed instruments. *Psychologica Belgica*, **39**, 163–87.

Ward, T. (2000). Sexual offenders' cognitive distortions as implicit theories. *Aggression and Violent Behavior*, **5**, 491–507.

Ward, T. (2003). The explanation, assessment and treatment of child sexual abuse. *International Journal of Forensic Psychology*, **1**, 10–25.

Ward, T. & Beech, A. R. (2006). An integrated theory of sexual offending. *Aggression and Violent Behavior*, **11**, 44–63.

Ward, T., Gannon, T. A. & Keown, K. (2006). Beliefs, values, and action: the judgment model of cognitive distortions. *Aggression and Violent Behavior: A Review Journal*, **11**, 323–40.

Ward, T., Hudson, S. M. & Keenan, T. (1998). A self-regulation model of the sexual offense process. *Sexual Abuse: A Journal of Research and Treatment*, **10**, 141–57.

Ward, T. & Keenan, T. (1999). Child molesters' implicit theories. *Journal of Interpersonal Violence*, **14**, 821–38.

Ward, T., Louden, K., Hudson, S. M. & Marshall, W. L. (1995). A descriptive model of the offense chain for child molesters. *Journal of Interpersonal Violence*, **10**, 452–72.

Ward, T. & Siegert, R. (2002). Toward a comprehensive theory of child sexual abuse: a theory knitting perspective. *Psychology, Crime and Law*, **8**, 319–51.

Wenzel, A. & Rubin, D. C. (2005). *Cognitive Methods and their Application to Clinical Research*. Washington, DC: American Psychological Society.

Chapter 5

RAPE-RELATED COGNITION: CURRENT RESEARCH

CALVIN M. LANGTON

University of Nottingham, and Peaks Unit, Rampton Hospital,
Nottinghamshire Healthcare Trust and University of Toronto

There are a number of theories of sexual offending (Ward, Polaschek & Beech, 2006), including several multifactorial models in which cognition is identified as an important factor (e.g., Hall & Hirschman, 1991; Malamuth, Heavey & Linz, 1993; Marshall & Barbaree, 1990). This chapter reviews recent examples of rape-related cognition research. I begin with a brief section in which a rationale is presented for drawing upon cognition research with both convicted rapists and sexually coercive men from university/student and community populations even though there has been curiously little cross-referencing and integration of these two broad literatures. I then introduce three facets of cognition, *structures*, *processes*, and *products* to provide a framework for the chapter. In the sections that follow, recent studies representing investigations of rape-related cognitive structures, products, and processes are reviewed and implications for assessment noted. A final section considers select research concerning intervention efforts targeting rape-related cognition undertaken with the various populations.

In this review, studies using convicted and nonconvicted samples will be included. The intention is to demonstrate that advances in the cognition research with these two populations will be most effectively realised when findings within the two general bodies of literature are considered together. Prevalence data also suggest a sharp distinction between criminal and noncriminal populations may not be particularly meaningful. Abbey *et al.* (2006) administered a modified version of the Sexual Experiences Survey (Koss & Oros, 1982) to a random community sample of 163 single men from a large metropolitan area and found that 39 % reported committing a sexual assault involving physical or verbal coercion and almost 25 % admitted attempted or completed rape. Studies of university men also reveal that as many as a third of respondents indicate a willingness to commit rape if assured that they would not be apprehended or punished (e.g., Malamuth,

Aggressive Offenders' Cognition: Theory, Research and Practice. Edited by T. A. Gannon, T. Ward, A. R. Beech and D. Fisher. © 2007 John Wiley & Sons, Ltd.

1981). Given that sexually coercive behaviour is something engaged in by a notable minority of the male population then, it is reasonable to postulate that there are dimensions on which men who have been arrested and convicted of sexual crimes against women do not meaningfully differ from those who have escaped such identification.

Convergence of conclusions from empirical findings also support a more inclusive approach to studies with criminal and noncriminal samples. For example, in an integrative review of cognition research completed with samples of university, marital, and incarcerated rapists, Ryan (2004) points to the shared role of rape-supportive attitudes, sexual pre-occupation (incorporating hypersexuality and deviant sexual arousal), sexual scripts (encompassing sexually coercive fantasies and planning), and the construct of hypermasculinity among these sexually aggressive men.

An interest in drawing together cognition research carried out with both convicted and university/community samples of sexual aggressors is not meant to imply, however, that they should be considered a homogenous group. Indeed, there is a marked heterogeneity among rapists, and their different characteristics, motivations, and offence behaviours (Knight, 1999; Knight & Prentky, 1990; Prentky & Knight, 1991), which invites theorising about differences across subtypes in domains such as cognitive processing (Langton & Marshall, 2001). Despite this, generic classifications appear the norm and the parsing of small, convenience samples of convicted rapists has generally not been undertaken presumably in part because of the reduced statistical power that analyses involving subgroups would afford (see Barbaree *et al.*, 1994; Beech *et al.*, 2005, Brown & Forth, 1997, and Kalichman *et al.*, 1989, for notable exceptions).

Within this chapter, the terms *sexual coercion*, *sexual aggression*, *rape* and variants are used interchangeably (although there are clearly valid distinctions to be drawn between the verbal and physical acts involved in these behaviours; see, for example, DeGue & DiLillo, 2005), and the terms *rapists* and *sexual offenders* are also used interchangeably with *sexually aggressive/coercive men*, in keeping with an inclusive approach to the research.

COGNITIVE DISTORTIONS

Cognitive distortions have been identified as components within both aetiological theories of sexually abusive behaviour (Finkelhor, 1984; Hall & Hirschman, 1991; Marshall & Barbaree, 1990; Ward & Siegert, 2002) as well as theories of the sexual recidivism process (Pithers, 1990; Ward & Hudson, 2000). They have been identified as important targets within comprehensive treatment programs for sexual offenders (Marshall *et al.*, 1998) and (in the form of offence-supportive attitudes) as predictors of sexual reoffence (Hanson & Harris, 2000; Hanson & Morton-Bourgon, 2005).

Despite this apparent consensus concerning the relevance of cognitive distortions, the literature is characterised by considerable variation in exactly what is meant by the term. Indeed, the term's limitations for furthering understanding of assessment and treatment issues as well as aetiology of sexual deviance and aggression have been repeatedly noted (Gannon & Polaschek, 2006; Mann & Beech, 2003; Maruna & Mann, 2006; Ward *et al.*, 1997). As should become clear, there are contrasting ways to conceptualise cognitive distortions. Perhaps most frequently, cognitive distortions have been viewed as attitudes and beliefs which offenders use to deny, minimise and rationalise their behaviour (Murphy, 1990), and which serve to precipitate and maintain sexually coercive behaviour (Abel, Becker & Cunningham-Rathner, 1984; Stermac & Segal, 1989; Ward, 2000). As such, they seem to be implicated at various stages of an offence cycle, giving the construct a rather broad, multifaceted role. Certainly, qualitative analyses of rapists' accounts of their offences by Polaschek and her colleagues (Polaschek *et al.*, 2001; Polaschek & Hudson, 2004) implicate maladaptive cognitive processing at various temporal phases within the offence pathways identified (see also Monahan, Marolla & Bromley, 2005).

SOCIAL COGNITION: STRUCTURES, PROCESSES, AND PRODUCTS

As a general approach to the study of the individual in a social context, social cognition is concerned with the types and content of information stored in memory, how this information is represented and organised, the influence that such information has on perceiving and interpreting social information, and how new information is integrated with existing knowledge and memories (Bodenhausen & Lambert, 2003; Sherman, Judd & Park, 1989). The approach has generated a considerable body of research that has greatly advanced understanding of the way people function as active social perceivers. Importantly, all individuals have limited cognitive resources (Fiske & Taylor, 1991; Muraven, Tice & Baumeister, 1998) so some processing must be automatic (that is, beyond conscious control – Bargh, 1994, 1999), involving heuristic strategies based on pre-existing knowledge (Macrae, Milne & Bodenhausen, 1994; Strack & Mussweiler, 2003) to offset the demands of engaging in systematic, effortful processing. In conjunction with motivations (see Higgins & Molden, 2003) the content and organisation of prior knowledge and memories is a key determinant, through the generation of expectancies and hypothesis-confirming biases of what is attended to and how it is appraised (Darley & Gross, 1983; Hamilton & Garcia-Marques, 2003). Given the active role of the social perceiver in this essentially subjective process, it is unsurprising that errors of interpretation and judgment can result (Nisbett & Ross, 1980; Tversky & Kahneman, 1974).

A number of clinical disorders and maladaptive behaviours have been productively considered from the social cognition and cognitive science approach (e.g., Crick & Dodge, 1994; Huesmann, 1998; Ingram, 1986; Wenzel & Rubin, 2005) and it has also been seen as promising in the study of sexual aggression (Drieschner & Lange, 1999; Gannon, Polaschek & Ward, 2005; Johnston & Ward, 1996; Segal & Stermac, 1990). In essence, sexual aggressors are thought to have maladaptive schema, or a cognitive orientation, that influences their processing of social information in a way that facilitates or increases the likelihood of committing a sexual assault. The dysfunctional biases and insensitivities also maintain the behaviour (by ensuring information is processed in a manner congruent with existing knowledge and memories) and prevent the formation of alternative, more balanced or realistic appraisals of the information.

McFall, Treat, and Viken (1997) cogently argue that clinical, social, and cognitive psychologists should view cognition as a reciprocal, recursive, dynamic process rather than as an event or experience, a discrete construct accessible through introspective methods of assessment. However, a considerable amount of research with sexually coercive men has employed self-report methodologies, which are reliant on introspection. Although conclusions based solely on such work would be ill advised (Hilton, Harris & Rice, 1998), it seems somewhat fastidious to discount the contribution of such work entirely. As should become clear from what follows, it is when research concerning facets of cognition triangulate that confidence in both the directions and implications of the work is garnered. From this perspective, rape-related cognition might be best construed as a latent construct that must be inferred from the pattern of data generated from direct measurement of aspects of the process. Although something of a didactic simplification, the present review will discuss the recent research in terms of three general facets of cognition (*structures*, *processes*, and *products*), which I briefly describe next.

Cognitive structures can be considered the architecture of an individual's stored knowledge and memories. These represent organisational units, associated networks of meaning containing semantic, episodic, and affective elements concerning abstract, situational, and interpersonal constructions. There is considerable variation in the terminology and conceptualisation of these constructions (Wyer, 2004). Here, it will suffice to simply note examples, which include: prototypes and stereotypes (Cantor, Mischel & Schwartz, 1982), scripts (Abelson, 1981), and schema (Scarvalone, Fox & Safran, 2005; Segal, 1988). These structures can be selectively and automatically activated (Bargh, 1989) depending on internal motivational states of the individual as well as external stimuli, and through repeated activation can become highly accessible (Andersen, Spielman & Bargh, 1992). Importantly, they enable individuals to make sense of their social world while preserving cognitive resources (White & Carlston, 1983); they provide the basis for resolving ambiguity in favour of prior experiences and knowledge (Dunning & Sherman, 1997) and for interpreting and anticipating events through the generation of expectancies and confirmatory biases that influence cognitive processes including encoding (Wittenbrink, Gist & Hilton, 1997) and retrieval (Bruch, Kaflowitz & Berger, 1988; Lenton & Bryan, 2005) as well as behaviour (Bargh, Chen & Burrows, 1996; Dijksterhuis & van Knippenberg, 1998).

The external environment and the individual's cognitive experience of it is mediated through various *cognitive processes*, which involve the use of heuristic mechanisms that determine what needs to be attended to, how it is perceived and what interpretations and attributions are made. Reflecting the reciprocal and recursive nature of the interactions, these cognitive processes are heavily influenced by the content and organisation of cognitive structures through expectancies and self-serving biases (Marx, Gross & Adams, 1999; Ross & Sicoly, 1979) but also by the individual's motivations (Ditto & Lopez, 1992; Kunda, 1990), affect (Forgas, 2001) and circumstances, hence the discrepancies between the general consistency in the way an individual thinks and acts and the situational specificity and temporal instability of an individual's cognitive products (Hollon & Kriss, 1984). Importantly, individuals have little or no introspective awareness of their cognitive processes nor, indeed, access to their cognitive structures (Nisbett & Wilson, 1977).

Emerging from these processes are the *cognitive products*, the thoughts, inferences, understandings, and imagery to which an individual does have some degree of introspective access and is therefore able to express. In this regard they could be considered surface cognition, providing hints and permitting inferences about underlying structures and processes but representing only the "tip of the iceberg" concerning the content, organisation, and systematic interrelationships between these cognitive facets (Hollon & Kriss, 1984, p. 39). Because information processing is reciprocal and recursive, these products are incorporated back into relevant components of the individual's underlying cognitive structures, either reinforcing or causing revision of them, and in turn influencing ongoing processing in current and future social situations.

RAPE-RELATED COGNITIVE STRUCTURES

In contrast to the considerable body of research concerning cognitive products related to sexual aggression (to which I turn shortly) there has, until recently, been relatively little work investigating cognitive structures or schemas in sexually coercive men. Ward and his colleagues (Ward, 2000; Ward & Keenan, 1999) have introduced the concept of *implicit theories*, drawing on both the broader social cognition and developmental literatures and acknowledging the conceptual overlap with schema (see Chapter 1 of this volume). These researchers suggest that just as individuals develop from childhood onwards an understanding of themselves, their beliefs, needs, behaviours, and those of the people with whom they interact, sexual offenders will have formulated and utilise causal theories, some of which will be specific to their sexually coercive or deviant behaviour, and which would be expected to exert an influence on their information processing.

Conceptualising certain cognitive structures as implicit theories affords a basis for hypothesising relations between various core stereotypes or schema, their influence on cognitive processes, and their associations with cognitive products.

The implicit theories of rapists and sexual murderers are discussed by Fisher and Beech (Chapter 2 of this volume; see also Beech, Ward & Fisher, 2006). As such, they are only briefly mentioned here. Following earlier efforts to identify the implicit theories of child molesters (Ward & Keenan, 1999), Polaschek and Ward (2002) examined a range of self-report scales and attitudinal statements concerning rape-supportive beliefs, and identified a number of core themes around which clusters of specific distortions could be organised. From these, they constructed five implicit theories intended to encompass the broad range of beliefs and desires considered conducive to sexually coercive behaviour and therefore likely held by sexually aggressive men. These were *women are unknowable* (e.g., "women are usually sweet until they've caught a man and then they let their true self show"), *women are sex objects* (e.g., "the degree of a woman's resistance should be a major factor in determining if a rape has occurred"), *male sex drive is uncontrollable* (e.g., "if a girl engages in necking or petting and she lets things get out of hand, it is her own fault if her partner forces sex on her"), *entitlement* (e.g., "women are there to meet men's sexual needs regardless of their own"), and *dangerous world* (e.g., "lots of people are out to get you").

Support for the validity of these implicit theories work comes from a number of recent studies. Polaschek and Gannon (2004) were able to place statements given by 37 convicted rapists regarding their offence processes into five categories representing these implicit theories (relabelling the first as *women are dangerous* to more accurately convey the underlying hostility perceived in women's behaviour). Demonstrating considerable overlap with these findings, Mann and Hollin (2001) used content analysis to infer what they described as underlying schemas from the explanations of sexual assaults provided by 45 rapists. They identified a number of general categories: *entitlement* (e.g., "she was my wife, it was my right"), *grievance* (e.g., "she lied to me and made me angry"), *control* (e.g., "it was my way of having the last word"), *self as victim* (e.g., "it always happens to me"), *disrespect for certain women* (e.g., "women who go to nightclubs are looking for sex"), *justifications* (e.g., "she encouraged me"), *minimisations* (e.g., "I only tied her with the belt to calm her down") and *excuses* (e.g., "I was under the influence of glue"). Similarly, Milner and Webster (2005) examined the autobiographical accounts provided by 12 rapists and compared these with the accounts of 12 child molesters and 12 nonsexual violent offenders. As expected, content analysis revealed that themes reflecting hostility to women and sexual entitlement were significantly higher among rapists than the other groups (bias-corrected effect sizes ranged from 0.72 to 1.60).

There are, however, limitations to the use of qualitative methodologies such as those used in these studies with convicted rapists because the inferences about the content and organisation of implicit theories or schemas are based solely on questionnaire items or interview data; that is, they are *explicit* measures of surface cognition. Importantly, explicit tests of cognition are subject to conscious control (Greenwald, McGhee & Schwartz, 1998) and may not adequately tap the content or organisation of underlying schema. In contrast, *implicit* measures reflect the automatic impact of cognitions on behaviour (De Houwer, 2006). From their review of a number of implicit memory studies with a range of clinical populations, Amir and Selvig (2005) concluded that the implicit measures provide "an innovative method of describing clinical conditions and may supplant information gained from self-report to help triangulate the clinical construct under study . . . " (p. 165). Adapting implicit measures for use with rapists clearly has potential, perhaps revealing enhanced implicit memory or distinct patterns of affective association in sexual aggressors for material relevant to women and sexually coercive behaviour (see Smith & Waterman, 2004, and Snowden *et al.*, 2004, for use of the Stroop Test and the Implicit Association Test, respectively, with other offender groups). By examining the performance in experimental investigations of implicit cognition researchers can overcome some of the limitations inherent in relying on what sexually aggressive men are willing (or even able) to tell us themselves.

RAPE-RELATED COGNITIVE PRODUCTS

In approaching the research concerning cognitive products it is helpful to discuss two kinds: general beliefs or attitudes and offence-specific accounts. Both are surface cognitions in that they represent information stored in memory of which the individual has awareness (in that he endorses certain items on a measure of attitudes or provides a description of his offence) and, clearly, both are susceptible to deliberate misrepresentation at the time they are assessed. It is important to note as well that although the contents and organisation of underlying cognitive structures can be inferred from these two types of cognitive products, these deep structures are not themselves being assessed.

Item endorsement of attitudes and beliefs that are generally untrue but supportive of sexually coercive behaviour (e.g., "women secretly want to be raped", "women actually mean 'yes' when they say 'no'") can be considered generalised *offence-supportive cognitive distortions* (Thornton & Shingler, 2001). The accounts provided by sexually coercive men (usually obtained through interview procedures) of their sexual assaults can be considered *offence-specific cognitive distortions* (Thornton & Shingler, 2001). These include the offender's own perceptions, attributions, and interpretations that are contrary to the accounts of the incident given by his victim, witnesses, and investigators. These distortions are frequently taken to represent examples of denial and/or minimisation. It remains unclear, however, whether (or when) such distortions are products of information processing errors or deliberate misrepresentations intended to divert blame or avoid negative self-evaluation.

The majority of investigations of cognition in sexual offenders have concentrated on attitudes and beliefs (see Gannon, Polaschek & Ward, 2005; Polaschek, Ward & Hudson, 1997) so I turn to this body of research first and review pertinent studies in three sub-sections.

Studies Concerning Discriminative Validity

Much of the evidence suggests that convicted rapists do not differ significantly in their responses to self-report measures designed to assess rape-supportive attitudes and beliefs compared with other groups of sexual offenders, usually child molesters (e.g., Blumenthal, Gudjonsson & Burns, 1999; Bumby, 1996; Feelgood, Cortoni & Thompson, 2005; Kroner, Boer & Mills, 2004; Segal & Stermac, 1984), or nonsexual offenders (e.g., Feelgood *et al.*, 2005; Kroner *et al.*, 2004; Marolla & Scully, 1986).

One possible reason for the mixed findings is that some level of acceptance or agreement with rape-related attitudes, beliefs and myths might be present in men in general. Alternatively, methodological and conceptual issues might account for the mixed findings. The small sample sizes and associated low statistical power that characterise many of the studies, particularly those involving convicted rapists, may have precluded finding significant differences. Consistent with this, Feelgood *et al.* (2005) found no significant differences between rapists ($n = 25$), child molesters ($n = 36$), and nonsexually violent offenders ($n = 25$) on Bumby's (1996) RAPE scale (a questionnaire assessing general attitudes and beliefs about sexual aggression towards women). However, these investigators also calculated effect sizes for comparisons between their groups and those described by Bumby (1996). Although generally in the small-to-medium range, the effect sizes were in the expected direction, leading the investigators to conclude that "the possibility that rape distortions are more distinctive in rapists relative to some comparison groups cannot be dismissed" (p. 165).

The vulnerability of self-report measures to social desirability response biases has also been noted by many, and circumstantial considerations such as the implications of a forensic assessment (versus participation in a research study assuring anonymity and confidentiality) might be thought highly conducive to "faking-good". Experimental information-processing paradigms looking at this issue (see Chapter 4 of this volume) have yet to be used with rapists. However, Kroner *et al.* (2004) found that statistically controlling for self-reported impression management did not explain the lack of differences on rape-supportive attitudes between their sample of rapists and other offender groups, which is also inconsistent with a simple fake-good response bias explanation of the data.

Of course, as windows onto the underlying cognitive structures of sexually coercive men, responses in questionnaires and in interviews are rather incomplete. As has been already noted, research from social psychology and cognitive science clearly shows that individuals do not have introspective access to the cognitive processes that underlie their motivations, perceptions, and behaviour. That said, any endorsement by convicted rapists of rape-supportive attitudes and beliefs in the context of a forensic assessment would appear worthy of attention.

Prediction Studies

Research to be reviewed here has investigated the association between rape-supportive cognitive products and sexual aggression, either in terms of convicted sexual offenders' criminal recidivism or university and community men's self-reported interest in or history of sexually coercive behaviour. First, I consider the findings of two recent quantitative reviews.

Hanson and Morton-Bourgon (2004) carried out a comprehensive meta-analysis of the predictors of sexual recidivism among sexual offenders and included among the many variables examined "attitudes tolerant of sexual crime" (which was distinct from a "child molester attitudes" variable). Using nine studies (total $N = 1,617$), the reported effect size for this variable was small but significant ($d = 0.22$, 95 % confidence interval = 0.05 to 0.38, with significant variability across studies). Firm conclusions about the predictive significance of the "attitudes tolerant of sexual crime" variable for rapists specifically are not possible because the studies used in the meta-analysis included both child molesters and rapists and Hanson and Morton-Bourgon did not report separate analyses for sexual offender types. The attitude measures in a number of the studies were also single-item ratings or classifications completed by clinicians or research assistants rather than self-report scales with established psychometric properties. Nevertheless, the findings are consistent with the view that rape-related cognition is associated with future sexually aggressive behaviour among identified sexual offenders.

The other meta-analysis of relevance here was carried out by Murnen, Wright and Kaluzny (2002). In contrast to the Hanson and Morton-Bourgon (2004) meta-analysis, this study focused on the link between university (and, in a few samples, university plus community) men's responses to questionnaire measures representing *masculine ideology* and either their self-reported history of sexually aggressive behaviour or self-reported likelihood of raping a women if assured it would go undetected and unpunished. Findings in 39 studies for 11 self-report measures were available (with some studies using more than one measure: Ns for each measure ranged from 712 to 5,995).

Effect sizes were statistically significant for 10 of the measures: absolute *d* values ranged from 0.27 for *sex role stereotyping* (Burt, 1980) to 0.61 for *hypermasculinity* (Mosher & Sirkin, 1984). As expected, the measures of general gender role attitudes had smaller effect sizes. Significant heterogeneity was generally found across studies, although for the two measures with the largest effect sizes, *hostile masculinity* (Malamuth, 1989a, 1989b; Malamuth *et al.*, 1995) and *hypermasculinity*, findings were homogenous. Overall, these correlational data with nonconvicted men confirm a small to moderate association between sexual aggression (history of, or willingness to engage in) and attitudes accepting of violence in relationships or that reflect hostility towards women (see also Anderson, Cooper & Okamura, 1997).

Two recent studies have also provided evidence implicating sexual offence-supportive cognition in sexual recidivism and warrant particular mention here. In the first of these, Hanson and Harris (2000) explicitly drew on social cognition theory in their investigation of dynamic variables (variables capable or demonstrated to have changed over time). Using a sample of 409 sexual offenders (including 137 rapists) under community supervision, these researchers found that a number of dynamic variables correlated with recidivism status. Among these were "rape attitudes" ($r = 0.19$), as well as attitudes reflecting "sexual entitlement" ($r = 0.29$) and "low remorse/victim blaming" ($r = 0.28$) (all $p < 0.001$). Although the variables were scored using information reported retrospectively by the offenders' community supervisors, the data are consistent with the meta-analytic results and, again, demonstrate a link between rape-related cognition and sexually aggressive behaviour.

In another prediction study, Langton *et al.* (in press) compared the post-treatment accounts provided by 102 sexual offenders of their offences with official records. Discrepancies were coded using a six-item minimisation scale, reflecting the extent to which the offender continued to: attribute blame to his victim (e.g., she seduced him); justify his behaviour using external factors (e.g., alcohol or drug use); justify his behaviour using internal factors (e.g., his own sexual victimisation); minimise the extent of his offending behaviour (e.g., its frequency or intrusiveness); minimise the harm caused (e.g., construed the experience as pleasurable or educational for the victim); and minimise his sexual deviance (e.g., claimed disinterest in sexually coercive behaviour). At follow-up after release, among the sexual offenders assessed as being higher risk for sexual recidivism (according to an actuarial assessment tool, Hanson, 1997), those with higher scores on the minimisation scale recidivated sexually at a significantly faster rate than those at the same level of risk but who had lower minimisation scores.

Langton *et al.* (in press) suggested that minimisation among sexual offenders may be better conceptualised in terms of different general types. Of relevance here, one type would be instances of minimisation that represent *offence-specific cognitive distortions* (i.e., the products of biased processing influenced by of-fence-supportive cognitive structures). These cognitive distortions would re-flect the offender's grossly inaccurate interpretations, attributions, and infer-ences about his victim and/or the assault but are believed by him nonetheless. Langton *et al.* reasoned that if these offence-specific cognitive distortions were present in the sample at post-treatment (despite cognitive restructuring work during the programme) the underlying offence-supportive cognitive structures must have remained intact in the sexual recidivists, resulting in biased infor-mation processing in their later offence cycles and consequent assaults. This interpretation of the data is consistent with the research presented above that links more general rape-supportive attitudes and beliefs with sexually coercive behaviour – and with the research on perceptual biases and insensitivities reviewed shortly.

Based in part on the earlier empirical evidence indicating that denial and mini-misation do not predict sexual recidivism (Hanson & Bussière, 1998; Hanson & Morton-Bourgon, 2005), as well as a broader body of evidence concerning explana-tory styles demonstrating positive effects for excuse-making, Maruna and Mann (2006) cogently argued for a shift in treatment emphasis from denial and minimi-sation (Thornton & Shingler's, 2001, and Langton *et al.*'s, in press, *offence-specific cognitive distortions*) to therapeutic work at the level of schemas. Although research and treatment efforts focused on schemas represent an important advance for the field (Mann & Beech, 2003), critiques of the methodology and conceptualisations used in the denial/minimisation studies included in the meta-analyses by Hanson and his colleagues suggest that conclusions regarding lack of prediction validity may be premature (Langton *et al.*, in press; Lund, 2000). Further investigations that combine innovative assessment methodologies with more refined conceptualisa-tions of denial and minimisation (see, for example, Jung, 2004, and Schneider & Wright, 2004) are clearly necessary.

Studies of Multifactorial Models

The third stream of research at the level of cognitive products related to sexual aggression has sought to identify the characteristics of sexually aggressive men within multifactorial models. The work of Malamuth and his colleagues has been particularly informative and influential in this line of investigation. Malamuth *et al.* (1991) collected cross-sectional, retrospective data from a nationally repre-sentative sample of US university men ($N = 2,652$) and used structural equation modelling to examine the relationships between a number of latent constructs (op-erationalised using a range of measured variables) implicated in earlier theoretical and empirical work as relevant to aggression. In the model they reported, forms of aggression (sexual and nonsexual, measured using self-reported occurrence and frequency) resulted from involvement in delinquency (having delinquent friends, running away) that followed hostile childhood experiences (parental violence and child abuse).

Aggression was predicted via two main pathways from the delinquency construct: the first, the *hostile masculinity* pathway, involved two latent constructs: *attitudes supporting aggression* (consisting of Burt's (1980) scales: Rape Myth Acceptance (RMA), Acceptance of Interpersonal Violence (AIV), and Adversarial Sexual Beliefs (ASB)) and *hostile masculinity* personality features (including Spence, Helmreich & Holahan's (1979) Negative Masculinity scale, and Check's (1985) Hostility Toward Women scale). The second pathway was labelled *sexual promiscuity* (operationalised by age at first sexual intercourse and number of sexual partners) and in later research as *impersonal sex*. The hostile masculinity pathway was found to lead to both sexual and nonsexual coercion towards women, with hostile masculinity strongly influenced by attitudes supporting aggression. The sexual promiscuity pathway led to sexual coercion; importantly, an interaction between characteristics from both pathways accounted for a unique portion of the variation in the prediction of sexual aggression.

In a later study involving a path-analytic approach, Malamuth *et al.* (1995) replicated their earlier findings and extended them using both cross-sectional and longitudinal data from a separate, combined sample of university men (see also Abbey *et al.*, 2006; Knight & Sims-Knight, 2003; Lussier, Proulx & LeBlanc, 2005; and Wheeler, George & Dahl, 2002, for recent reformulations of Malamuth's work). Reflecting the model's emphasis on the confluence of several variables, Malamuth *et al.* also reported a risk analysis demonstrating a significant difference in the level of sexual aggression shown as a function of the number of risk factors present. Essentially a positive linear relationship was evident. Among men with all five factors (impersonal sex, masculine role stress, proneness to general hostility, violence attitudes, and hostile masculinity variables), 89 % showed some level of sexual aggression.

RAPE-RELATED COGNITIVE PROCESSES

Research using written vignettes of social situations/sexual offences that require interpretations and evaluations of emotional states and experiences of others has shown that sexual offenders make perspective-taking errors (Hanson & Scott, 1995; Stermac & Segal, 1989). For example, Fernandez and Marshall (2003) found no differences between 27 rapists and 27 incarcerated nonsexual offenders in level of empathy towards an accident victim or empathy towards a woman who had been sexually victimised by an unknown assailant. However, compared to their own empathic responses to the women in these two scenarios, the rapists showed significantly less empathy towards their own victim, prompting the researchers to suggest that their rapists' victim-specific empathy deficits might actually be better construed as offence-specific cognitive distortions (see also Marshall, Hamilton & Fernandez, 2001) arising from a failure at the perspective-taking stage of an empathy response (Marshall *et al.*, 1995). Marshall and Moulden (2001) reported similar results for their sample of 32 rapists, and also found a significant negative correlation between the rapists' scores on self-report measures of hostility towards women and empathy towards the women in the scenarios.

These findings are consistent with the general postulation that sexually aggressive men's cognitive schema could undermine perspective-taking ability via perceptual biases and insensitivities to social, emotional, and sexual cues within heterosocial interactions, resulting in attributions and interpretations that facilitate sexual aggression in some way. For example, misperception of friendliness as sexual interest, if not resolved, could lead to forced sexual activity (Abbey, 1987). Perceiving sexual interest early in a social interaction could result in rejection of disconfirming information and pursuit of sexual relations despite later protestations or resistance. Indeed, such protestations could elicit frustration and anger at having been initially encouraged only to be refused, which might then be taken to justify continuing forcibly.

The work of Abbey and her colleagues with university samples has clearly demonstrated a bias in men towards the perception of sexual interest or attraction in a woman when not actually intended by her. These researchers have shown that both as participants in, and as observers of heterosexual interactions with women, men's perceptions and judgments tend to be in sexual terms (Abbey, 1982), a bias that increases when alcohol is consumed (Abbey *et al.*, 2003; Abbey, Zawacki & McAuslan, 2000) and evident whether women's nonverbal cues are ambiguous or not (Abbey & Melby, 1986). Abbey and Harnish (1995) found that men's interpretation of women's behaviour as sexual in written vignettes was also found to increase as a function of the men's endorsement of rape-supportive attitudes. Abbey, Zawacki and Buck (2005) found that self-acknowledged sexual aggressors reported greater sexual attraction to a female confederate than did nonaggressors, and trained coders observing their interactions were least confident that the sexual aggressors had attended to specific cues from the confederate.

This last finding, that sexually aggressive men might be insensitive to certain cues from women, has been explored by a number of other researchers too. Lipton, McDonel and McFall (1987) developed the Test of Reading Affective Cues (TRAC), consisting of a videotaped series of 72 30-second heterosocial interactions, to investigate 11 convicted rapists' ability to correctly classify the affect (bad mood, negative, neutral, positive and romantic) of men and women. The rapists were found to be significantly less accurate in reading the women's cues in first-date interactions than were comparison groups of 11 violent nonrapists and 11 nonviolent nonrapists, with judgment errors for the women's negative and bad mood cues accounting the greatest portion of total variance in group membership.

Among 50 university men, McDonel and McFall (1991) reported significant negative correlations between negative affect cue-reading accuracy in first date interactions using the TRAC and self-reported rape proclivity as well as rape-supportive attitudes. These researchers also found a significant association between performances on the TRAC and their Heterosexual Perception Survey (HPS). The latter measure requires participants read three scenarios involving a man and a woman in which the man is interested in having sex. The duration and quality of their relationship varies across scenarios. Participants also read five descriptions of the man's sexual advance and the woman's response, which increase in negativity. Participants then rate the justifiability of the man continuing his sexual advance given the woman's reaction. McDonel and McFall found that their participants' judgments about the justifiability of continuing unwanted sexual advances positively correlated with negative affect cue-reading inaccuracy.

In similar work, Malamuth and Brown (1994) had a sample of 174 university and community men view videotaped heterosocial interactions and rate their level of agreement with the extent to which both the man and woman in each were friendly, assertive, rejecting, seductive, and hostile towards the other. Data were also collected on sexual arousal to rape (using phallometry) and on self-report measures of attitudes supportive of interpersonal and sexual aggression, hostility towards women, dominance as a motive in sexual relations, general antisocial personality characteristics, and sexual (including aggressive) behaviour history.

The researchers sought to compare three explanations for differences in the way women's social behaviour were perceived by sexually aggressive men relative to other men. The first was an over-perception of seductiveness or hostility, involving a failure to distinguish such communications from those conveying friendliness or assertiveness (Harnish, Abbey & DeBono, 1990; Murphy, Coleman & Haynes, 1986). The second implicated a negative blindness, involving a failure to recognise negative or rejecting communications (Lipton et al., 1987; McDonel & McFall, 1991). The third suggested that suspicious schema cause doubt about the veridicality of women's romantic or sexual communications through decision rules and judgmental heuristics, leading to schema-driven expectancies and interpretations about women conducive to sexually coercive behaviour.

Malamuth and Brown (1994) found a pattern of significant associations between the men's perceptions of the women and the attitudinal and self-reported sexual aggression measures that was most consistent with the researchers' suspicious schema explanation. Further, Malamuth and Brown found that a suspicious schema perceptions index was a significant predictor of sexual aggression, accounting for a unique portion of the variance in various regression models, including those containing the sexual arousal to rape index as well as the measures of attitudes supportive of rape and interpersonal violence.

More recently, McFall and his colleagues have undertaken several studies using models and methodology from cognitive science that examine a number of parameters under which perceptual biases and insensitivities relevant to sexually coercive behaviour might be expected to occur and which also allow for inferences about the nature of the underlying cognitive structures involved. Farris et al. (2006) examined two mechanisms posited to lead to high-risk males' perceptual errors: one reflected an insensitivity to affective cues (sensitivity, defined as "the ability of the perceiver to discriminate one category from another accurately . . . e.g., women's sexual interest vs. friendliness", p. 870), and the other represented response preferences (bias, defined as the perceiver's "tendency to choose one response rather than another . . . e.g., to assume women's negative affect is rejection rather than just sadness or withdrawal", p. 870).

In a sample of 277 university men, the investigators found that sensitivity to depictions of sadness, rejection, and friendliness in photographs of women declined when the women were wearing provocative clothing although sensitivity to depictions of sexual interest increased (see also Abbey et al., 1987). Strong endorsement of rape-supportive attitudes among participants was associated with less sensitivity to depictions of sexual interest and rejection when the women were dressed incongruently with their affective display (e.g., sexually interested but dressed conservatively). Further, participants exhibited a positive-affect decisional bias, viewing women dressed provocatively as sexually interested rather than friendly. This bias was more pronounced for participants who strongly endorsed rape-supportive attitudes and these participants also viewed provocatively dressed women who were displaying negative affect as rejecting rather than sad (see also Lipton et al., 1987).

In another study, Treat et al. (2001) adapted performance-based tasks and analytical techniques from cognitive science (based on modelling procedures using multidimensional scaling and connectionist learning, as well as signal detection theory) to examine perceptual organisation, classification, and category learning relevant to sexual coercion. First, 74 university men completed a similarity ratings task using 14 photographs, presented in a total of 91 pairs, of women varying along dimensions of affect (positive to negative) and degree of physical exposure (modest to revealing clothing). This task revealed significant differences in the relative attention of the participants to the exposure and affect dimensions, suggesting two different perceptual organisations and permitting division of the participants into exposure-oriented (EO) and affect-oriented (AO) groups. Next, in an implicit classification task, the participants judged whether women in 26 slides, presented in four trial blocks, had an unnamed characteristic or not. Feedback given at the end of each block was random rather than related to the women's characteristics. The results showed that sensitivity was greater when the attribute (the woman's affect or exposure in the slide) was congruent with participants' perceptual organisation group (EO or AO).

In two category learning tasks that followed (one for affect and one for exposure), slides were again presented but accurate feedback was provided after each. The findings again showed that the groups' perceptual organisation grouping was predictive, with performance found to be relatively better in the congruent category learning task for each group. Treat et al. (2001) also found that, among the EO participants, the perceived justifiability of unwanted sexual advances (assessed using the HPS – McDonel & McFall, 1991) was less dependent on the degree of negative reaction from the woman than it was for the AO participants, indicating a relatively greater sensitivity to the negativity among the AO, consistent with their underlying perceptual organisation.

These studies by McFall and his colleagues are particularly noteworthy because they employed performance-based paradigms that involved implicit, rather than explicit, cognitive tasks (in essence, removing possible social desirability response biases), which enabled them to test for biases and insensitivities in the cognitive processes of the men and make relatively strong inferences about the organisation of underlying cognitive structures as these facets of cognition pertain to sexual aggression. Clearly, there is considerable potential for further development and testing of theory implicating rape-related cognition using these methodologies.

One direction would be to incorporate individual differences in attitudinal and experiential variables (Abbey et al., 2001), and to experimentally control the influence of situational and motivational factors conducive to sexual misperception and coercion. Whether studies adopt tests of explicit or implicit cognition, the influence on cognitive processes of priming arousal (see Tiedens, 2001, and Weisz & Earls, 1995) or manipulating the accessibility of specifically operationalised rape-related cognitive structures has implications for design and interpretation (see Lepore & Brown, 1997, and Schuette & Fazio, 1995) as well as the development of clinical assessment procedures. As one example of such effects, McKenzie-Mohr and Zanna (1990) found that among their sample of 60 undergraduate men, those high in masculinity whose sexual interest was primed (in a condition involving exposure to pornography) were more sexually motivated in their behaviour towards a female confederate (who was blind to conditions), and were focused more on her appearance and less on her verbalisations than were participants low in masculinity in the same condition or men high in masculinity exposed to nonsexual control material.

In a second example, Vass and Gold (1995) used guided imagery of a date in which participants had to imagine receiving either positive or negative feedback from a woman about their sexual performance (a neutral condition involved no imagined feedback). Men scoring in the upper and lower thirds of an index of hypermasculinity (Mosher & Sirkin, 1984) were randomly assigned to these imagined conditions. The findings revealed that the high-hypermasculinity men exhibited more anger and less empathy towards the woman in the negative feedback (and neutral) conditions than the low-hypermasculinity men, suggesting a lower threshold among the high masculinity men for activating schema conducive to negative and aggressive behaviour towards women, which then impacted directly on their behaviour.

TREATMENT EFFORTS

Cognitive Products and Structures

Evaluations of sexual assault prevention initiatives with university and community men show that both fact-based and empathy-focused programmes produce positive change in rape-supportive attitudes and empathy towards rape survivors (e.g., Foubert & Newberry, 2006; Johansson-Love & Geer, 2003), with effects still evident at follow-ups months and years later (e.g., Gilbert, Heesacker & Gannon, 1991; Lonsway et al., 1998). In a meta-analytic review of the effectiveness of sexual assault education programmes, Anderson and Whiston (2005) looked at change in a number of outcomes including rape attitudes, rape-related attitudes, rape knowledge, behavioural intent, and incidence using 69 studies that included control groups ($N = 18,172$). Significant effect sizes were reported for these five outcomes ($d = 0.21, 0.13, 0.57, 0.14$, and 0.10, respectively). However, the clinical significance of programme impact on rape-related attitudes, behavioural intent and incidence is debatable given the small magnitude of their effect sizes. Furthermore, there is evidence to suggest that programmes such as these are least effective for the men most in need of intervention because they are high risk according to their self-reported history of sexual coerciveness, self-rated likelihood of sexual abusing, raping, and harassing, or endorsement of rape-related attitudes (Schewe & O'Donohue, 1993; Stephens & George, 2004).

With convicted sexual offenders there has been little research concentrating on treatment-related change in cognitive targets (Langton & Marshall, 2000). Beech *et al.* (2005) recently reported significant positive changes from pre- to post-treatment on a number of self-report measures relevant to sexual aggression (e.g., Bumby's (1996) RAPE scale, and Mosher & Sirkin's (1984) Hypermasculinity Inventory) in a combined sample of 112 rapists and 36 sexual murderers, consistent with similar findings with child molesters (Hudson *et al.*, 2002). However, an association between these positive changes pre- to post-treatment and rapists' sexual recidivism has still to be shown. It also remains to be demonstrated that such observable change corresponds to change in the content, organisation, or influence of underlying offence-supportive cognitive structures.

Ward and his colleagues (Drake *et al.*, 2001; Ward & Keenan, 1999) have recommended that treatment efforts directly address sexual offenders' implicit theories in order to be effective (for similar arguments concerning a therapeutic focus at the level of schemas see Mann & Beech, 2003). Shingler and Carter (2001) describe how sexual offenders' *life maps*, autobiographical accounts graphically depicted along with text notes, can be used in treatment to help the offenders identify and organise their general thinking patterns and so understand how these developed and influence their day to day experiences. Dysfunctional or offence-supportive schema are inferred from the offenders' work and addressed in treatment.

Following on from this, Thornton and Shingler (2001) reported encouraging preliminary outcome data for two sequentially administered programmes using a combined sample of sexual offenders within the prison service in the UK. Treatment focused on offenders' cognitive distortions about their offences in the initial, core programme and, in the extended programme, on offenders' recognition and management of inferred schema. Among the measures used was one reflecting a sense of *sexual entitlement* and a view of *women as deceitful*. Significant reductions in both, as well as in minimisations of the offenders' own offence was found following participation. However, it was not clear from the data presented that rapists in the samples made statistically or clinically significant gains.

As has already been discussed, it is possible that sexual offenders are simply able to express prosocial sentiments in treatment and assessment interviews, and to identify and endorse socially appropriate items on self-report questionnaires regardless of their own views. Certainly, through treatment the offender is presented with the knowledge to identify and reject offence-supportive attitudes and beliefs; the measures of these constructs are relatively transparent and it is clearly in his best interest to demonstrate this knowledge and ability (see Gannon & Polaschek, 2005, for further discussion of this issue) but such identification and rejection does not equate to change at deeper cognitive levels.

Indeed, findings in the broader social psychology literature do not permit the assumption of direct correspondence between surface change and change in underlying cognitive structures. For example, when individuals have strong opinions and beliefs they evaluate information in a biased fashion, accepting confirming evidence without question but subjecting disconfirming evidence to scrutiny, which often produces attitude polarisation rather than attitude change (Edwards & Smith, 1996; Lord, Ross & Lepper, 1979). Individuals also tend to persist in holding their initial explanations for outcomes even when discrediting information is presented (Jennings, Lepper & Ross, 1981), particularly when these explanations or impressions are underscored by their own causal theories (Anderson, Lepper & Ross, 1980). Instead, the contradictory information is trivialised (Simon, Greenberg & Brehm, 1995) or construed as an exception to individuals' own rules rather than as grounds for changing their beliefs (Wilder, Simon & Faith, 1996).

Findings such as these should not discourage cognitive restructuring efforts with sexual offenders but they pose a challenge to assumptions about what measures of cognitive products may actually reveal concerning clinically relevant change in rape-related cognition. As awareness of assessment methodologies increases, investigations of the interrelationships between cognitive facets, and the impact of treatment on these, in sexually aggressive men should be illuminating.

Cognitive Processes

Although empirical research on the malleability of sexual aggressors' cognitive processes has received scant attention, one aspect that has been considered concerns mental control in relation to deviant sexual thoughts (Johnston, Ward & Hudson, 1997). Much of the evidence reviewed above indicates a bias towards sexual interpretations of women's behaviour among men in general. Among convicted rapists, negative affective states of anger, loneliness and humiliation arising through interpersonal conflict have been found to coincide with overwhelming deviant sexual fantasising and masturbation to these fantasies (Proulx, McKibben & Lusignan, 1996). It is possible that there is an automaticity involved in such processes that is unintended or involuntary but about which there is awareness (Amir & Selvig, 2005). At least some sexually aggressive men may experience their sexual thoughts, fantasies, and general preoccupation with sex (see Ryan, 2004) as obsessive or intrusive in nature (Egan, Kavanagh & Blair, 2005; Marshall & Langton, 2005).

It seems reasonable, then, to address these processes in treatment too. However, consistent with paradoxical effects reported in the wider literature on thought suppression, Johnston, Hudson and Ward (1997) found that sex-related and child-related words were *more* accessible in an implicit cognition task after suppression instructions among their sample of preferential child molesters. Although this finding is clearly cautionary and underscores the importance of broader efforts focusing on, for example, stress management and the development of adaptive coping strategies (cf., Cortoni & Marshall, 2001), considerable work remains to be done to better understand the parameters of this phenomenon in sexual offenders and rapists specifically. In recent work by Gordijn *et al.* (2004) with university students, hyper-accessibility of suppressed thoughts was found to occur only when participants' *internal* suppression motivation was low, suggesting that greater attention to motivational factors will be important in clinical research and treatment relating to mental control and thought suppression with sexual offenders.

Rapist-Specific Treatment

As a final point, the possibility must be seriously considered that treatment efficacy with rapists will be enhanced if the "one-size-fits-all" approach for sexual offender treatment is replaced or at least complimented by treatment programmes or components that more specifically address features particular to rapists (see Chapter 7 of this volume; Marshall, 1993; Polaschek & King, 2002). As one example of a clinical technique specific to work with rapists, consider a process of experiential disconfirmation, involving falsifiable behavioural experiments (Polaschek & Hudson, 2004). This would involve rapists explicitly testing their ideas, expectations, and interpretations during heterosocial interactions by asking questions and seeking feedback in order to identify errors and reframe their understanding. This process might be differentiated from evidential disconfirmation methods, the most obvious examples of which form the basis of the sexual assault education programmes discussed above. Whether experiential disconfirmation can be reliably measured in applied research and clinical contexts remains to be demonstrated but, in contrast to therapeutic work with child molesters, a technique involving a process of disconfirmation represents a potentially practical and realistic element in a comprehensive cognitive restructuring approach with rapists.

CONCLUSIONS

A large body of empirical evidence has emerged since the mid-1980s clearly demonstrating an association between rape-related cognition and the sexually aggressive behaviour of men towards women. Progress in conceptualisation and theorising have led to research on different facets of cognition. There has been a coalescence of key findings from studies with convicted rapists as well as university and community men and from investigations using both qualitative and quantitative methods. The integration of this work in broader theoretical formulations now warrants attention (e.g., Malamuth, 1998). The research paradigms and methods from cognitive science offer considerable promise for advancing understanding of the mechanisms by which the various facets of cognition influence the expression of sexually coercive behaviour against women. However, little impact is yet evident on the approaches to assessment and treatment found in clinical contexts for sexual aggressors (or, indeed, in community prevention programmes). Eventually, it is hoped that these more refined conceptualisations of rape-related cognition and the ways these facets function in reciprocal, dynamic fashion, will find their way into applied work and, with them, the advances being made in assessment procedures. Such progress should have profound implications for prevention as well as case planning, management, and treatment evaluation efforts.

REFERENCES

Abbey, A. (1982). Sex differences in attributions for friendly behavior: do males misperceive females' friendliness? *Journal of Personality and Social Psychology*, **42**, 830–38.

Abbey, A. (1987). Misperceptions of friendly behavior as sexual interest: a survey of naturally occurring incidents. *Psychology of Women Quarterly*, **11**, 173–94.

Abbey, A., Buck, P. O., Zawacki, T. & Saenz, C. (2003). Alcohol's effects on perceptions of a potential date rape. *Journal of Studies on Alcohol*, **64**, 669–77.

Abbey, A., Cozzarelli, C., McLaughlin, K. & Harnish, R. J. (1987). The effects of clothing and dyad sex composition on perceptions of sexual intent: do women and men evaluate these cues differently. *Journal of Applied Social Psychology*, **17**, 108–26.

Abbey, A. & Harnish, R. J. (1995). Perception of sexual intent: the role of gender, alcohol consumption, and rape supportive attitudes. *Sex Roles*, **32**, 297–313.

Abbey, A., McAuslan, P., Zawacki, T. *et al.* (2001). Attitudinal, experiential, and situational predictors of sexual assault perpetration. *Journal of Interpersonal Violence*, **16**, 784–807.

Abbey, A. & Melby, C. (1986). The effects of nonverbal cues on gender differences in perceptions of sexual intent. *Sex Roles*, **15**, 284–98.

Abbey, A., Parkhill, M. R., BeShears, R. *et al.* (2006). Cross-sectional predictors of sexual assault perpetration in a community sample of single African American and Caucasian men. *Aggressive Behavior*, **32**, 54–67.

Abbey, A., Zawacki, T. & Buck, P. O. (2005). The effect of past sexual assault perpetration and alcohol consumption on men's reactions to women's mixed signals. *Journal of Social and Clinical Psychology*, **24**, 129–55.

Abbey, A., Zawacki, T. & McAuslan, P. (2000). Alcohol's effects on sexual perception. *Journal of Studies on Alcohol*, **61**, 688–97.

Abel, G. G., Becker, J. V. & Cunningham-Rathner, J. (1984). Complications, consent, and cognitions in sex between children and adults. *International Journal of Law and Psychiatry*, **7**, 89–103.

Abelson, R. P. (1981). Psychological status of the script concept. *American Psychologist*, **36**, 715–29.

Amir, N. & Selvig, A. (2005). Implicit memory tasks in clinical research. In A. Wenzel & D. C. Rubin (eds), *Cognitive Methods and their Application to Clinical Research* (pp. 153–71). Washington, DC: American Psychological Association.

Anderson, K. B., Copper, H. & Okamura, L. (1997). Individual differences and attitudes toward rape: A meta-analytic review. *Personality and Social Psychology Bulletin*, **23**, 295–315.

Anderson, C. A., Lepper, M. R. & Ross, L. (1980). Perseverance of social theories: the role of explanation in the persistence of discredited information. *Journal of Personality and Social Psychology*, **39**, 1037–49.

Andersen, S. M., Spielman, L. A. & Bargh, J. A. (1992). Future-event schemas and certainty about the future: automaticity in depressives' future-event predictions. *Journal of Personality and Social Psychology*, **63**, 711–23.

Anderson, L. A. & Whiston, S. C. (2005). Sexual assault education programs: a meta-analytic examination of their effectiveness. *Psychology of Women Quarterly*, **29**, 374–88.

Barbaree, H. E., Seto, M. C., Serin, R. C. *et al.* (1994). Comparisons between sexual and nonsexual rapist sub-types: sexual arousal to rape, offense precursors, and offense characteristics. *Criminal Justice and Behavior*, **21**, 95–114.

Bargh, J. A. (1989). Conditional automaticity: Varieties of automatic influence in social perception and cognition. In J. S. Uleman & J. A. Bargh (eds), *Unintended Thought* (pp. 3–51). New York: Guilford Press.

Bargh, J. A. (1994). The four horsemen of automaticity: Awareness, intention, efficiency, and control in social cognition. In R. S. Wyer & T. K. Srull (eds), *Handbook of Social Cognition: Basic Processes* (Vol. 1, pp. 1–40). Hillsdale, NJ: Erlbaum.

Bargh, J. A. (1999). The cognitive monster: the case against the controllability of automatic stereotype effects. In S. Chaiken & Y. Trope (eds), *Dual-process Theories in Social Psychology* (pp. 361–82). New York: Guilford Press.

Bargh, J. A., Chen, M. & Burrows, L. (1996). Automaticity of social behavior: direct effects of trait construct and stereotype activation on action. *Journal of Personality and Social Psychology*, **71**, 230–44.

Beech, A., Oliver, C., Fisher, D. & Beckett, R. (2005). *STEP 4: The Sex Offender Treatment Programme in Prison: Addressing the Offending Behaviour of Rapists and Sexual Murderers*. Birmingham: The Centre for Forensic and Family Psychology, University of Birmingham.

Beech, A. R., Ward, T. & Fisher, D. (2006). The identification of sexual and violent motivations in men who assault women: Implication for treatment. *Journal of Interpersonal Violence*, **21**, 1635–53.

Blumenthal, S., Gudjonsson, G. & Burns, J. (1999). Cognitive distortions and blame attribution in sex offenders against adults and children. *Child Abuse & Neglect*, **23**, 129–43.

Bodenhausen, G. V. & Lambert, A. J. (ed.). (2003). *Foundations of Social Cognition: A Festschrift in Honor of Robert S. Wyer, Jr.* Mahwah, NJ: Lawrence Erlbaum Associates.

Brown, S. L. & Forth, A. E. (1997). Psychopathy and sexual assault: static risk factors, emotional precursors, and rapist subtypes. *Journal of Consulting and Clinical Psychology*, **65**, 848–57.

Bruch, M. A., Kaflowitz, N. G. & Berger, P. (1988). Self-schema for assertiveness: Extending the validity of the self-schema construct. *Journal of Research in Personality*, **22**, 424–44.

Bumby, K. M. (1996). Assessing the cognitive distortions of child molesters and rapists: development and validation of the MOLEST and RAPE scales. *Sexual Abuse: A Journal of Research and Treatment*, **8**, 37–54.

Burt, M. R. (1980). Cultural myths and supports for rape. *Journal of Personality and Social Psychology*, **38**, 217–30.

Cantor, N., Mischel, W. & Schwartz, J. (1982). Social knowledge: structure, content, use, and abuse. In A. H. Hastorf & A. M Isen (eds), *Cognitive Social Psychology* (pp. 33–72). New York: Elsevier.

Check, J. V. P. (1985). *The Hostility Toward Women Scale*. Unpublished doctoral dissertation, University of Manitoba, Winnipeg.

Cortoni, F. & Marshall, W. L. (2001). Sex as a coping strategy and its relationship to juvenile sexual history and intimacy in sexual offenders. *Sexual Abuse: A Journal of Research and Treatment*, **13**, 27–43.

Crick, N. R. & Dodge, K. A. (1994). A review and reformulation of social information-processing mechanisms in children's social adjustment. *Psychological Bulletin*, **115**, 74–101.

Darley, J. M. & Gross, P. H. (1983). A hypothesis-confirming bias in labeling effects. *Journal of Personality and Social Psychology*, **44**, 20–33.

DeGue, S. & DiLillo, D. (2005). "You would if you loved me": toward an improved conceptual and etiological understanding of nonphysical male sexual coercion. *Aggression and Violent Behavior*, **10**, 513–32.

De Houwer, J. (2006). What are implicit measures and why are we using them? In R. W. Wiers & A. W. Stacy (eds), *Handbook of Implicit Cognition and Addiction* (pp. 11–28). Thousand Oaks, CA: Sage.

Dijksterhuis, A. & Van Knippenberg, A. (1998). The relation between perception and behavior, or how to win a game of Trivial Pursuit. *Journal of Personality and Social Psychology*, **74**, 865–77.

Ditto, P. H. & Lopez, D. F. (1992). Motivated skepticism: Use of differential decision criteria for preferred and nonpreferred conclusions. *Journal of Personality and Social Psychology*, **63**, 568–84.

Drake, C. R., Ward, T., Nathan, P. & Lee, J. K. P. (2001). Challenging the cognitive distortions of child molesters: an implicit theory approach. *Journal of Sexual Aggression*, **7**, 25–40.

Drieschner, K. & Lange, A. (1999). A review of cognitive factors in the etiology of rape: Theories, empirical studies, and implications. *Clinical Psychology Review*, **19**, 57–77.

Dunning, D. & Sherman, D. A. (1997). Stereotypes and tacit inferences. *Journal of Personality and Social Psychology*, **73**, 459–71.

Edwards, K. & Smith, E. E. (1996). A disconfirmation bias in the evaluation of arguments. *Journal of Personality and Social Psychology*, **71**, 5–24.

Egan, V., Kavanagh, B. & Blair, M. (2005). Sexual offenders against children: The influence of personality and obsessionality on cognitive distortions. *Sexual Abuse: A Journal of Research and Treatment*, **17**, 223–40.

Farris, C., Viken, R. J., Treat, T. A. & McFall, R. M. (2006). Heterosocial perceptual organization: application of the Choice Model to sexual coercion. *Psychological Science*, **17**, 869–75.

Feelgood, S., Cortoni, F. & Thompson, A. (2005). Sexual coping, general coping and cognitive distortions in incarcerated rapists and child molesters. *Journal of Sexual Aggression*, **11**, 157–70.

Fernandez, Y. M. & Marshall, W. L. (2003). Victim empathy, social self-esteem, and psychopathy in rapists. *Sexual Abuse: A Journal of Research and Treatment*, **15**, 11–26.

Finkelhor, D. (1984). *Child Sexual Abuse: New Theory and Research*. New York: Free Press.

Fiske, S. T. & Taylor, S. E. (1991). *Social Cognition* (2nd edn). New York: McGraw-Hill.

Forgas, J. P. (Ed.). (2001). *Affect and Social Cognition*. Mahwah, NJ: Lawrence Erlbaum Associates.

Foubert, J. D. & Newberry, J. T. (2006). Effects of two versions of an empathy-based rape prevention program on fraternity men's survivor empathy, attitudes, and behavioral intent to commit rape or sexual assault. *Journal of College Student Development*, **47**, 133–48.

Gannon, T. A. & Polaschek, D. L. L. (2005). Do child molesters deliberately fake good on cognitive distortion questionnaires? An information processing-based investigation. *Sexual Abuse: A Journal of Research and Treatment*, **17**, 183–200.

Gannon, T. A. & Polaschek, D. L. L. (2006). Cognitive distortions in child molesters: A re-examination of key theories and research. *Clinical Psychology Review*, **26**, 1000–19

Gannon, T. A., Polaschek, D. L. L. & Ward, T. (2005). Social cognition and sex offenders. In M. McMurran & J. McGuire (eds), *Social Problem Solving and Offending: Evidence, Evaluation, and Evolution* (pp. 223–47). New York: John Wiley & Sons.

Gilbert, B. J., Heesacker, M. & Gannon, L. J. (1991). Changing the sexual aggression-supportive attitudes of men: a psychoeducational intervention. *Journal of Counseling Psychology*, **38**, 197–203.

Gordijn, E. H., Hindriks, I., Koomen, W. *et al.* (2004). Consequences of stereotype suppression and internal suppression motivation: a self-regulation approach. *Personality and Social Psychology Bulletin*, **30**, 212–24.

Greenwald, A. G., McGhee, D. E. & Schwartz, J. L. K. (1998). Measuring individual differences in implicit cognition: the implicit association test. *Journal of Personality and Social Psychology*, **74**, 1464–80.

Hall, G. C. N. & Hirschman, R. (1991). Toward a theory of sexual aggression: a quadripartite model. *Journal of Consulting and Clinical Psychology*, **59**, 662–9.

Hamilton, D. L. & Garcia-Marques, L. (2003). Effects of expectancies on the representation, retrieval, and use of social information. In G. V. Bodenhausen & A. J. Lambert (eds), *Foundations of Social Cognition: A Festschrift in Honor of Robert S. Wyer, Jr.* (pp. 25–50). Mahwah, NJ: Lawrence Erlbaum Associates.

Hanson, R. K. (1997). *The Development of a Brief Actuarial Risk Scale for Sexual Offense Recidivism* (User report 1997-04). Ottawa: Department of the Solicitor General of Canada.

Hanson, R. K. & Bussière, M. T. (1998). Predicting relapse: a meta-analysis of sexual offender recidivism studies. *Journal of Consulting and Clinical Psychology*, **66**, 348–62.

Hanson, R. K. & Harris, A. J. R. (2000). Where should we intervene? Dynamic predictors of sexual assault recidivism. *Criminal Justice and Behavior*, **27**, 6–35.

Hanson, R. K. & Morton-Bourgon, K. (2004). *Predictors of Sexual Recidivism: An Updated Meta-analysis*. Ottawa: Public Works and Government Services Canada.

Hanson, R. K. & Morton-Bourgon, K. E. (2005). The characteristics of persistent sexual offenders: a meta-analysis of recidivism studies. *Journal of Consulting and Clinical Psychology*, **73**, 1154–63.

Hanson, R. K. & Scott, H. (1995). Assessing perspective-taking among sexual offenders, nonsexual criminals, and nonoffenders. *Sexual Abuse: A Journal of Research and Treatment*, **7**, 259–77.

Harnish, R. J., Abbey, A. & DeBono, K. G. (1990). Toward an understanding of "the sex game": the effects of gender and self-monitoring on perceptions of sexuality and likability in initial interactions. *Journal of Applied Social Psychology*, **20**, 1333–44.

Higgins, E. T. & Molden, D. C. (2003). How strategies for making judgments and decisions affect cognition: Motivated cognition revisited. In G. V. Bodenhausen & A. J. Lambert (eds), *Foundations of Social Cognition: A Festschrift in Honor of Robert S. Wyer, Jr.* (pp. 211–35). Mahwah, NJ: Lawrence Erlbaum Associates.

Hilton, N. Z., Harris, G. T. & Rice, M. E. (1998). On the validity of self-reported rates of interpersonal violence. *Journal of Interpersonal Violence*, **13**, 58–72.

Hollon, S. D. & Kriss, M. R. (1984). Cognitive factors in clinical research and practice. *Clinical Psychology Review*, **4**, 35–76.

Hudson, S. M., Wales, D. S., Bakker, L. & Ward, T. (2002). Dynamic risk factors: The Kia Marama evaluation. *Sexual Abuse: A Journal of Research and Treatment*, **14**, 103–19.

Huesmann, L. R. (1998). The role of social information processing and cognitive schema in the acquisition and maintenance of habitual aggressive behavior. In R. G. Geen & E. Donnerstein (eds), *Human Aggression: Theories, research, and implications for social policy* (pp. 73–109). San Diego: Academic Press.

Ingram, R. E. (ed.) (1986). *Information Processing Approaches to Clinical Psychology*. New York: Academic Press.

Jennings, D. L., Lepper, M. R. & Ross, L. (1981). Persistence of impression of personal persuasiveness: perseverance of erroneous self-assessments outside the debriefing paradigm. *Personality and Social Psychology Bulletin*, **7**, 257–63.

Johansson-Love, J. & Geer, J. H. (2003). Investigation of attitude change in a rape prevention program. *Journal of Interpersonal Violence*, **18**, 84–99.

Johnston, L., Hudson, S. M. & Ward, T. (1997). The suppression of sexual thoughts by child molesters: a preliminary investigation. *Sexual Abuse: A Journal of Research and Treatment*, **9**, 303–19.

Johnston, L. & Ward, T. (1996). Social cognition and sexual offending: A theoretical framework. *Sexual Abuse: A Journal of Research and Treatment*, **8**, 55–80.

Johnston, L., Ward, T. & Hudson, S. M. (1997). Deviant sexual thoughts: mental control and the treatment of sexual offenders. *The Journal of Sex Research*, **34**, 121–30.

Jung, S. (2004). *Assessing denial among sex offenders*. Unpublished doctoral dissertation, University of Victoria, Canada.

Kalichman, S. C., Craig, M. E., Shealy, L. S. *et al.* (1989). An empirically derived typology of adult sex offenders based on the MMPI: a cross validation study. *Journal of Psychology and Human Sexuality*, **2**, 165–82.

Knight, R. A. (1999). Validation of a typology for rapists. *Journal of InterpersonalViolence*, **14**, 303–30.

Knight, R. A. & Prentky, R. A. (1990). Classifying sexual offenders: The development and corroboration of taxonomic models. In W. L. Marshall, D. R. Laws & H. E. Barbaree (Eds.), *Handbook of Sexual Assault: Issues, Theories, and Treatment of the Offender* (pp. 23–52). New York: Plenum Press.

Knight, R. A. & Sims-Knight, J. E. (2003). The developmental antecedents of sexual coercion against women: testing alternative hypotheses with structural equation modeling. *Annals New York Academy of Sciences*, **989**, 72–85.

Koss, M. P. & Oros, C. J. (1982). The Sexual Experiences Survey. *Journal of Consulting and Clinical Psychology*, **55**, 162–70.

Kroner, D. G., Boer, D. P. & Mills, J. F. (2004). Explaining rape-supportive attitudes among rapists. *American Journal of Forensic Psychology*, **22**, 65–76.

Kunda, Z. (1990). The case for motivated reasoning. *Psychological Bulletin*, **108**, 480–98.

Langton, C. M., Barbaree, H. E., Harkins, L. *et al.* (in press). *Denial and Minimization among Sexual Offenders: Post-treatment Presentation and Association with Sexual Recidivism*. Criminal Justice and Behavior.

Langton, C. M. & Marshall, W. L. (2000). The role of cognitive distortions in relapse prevention programs. In D. R. Laws, S. M. Hudson & T. Ward (eds), *Remaking Relapse Prevention with Sex Offenders: A Source Book* (pp. 167–86). Thousand Oaks, CA: Sage Publications.

Langton, C. M. & Marshall, W. L. (2001). Cognition in rapists: Theoretical patterns by typological breakdown. *Aggression and Violent Behavior*, **6**, 499–518.

Lenton, A. P. & Bryan, A. (2005). An affair to remember: the role of sexual scripts in perceptions of sexual intent. *Personal Relationships*, **12**, 483–98.

Lepore, L. & Brown, R. (1997). Category and stereotype activation: Is prejudice inevitable? *Journal of Personality and Social Psychology*, **72**, 275–87.

Lipton, D. N., McDonel, E. C. & McFall, R. J. (1987). Heterosocial perception in rapists. *Journal of Consulting and Clinical Psychology*, **55**, 17–21.

Lonsway, K. A., Klaw, E. L., Berg, D. R. *et al.* (1998). Beyond "no means no": outcomes of an intensive program to train peer facilitators for campus acquaintances rape education. *Journal of Interpersonal Violence*, **13**, 73–92.

Lord, C. G., Ross, L. & Lepper, M. R. (1979). Biased assimilation and attitude polarization: the effects of prior theories on subsequently considered evidence. *Journal of Personality and Social Psychology*, **37**, 2098–109.

Lund, C. A. (2000). Predictors of sexual recidivism: did meta-analysis clarify the role and relevance of denial? *Sexual Abuse: A Journal of Research and Treatment*, **12**, 273–85.

Lussier, P., Proulx, J. & LeBlanc, M. (2005). Criminal propensity, deviant sexual interests and criminal activity of sexual aggressors against women: a comparison of explanatory models. *Criminology*, **43**, 249–81.

Macrae, C. N., Milne, A. B. & Bodenhausen, G. V. (1994). Stereotypes as energy-saving devices: a peek inside the cognitive toolbox. *Journal of Personality and Social Psychology*, **66**, 37–47.

Malamuth, N. M. (1981). Rape proclivity among males. *Journal of Social Issues*, **37**, 138–57.

Malamuth, N. M. (1989a). The attraction to sexual aggression scale: I. *Journal of Sex Research*, **26**, 26–49.

Malamuth, N. M. (1989b). The attraction to sexual aggression scale: II. *Journal of Sex Research*, **26**, 324–54.

Malamuth, N. M. (1998). An evolutionary-based model integrating research on the characteristics of sexually coercive men. In J. G. Adair, D. Bélanger & K. L. Dion (eds), *Advances in Psychological Science, Volume 1: Social, Personal, and Cultural Aspects* (pp. 151–84). Hove: Psychology Press.

Malamuth, N. M. & Brown, L. M. (1994). Sexually aggressive men's perceptions of women's communications: Testing three explanations. *Journal of Personality and Social Psychology*, **67**, 699–712.

Malamuth, N. M., Heavey, C. L. & Linz, D. (1993). Predicting men's antisocial behavior against women. In G. C. N. Hall, R. Hirschman, J. R. Graham & M. S. Zaragoza (eds), *Sexual Aggression: Issues in Etiology, Assessment, and Treatment* (pp. 63–97). Washington, DC: Taylor & Francis.

Malamuth, N. M., Linz, D., Heavey, C. L. *et al.* (1995). Using the Confluence Model of sexual aggression to predict men's conflict with women: a 10-year follow-up study. *Journal of Personality and Social Psychology*, **69**, 353–69.

Malamuth, N. M., Sockloskie, R., Koss, M. P. & Tanaka, J. (1991). The characteristics of aggressors against women: Testing a model using a national sample of college students. *Journal of Consulting and Clinical Psychology*, **59**, 670–81.

Mann, R. E. & Beech, A. R. (2003). Cognitive distortions, schemas, and implicit theories. In T. Ward, D. R. Laws & S. M. Hudson (Eds.), *Sexual Deviance: Issues and Controversies* (pp. 135–53). Thousand Oaks, CA: Sage.

Mann, R. E. & Hollin, C. (2001). *Schemas: A Model for Understanding Cognition in Sexual Offending.* Paper presented at 20th annual conference of the Association for the Treatment of Sexual Abusers (ATSA), San Antonio, Texas.

Marolla, J. & Scully, D. (1986). Attitudes toward women, violence, and rape: a comparison of convicted rapists and other felons. *Deviant Behavior*, **7**, 337–55.

Marshall, W. L. (1993). A revised approach to the treatment of men who sexually assault adult females. In G. C. N. Hall, R. Hirschman, J. R. Graham & M. S. Zaragoza (eds), *Sexual Aggression: Issues in Etiology, Assessment, and Treatment* (pp. 143–65). Philadelphia, PA: Taylor & Francis.

Marshall, W. L. & Barbaree, H. E. (1990). An integrated theory of the etiology of sexual offending. In W. L. Marshall, D. R. Laws & H. E. Barbaree (eds), *Handbook of Sexual Assault: Issues, Theories, and Treatment of the Offender* (pp. 257–75). New York: Plenum Press.

Marshall, W. L., Fernandez, Y. M., Hudson, S. M. & Ward, T. (eds), (1998). *Sourcebook of Treatment Programs for Sexual Offenders.* New York: Plenum Press.

Marshall, W. L., Hamilton, K. & Fernandez, Y. (2001). Empathy deficit and cognitive distortions in child molesters. *Sexual Abuse: A Journal of Research and Treatment*, **13**, 123–30.

Marshall, W. L., Hudson, S. M., Jones, R. & Fernandez, Y. M. (1995). Empathy in sex offenders. *Clinical Psychology Review*, **15**, 99–13.

Marshall, W. L. & Langton, C. M. (2005). Unwanted thoughts and fantasies experienced by sexual offenders. In D. A. Clark (ed.), *Intrusive Thoughts in Clinical Disorders: Theory, Research, and Treatment* (pp. 199–25). New York: The Guilford Press.

Marshall, W. L. & Moulden, H. (2001). Hostility toward women and victim empathy in rapists. *Sexual Abuse: A Journal of Research and Treatment*, **13**, 249–55.

Maruna, S. & Mann, R. E. (2006). A fundamental attribution error? Rethinking cognitive distortions. *Legal and Criminological Psychology*, **11**, 155–77.

Marx, B. P., Gross, A. M. & Adams, H. E. (1999). The effect of alcohol on the responses of sexually coercive and noncoercive men to an experimental rape analogue. *Sexual Abuse: A Journal of Research and Treatment*, **11**, 131–45.

McDonel, E. C. & McFall, R. M. (1991). Construct validity of two heterosocial perception skill measures for assessing rape proclivity. *Violence and Victims*, **6**, 17–30.

McFall, R. M., Treat, T. A. & Viken, R. J. (1997). Contributions of cognitive theory to new behavioral treatments. *Psychological Science*, **8**, 174–76.

McKenzie-Mohr, D. & Zanna, M. P. (1990). Treating women as sexual objects: Look to the (gender schematic) male who has viewed pornography. *Personality and Social Psychology Bulletin*, **16**, 296–308.

Milner, R. J. & Webster, S. D. (2005). Identifying schemas in child molesters, rapists, and violent offenders. *Sexual Abuse: A Journal of Research and Treatment*, **17**, 425–39.

Monahan, B. A., Marolla, J. A. & Bromley, D. G. (2005). Constructing coercion: The organization of sexual assault. *Journal of Contemporary Ethnography*, **34**, 284–316.

Mosher, D. L. & Sirkin, M. (1984). Measuring a macho personality constellation. *Journal of Research in Personality*, **18**, 150–63.

Muraven, M., Tice, D. M. & Baumeister, R. F. (1998). Self-control as limited resources: Regulatory depletion patterns. *Journal of Personality and Social Psychology*, **74**, 774–89.

Murnen, S. K., Wright, C. & Kaluzny, G. (2002). If "boys will be boys," then girls will be victims? A meta-analytic review of the research that relates masculine ideology to sexual aggression. *Sex Roles*, **46**, 359–75.

Murphy, W. D. (1990). Assessment and modification of cognitive distortions in sex offenders. In W. L. Marshall, D. R. Laws & H. E. Barbaree (eds), *Handbook of Sexual Assault: Issues, Theories, and Treatment of the Offender* (pp. 331–42). New York: Plenum Press.

Murphy, W. D., Coleman, E. M. & Haynes, M. R. (1986). Factors related to coercive sexual behavior in a nonclinical sample of males. *Violence and Victims*, **1**, 255–78.

Nisbett, R. E. & Ross, L. (1980). *Human Inference: Strategies and Shortcomings of Social Judgment*. Englewood Cliffs, NJ: Prentice-Hall.

Nisbett, R. E. & Wilson, T. D. (1977). Telling more than we can know: verbal reports on mental processes. *Psychological Review*, **84**, 231–59.

Pithers, W. D. (1990). Relapse prevention with sexual aggressors: A method for maintaining therapeutic gain and enhancing external supervision. In W. L. Marshall, D. R. Laws & H. E. Barbaree (eds), *Handbook of Sexual Assault: Issues, Theories, and Treatment of the Offender* (pp. 343–61). New York: Plenum Press.

Polaschek, D. L. L. & Gannon, T. A. (2004). The implicit theories of rapists: what convicted offenders tell us. *Sexual Abuse: A Journal of Research and Treatment*, **16**, 299–314.

Polaschek, D. L. L. & Hudson, S. M. (2004). Pathways to rape: preliminary examination of patterns in the offence processes of rapists and their rehabilitation implications. *Journal of Sexual Aggression*, **10**, 7–20.

Polaschek, D. L. L., Hudson, S. M., Ward, T. & Siegert, R. J. (2001). Rapists' offense processes: A preliminary descriptive model. *Journal of Interpersonal Violence*, **16**, 523–44.

Polaschek, D. L. L. & King, L. L (2002). Rehabilitating rapists: reconsidering the issues. *Australian Psychologist*, **37**, 215–21.

Polaschek, D. L. L. & Ward, T. (2002). The implicit theories of potential rapists: What our questionnaires tell us. *Aggression and Violent Behavior*, **7**, 385–406.

Polaschek, D. L. L., Ward, T. & Hudson, S. M. (1997). Rape and rapists: theory and treatment. *Clinical Psychology Review*, **17**, 117–44.

Prentky, R. A. & Knight, R. A. (1991). Identifying critical dimensions for discriminating among rapists. *Journal of Consulting and Clinical Psychology*, **59**, 643–61.

Proulx, J., McKibben, A. & Lusignan, R. (1996). Relationships between affective components and sexual behaviors in sexual aggressors. *Sexual Abuse: A Journal of Research and Treatment*, **8**, 279–89.

Ross, M. & Sicoly, F. (1979). Egocentric biases in availability and attribution. *Journal of Personality and Social Psychology*, **37**, 322–36.

Ryan, K. M. (2004). Further evidence for a cognitive component of rape. *Aggression and Violent Behavior*, **9**, 579–604.

Scarvalone, P., Fox, M. & Safran, J. D. (2005). Interpersonal schemas: Clinical theory, research, and implications. In M. W. Baldwin (ed.), *Interpersonal Cognition* (pp. 359–87). New York: Guilford Press.

Schewe, P. A. & O'Donohue, W. (1993). Sexual abuse prevention with high-risk males: The roles of victim empathy and rape myths. *Violence and Victims*, **8**, 339–51.

Schneider, S. L. & Wright, R. C. (2004). Understanding denial in sexual offenders: A review of cognitive and motivational processes to avoid responsibility. *Trauma, Violence and Abuse*, **5**, 3–20.

Schuette, R. A. & Fazio, R. H. (1995). Attitude accessibility and motivation as determinants of biased processing: A test of the MODE model. *Personality and Social Psychology*, **21**, 704–10.

Segal, Z. V. (1988). Appraisal of the self-schema construct in cognitive models of depression. *Psychological Bulletin*, **103**, 147–62.

Segal, Z. V. & Stermac, L. E. (1984). A measure of rapists' attitudes towards women. *International Journal of Law and Psychiatry*, **7**, 437–40.

Segal, Z. V. & Stermac, L. E. (1990). The role of cognition in sexual assault. In W. L. Marshall, D. R. Laws & H. E. Barbaree (eds), *Handbook of Sexual Assault: Issues, Theories and Treatment of the Offender* (pp. 161–72). New York: Plenum Press.

Sherman, S. J., Judd, C. M. & Park, B. (1989). Social cognition. *Annual Review of Psychology*, **40**, 281–326.

Shingler, J. & Carter, A. (2001, November). *Therapeutic Techniques for Working with Sexual Offenders' Dysfunctional Schemas*. Paper presented at 20th annual conference of the Association for the Treatment of Sexual Abusers (ATSA), San Antonio, Texas.

Simon, L., Greenberg, J. & Brehm, J. (1995). Trivialization: The forgotten mode of dissonance reduction. *Journal of Personality and Social Psychology*, **68**, 247–60.

Smith, P. & Waterman, M. (2004). Processing bias for sexual material: The emotional stroop and sexual offenders. *Sexual Abuse: A Journal of Research and Treatment*, **16**, 163–71.

Snowden, R. J., Gray, N. S., Smith, J. *et al.* (2004). Implicit affective associations to violence in psychopathic murderers. *The Journal of Forensic Psychiatry & Psychology*, **15**, 620–41.

Spence, J. T., Helmreich, R. L. & Holahan, C. K. (1979). The negative and positive components of psychological masculinity and femininity and their relationships to self-reports of neurotic and acting out behaviors. *Journal of Personality and Social Psychology*, **37**, 1673–82.

Stephens, K. A. & George, W. H. (2004). Effects of anti-rape video content on sexually coercive and noncoercive college men's attitudes and alcohol expectancies. *Journal of Applied Social Psychology*, **34**, 402–16.

Stermac, L. E. & Segal, Z. V. (1989). Adult sexual contact with children: an examination of cognitive factors. *Behavior Therapy*, **20**, 573–84.

Strack, F. & Mussweiler, T. (2003). Heuristic strategies for estimation under uncertainty: The enigmatic case of anchoring. In G. V. Bodenhausen & A. J. Lambert (eds), *Foundations of Social Cognition: A Festschrift in Honor of Robert S. Wyer, Jr.* (pp. 79–95). Mahwah, NJ: Lawrence Erlbaum Associates.

Thornton, D. & Shingler, J. (2001). *Impact of schema level work on sexual offenders' cognitive distortions*. Paper presented at 20th annual conference of the Association for the Treatment of Sexual Abusers (ATSA), San Antonio, Texas, November.

Tiedens, L. Z. (2001). The effect of anger on the hostile inferences of aggressive and nonaggressive people: specific emotions, cognitive processing, and chronic accessibility. *Motivation and Emotion*, **25**, 233–51.

Treat, T. A., McFall, R. M., Viken, R. J. & Kruschke, J. K. (2001). Using cognitive science methods to assess the role of social information processing in sexually coercive behavior. *Psychological Assessment*, **13**, 549–65.

Tversky, A. & Kahneman, D. (1974). Judgment under uncertainty: Heuristics and biases. *Science*, **185**, 1124–31.

Vass, J. J. & Gold, S. R. (1995). Effects of feedback on emotion in hypermasculine males. *Violence and Victims*, **10**, 217–26.

Ward, T. (2000). Sexual offenders' cognitive distortions as implicit theories. *Aggression and Violent Behaviour*, **5**, 491–507.

Ward, T. & Hudson, S. M. (2000). A self-regulation model of relapse prevention. In D. R. Laws, S. M. Hudson & T. Ward (Eds.), *Remaking Relapse Prevention with Sexual Offenders: A Sourcebook* (pp. 79–101). Thousand Oaks, CA: Sage.

Ward, T., Hudson, S. M., Johnston, L. & Marshall, W. L. (1997). Cognitive distortions in sex offenders: An integrative review. *Clinical Psychology Review*, **17**, 479–507.

Ward, T. & Keenan, T. (1999). Child molesters' implicit theories. *Journal of Interpersonal Violence*, **14**, 821–38.

Ward, T., Polaschek, D. L. L. & Beech, A. R. (2006). *Theories of Sexual Offending*. Chichester: John Wiley & Sons.

Ward, T. & Siegert, R. (2002). Toward a comprehensive theory of child sexual abuse: a theory knitting perspective. *Psychology, Crime and Law*, **8**, 319–51.

Weisz, M. G. & Earls, C. M. (1995). The effects of exposure to filmed sexual violence on attitudes toward rape. *Journal of Interpersonal Violence*, **10**, 71–84.

Wenzel, A. & Rubin, D. C. (eds), (2005). *Cognitive Methods and their Application to Clinical Research*. Washington, DC: American Psychological Association.

Wheeler, J. G., George, W. H. & Dahl, B. J. (2002). Sexually aggressive college males: Empathy as a moderator in the "Confluence Model" of sexual aggression. *Personality and Individual Differences*, **33**, 759–76.

White, J. D. & Carlston, D. E. (1983). Consequences of schemata for attention, impression, and recall in complex social interactions. *Journal of Personality and Social Psychology*, **45**, 538–49.

Wilder, D. A., Simon, A. F. & Faith, M. (1996). Enhancing the impact of counterstereotypic information: Dispositional attributions for deviance. *Journal of Personality and Social Psychology*, **71**, 276–87.

Wittenbrink, B., Gist, P. L. & Hilton, J. L. (1997). Structural properties of stereotypic knowledge and their influences on the construal of social situations. *Journal of Personality and Social Psychology*, **72**, 526–43.

Wyer, R. S. Jr. (2004). *Social Comprehension and Judgment: The Role of Situation Models, Narratives, and Implicit Theories*. Mahwah, NJ: Lawrence Erlbaum Associates.

Chapter 6

CHANGING CHILD SEXUAL ABUSERS' COGNITIONS

CHRISTOPHER DEAN, RUTH E. MANN AND REBECCA MILNER

HM Prison Service, London, UK

SHADD MARUNA

Queen's University Belfast, Northern Ireland

It is generally accepted that the most effective approach to treating adult male sexual offenders is cognitive-behavioural. Cognitive-behavioural therapy involves the application of modification and relearning principles to both cognitions and behaviours. The underlying principle of the cognitive behavioural approach is that to change behaviour, we should first address the cognitions that precede the behaviour.

Early writing on criminal thinking suggested that rationalisations for crime reflect the cognitions that preceded the crime, and consequently such rationalisations must be removed from the offender's presentation for him to be considered less dangerous (e.g., McCaghy, 1968). In the sex offender field, this assumption was translated into the direction that workers must eliminate all external attributions for offending (and even some internal attributions) (e.g., Salter, 1988). This direction has had an overwhelming impact on sex offender treatment and is still widely believed and practised today. In this chapter we will argue that this prevailing belief may be mistaken. Two sources of error are suggested. First, it may be erroneous to assume that external attributions of cause are dangerous (Maruna & Mann, 1996). Second, what an offender says about his offending is not necessarily what he thinks about his offending and, arguably, is even less likely to represent what he thought at the time of offending.

The first of many complications when working with sexual offenders is that cognitions are only accessed through self-report, and there are problems with how accurately people report their cognitions (see also Chapter 4 of this volume). For example, cognitive therapy theory suggests that some underlying cognitions,

Aggressive Offenders' Cognition: Theory, Research and Practice. Edited by T. A. Gannon, T. Ward, A. R. Beech and D. Fisher. © 2007 John Wiley & Sons, Ltd.

such as schemas, may not be consciously accessible to a person, so they may not be able to self-report beliefs of which they are not aware (Beck, 1996). Furthermore, in the kinds of situations where child sexual abusers enter therapy – i.e., usually court-ordered or in a penal or probation setting – there are many reasons why an offender may choose to misreport or hide cognitions. For most offenders, gaining back their liberty or reducing their restrictions is dependent on convincing the authorities that they are not risky. In such a context, when there is much to lose and much to gain, there is a strong likelihood that the offender will conceal cognitions that he realises are not socially desirable. Offenders, like many people in many everyday situations, do not always say what they think, or think what they say.

In practice, those working with sexual abusers tend to assume that their verbalised statements about their offending are a direct representation of their cognitions. In particular, workers frequently assume that when an offender describes or explains his offending, he is revealing something about his cognitive patterns. We therefore begin this chapter by urging clinicians to be cautious about what they assume from what they hear. Clinicians must remember that what an offender *reports* to be, or have been thinking, cannot be assumed to be a faithful representation of his actual cognitions. To keep this caution in the reader's mind, we will frequently refer in this chapter to "statements of cognition" rather than the simpler, but less accurate term, "cognitions".

In this chapter, we will discuss treatment techniques for various different types of cognition. We will explore issues for therapists in accessing and recognising statements of cognitions, and deciding which to prioritise for intervention. We will suggest techniques for changing specific beliefs about the legitimacy of sexual offending e.g., beliefs that sexual offending is harmless or desirable. We will also review methods for changing offence-related elements of cognitive schemas (also known as implicit theories). These are not beliefs directly about offending but are more general forms of dysfunctional thinking (e.g., entitlement) which may predispose someone towards choosing sexual assault as a course of action in certain circumstances.

ACCESSING AND RECOGNISING OFFENDING-RELEVANT COGNITIONS

Typically, clinicians interested in determining cognitions relevant to sexual offending focus on three types of statement:

- Statements of attitude or belief about offending; e.g., "children are sexually provocative".
- Reports of specific thoughts that the offender experienced at the time of the offence: 'she is happy doing this."
- Statements that give reasons why the offence occurred. These statements may attribute responsibility for the offence to someone or something. The offender may say he is responsible: "I did it because I have twisted desires." He may say the victim is responsible: "She asked me to touch her." Or he may say that the offence occurred because of external or internal circumstances, often noting

that these were transitory states: "I was stressed" or "I was drunk" or "I was depressed".

Access to such potential cognitions is also sought through attitude scales, which have been constructed to measure any or all of these three phenomena in a quantitative way (e.g., Abel *et al.*, 1989; Bumby, 1996; Hanson, Gizzarelli & Scott, 1994; Mann *et al.*, 2007).

The third category of statements – statements of reason for offending – is particularly contentious. When an offender gives reasons for his offence, his statements are frequently labelled "cognitive distortions". That is, "Self-statements made by offenders that allow them to deny, minimize, rationalize or justify their behaviour" (Murphy, 1990, p. 332). Fifty years of neutralisation theory (see Maruna & Copes, 2005) have resulted in criminal justice workers expecting offenders to try to explain away the badness of their offending by making excuses for their actions. In an unpublished paper, Mann and Webster (2001) found that clinicians working with sexual offenders appeared to think that *any* reason for offending must be a neutralisation – and so offenders in treatment got the message that the only statement of reason that the authorities would find acceptable was "I did it because I wanted to". It is no exaggeration to say that the criminal justice system is obsessed with the desire to hear offenders "taking responsibility for their behaviour".

Maruna and Mann (2006) analysed the assumption that taking responsibility for offending reduces the likelihood of further criminality. They argued that this assumption is an example of a fundamental attribution error: the preference for explaining other people's behaviour in terms of internal disposition rather than by locating it in an external situation. In line with this, people prefer to explain their *own* behaviour by ensuring that they describe the circumstances in which it took place. Maruna and Mann suggested that offenders' tendency to explain their behaviour with reference to external circumstances is not abnormal or unhealthy. Offenders are only doing what all human beings do, and are expected to do, following a transgression. Maruna and Mann even hypothesised that to demand that an offender "takes responsibility" for his offending (i.e., adopts an explanation that involves internal, stable, attributions) may be counterproductive, forcing the offender to adopt a "doomed to deviance" script which is associated with persistence rather than desistance from offending (Maruna, 2001).

Furthermore, Maruna and Mann demonstrated that the concept of "cognitive distortion" has reached a level of fuzziness whereby it is no longer of any value to those evaluating, treating or researching sexual offenders (see also Mann & Beech, 2003). In this chapter, therefore, we will adopt the notion proposed by Maruna and Mann that a number of different cognitive phenomena are likely to be of relevance when working with sexual offenders and that these should be understood (and, by extension, treated) differently.

Therefore, following the arguments of Maruna and Mann (2006), we propose in this chapter that there are different forms of cognition related to child sexual offending. First, statements of *cause* or *reason* involve the explanations that an offender gives for his offending. These typically involve a mixture of internal and external attributions, as might be seen in the following statement: "I suppose I did it for a number of reasons: I was lonely, I was sexually frustrated, I was angry and I was drunk." Maruna and Mann (2006) and Mann and Hollin (2007) pointed out that such statements, often dismissed as "cognitive distortions", actually provide useful signposts to established dynamic risk factors for sexual offending. So, in the example statement above, the offender recognises he has problems with sexual self-regulation, anger management, and lack of emotional intimacy; all of which are identified criminogenic needs for sexual offenders (e.g., Hanson & Morton-Bourgon, 2005).

We distinguish one particular type of explanation as a separate second category for treatment purposes. This is the suggestion that the offence occurred because the victim was encouraging or provocative. Rather than class this explanation with other statements of reason, we believe it should be treated separately. Mann *et al.* (2007) demonstrated that statements that ascribe some or all responsibility for the offence to the victim's behaviour are correlated with underlying attitudes that sexual abuse of children is not harmful. Thus, we class this reason for offending as an indicator of an underlying offence-supportive attitude. There is some justification for this separation in the risk factor literature: Hanson and Morton-Bourgon (2005) noted that presence of offence-supportive attitudes weakly predicted recidivism, whereas "taking responsibility for offending" was not linked with lower recidivism rates.

The third distinct type of offence-relevant cognition is the schema (Mann & Beech, 2003; Mann & Hollin, 2007). A schema is a structure that contains core beliefs about the self, others and the outside world. The schema directs the processing of events (Beck, 1999), leading to schema-consistent interpretations of events (particularly those events that are ambiguous or threatening). Schemas relevant to sexual offending include the *dominance* schema, where respect and vengeance are over-valued; and the *disadvantaged* schema, where the offender feels irreparably damaged by others and controlled by his past, and ruminates resentfully on his lot (Mann, 2005). Researchers have also noted a *suspiciousness* schema, where the offender inherently distrusts the meaning of apparent messages conveyed by women (Malamuth & Brown, 1994) and an *entitlement* schema, where the offender has an inflated sense of his own rights, especially in the sexual arena (Hanson, *et al.*, 1994). *Implicit theories* (see Chapter 1 of this volume) are conceptually very similar to schemas and characteristic implicit theories have been outlined for child sexual abusers. For example: *children as sexual beings* (children are inherently sexual who enjoy and seek out sex from adults), *dangerous world* (the world is a dangerous place containing hostile and abusive adults) and *uncontrollability* (one's actions are a function of external rather than forces) (Ward & Keenan, 1999).

MANAGING STATEMENTS ABOUT COGNITIONS

The previous discussion raises key questions about how we categorise and demarcate types of thinking associated with sexual offending behaviour. There are associated issues for therapists about working with different types of cognition in treatment.

Given the argument that addressing certain thinking patterns (e.g., excuses or justifications) may be detrimental to an offender's desistance from offending or to their general mental health (Maruna & Copes, 2005; Maruna & Mann, 2006), therapists need to be mindfully aware about how they respond to such statements. Therapists face a dilemma when considering how to manage these statements. On the one hand, if they do not encourage individuals to identify and address particular cognitions they may reinforce, support or collude with thoughts that are distorted, inaccurate or offence promoting. On the other hand, if therapists challenge all an offender's statements of cause, believing them to be excuses or justifications, they may remove those thinking patterns that may enable the offender to desist from further offending. In addition, challenging statements that attribute responsibility to external causes may prevent therapists and offenders from identifying other dynamic risk factors where change needs to occur to reduce risk of re-offending (see Mann & Hollin, 2007). This, in turn, may reduce the collaborative insight that therapists and offenders can gain into the type and range of alternative cognitions and behaviours required for effective behaviour change.

Therapists working with child sexual abusers therefore need to consider when and how they should address cognitive statements, taking into account the need to protect the health of the offender whilst also acting to prevent future harm to victims. We outline three suggested activities in this chapter to assist therapists in making appropriate, confident decisions about how to manage such statements. By "manage", we mean the decisions taken by therapists to ignore or address a given statement. These approaches are an attempt to translate the theoretical issues referred to earlier in this chapter into guidance for applied practice. For example, a therapist can choose whether to ignore a statement; draw the attention of the group or individual to a statement; support the statement through positive reinforcement; or challenge the statement directly.

We suggest three activities are crucial in making appropriate decisions regarding offenders' cognitions. These are:

- Exploring the function of cognitions.
- Empowering individuals to take active responsibility for changing cognitions.
- Prioritising cognitions based on their significance to offending behaviour.

Exploring the Function of Cognitions

As discussed earlier in this chapter, a debate exists in the academic literature about the ambiguous definition of the term "cognitive distortion" (see Chapter 4 of this volume; Maruna & Copes, 2005; Maruna & Mann, 2006; Neidigh & Krop, 1992; Ward et al., 1997). Alongside, there has been debate about how different cognitions may be present at different phases of sexual offending and therefore play different roles in the occurrence of sexual offences. There are those who argue that some excuses and justifications contribute to or cause an offence to occur (Finkelhor, 1984; Hartley, 1998). Others suggest that excuses and justifications play a maintenance function in offending behaviour by reducing guilt following an offence (Abel et al., 1989; Murphy, 1990). These debates are unresolved but a solution to this uncertainty may be to focus on the function of different types of thoughts and how they may be relevant to sexual offending behaviour (Maruna & Mann, 2006; Ward et al., 1997). More research is required to guide therapists further regarding the types of cognition that it may be most important to address (see Ward, 2000, and his debate between focusing on schemas and attitudes underlying offending behaviour rather than "surface" distortions). In the meantime, clinical exploration of how particular cognitions function for individual offenders seems important. Exploring the function of cognitions is suggested as an appropriate way to evaluate with more clarity how different cognitions should be managed, to differentiate those that need to be addressed in treatment from those that do not.

Therapists need not become overly concerned about applying labels or categorisations to cognitions verbalised in treatment. Ascribing the "correct" label to a statement of cognition is less of a priority than understanding how the cognition functions for the offender generally and in terms of his offending behaviour. Through discussion and targeted Socratic questions, a therapist can elicit information about when and why a belief may have developed, and whether and why it remains. For example, asking as simple a question as "Was this thought present at the time of your offence?" may provide vital information about the role of this thought in their offending and whether it developed before, during or after the offence occurred. Associated questions might be "When do you first recall having that thought?" and, "When do you particularly find yourself having that thought?" If an offender reports that a thought occurred after his offence, this may then provide clues that this cognition functions in a protective manner (e.g., preserving self-esteem, minimising sense of shame). Exploring and identifying protective cognitions is particularly important when working with child sexual abusers, given that feelings of shame, guilt and stigma have been identified as typically characteristic of this group and may raise risk of continued offending (Proeve & Howells, 2006). Therefore, therapists should be cautious about challenging cognitions that serve to protect the offender from dysfunctional guilt and shame.

An additional strategy is for therapists to explain to offenders that thoughts have different functions for individuals, generally and in terms of sexual offending behaviour. Some thoughts will be more significant to address and challenge than others, so offenders and therapists need to work collaboratively to understand these functions. The explanation may take the form of a psycho-educational discussion, which differentiates thoughts that may help to protect a sense of self-esteem from those that directly link with offending behaviour (e.g., offence-supportive attitudes). Follow-up Socratic questions could be used to probe the function of specific cognitions, e.g., "How do you think this thought could be linked to making you feel better about what you did?" or "Were there any ways in which this type of thought led to your offence occurring?" This strategy strengthens therapeutic collaboration through making transparent why the therapist asks certain questions, and ensures that discussion remains focused on those thoughts that are likely to be the most important targets for change.

Empowering Active Responsibility for Cognitive Change

As discussed earlier in this chapter, Maruna and Mann (2006) suggested that making offenders "take responsibility" for their past offending behaviour may be ineffective, even counterproductive, to the effort to encourage desistance from sexual offending (see also Maruna & Copes, 2005). In particular, it may not be necessary to challenge post-offence cognitions that seem to excuse, justify or blame offending behaviour on external causes. Maruna and Mann (2006) argued that instead of avoiding the issue of responsibility altogether, focus should be on what Bovens (1998) defined as *active* rather than *passive* responsibility. *Active* responsibility involves seeing oneself as responsible for changing one's behaviour for the better, in the future. In contrast, *passive* responsibility involves seeing oneself as responsible for past actions. Encouraging active responsibility places the focus of treatment on assisting offenders to construct alternative thoughts, behaviours and relationships that will both protect them from future sexual offending and enhance their lives more generally.

Many interventions for sexual offenders encourage offenders to disclose information about their past thinking patterns, emotions, behaviour and relationships, both generally and also specifically in the lead-up to their sexual offences (Hudson & Ward, 1996; Mann & Thornton, 1998). Focusing on *active* responsibility, does not mean that analysis of past offending should stop but such analysis should not be an end in itself. Offenders should still be required to identify the factors (especially cognitions, in accordance with the cognitive-behavioural model) that may have led to their offences occurring. This process is required to help identify key areas of treatment need where change is necessary. Identifying previous problems will provide offenders with guidance on where they need to develop alternative thinking, behaviour, and ways of relating to others in order to be *actively* responsible.

Therapists can encourage active responsibility by ensuring that they positively reinforce statements made by individuals that indicate *active* personal responsibility for their future actions. This includes statements made that suggest individuals are distancing themselves from their offending identity and opting for a more prosocial identity. For example, "I wasn't really being me at the time of the offence, I don't want to be a person who hurts children, I want to do things differently to be a better person." Evidence of change in offence-related cognitions themselves is perhaps the best indicator of an individual engaging in the pursuit of being *actively* responsible. This is consistent with treatment approaches that focus on getting offenders to develop and practice alternative thoughts and behaviour to protect themselves from future offending and to live "better lives" in general e.g., the good lives model (Ward & Marshall, 2004).

Prioritising Cognitions in Treatment

Therapists must decide not only how cognitions should be managed but which cognitions should be addressed and why. This question takes on a greater significance in a treatment setting when an offender may verbalise multiple cognitions and a therapist faces the challenge of having to manage all effectively. The therapeutic environment demands that therapists spontaneously make decisions about the direction that a treatment session takes, in order to achieve their overall goal. So, therapists have to make multiple decisions: which cognitions to focus on, which to focus on first, and what approach to take in each case. Whilst such decisions are hard enough to take quickly in individual therapy, many therapists are working with sexual offenders in a group setting, which means that different individuals may verbalise different cognitions at the same time. The demand of having to decide what to focus on at any one time means that therapists require a way of filtering the statements that they hear. The filter should discriminate those cognitions that are most significant to address from those that are less significant. In this section, therefore, we discuss the types of cognitions to prioritise in treatment as targets for change. These are: offence-supportive attitudes, obstacles to active responsibility, toxic cognitions, and schema-driven beliefs about the self and others.

Offence-supportive Attitudes

The risk principle of offender rehabilitation (Andrews & Bonta, 2003) requires clinicians to prioritise factors that have empirically determined relationships with recidivism likelihood. Fortunately, for those of us who work with sexual offenders, the evidence base for such "dynamic risk factors" is now strong enough to enable a clear sense of what the priority issues are (e.g., Hanson & Bussière, 1998; Hanson & Mourton-Bourgon, 2005). In particular, the presence of cognitions that excuse, justify or rationalise offending behaviour, perhaps by appealing to external or temporary circumstances, has little if any impact on risk. Offence-supportive attitudes, such as beliefs that offending is harmless, or desirable, do raise risk somewhat when present (Hanson & Mourton-Bourgon, 2005). Therefore, Maruna and Mann (2006) suggested that these attitudes are separate from other "rationalisations".

Therefore, we suggest therapists should prioritise for intervention any statements that indicate the presence of attitudes that support offending behaviour against children (e.g., children as sexualised beings). The statement: "She was teaching me a thing or two about sex, she knew what she was doing" seems likely to be a manifestation of attitudes supporting the sexual abuse of children. Such a statement would therefore be important to target for intervention. In the therapeutic setting, when hearing a statement of cognition, therapists can ask the useful question: "Does this sound like a thought that is associated with an offence-supportive attitude?"

We do not suggest that therapists should abandon challenging surface cognitions associated with offence-supportive attitudes. At present, there is insufficient evidence to justify such a departure from current established practice. In fact, processes that typically address and modify offence-supportive attitudes often rely on challenging the specific, surface-cognitions associated with the underlying attitude (see Jenkins-Hall, 1989).

Obstacles to Active Responsibility

Certain cognitions may prevent or reduce the amount of disclosure offenders make about their past thoughts, feelings, behaviour or relationships, including immediately before and during their offence. For example, the belief that "Things just happened; I didn't really think or feel anything before it happened." Such thoughts can prevent both individual and therapist gaining insight into those aspects of the offender that contributed to their previous offence/s. Without this insight, the offender may not see the need to make changes to prevent re-offending. In other words, such cognitions may prevent the offender taking active responsibility for change. One explanation for such vagueness about the cognitions that were experienced during sexual assault may be found in cognitive deconstruction theory (Ward, Hudson & Marshall, 1995). This theory suggests that in a state of stress-induced cognitive deconstruction (Baumeister, 1991) a sex offender may process only information that is consistent with his desired goals (e.g., achieving sexual intimacy). Thinking is concrete and not analytical. Once sexual satisfaction is achieved, the state of cognitive deconstruction lifts and the memory of events is biased, superficial, and self-justifying.

Toxic Cognitions

Maruna (2004) identified certain cognitions as "toxic" that are internal, stable and global (e.g., "This is just who I am"). Maruna emphasised how cognitions that serve to preserve self-identity are especially resilient. Therapists should consider in treatment whether statements made by the offender suggest internal, stable, global attributions that may make personal change more difficult.

Schema-related Beliefs

The emphasis on offence-supportive attitudes should not preclude consideration of cognitions more indirectly related to offending. Some cognitions may increase the significance of other risk factors associated with child sexual abuse (e.g., lack of intimate relationships with adults, distorted intimacy balance, inadequacy, grievance thinking, poor emotional control). For example, Maruna (2004) emphasised the association of hostile attributions (e.g., "everyone is against me") with persistent criminality. We have noted earlier in this chapter that there are patterns of thinking (schemas) that are not directly offence-related but which may increase vulnerability to offend, perhaps by creating an aversive emotional state where the offender is less motivated to resist feelings of sexual arousal (Mann, 2005). Other cognitions may support emotional intimacy with children rather than adults (e.g., "Children trust you more than adults, and never let you down"). These types of cognitions are similar to *implicit theories* identified as being held by child sexual abusers (e.g., *dangerous world*; see Chapter 1 of this volume; Ward & Keenan, 1999). Therefore, in addition to targeting offence-related cognitions with direct links to recidivism, therapists should aim to identify and address cognitions that may have an indirect effect on recidivism. In this category, we place schema-driven thinking, and cognitions that form obstacles to relating intimately to adults.

Lower Priority Cognitions

Some types of cognition may be less important to target with child sexual abusers in treatment. Certain statements of cognition may have developed after an offence occurred. For example, "I only touched her over her clothes and I only did it the once." An offender may develop such a representation of the offence to protect self-esteem or worth, to reduce feelings of guilt, to protect identity or to reduce feelings of stigmatisation. If such thoughts prevent exposure to aversive emotions, or occurred only after offences had been committed, it is possible that there is less purpose in addressing these thoughts. Therapists should therefore consider on each occasion the purpose of addressing statements that do not correspond with the facts of a case (e.g., the offender touched their victim under her clothes and more than once). It is hard for therapists, usually attuned to the rights and needs of the victims of sexual abuse, to be able to tolerate statements that minimise the offence. However, it is sometimes difficult to understand how full admission of all facts would provide any further information about the nature of change needed to prevent sexual reoffending. When an offender distorts the facts of a case, therapists should ask themselves "How would the offender admitting to the accuracy of the facts help him to change?" or "Will challenging such thoughts allow any further information or insight that will enable change to occur?" If answers to such questions suggest there is little to gain, it seems justifiable to tolerate some distortion of the facts of a case. In some cases, the therapist may conclude that admission of additional facts *is* relevant in enabling the offender to take active responsibility. As Mann and Marshall (in press) note, "it does not matter if an offender denies that his victim was aged six, insisting that she was aged eight. Either way, he acknowledges that he abused a pre-pubescent child. It does matter if he denies that she was six, insisting that she was sixteen, because this denial would preclude him from discussing sexual arousal to younger children."

There are various limitations to the approach outlined. One limitation is that the influence of post-offence cognitions that then contribute to further offences being committed may be neglected or deprioritised. This may particularly be the case if individuals emphasise that such thoughts were not present during initial offences (or index offences) but developed after the offence. Such cognitions could become confused as being present to protect self-esteem or identity. Another limitation is that cognitions based on offence-supportive attitudes may be emphasised at the expense of other thoughts or attitudes that may be equally as significant in an individual's offending. Therefore, therapists need to be aware of the possibility of idiosyncratic beliefs that are not (yet) established as cognitive risk factors for recidivism, but which in a particular case clearly played an important role in enabling the offender to abuse a child. In addition, it is possible that some cognitions are multifunctional in that they may allow offending behaviour to be maintained and are based on offence-supportive attitudes yet also protect self-esteem and reduce a sense of shame. In such a situation, the therapist may be uncertain whether to challenge the cognitions, or not address them at all. Until we have further research into the characteristics and functions of cognitions, such ambiguity will remain.

We also acknowledge that these approaches may be harder to apply in practice than they are in theory. Under the demanding conditions of a group treatment setting, making multiple, considered decisions about the significance of verbalised cognitions amidst managing other events and decisions arising in this setting may not always be possible.

Beyond the three specific approaches outlined here, the broader message about addressing sexual abusers' cognitions is that therapists should take a highly reflective approach in considering when, what, how and why they address, challenge and prioritise cognitions that emerge in treatment. This message contrasts with earlier texts on sex offender treatment, where therapists were given simple guidance to "challenge cognitive distortions" (e.g., McCaghy, 1968; Salter, 1988). We emphasise that therapists need to work collaboratively with individual offenders, to establish what the function of their thoughts are and to prioritise areas for change based on their likely significance to their sexual offending. Therapists should understand how offenders' statements of cognition can indicate targets for change, but also how cognitions may enable or prevent offenders from taking active responsibility for personal change to occur. Therapists also need to consider how statements of cognition may be associated with other areas of risk and give such cognitions as much priority as cognitions directly concerned with sexual offending.

ADDRESSING OFFENCE-SUPPORTIVE COGNITIONS IN TREATMENT

The focus of this section is on how therapists address those cognitions that they have identified as targets for change. A therapist needs particular knowledge and skills to address cognitions effectively. We will look at strategies to address both situation-specific cognitions and deeper offence-supportive attitudes that permit or minimise sexual abuse.

There is a distinction between *addressing* and *challenging* cognitions. The process of *addressing* a cognition is conceptualised as the decision by a therapist not to ignore a cognitive statement but to work with a statement with the aim of achieving a change of view. The process of *challenging* a cognition is conceptualised as one method of addressing a cognition. Challenging a statement is not always necessary or ideal. A statement can be addressed without being verbally challenged: the therapist can simply draw the attention of the group or individual to a statement; can support only part of a statement through selective positive reinforcement; can model alternative options without making a direct challenge; or can ask Socratic questions to explore the meaning and significance of the statement. There are many reasons why a therapist may want to address a statement but not challenge it. Some offenders expect, respect and respond to challenge; others can become defensive and resistant. So in many cases, challenging may be too high risk a strategy to embark on, at least until the therapist is sure that the strategy will be effective. The therapist may also be wise to address rather than challenge a statement if it is not clear that a cognition is associated with an underlying attitude. Further, addressing rather than challenging can allow group exploration (particularly if others may share similar thoughts) and reinforcement of alternative, pro-social thinking in the group to develop cohesion and progress.

The distinction between addressing and challenging therefore emphasises that whilst challenging distorted cognitions can be productive in some situations (Langton & Marshall, 2000), there are other effective methods also available for therapists to produce cognitive change.

Therapists also need to recognise *when* to address offence-related cognitions. Even if an offender verbalises a cognition that appears to indicate an offence-supportive attitude (e.g., "He was smiling, he was enjoying it, he knew what sex was all about"), a change of view is unlikely before the group (or the therapeutic relationship) has developed cohesion and trust. To address statements (particularly via the method of challenging) too early in treatment is likely to be detrimental to the process of change.

When an offender makes a statement of cognition in treatment, the therapist needs to be able to detect the component of a statement that requires addressing. The knowledge required to make this decision is gained from personal experience, research, professional training, the experience of others, or other sources of general information (e.g., media, social groups, peers). A therapist needs to evaluate statements and verbalisations made in treatment against their own knowledge, as well as that of their co-therapist and other group members. Without such knowledge, a therapist may be unable to detect when unhelpful cognitions occur in such settings and therefore such cognitions may remain unchallenged. For example, when an offender verbalises, "At the time of the offence I remember thinking he seemed happy, he was smiling, I thought he was enjoying it" a therapist needs to appreciate why this belief could be very important to the offender. Only then can the therapist effectively discuss why this is an unhelpful belief to possess and what it is about this way of thinking that needs to change. The clinician also needs to be aware that the offender is not necessarily lying – the victim's behaviour may have been as he said. It could therefore be quite counterproductive to argue that the victim would have been unlikely to behave that way. Therapists who have good knowledge of the complexities of victim reactions during sexual abuse will understand that the *meaning* attributed to the behaviour – that the victim enjoyed the abuse – is a more important issue to address than the *description* of the behaviour – that the victim smiled. The therapist's aim is to assist the individual in sharing this understanding.

When challenging a child sexual abuser, therapists consider the source, method and approach of challenge. The *source* of the challenge refers to where the information or knowledge that can challenge a viewpoint will come from (is it within the offender themselves, from the therapist, another group member, research, etc.). The *method* of the challenge refers to how the therapist then conveys that knowledge (e.g., through group discussion, role-play, video presentation, behavioural experiment, etc.). The *approach* of the challenge refers to whether the therapist delivers the challenge reflectively or directly (i.e., through Socratic questioning versus direct feedback). Different offenders are likely to be responsive to different combinations of sources, methods and approaches of challenge. The more a therapist can engage a variety of combinations, responding flexibly to the offender and the time and place, the more likely that challenges will be successful.

Methods for Addressing Cognitions

If we are to assume that certain cognitions contributed to a previous sexual offence occurring, it seems rational to argue that such cognitions should be changed or modified in order to minimise their influence in contributing to future offences. A key process in enabling this to happen in treatment is "cognitive restructuring", essentially the process of identifying and challenging dysfunctional thoughts and developing alternatives to these thoughts (Meichenbaum, 1977). Therapists (and group members if present in treatment) encourage individuals to actively challenge and re-evaluate the validity or helpfulness of their previous way of thinking.

Socratic Questioning

One approach to cognitive restructuring is to use questions to encourage the offender to generate evidence that is contrary to their way of thinking through Socratic questioning (Overholser, 1993). The aim of Socratic questioning is to help the offender to re-evaluate the particular validity of their pattern of thinking (see Jenkins-Hall, 1989). For example, a therapist may ask an offender, "What other reasons could there be why your victim smiled during the abuse? Why might your victim not have enjoyed the abuse even though they may not have shown this on their face? When might people express feelings which are different to what they express inside?" In group settings, therapists can also ask other group members such questions to try and elicit alternative views for the offender to consider. Likewise, therapists themselves can offer alternative suggestions as to why a child may respond in this way for an offender to consider.

Behavioural Experiments

Another approach is for individuals to create or recall specific experiences that disconfirm their ways of thinking (Hollon & Garber, 1988). This is similar to a behavioural experiment approach in which individuals actively have to create or expose themselves to situations that will challenge their patterns of thinking. For example, offenders could be asked to observe occasions when they themselves may express enjoyment or happiness at times when they do not feel either of these things. They could be asked more broadly to report times when they hid emotions from others and the reasons why they may do this.

Provision of Knowledge

Another technique is the presentation of videos and victim-impact statements to encourage offenders to understand the possible perspective of their victims and others (see Pithers, 1994). This approach presents the offender with new information about a perspective, rather than trying to encourage him to generate this for himself. For example, continuing the example given above, the therapist could locate an account of an abuse survivor who describes why they tried to keep smiling during their abuse for reasons other than enjoying the abuse that was occurring to them.

Role-plays

The use of role-plays can also be effective in a similar way (Mann, Daniels & Marshall, 2002). The role-play allows the offender to recognise the thoughts and feelings of others; enabling him to develop empathy and perspective taking.

Offenders who have committed offences against children are invited to "step into the shoes" of their victim and consider the abuse experience from that perspective, which may challenge their interpretation of the victim's responses and thoughts during the offence.

This kind of process is usually thought of as "victim empathy development". The value of victim empathy work has recently been in question, given the finding that victim empathy appears unrelated to recidivism risk (Hanson & Morton-Bourgon, 2005). Current thinking (e.g., Mann & Marshall, in press) is that work previously conceptualised as "developing victim empathy" may in fact serve the purpose of addressing beliefs that sexual abuse (either in general or in relation to the offender's specific abusive behaviour) was harmless or beneficial to the victim.

Recognising Change

Therapists need to be able to recognise when an offender understands something differently, that is, when he has altered his cognitions. For example, an offender could verbalise that, "Actually maybe he was smiling because he didn't want to hurt my feelings or to show me his true feelings, he could have been scared about what I was doing, it could have been the only way he knew how to deal with it." This statement indicates that the offender has explored his earlier belief that smiling was an indicator of sexual pleasure and has adjusted that belief. When there is evidence of cognitive change, therapists should recognise and reinforce (through praise, approval, or direct feedback) the change. They should immediately consider – and check – whether related beliefs have also changed, to capitalise on the offender's progress.

ADDRESSING COGNITIONS THAT INCREASE VULNERABILITY TO OFFEND

As noted earlier, offence-related attitudes are not the only form of cognition that can promote sexual offending. It is also important to consider cognitions that contribute to the emergence and maintenance of other factors associated with sexual offending against children (e.g., cognitions about personal inadequacy, poor emotional control, fear of adults). For example, a child sexual abuser may truly believe he can trust children more than adults, and so view children as easier to be intimate with. The treatment literature to date has focused on this aspect of cognition much less thoroughly and there is little written direction for sex offender treatment providers about how to treat schema-driven thinking (see, however, Mann & Shingler, 2005).

Greater creativity may be required in both the sources and methods used to challenge these sorts of cognitions. For example, a man who fears adult intimacy may find it helpful to hear personal accounts of adults who have overcome mistrust of adults and have changed their interpretations during this process. He may also respond to behavioural approaches such as being supported in an opportunity to experience adult intimate relationships.

SCHEMA-FOCUSED THERAPY WITH SEXUAL OFFENDERS

Modern cognitive therapy texts (e.g., Beck, 1995) provide considerable direction on schema-focused therapy. Many cognitive therapy techniques are relevant and effective for sex offender treatment. However, it requires considerable familiarity and skill at cognitive therapy to work successfully with schemas and core beliefs. Often, sex offender treatment providers do not have adequate training in this area. Hence, they may be in danger of falling back on "challenging" schema-driven beliefs, as though these beliefs are consciously adopted for a self-serving purpose. This chapter cannot serve as a replacement for cognitive therapy training. However, we can draw attention to some useful techniques and encourage therapists to seek formal training in this approach.

Cognitive approaches to changing schemas generally emphasise the present, but they also make use of the client's past experiences as a vehicle for developing a clearer understanding of their current experiences (Beck, 1995). A life history presentation allows each offender to recount formative events that probably shaped his thinking. By tracing the development of cognitions and life experiences, the offender and the therapist develop an understanding of patterns of dysfunctional thinking (schemas) and how they function (Winter & Kuiper 1997). We particularly recommend the provision of schema focused therapy via group work sessions. Therapists and other group members can assist the offender to re-evaluate his schemas and to start to build more adaptive ways of thinking. Using a variety of cognitive therapy methods, therapists can help offenders to consider that their beliefs are hypotheses to be tested rather than absolute truths. Time is spent looking at the evidence for and against the belief, and also the advantages and disadvantages of revising it. This motivational work is important as schemas serve an important function in helping us understand and feel comfortable in the world (even though they may be dysfunctional). Role-plays which enable the offender to practice holding a different schema, or view his own schema from a different perspective, are useful tasks to set up in groups. For example, a therapist may ask a group member to argue against his own belief, whilst the therapist (or another group member) holds his old belief. Self-monitoring in the form of a schema log (Padesky & Greenberger, 1995) is also a key part of this modification process.

Treatment should enable offenders to create alternative and more adaptive ways of thinking: Schema change involves a simultaneous focus on weakening old schemas and strengthening new ones (Padesky, 1994). A variety of techniques are available to help offenders create positive alternative schemas. Group members identify what the positive schema may look like, how it may feel, associated behaviour and moods. Imagery can be a useful tool here. Continuum/scale work enables offenders to rate how much they believe the new schema, and then start to collect evidence for the new belief. The "stepping stones" technique is used to help offenders look at how they will get to new schema, e.g., setting themselves small tasks that will help to achieve alternative thinking. The "Life through a different lens" technique (Leahy, 2003) asks the group member to consider how life would have been different with a more positive alternative schema. This technique also asks how life will be different in the future with a new alternative schema. Areas that can be considered "through the lens" include friendships, partner, sex life, offending, choice of jobs, health, leisure, prison life, relationship with prison/probation staff, and group work relationships.

Practising the adaptive schemas in real life is also an important activity. Behavioural experiments are a key component of most effective cognitive therapy packages and are a particularly powerful method for producing cognitive change (Bennett-Levy *et al.*, 2004).

Research into the role of schemas in sexual offending is ongoing but we believe that there is sufficient evidence from studies with other types of psychological dysfunction and more recently from sexual offending to support a schema-focused approach with sex offenders. The main task for the therapist is to encourage sexual offenders to evaluate and modify their dysfunctional schemas and their role in offending. However, evaluation of the impact of such work on relevant attitudes and socio-affective variables, and ultimately sexual re-offending, is required.

CONCLUSION

Recent developments in research have challenged previously held views about the nature of child sexual abusers' cognitions and how these should be addressed in treatment settings. Criticism of the label "cognitive distortion" and the possible negative consequences of challenging some cognitions, collectively challenge therapists to reconsider how they address cognitive statements in treatment. This chapter has aimed to outline possible approaches and techniques through which therapists can respond to this challenge.

It is argued that therapists need to move away from a one-dimensional approach of seeing all cognitive statements as cognitive distortions that simply need to be challenged. Therapists need to take a more considered, reflective approach towards such statements, acknowledging that cognitions vary and have different functions that need to be addressed in different ways for effective treatment outcome. For this to occur, therapists, in collaboration with child sexual abusers, need to explore the function of their cognitions, empower offenders to take active responsibility for change and to prioritise cognitions that most need addressing. The primary focus of this approach is to encourage offenders to understand and use alternative cognitions to those that contributed to their offending behaviour (in order to enable change to occur), rather than making offenders describe and disclose fully the facts of their case with no specific purpose in mind.

Therapists must also decide *how* cognitive statements will most effectively be addressed. The act of challenging cognitions is a key method, but only one method from those available. The process of addressing cognition requires the combined use of different methods and approaches drawing on different sources of knowledge. Certain therapies, such as schema-focused therapy, provide promising, flexible strategies through which different types of cognition can be addressed effectively, using different sources of knowledge, approaches and methods. The ongoing challenge for practitioners and researchers alike, is to develop our understanding about which combinations of approach, method and sources of knowledge work most effectively to change different cognitions characteristic of child sexual abusers.

REFERENCES

Abel, G. G., Gore, D. K., Holland, C. L. *et al.* (1989). The measurement of the cognitive distortions of child molesters. *Annals of Sex Research*, **2**, 135–53.

Andrews, D. A. & Bonta, J. (2003). *The Psychology of Criminal Conduct*. Cincinnati, OH: Anderson Publishing.

Baumeister, R. F. (1991). *Escaping the Self*. New York: Basic Books.

Beck, A. T. (1996). Beyond belief: a theory of modes, personality, and psychopathology. In P.M. Salkovskis (Ed.), *Frontiers of Cognitive Therapy* (pp. 1–25). New York: Guilford Press.

Beck, A. T. (1999). *Prisoners of Hate: The Cognitive Basis of Anger, Hostility and Violence*. New York: HarperCollins.

Beck, J. (1995). *Cognitive Therapy: Basics and Beyond*. New York: Guilford Press.

Bennett-Levy, J., Butler, G., Fennell, M. *et al.* (2004). *Oxford Guide to Behavioural Experiments in Cognitive Therapy*. Oxford University Press.

Bovens, M. (1998). *The Quest for Responsibility*. Cambridge: Cambridge University Press.

Bumby, K. (1996). Assessing the cognitive distortions of child molesters and rapists: development and validation of the RAPE and MOLEST scales. *Sexual Abuse: A Journal of Research and Treatment*, **8**, 37–54.

Finkelhor, D. (1984). *Child Sexual Abuse: New Theory and Research*. New York: Free Press.

Hanson, R. K. & Bussière, M. T. (1998). Predicting relapse: a meta-analysis of sex offender recidivism studies. *Journal of Consulting and Clinical Psychology*, **73**, 1154–63.

Hanson, R. K., Gizzarelli, R. & Scott, H. (1994). The attitudes of child molesters: sexual entitlement and acceptance of sex with children. *Criminal Justice and Behaviour*, **21**, 187–202.

Hanson, R. K. & Morton-Bourgon, K. E. (2005). The characteristics of persistent sexual offenders: A meta-analysis of recidivism studies. *Journal of Consulting and Clinical Psychology*, **73**, 1154–63.

Hartley, C. C. (1998). How incest offenders overcome internal inhibitions through the use of cognitions and cognitive distortions. *Journal of Interpersonal Violence*, **13**, 25–39.

Hollon, S. D. & Garber, J. (1988). Cognitive therapy. In L. Y. Abramson (ed.), *Social Cognition and Clinical Psychology: A Synthesis* (pp. 204–53). New York: Guilford.

Hudson, S. M. & Ward, T. (1996). Relapse prevention: future directions. *Sexual Abuse: A Journal of Research and Treatment*, **8**, 249–56.

Jenkins-Hall, K. D. (1989). Cognitive restructuring. In D. R. Laws (ed.), *Relapse Prevention with Sex Offenders* (pp. 47–55). New York: Guilford.

Langton, C. M. & Marshall, W. L. (2000). Cognition in rapists: theoretical patterns by typological breakdown. *Aggression and Violent Behaviour*, **6**, 499–518.

Leahy, R. L. (2003). *Cognitive Therapy Techniques: A Practitioner's Guide*. New York: Guilford.

Malamuth, N. M. & Brown, L. M. (1994). Sexually aggressive men's perceptions of women's communications: testing three explanations. *Journal of Personality and Social Psychology*, **67**, 699–712.

Mann, R. E. (2005). *An investigation of the nature, content and influence of schemas in sexual offending*. Unpublished doctoral thesis: University of Leicester.

Mann, R. E. & Beech, A. R. (2003). Cognitive distortions, schemas, and implicit theories. In T. Ward, D. R. Laws & S. M. Hudson (eds), *Sexual Deviance: Issues and Controversies* (pp. 135–53). Thousand Oaks, CA: Sage.

Mann, R. E., Daniels, M. & Marshall, W. L. (2002). The use of role-plays in developing empathy. In Y. Fernandez (ed.) *In Their Shoes*. Oklahoma: Wood 'N' Barnes.

Mann, R. E. & Hollin, C. R. (2007). *Sexual Offenders' Explanations for their Offending*. Journal of Sexual Aggression, **13**, 3–9.

Mann, R. E. & Marshall, W. L. (in press). Advances in the treatment of sexual offenders. In A. Beech, L. Craig & K. Browne (Eds.), *Handbook of Assessment, Conceptualization, and Treatment of Sex Offenders. Vol. 1, Adult disorders*. Chichester: Wiley.

Mann, R. E. & Shingler, J. (2005). Schema-driven cognition in sexual offenders: theory, assessment and treatment. In W. L. Marshall, Y. M. Fernandez, L. E. Marshall & G. A.

Serran (eds), *Sexual Offender Treatment: Controversial Issues* (pp. 173–86). Chichester, UK: Wiley.

Mann, R. E. & Thornton, D. (1998). The evolution of a multi-site sexual offender treatment programme. In W. L. Marshall, Y. M. Fernandez, S. M. Hudson & T. Ward (eds). *Sourcebook of Treatment Programmes for Sexual Offenders* (pp. 47–57). New York: Plenum Press.

Mann, R. E. & Webster, S. D. (2001). *Explanations or Excuses?* Unpublished paper, available from HM Prison Service, Offending Behaviour Programme Unit, Cleland House, Page Street, London, England.

Mann, R. E., Webster, S. D., Wakeling, H. C. & Marshall, W. L. (2007). The measurement and influence of child sexual abuse supportive beliefs. *Psychology, Crime and Law,* **00** (0) 1–16.

Maruna, S. (2001). *Making Good: How Ex-convicts Reform and Rebuild their Lives*. Washington, DC: American Psychological Association Books.

Maruna, S. (2004). Desistance and explanatory style: A new direction in the psychology of reform. *Journal of Contemporary Criminal Justice,* **20**, 184–200.

Maruna, S. & Copes, H. (2005). What have we learned in five decades of neutralisation research? *Crime and Justice: A Review of Research,* **32**, 221–320.

Maruna, S. & Mann, R. E. (2006). A fundamental attribution error? Rethinking cognitive distortions. *Legal and Criminological Psychology,* **11**, 155–78.

McCaghy, C. H. (1968). Drinking and deviance disavowal: the case of child molesters. *Social Problems,* **16**, 43–9.

Meichenbaum, D. (1977). *Cognitive-behavior Modification*. New York: Plenum.

Murphy, W. D. (1990). Assessment and modification of cognitive distortions in sex offenders. In W. L. Marshall, D. R. Laws & H. E. Barbaree (eds), *Handbook of Sexual Assault* (pp. 331–42). New York: Plenum Press.

Neidigh, L. & Krop, H. (1992). Cognitive distortions among child sex offenders. *Journal of Sex Education and Therapy,* **18**, 208–15.

Overholser, J. (1993). Elements of the Socratic method: I. Systematic questioning. *Psychotherapy,* **30**, 67–74.

Padesky, C. (1994). Schema change processes in cognitive therapy. *Clinical Psychology and Psychotherapy,* **1**, 267–78.

Padesky C. & Greenburger, D. (1995). *Mind over Mood: Change How you Feel by Changing the Way You Think*. New York: Guilford.

Pithers, W. D. (1994). Process evaluation of a group therapy component designed to enhance sex offenders' empathy for sexual abuse survivors. *Behaviour Research and Therapy,* **32**, 565–70.

Proeve, M. & Howells, K.H. (2006). Shame and guilt in child molesters. In W. L. Marshall, Y. M. Fernandez, L. E. Marshall & G. A. Serran (eds), *Sexual Offender Treatment: Controversial Issues* (pp. 125–39). Chichester: John Wiley & Sons.

Salter, A. C. (1988). *Treating Child Sex Offenders and their Victims: A Practical Guide*. Newbury Park, CA: Sage Publications.

Ward, T. (2000). Sexual offenders' cognitive distortions as implicit theories. *Aggression and Violent Behaviour,* **5**, 491–507.

Ward, T., Hudson, S. M., Johnston, L. & Marshall, W. L. (1997). Cognitive distortions in sex offenders: an integrative review. *Clinical Psychology Review,* **17**, 479–507.

Ward, T., Hudson, S. M. & Marshall, W. L. (1995). Cognitive distortions and affective deficits in sex offenders: A cognitive deconstructionist interpretation. *Sexual Abuse: A Journal of Research and Treatment,* **7**, 67–83.

Ward, T. & Keenan, T. (1999). Child molesters' implicit theories. *Journal of Interpersonal Violence,* **14**, 821–38.

Ward, T. & Marshall, W.L. (2004). Good lives, aetiology and the rehabilitation of sex offenders: A bridging theory. *Journal of Sexual Aggression,* **10**, 153–69.

Winter, K. A. & Kuiper, N. A. (1997). Individual differences in the experience of emotions. *Clinical Psychology Review,* **17**, 791–821.

Chapter 7

COGNITIVE TREATMENT "JUST FOR RAPISTS": RECENT DEVELOPMENTS

Lynne Eccleston

The University of Melbourne, Australia

Karen Owen

Sex Offender Programs, Corrections Victoria, Australia

Theories of sexual offending (Finkelhor, 1984; Hall & Hirschman, 1991; Marshall & Barbaree, 1991; Ward & Siegert, 2002) contend that rape and other forms of sexual assault are facilitated by pro-offending attitudes and beliefs that maintain the deviant behaviour. These attitudes or beliefs function in sexual offenders to minimise, rationalise, or justify offending behaviour (Beech, Ward & Fisher, 2006b; Drieschner & Lange, 1999; Gannon, Polaschek & Ward, 2005; Marx, Miranda & Meyerson, 1999). These belief systems, or cognitive distortions have therefore become the focus of empirical research during the last two decades (Drieschner & Lange, 1999; Maruna & Mann, 2006). Despite this focus, intense confusion exists within the sexual offender literature relating to how professionals define "cognitive distortions" (Maruna & Mann, 2006). Maruna and Mann posit that the inconsistencies in defining cognitive distortions, coupled with a lack of empirical evidence suggesting that offending is preceded by rationalisations, is problematic (Beech & Mann, 2002; Beech *et al.*, 2006a; Ward, 2000).

To illustrate the level of complexity, descriptions of cognitive distortions have been conceptualised ranging from overarching beliefs and attitudes (Drieschner & Lange, 1999); a continuum of cognitive processes from denial to minimisation (Barbaree, 1991); or a concept as specific as psychological deception (Rogers, 1988). Recent conceptualisations include cognitive distortions as fundamental attribution errors (Maruna & Mann, 2006), and dysfunctional "social cognitions" that reflect the way a person thinks, perceives, understands and reasons, interrelated with how they behave and function in their social world (Gannon, Polaschek & Ward, 2005; Johnston & Ward, 1996; see also Chapter 4 of this volume). In summary,

Aggressive Offenders' Cognition: Theory, Research and Practice. Edited by T. A. Gannon, T. Ward, A. R. Beech and D. Fisher.   © 2007 John Wiley & Sons, Ltd.

descriptions include complex and often overlapping phenomena used to refer to offence-supportive attitudes, cognitive processing during the offence, and cognitive reasoning post-offence. In this chapter, we describe the treatment for heterogeneous sexual offenders, and treatment issues for rapists focusing on how rapists differ from child sexual abusers in relation to cognitive distortions. We then introduce a prison-based Sexual Offender Treatment Programme for Rapists recently developed in Victoria, Australia. We discuss the logistics of running the programme, process issues with this type of offender, and therapists' reflections on their experience running the group. The chapter concludes with a discussion of the future direction of cognitive treatment for rapists.

RAPISTS AND CHILD SEXUAL ABUSERS – DIFFERENT TREATMENT NEEDS?

In an attempt to target sexual offender's cognitive distortions, therapists have developed a number of sophisticated multiple-component treatment approaches, based on cognitive behavioural concepts (Beyko & Wong, 2005). The focus of these treatment programmes is to address the multiple determinant nature of sexual assault by: challenging cognitive distortions; targeting and controlling deviant sexual arousal patterns; equipping offenders with social and coping skills; addressing intimacy needs, empathy deficits and self-esteem; and initiating relapse prevention plans. Moreover, studies have demonstrated that sexual offender programmes using such cognitive behaviour therapy (CBT) interventions have successfully reduced sexual recidivism (Hall, 1995; Hanson et al., 2002; Harkins & Beech, 2007; Kenworthy et al., 2004; Lösel & Schmucker, 2005).

Building on earlier research (see Hall, 1996; Marshall & Barbaree, 1991), Thornton (2002) examined sexual offenders' attitudes and beliefs and reported the presence of a four-domain framework of dynamic risk factors. The four domains were: offence-related *sexual interests* (towards children and/or adults); *distorted attitudes* relating to offences, sexuality or victims; *socioaffective functioning* whereby factors such as low self-esteem, emotional loneliness, anger or external locus of control motivate interpersonal interactions and *self-management* reflecting offenders' ability to plan, solve problems and regulate emotions and impulsivity to achieve their goals. Arguably, given that rapists have been found to be more impulsive, psychopathic, antisocial, hostile and less empathic than child sexual abusers (Beech et al., 2006b; Polaschek & Ward, 2002; Quinsey, Harris, Rice & Cormier, 2006) and generally hold characteristics similar to violent men (see Alder, 1984; Gannon & Ward, in press) their cognitive distortions are likely to differ substantially from those of child sexual abusers and may require different treatment approaches.

Although treatment interventions have developed and improved dramatically during recent years and now offer a broader range of offence-related components, these programmes have been developed predominantly to meet the needs of child sexual abusers (Marshall, 1993). The current tendency in treatment is for professionals to treat different types of sexual offenders within the same programme using essentially the same treatment components (Brown, 2005; Jennings

& Sawyer, 2003; McGrath *et al.*, 2003; Marshall & Laws, 2003; Ward *et al.*, 1997a). Typically, offences are mixed including sexual acts against adult victims, against children, exhibitionism and lately child Internet pornographers. There are, however, substantial differences between child sexual abusers and rapists particularly in relation to cognitive distortions, empathy deficits, deviant arousal and anti-social personality characteristics (Beech *et al.*, 2006a; Drieschner & Lange, 1999; Gannon & Ward, in press). To illustrate, rapists display cognitive distortions that women should be submissive and controlled by men, men are entitled to have sex to gratify their sexual needs and that rape is justified if the woman behaves or dresses inappropriately (Beech *et al.*, 2006a; Thornton, 2002).

These differences necessarily have implications for the treatment of rapists. Given that offence-supportive beliefs may be similar for rapists and nonsexual violent offenders (see Beech, Ward & Fisher, 2006b; Milner & Webster, 2005) rapists may have different identifiable themes in their underlying thinking patterns than child sexual abusers. This implies that clinicians should be focusing on the underlying cognitive structures and processes rapists possess, rather than surface-level cognitions (Beech *et al.*, 2006a; Milner & Webster, 2005).

One treatment component identified in research that could be seen as critical in targeting rapists' cognitive distortions effectively is embedded in the therapeutic relationship and the "process" aspects of therapy (Anechiarico, 1998; Blanchard, 1995; Marshall & Serran, 2004). Beech and Fordham (1997), for example examined group based sexual offender treatment programmes in the United Kingdom and argued that to achieve a desired level of cohesiveness, good group processes had to be led and activated by therapists. The most effective group leaders were those who were supportive and modelled effective interpersonal interactions. Therapists' engagement style had a significant influence on the effectiveness of treatment. Arguably, these therapist process factors may be particularly crucial for breaking down hostility, suspiciousness and distrust in rapists.

ADDRESSING RAPISTS' TREATMENT NEEDS

Decisions about whether to treat rapists separately from child sexual abusers and other sexual offenders are complex. There are potential strengths and weaknesses in either approach given that both rapists and child sexual abusers exhibit offence-supportive cognition, social skills deficits, intimacy deficits, and poor self-esteem (Marshall, 2004). Therapists are cautious in placing too many rapists into a group programme in line with research suggesting that engaging such offenders in treatment is much more difficult (Marques, Nelson, West & Day, 1994; Marshall, 1993). Marques and his colleagues (1994) reported that in the California Sex Offender Treatment and Evaluation Project, 44% of child sexual abusers and only 24.3% of rapists volunteered to take part, with a completion rate of those selected for the programme of 67% for child sexual abusers and 34% for rapists.

The larger attrition rates and noncompletion rates for rapists undergoing group treatment raises several issues including treatment intensity, the treatment context, pre-treatment motivational interventions, and how interventions might have to be modified from those used with other sexual offenders (Ward *et al.*, 1997b). In line with the Risk-Needs-Responsivity Model (Andrews & Bonta, 1998) treatment intensity needs to be matched to the level of risk posed by rapists and the extensiveness and diverse nature of their criminogenic needs. The heterogeneity of deficits in rapists also suggests that their treatment needs should be carefully assessed and treatment should be tailored to meet their individual needs. For example, deficits could include poor conversation skills, absence of conflict resolution skills, inability to manage anger or stress, or pervasive rape fantasies. Many rapists also exhibit deficits in social and interpersonal skills that impact on their ability to develop and sustain meaningful interpersonal relationships (Gannon, Polaschek & Ward, 2005; Jennings & Sawyer, 2003; Milner & Webster, 2005; Polaschek, Ward & Hudson, 1997). Clinicians (Marshall, Eccles & Barbaree, 1993; Polaschek, Ward & Hudson, 1997) have acknowledged, however, that given the difference between rapists and child sexual abusers, and the difficulties engaging rapists in treatment, it might be beneficial to run separate programmes.

An additional therapeutic goal is to help rapists develop victim empathy, and learn to understand and value other individuals by highlighting the consequences of victimisation. Sexual reconditioning and/or fantasy retraining procedures may be crucial for particular offenders who have difficulty controlling their own sexual arousal, are motivated to coerce others into sexual acts, or are prone to frequent, intrusive rape fantasies (Johnston, Hudson & Marshall, 1992). Moreover, research has found that rapists with psychopathic characteristics and deviant sexual preferences recidivated more frequently than other groups of rapists (Hildebrand, De Ruiter & De Vogel, 2004).

The aim of empathy training is to challenge and dispel offence-supportive cognitions and increase the offender's awareness of the harm inflicted on the victim (Marshall, 1993; Marx, Miranda & Meyerson, 1999). It is important to note, however, that the motivation of rapists, according to Knight and Prentky (1990) and Beech *et al.* (2006a), can be either sexual or nonsexual. Research has also reported that nonsexual subtypes of rapists report less sexual arousal to rape scenarios than sexual subtypes and would be expected to score low on measures of rape supportive cognition (Barbaree, Seto, Serin, Amos & Preston 1994; Feelgood, Cortoni & Thompson, 2005). Consistent with this sub-typing, deviant sexual arousal may be relevant to a specific group of rapists (Marshall, 2004; Marshall & Fernandez, 2000), who hold higher levels of rape supportive cognition. Thus, providing nonsexually deviant rapists with high levels of therapy on deviant arousal and its associated cognition may be a waste of valuable resources, and reduce motivation to engage in treatment.

A further confounding factor in treatment is that research has revealed that rapists in particular do not experience empathy deficits towards sexual assault victims in general, but instead demonstrate least empathy for their own victims (Fernandez & Marshall, 2003). Fernandez and Marshall argued that since rapists recognised the harm committed against victims in general, there seems little value in attempting to make them understand the impact of sexual assault committed by other sexual offenders. The authors inferred that rapists may construe the harm they have inflicted on their specific victims quite differently, and their motivations and beliefs related to the rape may require alternative treatment than that offered in standard empathy modules.

Empathy skills training for rapists is further complicated for those offenders who exhibit antisocial or psychopathic traits. Research has shown that rapists have difficulty recognising emotions in others and in particular confuse anger, disgust, and fear – typically the emotions portrayed by their victims (Beech *et al.*, 2006a; Hudson *et al.*, 1993). Malamuth and Brown (1994) also reported that rapists were unable to perceive women's facial affect accurately, viewing friendly and seductive women as hostile. The treatment implications for rapists with antisocial personality characteristics suggests they will require more empathy training than for other sexual offenders given their emotional processing deficits. Treatment will need to focus on teaching them how to recognise their own emotional states as a first step towards being able to recognise facial affect and emotional states in others if they are to elicit empathy for their victims (Beech, Ward & Fisher, 2006b; Marshall, 2004; Marshall *et al.*, 1995). Further work with psychopathic rapists needs to tread carefully since they may well use such training to impact further harm on future victims.

Research and clinical experience also suggests that a direct, confrontational approach to the treatment of rapists is likely to result in increased treatment resistance (Kear-Colwell & Pollack, 1997). Marshall advocates for the use of respect, support, confidence, emotional responsivity, self-disclosure, flexibility and humour as a way of improving offenders' coping skills, perspective-taking, responsibility-taking and accepting future risk (Marshall *et al.* 2003). A UK prison study (Thornton, Mann & Williams, 2000; cited in Mann, 2004) reported reductions in denial and minimisation of pro-offending attitudes (rape myths) when offenders were exposed to both warm and supportive therapists and challenging questioning. Interestingly, only those offenders treated by "warm" therapists displayed less entitlement, distrust of women, subjective personal distress and impulsiveness (Beech & Hamilton-Giachritsis, 2005).

The predominant rationale for running mixed groups is to challenge the cognitions and attitudes offenders possess related to their offences (Harkins & Beech, in press). For example, our clinical experience informs us that a hierarchy exists among sexual offenders – rapists tend to make moral judgments about child sexual abusers and perceive paedophiles as inferior. One advantage of running a mixed group, and a key therapeutic aim, is for rapists to modify their self-proclaimed elevated status and to begin to view paedophiles as people.

Ward *et al.* (1997b) also argued that it can be advantageous to treat rapists with other sexual offenders if the rapists exhibit no evidence of rape fantasising, and there is an absence of a distinct offence cycle. Notwithstanding, it could also be argued that rapists with impulsivity problems may benefit initially from being placed in a cognitive skills programme that teaches offenders to concentrate and think more effectively prior to engaging in a group that focuses on the relationship between their offence-supportive cognition and sexual offending (Beech *et al.*, 2006a).

However, a distinct disadvantage of running heterogeneous sexual offender groups with several modules focusing on different treatment needs is that participants may regard some modules as being irrelevant. In this event offenders are likely to be disengaged and less motivated to participate in treatment. It is important to note that the majority of sexual offenders are mandated to treatment by the criminal justice system and may participate in programmes to avoid legal consequences, or to increase their chance of being granted parole (Birgden & Vincent, 2000). Given that offenders do not enter treatment voluntarily they may already lack motivation to engage fully in the treatment process.

Increasingly, both researchers and therapists are paying attention to the issue of assessing an offender's level of motivation and readiness for treatment. Ward *et al.* (2004) have recently developed a model that assesses a violent offender's suitability for entry into a rehabilitation programme. The model includes consideration of the offender's personal characteristics, and the situational factors, internal and external, that are likely to affect engagement in therapy. The internal factors that impact on motivation towards treatment are cognitive (beliefs, cognitive strategies), affective (emotions), volitional (goals, wants or desires), and behavioural (skills and competencies; Ward *et al.*, 2004).

These internal factors are important considerations in deciding whether to treat rapists separately from child sexual abusers. Rapists in particular tend to be less willing than other sexual offenders to participate in treatment, accept less responsibility for the consequences of their behaviour, and have higher attrition rates (Marques *et al.*, 1994; Marshall, 1993). In a pioneering study, Beech *et al.* (2006a) examined rapists' motivation to change pre-treatment and post-treatment. They reported that the majority of rapists were contemplating working on their problems prior to engaging in treatment, and following treatment they were motivated to change and engaged in more therapeutic interventions. Thus far, we have provided a broad overview of the different treatment needs of rapists. We now focus on some differences in rapists specifically in the area of cognition.

Rapists' Antisocial Attitudes, Beliefs and Behaviours

Research has reported that rapists, more so than other sexual offenders, meet the criteria for a diagnosis of antisocial personality disorder or possess psychopathic personality characteristics (Drieschner & Lange, 1999; Moore, Bergman & Knox, 1999; Polaschek, Ward & Hudson, 1997; Quinsey *et al.*, 2006; Thornton, 2002). The prevalence of antisocial behavioural characteristics impacts on treatment in that rapists exhibit greater impulsiveness, aggression and disruptive behaviour during group programmes (Marques *et al.*, 1994). Rapists also have more nonviolent institutional offences, and engage in more criminalised behaviours than other sexual offenders (Beyko & Wong, 2005).

Drieschner and Lange (1999) reviewed the cognitive determinants of rape and reported that rapists exhibit attitudes consistent with rape myths or victim blame, for example, "if women dress seductively they deserve to get raped". In addition, rapists who possess macho attitudes idealise power, toughness, competitiveness and aggression and view rape as their right to assert their masculinity. Given the presence of anger, aggression and extreme violence prevalent in antisocial rapists, research has attempted to investigate sexual offenders' motivation to rape in an attempt to understand the specific pro offending cognitions that exist in different types of rapists (Knight & Prentky, 1990).

Given the higher levels of aggressive behaviour noted in rape, rapists are likely to benefit from additional treatment modules to target their broad antisocial cognitions more than some other sexual offenders (see Chapter 9 of this volume for information relating to broad antisocial cognitions). Modules such as anger and stress management and violence-reducing interpersonal skills training may be more effective in reducing entrenched cognitions underlying hostility, entitlement, suspiciousness of women, and minimisation (Ward *et al.*, 1997a). Moreover, since many rapists have substance-abuse histories interrelated with their violence they may find that drug and alcohol interventions are likely to be useful (Marshall, 1996). Pithers (1993) also inferred that due to their higher levels of impulsivity, rapists are less likely to be able to identify their relapse precursors. In practical terms this means that rapists who act impulsively may be unaware of the triggers to their offending, and may need some work to learn how to become cognisant of their behaviour. They may therefore need to spend more time in treatment on identifying the triggers – in their offence chain – to reduce their risk of recidivism than other less impulsive sexual offenders such as child sexual abusers.

In summary, the prevalence of antisocial personality characteristics, aggressiveness and impulsivity suggests that rapists would benefit from additional modules that specifically target the cognitions underlying these components. For many rapists their propensity towards violence stems from dysfunctional violent childhoods and they exhibit longstanding problems. Marshall (1993) suggested that to address rapists' higher incidence of hostile masculinity treatment interventions are required to reconstruct the rapist's sense of self by enhancing self-efficacy skills. He argued that this provides rapists with an alternative sense of power and control previously derived from their sexual offending. Moreover, since rapists are heterogeneous in regard to the level of aggression used in rape they are also likely to differ in their pro-offending cognitions.

Rapists' Cognitive Distortions and Implicit Theories

Building on Ward's earlier established *implicit theories* in child sexual abusers (Ward & Keenan, 1999), Polaschek and Ward (2002) introduced the notion of implicit theories in rapists (see Chapter 2 of this volume). In brief, implicit theories are the underlying causal theories or schemas that rapists hold about the nature of their victims, themselves, and world around them. Implicit theorising allows rapists – like other people – to anticipate how they or other people will respond to particular experiences, and to decide what future actions they will take as a result. From examining existing questionnaire measures of rapists' offence-supportive cognition, Polaschek and Ward hypothesised that rapists held five main implicit theories: *women are unknowable, women are sex objects, male sex drive is uncontrollable, entitlement,* and *dangerous world*. Polaschek and Gannon (2004) tested the rapist implicit theory model by examining imprisoned rapists' narrative statements and found support for the five implicit theories (although *women are unknowable, women as sex objects,* and *entitlement* were most common) renaming *women are unknowable* as women are *dangerous* to highlight the fact that rapists' appeared to view women as more menacing and vindictive than previously thought.

Beech, Ward and Fisher (2006b) further tested the implicit theory model and identified three main groups of rapists according to their specific implicit theory.

The first group was violently motivated and held the implicit theory of "dangerous world" and/or the absence of "women as sexual objects". The second group was sexually motivated and exhibited the implicit theory "women as sexual objects" and/or the absence of "dangerous world". The third group was sadistically motivated and the implicit theories "women as sexual objects" and "dangerous world" were both present (see Chapter 2 of this volume for more details).

Polaschek and Ward (2002) further argued that although implicit theories are significant contributors towards predisposing some men to commit rape, they are limited in utility. They suggested that there did not appear to be a clear relationship between rape-specific attitudes and beliefs (rape myths/world view/sex role stereotyping), general rape-related cognitions (i.e., hostile schemas towards women, condoning of interpersonal violence towards women) and the individual committing a rape.

Importantly, research has found that rapists' cognitions are more similar to those of nonsexual violent offenders than to other sexual offenders (e.g., in terms of general violent-supportive themes – Beech, Ward & Fisher, 2006b – and "grievance" or feeling wronged – Milner & Webster, 2005). One study reported that sexually aggressive men held a "suspiciousness of women" schema and believed that women did not tell the truth in sexual matters (Malamuth & Brown, 1994). Eckhardt and Dye (2000) also reported the presence of a "suspicion/hostility to women" schema in men who were violent towards their intimate partners (see also Chapter 13 of this volume). Beck (1999) inferred that these schemas served a protective purpose to perceived threats from others. Later research identified five categories of schemas in a sample of 45 rapists: *grievance, entitlement, self as victim; control* and *disrespect for certain women* (Mann & Beech, 2003; Mann & Hollin, 2001).

We now turn our focus to describing a new rapist treatment programme developed in Victoria, Australia.

CORRECTIONS VICTORIA – RAPISTS' SEX OFFENDER PROGRAMME

The first rapist group we delivered was at one of Victoria's rural prisons where we had successfully been delivering other programmes for several years. The group programme ran for one year. Another rapist group is currently being delivered at a new prison in Victoria that operates in line with the philosophy of therapeutic jurisprudence and rehabilitation.

When we first considered the idea of starting a cognitive treatment programme "just for rapists" we essentially had little to base it on apart from research that informed us that rapists were more like violent offenders than other sexual offenders. Our clinical experience, based on some of the process issues we had experienced mixing rapists with other sexual offenders, confirmed that rapists were more antisocial. Prior to starting the programme we contacted the managers of other programmes in Australia and internationally to gauge their opinion about running a mainstream purely rapist group and every single response was "don't do it". The consensus was that running a purely rapist group required creativity and adaptation from other types of treatment programmes that deal with violent offenders.

An additional concern was that with a pure group of rapists you would expect to have greater group affiliation, and as a group offenders would band together and be more supportive and less challenging of each other's cognitions, particularly their antisocial attitudes and beliefs about women. Another argument against a pure rapist group was that therapeutically it was extremely difficult for the therapist in terms of facilitating the group process and engaging offenders in therapy, in addition to being psychologically draining.

Assessment Strategies and Protocols

Corrections Victoria has a standard assessment protocol for all its prison and community programmes. An extensive battery of assessment tools is administered to each offender, in addition to a lengthy interview process, that requires approximately 16 hours in total to complete.

Offenders included in the programme must be within the last 18 months or two years of their sentence and they must voluntarily consent to treatment. The rape offences for this group of sexual offenders all occurred in the context of an established prior relationship with the victim, either whilst they were in a relationship or following the breakdown of a relationship. This cohort of offenders was not explicitly singled out to participate in the treatment programme but rather represented the cohort of rape offenders based at the particular prison location.

A number of structured assessments such as the Bumby Rape Myth Scale (Bumby, 1996), The Rape Myth Acceptance Scale (Burt, 1980), the Interpersonal Reactivity Index (Davis, 1983) and the Multiphasic Sex Inventory (Nichols & Molinder, 1984) were used as pre- and post-treatment measures. The most useful tool, however, for identification of the rapists' cognitions and post treatment change, was the in-group focus on the life story exercises. Following initial psychoeducational sessions that enabled the offenders to understand the concept of underlying thinking patterns the concepts were applied to generalised ways of behaving. Later in the offence process module-specific application to offence-related cognitions allowed more individualised identification of underlying cognitions or implicit theories. A range of experiential activities and tasks were used to develop the rapist's understanding of both generalised and offence specific interrelationships between values, attitudes, beliefs, thoughts, feelings, and behaviours. Of greatest value in assessing change was offenders' participation in these exercises and their demonstration of understanding about their own cognitions throughout the programme but especially in the relapse prevention and healthy lifestyles module.

Motivation to engage in treatment is always difficult and the majority of the rapists we assessed were only interested in being included in the group because the Parole Board had directed them to treatment. We had the same expectations that we had for any group; essentially the first stage of treatment is about motivating offenders to perceive treatment as beneficial and worthwhile. However, as the literature discussed earlier suggested, we found that the rapists were much less motivated than other rapists (Beech et al., 2006a; Polaschek, Ward & Hudson, 1997; Ward et al., 1997b).

Logistics

Consistent with the advice we had been given, we found that the rapist group was more difficult to deliver (discussed below) and on reflection we decided we would start future programmes with smaller numbers than with other groups of mixed offenders. Our rationale for smaller numbers was to facilitate optimum therapeutic effectiveness and group cohesion. In general, therapists delivered two or three sessions a week.

Corrections Victoria normally delivers its sexual offender programmes as rolling groups – that is, new participants can join the group at any time. Our rationale for this group format is that group members who have been in treatment for several months play a vital role in challenging newer group members' cognitive distortions. The rapist group, however, was delivered as a static group because we did not have a pool of rapists we could bring into the group at a later time. Major issues of trust exist with these groups of violent offenders, particularly if new members are brought into the programme and interrupt group cohesion. In fact, we found that even with a static group there was no guarantee they would trust each other by the end of the programme.

Content

The first time we delivered the rapist programme we endeavoured to cover the content we normally covered in our other treatment programmes. There are four core modules in which all offenders recommended for treatment must participate. In addition, there are tailored modules – these are recommended on an as-needs basis. The core modules are: Commencement Module; Offence Process; Victim Empathy; and Relapse Prevention and Healthy Lifestyle. The additional modules are: Fantasy Reconditioning; Affect Management; Intimacy and Social Competence; and Maintaining Change.

To guide our cognitive intervention work – which formed an important thread throughout many of the modules – an implicit theories matrix was developed based on the work of Beech *et al.* (2006a), Polaschek and Gannon (2004) and Polaschek and Ward (2002).

To enable exploration of the implicit theories, the first treatment task involved each participant presenting a life story. It was not our aim to obtain a complete disclosure, but rather to focus on salient aspects to identify an offender's beliefs, origins, and maintaining factors in relation to their offence. Participants were encouraged to explore their own beliefs, attitudes and expectations, and to explicitly clarify the themes observed and identified throughout sessions. Several strategies were used including use of photo-language, exploring relationships using ideals and making "values" posters. Focusing on cognitive content activity based visual tasks was more successful in engaging offenders in the treatment process for sustained periods of time. The group then progressed to making links between the identified salient beliefs, themes labelled "thinking patterns", and to drawing out examples of the thinking patterns preceding their offences.

Consistent with the findings of Beech *et al.* (2006a) participants universally fell into the "dangerous world" implicit theory, which appeared primarily motivated by grievance, anger and resentment towards women. In line with other therapeutic programmes (Beech *et al.* 2006a; Polaschek & King, 2002) we found that group members had high levels of rape-supportive beliefs and victim-blaming attitudes. Additionally, two participants were considered to also present with the "women as unknowable" implicit theory.

As the group progressed we found that we were placing more of an emphasis on offence-related rather than offence-specific content, albeit related to their underlying implicit theories. For example, we focused on everyday interactions to target offenders' beliefs that enacting revenge/retaliation is necessary and justified to maintain power and control over others. Moreover, these rapists had not participated in other prison programmes to teach basic cognitive skills such as problem solving or consequential thinking. Our view at the commencement of the treatment programme was that it would have been valuable for such programmes to be undertaken prior to entry into the treatment programme. We found that offenders had pro-offence cognitions emanating from underlying implicit theories related to their generalised behaviour such as their antisocial attitudes and hostility that interfered with their motivation to engage in sexual offender treatment. We therefore found that we were not able to commence with the offence process work until we had devoted a great deal more time to readiness for change therapy. None of the rapists exhibited "male sex drive as uncontrollable" nor demonstrated deviant sexual arousal that required deviant arousal reconditioning. We also found that although we had rapists who exhibited the "women as sexual beings" implicit theory, their cognitive distortions were related to their antisocial attitudes and beliefs about women and revenge motives rather than to deviant sexual arousal. This is different from other treatment programmes (e.g., Beech *et al.*, 2006a) with offenders who presented with sexually and/or sadistic deviant fantasies and arousal. It is probable that we had a skewed sample of rapists in that they were predominantly in "consenting" sexual relationships prior to committing rape.

The focus on cognitive aspects continued in the affect regulation module. There is increasing support for the idea of distress tolerance, a key concept in dialectical behaviour therapy, a pioneering therapy designed for clients who have been diagnosed with borderline personality disorder (Linehan, 1993). Linehan comments that "Pain and distress are part of life; they cannot be avoided or removed" (p. 147). Clients are not encouraged to try to "think positively" about situations that elicit negative affect, but to recognise it for what it is and keep it in proportion. This is a very pragmatic approach, and it is reminiscent of the comments made by Gross (1998), about not over-regulating negative emotions. Whilst a key skill taught in this module is that of emotion management via cognitive processes, group members are introduced to other mood-management strategies, especially distress tolerance, to ensure that they have a wide range of skills at their disposal. Likewise, the intimacy and relationships module involved a range of activity, role-play and discussion to elicit relevant cognitions related to intimacy relationships and sexuality. Each of these was processed in terms of the importance of practising thinking patterns that will create better or more manageable emotional experiences.

There is considerable literature describing the early experiences of sexual offenders, and the relationship between these experiences and later sexual offending. Likewise, the work of Linehan (1993) has some distinct parallels with sexual offending. Linehan construes borderline personality disorder primarily as a disorder of emotional regulation. Linehan makes clear links between early experiences that emanate from childhood or adolescence, and subsequent problems in emotion regulation. Specifically, family disruption, divorce, antisocial influences, physical and sexual abuse, school and vocational failure, poor parenting, and substance abuse, characterise these offenders' lives. We suggest that the same pattern described by Linehan may exist for men who go on to sexually offend – as children their learning experiences shape their approach towards, and skills in, emotion regulation. Further support for the idea comes from literature on schemas and proposed links between schemas and the experience of emotion, and links the idea of cognitive schema with emotion (e.g. Beck, 1976; Winter & Kuiper, 1997; Young, 1999). Typically, these offenders display disproportionately intense emotions that impact on their cognitive processes – as they are unable to tolerate distress their maladaptive schemas dominate and they exhibit emotional and behavioural dysregulation (Eccleston & Sorbello, 2006).

On this basis we integrated several dialectical behaviour therapy practices into the treatment programme. For example, interpersonal effectiveness skills training was integrated into the intimacy and social competence module. This focused on learning to communicate one's needs effectively, and dealing with interpersonal conflict. Likewise exercises of distress tolerance skills and learning how to reduce emotional vulnerability and decreasing emotional suffering were included in the affect regulation module. The exercises we used followed Linehan's dialectical behaviour therapy models and are sufficiently robust to enable focus on offence specific cognitions without specific adaptation to sexual offender samples.

Cognitive-Driven Process Issues

One of the initial problems we had with the rapist group was that we had to modify the group rules and be more flexible about tolerating their antisocial cognitions and behaviour. We usually operate according to a "three strikes and you're out rule" which means that if an offender fails to attend, is disruptive or leaves a session on more than three occasions they are required to leave the group. However, if we had applied this rule to the rapist programme we would have lost all our group members within the first two days! We found that when offenders were challenged about their offence-supportive cognitions, such as their attitudes towards women they were constantly storming out of sessions and then coming back. We were forced to change the rules to be more accommodating of their hostility and impulsivity to ensure we retained group members in a static group. We also found that we needed to spend more time involved in individual work outside of the group to teach the offenders strategies to deal with being in group. One of the strengths in persevering with this approach is that the issues are dealt with by the group who are familiar with each other's history and how each offender behaves.

Another process issue we encountered was that the group was more expressive than mixed groups in terms of demonstrating their anger and resistance to treatment. Group members were less tolerant to group rules that impacted on the time we were able to spend on content. Normally the group and therapists within the first part of the initial group session developed the group rules. However, it took three sessions with the rapist group before we managed to reach agreement on the group rules. The group was resistant to boundaries, even those suggested by other group members and were argumentative. They frequently left the group session after disagreeing with each other and often returned minutes later – their impulsivity and lack of control was constant.

Compared to our groups with child sexual abusers, rapists have much less of a need for affiliation, and were less compliant and motivated towards treatment. Child sexual abusers often appeared more needing of other people's approval, wanting to be part of the group, and wanting to be perceived to be participating. One of the reasons we had difficulty with the rapist group was that when they banded together they banded very tightly, but when one of them fell out of line, there was no negotiation, no problem solving capacity, and no understanding of someone else's point of view. However, when they were challenged the attitude they expressed was typically, "I don't give a shit whether you like what I say or not, that's the way it is". We found that when an offender could not win their argument they would elect to leave the group session and it was difficult to persuade them to return without "losing face" in front of other group members. We spent a great deal of time outside of group doing individual work trying to really coax them back into the group and explaining the benefits of them returning to the group.

Once the rapist group was established we found that they were much more cohesive than any other group we had experienced. There was a real sense of "mateship" amongst group members and that extended to their distortions to a large degree more so than we had experienced with mixed groups. For example, offenders colluded with each other in terms of supporting each other's offence-supportive cognitions and attitudes towards women in general. In general, the rapists were much more difficult to break down, and much more vocal about challenging the therapists if they perceived that the therapists were being particularly hard on an individual in the group. The group superficially bonded against a common enemy, in this case the therapists.

Therapists' Reflections on Reframing Cognitive Distortions

In general, delivering a rapist group is much harder for the therapists and more confronting due to the constant hostility, impulsivity and resistance to changing their antisocial cognitions. Despite the warnings from our colleagues about the difficulties delivering a pure rapist group, we have commenced our second group. The therapists entered the new group with a different mind-set and revised expectations of what they can expect to achieve. In the first group the therapists experienced anxiety early in the programme because they were spending so much time dealing with process issues they were unable to make progress with the content and effectively challenging cognitive distortions. The impact on the therapists was that they were feeling extremely stressed. About four weeks into the programme they had only been able to cover three days of content material and felt they were not achieving anything. As much as we try to move therapists away from "cook book" manuals to using their therapeutic skills, they nonetheless still have an ingrained sense that "this is week 10 and I should be up to session 20". The therapists could not achieve this in the rapist programme and had to move through content more slowly due to process issues. One key lesson we learned was that any progress is good progress – this includes being able to keep everyone in a room for a session given their extreme impulsivity and volatile behaviour.

One of the advantages we found delivering the rapist group was that it gave us the capacity to set up the treatment programme and focus on issues that were pertinent to their kind of offending. The major disadvantage was that we spent so much time on process issues than we did with any other group and much less time on content. We learned, however, to turn this around and view it as a therapeutic advantage. The difficulties we encountered with process issues such as hostility, impulsivity, and resistance to treatment reflect the way these men operate in the world and are real issues that need to be managed.

Each time we have delivered the programme we have ensured that we have a gender mix of group facilitators. We paired female therapists with male therapists who had either a physically imposing presence and/or an authoritarian style. The male therapists found that they took on a protective role. There was a pronounced degree of projection onto the female therapists in that they were seen to represent everything bad in women. Rapists' attitudes towards the female therapists were derogatory and hostile consistent with their implicit theories "world is a dangerous place", "women as unknowable" and "women as sexual beings".

In summary, the rapists in our group developed some skills to prevent themselves reoffending but their attitudes and cognitive distortions towards women and their acceptance of interpersonal violence were intractable and extremely resistant to change. As therapists we traditionally measure change for treatment by looking for change in cognitions, that is, internal control. For the rapist group it is quite different. They will happily state that "women are scum but I'm not going to rape anymore, because. . . ". In essence, rapists' cognitions are different and more closely resemble those of generic violent offenders rather than the cognitions displayed by child sexual abusers, exhibitionists, or child internet pornographers. Consistent with other therapists (Beech *et al.*, 2006a; Polaschek & Ward, 2002) we found that rapists have distinct implicit theories or schemas that underlie their cognitive distortions about women – these directly impact on their offending behaviour. We also learned that we had to deal differently with the issues the rapists brought to group. Prior to challenging their offence-supportive cognitions we had to teach them how to problem solve and how to negotiate. By the end of the programme the therapists felt they had achieved some gains with the men, but it was more difficult for them to identify what the changes actually were. We hope that we can further fine-tune our work, especially our work regarding entrenched pro offending cognition, to achieve more gains from our next rapist-specific treatment endeavour.

CONCLUSIONS

Our experience with the rapist group challenges the content we apply in our traditional sexual offender programmes that typically contain one or two rapists mixed with child sexual abusers. Although a pure rapist group is more difficult to process therapeutically, by mixing rapists in with other sexual offenders we may not be addressing their treatment needs effectively. Greater attention must be paid to rapists' implicit theories such as "women are sexual objects" to effectively challenge their extreme distrust of women and acceptance of interpersonal violence. Moreover, in a mixed group rapists go through a structured treatment programme that is focused on the needs of child sexual abusers and other sexual offenders. They are not spending the additional time needed on problem solving, and maintaining their behaviour, impulsivity, and antisocial attitudes. Ward *et al.* (1997b) suggested that there may be other treatment interventions to address impulsivity in the wider offender rehabilitation field that could be used with rapists (e.g., Serin & Kuriychuk, 1994). Rapists may also benefit from more motivational pre-treatment interventions such as those developed in the drug and alcohol field to engage them in treatment programmes. Alternatively, there may be some benefit to including more focused cognitive problem solving components within offence specific treatment programmes to enable greater connection between more generalised underlying cognitions or implicit theories and offence-related behaviours. Given the difficulty experienced by the participants in this group in identifying their offence-related cognitions such an extended model may well enhance the treatment process. In addition, one must consider that the underlying cognitions that facilitate offending are the exact implicit theories that also facilitate other antisocial and impulsive behaviours observed in this population.

The differences we experienced, particularly in content and process issues, were significant enough to make us really review what we do with rapists in mixed groups. Therapists need to change their mind-set and expectations of what they can successfully achieve in sessions. A great deal more emphasis needs to be placed on teaching rapists skills to manage their impulsivity, poor problem solving and relationship problems. In summary, the focus of interventions should shift away from individual's rationalisations, minimisations and denial, and concentrate on addressing aspects of self-identify such as beliefs, schemas, and implicit theories. Treatment should therefore concentrate on cognitive skills, use of aggression, conflict resolution, problem solving, and more focus on lifestyle and peer standards and relationship skills.

Delivering the rapist group also leaves us with concerns about the extent to which we meet the needs of rapists in mixed sexual offender groups, and particularly community based treatment programmes. There is a much younger cohort of high-risk rapists in our community based group programmes than in prison. The next phase would be to develop a community based treatment programme for rapists because currently we anticipate that their needs are not being met in a mixed group. Rapists would benefit from participating in a joint violence/sexual offender programme given they display some cognitive similarities with violent men. There would of course be logistical difficulties involved in maintaining security if protection and mainstream prisoners were mixed. In an ideal world violence and sexual offender programmes would be modular and when rapists progress to a particular part for violence against women offenders from the pure violence and the sex-offender violence would be in a group together. In this brave new world, having reached this advanced stage of treatment, offenders should have acquired enough skills to be able to sit in a room together, but this would require months of therapy.

REFERENCES

Alder, C. (1984). The convicted rapist. *Criminal Justice and Behavior*, **11**, 157–77.

Andrews, D. A. & Bonta, J. (1998). *The psychology of criminal conduct* (2nd edn). Cincinnati, OH: Anderson Publishing Co.

Anechiarico, B. (1998). A closer look at sex offender character pathology and relapse prevention: An integrative approach. *International Journal of Offender Therapy and Comparative Criminology*, **42**, 16–26.

Barbaree, H. E. (1991). Denial and minimization among sex offenders: Assessment and treatment outcomes. *Forum on Corrections Research*, **3**, 30–3.

Barbaree, H. E., Seto, M., Serin, R. C. *et al.* (1994). Comparisons between sexual and non-sexual rapist subtypes: sexual arousal to rape, offence precursors, and offence characteristics. *Criminal Justice and Behavior*, **21**, 95–114.

Beck, A. T. (1976). *Cognitive Therapy and the Emotional Disorders*. New York: International Universities Press.

Beck, A. T. (1999). *Prisoners of Hate: The Cognitive Basis of Anger, Hostility and Violence*. New York: HarperCollins.

Beech, A. R. & Fordham, A. S. (1997). Therapeutic climate of sex offender treatment programmes. *Sexual Abuse: A Journal of Research and Treatment*, **9**, 219–37.

Beech, A. R. & Hamilton-Giachritsis, C. E. (2005). Relationship between therapeutic climate and treatment outcome in a group-based sexual offender programme. *Sexual Abuse: A Journal of Research and Treatment*, **17**, 127–40.

Beech, A. R. & Mann, R. (2002). Recent developments in the assessment and treatment of sexual offenders. In J. McGuire (ed.), *Offender Rehabilitation and Treatment: Effective Programmes and Policies to Reduce Re-offending* (pp. 259–88). Chichester: Wiley.

Beech, A., Oliver, C., Fisher, D. & Beckett, R. C. (2006a). *STEP 4: The Sex Offender Treatment Programme in prison: Addressing the needs of rapists and sexual murderers*. Birmingham: University of Birmingham. Available electronically from www.hmprisonservice.gov.uk/assets/documents/100013DBStep_4_SOTP_report_2005.pdf.

Beech, A. R., Ward, T. & Fisher, D. (2006b). The identification of sexual and violent motivations in men who assault women: implications for treatment. *Journal of Interpersonal Violence*, **21**, 1635–53.

Beyko, M. J. & Wong, S. C. P. (2005). Predictors of treatment attrition as indicators for program improvement not offender shortcomings: A study of sex offender treatment attrition. *Sexual Abuse: A Journal of Research and Treatment*, **17**, 375–89.

Birgden, A. & Vincent, F. (2000). Maximising therapeutic effects in treating sexual offenders in the Australian correctional system. *Behavioural Sciences and The Law*, **18**, 479–88.

Blanchard, G. T., (1995). *The Difficult Connection: The Therapeutic Relationship in Sex Offender Treatment*. Brandon, VT: Safer Society Press.

Brown, S. J. (2005). *Sex Offender Treatment Programmes*. Cullompton, Devon: Willan.

Bumby, K. M. (1996). Assessing the cognitive distortions of child molesters and rapists: Development and validation of the MOLEST and RAPE scales. *Sexual Abuse: A Journal of Research and Treatment*, **8**, 37–54.

Burt, M. (1980). Cultural myths and support for rape. *Journal of Personality and Social Psychology*, **39**, 217–30.

Davis, M. H. (1983). Measuring individual differences in empathy: Evidence for a multidimensional approach. *Journal of Personality and Social Psychology*, **44**, 113–26.

Drieschner, K. & Lange, A. (1999). A review of cognitive factors in the etiology of rape: Theories, empirical studies, and implications. *Clinical Psychology Review*, **19**, 57–77.

Eccleston, L. & Sorbello, L. (2006). A structured intervention for prisoners who are at risk of self harm. In G. E. Dear (ed.). *Preventing Suicide and Other Self-harm in Prison* (pp. 74–87). Basingstoke: Palgrave Macmillan.

Eckhardt, C. I. & Dye, M. L. (2000). The cognitive characteristics of martially violent men: Theory and evidence. *Cognitive Theory and Research*, **24**, 139–58.

Feelgood, S., Cortoni, F. & Thompson, A. (2005). Sexual coping, general coping and cognitive distortions in incarcerated rapists and child molesters. *Journal of Sexual Aggression*, **11**, 157–70.

Fernandez, Y. M. & Marshall, W. L. (2003). Victim empathy, social self-esteem, and psychopathy in rapists. *Sexual Abuse: A Journal of Research and Treatment*, **15**, 11–26.

Finkelhor, D. (1984). *Child Sexual Abuse: New Theory and Research*. New York: Free Press.

Gannon, T. A., Polaschek, D. L. L. & Ward, T. (2005). Social cognition and sexual offenders. In M. McMurran & J. McGuire (eds), *Social Problem Solving and Offender: Evidence, Evaluation and Evolution* (pp. 223–47). Chichester: Wiley.

Gannon, T. A. & Ward, T. (in press). Rape: psychopathology and theory. In D. R. Laws & W. O'Donohue. *Sexual Deviance: Theory, Assessment, and Treatment* (2nd edn). New York: Guilford Press.

Gross, J. J. (1998) The emerging field of emotional regulation: an integrative review. *Review of General Psychology*, **2**, 271–99.

Hall, G. C. N. (1995). Sexual offender recidivism revisited: A meta-analysis of recent treatment studies. *Journal of Consulting and Clinical Psychology*, **63**, 802–9.

Hall, G. C. N. (1996). *Theory Based Assessment, Treatment and Prevention of Sexual Aggression*. Oxford: Oxford University Press.

Hall, G. C. N. & Hirschman, R. (1990). Toward a theory of sexual aggression: A quadripartite model. *Journal of Consulting and Clinical Psychology*, **59**, 662–9.

Hanson, R. K., Gordon, A. J. R., Marques, J. K. *et al.* (2002). First report of the collaborative outcome-data project on the effectiveness of psychological treatment for sex offenders. *Sexual Abuse: A Journal of Research and Treatment*, **14**, 169–94.

Harkins, L. & Beech, A.R. (2007). Measurement of the effectiveness of sex offender treatment. *Aggression and Violent Behavior*, **12**, 36–44.

Harkins, L. & Beech, A. R. (in press). Examining the impact of mixing child molesters and rapists in group-based cognitive behavioural treatment for sexual offenders. *International Journal of Offender Therapy and Comparative Psychology*.

Hildebrand, M., De Ruiter, C. & De Vogel, V. (2004). Psychopathy and sexual deviance in treated rapists: Association with sexual and nonsexual recidivism. *Sexual Abuse: A Journal of Research and Treatment*, **16**, 1–24.

Hudson, S. M., Marshall, W. L., Wales, D. *et al.* (1993). Emotional recognition of sex offenders. *Annals of Sex Research*, **6**, 199–211.

Jennings, J. L. & Sawyer, S. (2003). Principles and techniques for maximizing the effectiveness of group therapy with sex offenders. *Sexual Abuse: A Journal of Research and Treatment*, **15**, 251–67.

Johnston, L. & Ward, T. (1996). Social cognition and sexual offending. *Sexual Abuse: A Journal of Research and Treatment*, **8**, 55–80.

Johnston, P., Hudson, S. M. & Marshall, W. L. (1992). The effects of masturbatory reconditioning with nonfamilial child molesters. *Behaviour Research and Therapy*, **30**, 559–61.

Kear-Colwell, J. & Pollack, P. (1997). Motivation or confrontation: which approach to the child sex offender? *Criminal Justice and Behavior*, **24**, 20–33.

Kenworthy, T., Adams, C. E., Bilby, C. *et al.* (2004). Psychological interventions for those who have sexually offended or are at risk of offending. *Cochrane Database of Systematic Reviews*. Issue 4. Art. No.: CD004858. DOI: 10.1002/ 14651858. CD004858.

Knight, R. A. & Prentky, R. A. (1990). Classifying sexual offenders: the development and corroboration of taxonomic models. In W. L. Marshall, D. R. Laws & H. E. Barbaree (eds), *Handbook of Sexual Assault: Issues, Theories and Treatment of the Offender* (pp. 23–53). New York: Plenum.

Linehan, M. M. (1993). *Cognitive-behavioral Treatment of Borderline Personality Disorder.* New York: Guilford Press.

Lösel, F. & Schmucker, M. (2005). The effectiveness of treatment for sexual offenders: A comprehensive meta-analysis. *Journal of Experimental Criminology, 1,* 117–146.

Malamuth, N. M. & Brown, L. M. (1994). Sexually aggressive men's perceptions of women's communications: Testing three explanations. *Journal of Personality and Social Psychology,* **67,** 699–712.

Mann, R. (2004). Innovations in sex offender treatment. *Journal of Sexual Aggression,* **10,** 141–52.

Mann, R. & Beech, A. R. (2003). Cognitive distortions, schemas and implicit theories. In T. Ward, D. R. Laws & S. M. Hudson (eds), *Theoretical Issues and Controversies in Sexual Deviance* (pp. 135–53). London: Sage.

Mann, R. & Hollin, C. R. (2001, November). *Schemas: a model for understanding cognition in sexual offending.* Paper presented at the 20th Annual Research and Treatment Conference, Association for the Treatment of Sexual Abusers, San Antonio, TX.

Marques, J., Day, D., Nelsen, C. & West, M. (1994). Effects of cognitive-behavioural treatment on sex offender recidivism. *Criminal Justice and Behavior,* **21,** 28–54.

Marshall, W. L. (1993). A revised approach to the treatment of men who sexually assault adult females. In G. C. N. Hall, R. Hirschman, J. R. Graham & M. S. Zaragoza (eds), *Sexual Aggression: Issues in Etiology, Assessment, and Treatment* (pp. 143–65). Washington, DC: Taylor & Francis.

Marshall, W. L. (1996). Assessment, treatment, and theorizing about sex offenders. *Criminal Justice and Behavior,* **23,** 162–99.

Marshall, W. L. (2004). Adult sexual offenders against women. In C. R. Hollin (ed.), *The Essential Handbook of Offender Assessment and Treatment* (pp. 147–62). Chichester: Wiley.

Marshall, W. L. & Barbaree, H. E. (1991). An integrated theory of the etiology of sexual offending. In W. L. Marshall, D. R. Laws & H. E. Barbaree (eds), *Handbook of Sexual Assault: Issues, Theories and Treatment of the Offender* (pp. 257–75). New York: Plenum.

Marshall, W. L., Eccles, A. & Barbaree, H. E. (1993). A three tiered approach to the rehabilitation of incarcerated sex offenders. *Behavioral Sciences and the Law,* **11,** 441–55.

Marshall, W. L. & Fernandez, Y. M., (2000). Phallometric testing with sexual offenders: limits to its value. *Clinical Psychology Review,* **20,** 807–22.

Marshall, W. L., Fernandez, Y. M., Serran, G. A. *et al.* (2003). Process issues in the treatment of sexual offenders: a review of relevant literature. *Aggression and Violent Behavior,* **8,** 205–34.

Marshall, W. L., Hudson, S. M., Jones, R. & Fernandez, Y. M. (1995). Empathy in sex offenders. *Clinical Psychology Review,* **15,** 99–113.

Marshall, W. L. & Laws, D. R., (2003). A brief history of behavioral and cognitive behavioral approaches to sexual offender treatment: Part 2. The modern era. *Sexual Abuse: A Journal of Research and Treatment,* **15,** 93–120.

Marshall, W. L & Serran, G. A. (2004). The role of the therapist in offender treatment. *Psychology, Crime and Law,* **10,** 309–20.

Maruna, S. & Mann, R. E. (2006). A fundamental attribution error? Rethinking cognitive distortions. *Legal and Criminological Psychology,* **11,** 155–77.

Marx, B. P., Miranda, J. & Meyerson, L. A. (1999). Cognitive-behavioral treatment for rapists: can we do better? *Clinical Psychology Review,* **19,** 875–94.

McGrath, R. J., Cumming, G., Livingston, J. A. & Hoke, S. E. (2003). Outcome of a treatment program for adult sex offenders. *Journal of Interpersonal Violence,* **18,** 3–17.

Milner, R. J. & Webster, S. D. (2005). Identifying schemas in child molesters, rapists, and violent offenders. *Sexual Abuse: A Journal of Research and Treatment,* **17,** 425–39.

Moore, D., Bergman, B. & Knox, P. (1999). Predictors of sex offender treatment completion. *Journal of Child Sexual Abuse,* **7,** 73–88.

Nichols, H. R. & Molinder, I. (1984). *Multiphasic Sex Inventory Manual.* Available from Nichols and Molinder, 437 Bowes Drive, Tacoma, WA. 98466, USA.

Pithers, W. D. (1993). Treatment of rapists: Reinterpretation of early outcome data and exploratory constructs to enhance therapeutic efficacy. In G. C. N. Hall, R. Hirschman,

J. R. Graham & M. S. Zaragoza (eds), *Sexual Aggression: Issues in Etiology, Assessment, and Treatment* (pp. 167–96). Washington: Taylor & Francis.

Polaschek, D. L. L. & Gannon, T. A., (2004). The implicit theories of rapists: What convicted offenders tell us. *Sexual Abuse: A Journal of Research and Treatment*, **16**, 299–314.

Polaschek, D. L. L. & King, L. L. (2002). Rehabilitating rapists: reconsidering the issues. *Australian Psychologist*, **37**, 215–21.

Polaschek, D. L. L. & Ward, T. (2002). The implicit theories of potential rapists: What our questionnaires tell us. *Aggression and Violent Behavior*, **7**, 385–406.

Polaschek, D. L. L., Ward, T. & Hudson, S. M. (1997). Rape and rapists: Theory and treatment. *Clinical Psychology Review*, **17**, 117–144.

Quinsey, V. L., Harris, G. T., Rice, M. E. & Cormier, C. A. (2006). *Violent Offenders: Appraising and managing risk* (2nd edn). Washington: American Psychological Association.

Rogers, R., (1988). Introduction. In R. Rogers (ed.), *Clinical Assessment of Malingering and Deception* (pp. 1–9). New York: Guilford Press.

Serin, R. C. & Kuriychuk, M. (1994). Social and cognitive processing deficits in violent offenders: Implications for treatment. *International Journal of Law and Psychiatry*, **17**, 431–41.

Thornton, D. (2002). Constructing and testing a framework for dynamic risk assessment. *Sexual Abuse: A Journal of Research and Treatment*, **14**, 139–53.

Thornton, D., Mann, R. E. & Williams, F. M. S. (2000). *Therapeutic style in sex offender treatment*. Available from Offending Behaviour Programmes Unit, HM Prison Service, Abell House, John Islip St, London, SW1P 4LH.

Ward, T. (2000). Sexual offenders' cognitive distortions as implicit theories. *Aggression and Violent Behavior*, **5**, 491–507.

Ward, T., Day, A., Howells, K. & Birgden, A. (2004). The multifactor offender readiness model. *Aggression and Violent Behavior*, **9**, 645–73.

Ward, T., Hudson, S. M., Johnston, L. & Marshall, W. L. (1997a). Cognitive distortions in sex offenders: An integrative review. *Clinical Psychology Review*, **17**, 479–507.

Ward, T. & Keenan, T. (1999). Child molesters' implicit theories. *Journal of Interpersonal Violence*, **14**, 821–38.

Ward, T., McCormack, J., Hudson, S. M. & Polaschek, D., (1997b). Rape: assessment and treatment. In D. R. Laws & W. T. O'Donohue (eds). *Sexual Deviance: Theory, Assessment and Treatment* (pp. 356–93). New York: Guilford Press.

Ward, T. & Seigert, R. (2002). Toward a comprehensive theory of child sexual abuse: a theory knitting perspective. *Psychology, Crime and Law*, **8**, 319–51.

Winter, K. A. & Kuiper, N. A. (1997). Individual differences in the experience of emotions. *Clinical Psychology Review*, **17**, 791–821.

Young, J. E. (1999) *Cognitive Therapy for Personality Disorders: A Schema Focused Approach* (3rd edn). Sarasota: Professional Resource Press.

PART II

VIOLENT OFFENDERS

Chapter 8

THEORETICAL EXPLANATIONS OF AGGRESSION AND VIOLENCE

Marc A. Sestir

University of North Carolina at Chapel Hill, USA

Bruce D. Bartholow

University of Missouri at Columbia, USA

Virtually all creatures great and small have shown an inclination to aggress; that aggression is a central and innate impulse has never been in question. What appears to separate human beings from most other species in the realm of aggressive behaviour is what separates us in most other domains as well: the complexity and ubiquity of our higher cognitive abilities. We seem as a species uniquely able to use higher mental processes to mediate and subvert even our most primal impulses, often in the service of superordinate goals for self-presentation or expression. Only a human being could surround itself with food and choose to resist the instinct to eat to the point of severe malnutrition or death, or live a life of celibacy despite the presence of gnawing sexual urges. Aggression is no exception to this rule, either. While the instinct to aggress is clearly a part of the human character, a good deal of individuals live peaceful lives free from acts of extreme aggression or violence. And some individuals – characterised by strong aggressive impulses – eventually abandon a life of violence to become wholly peaceful. Thus, individuals are capable of reducing or eliminating the effects of aggressive impulses on their behaviours – and the use of cognitive resources as a mediator appears to often be the mechanism by which they do so.

On the other hand, however, our cognitive processes can also be a mechanism by which aggressive tendencies are strengthened and given root. People who grow up in a more violent environment tend to come to see the world as a more hostile place and violence itself as a currency for conflict resolution (Hughes & Hasbrouck, 1996; Lochman & Dodge, 1994). The internalisations of beliefs about a hostile world and the development and justification of behavioural scripts calling for swift and

Aggressive Offenders' Cognition: Theory, Research and Practice. Edited by T. A. Gannon, T. Ward, A. R. Beech and D. Fisher. © 2007 John Wiley & Sons, Ltd.

violent actions can multiply the frequency and intensity of aggressive acts and even result in the chronic suppression of more pro-social instincts (Anderson & Bushman, 2002).

Aggression is generally defined as behaviour proposed to harm an individual, where the individual seeks to evade that harm (see Anderson & Bushman, 2001). Only when aggression departs the mind and enters the fists (so to speak) does it become a societal problem and a more extreme form of aggression commonly described as "violence" (Anderson & Bushman, 2001). This chapter is nearly exclusively focused on aggressive cognitions, but does so in the interest of establishing a primary mediator between the aggressive instincts that everyone possesses and the violent behaviour that a minority exhibits.

The aim of this chapter is to provide an overview of recent theory and research examining how human aggression can be shaped by the ways in which our minds perceive, process, store, and retrieve information. In other words, we propose that to fully understand the nature of human aggression and violence, we must understand how it functions at the level of cognition. First, we will briefly examine early theoretical conceptualisations of aggression and violence, highlighting the initial absence of cognitive factors. Then, we will evaluate current theoretical conceptualisations that focus only on individual cognitive factors related to aggressive behaviour. Following this, we will move on to discuss and evaluate current multifactorial theories incorporating cognition to explain aggressive acts. Where possible, we will examine some of the research investigating each theory, in order to make conclusions about each theory's empirical validity. We will also evaluate the clinical utility and application of each individual theory. Finally, after evaluating these theories, we will attempt to draw together core conclusions about current knowledge in this arena and make some suggestions for future work.

EARLY THEORETICAL CONCEPTUALISATIONS

Unsurprisingly for such a universal and problematic tendency, theorists from a variety of backgrounds have continually devised and revised theories of the mechanisms underlying aggression and violence. Of course, most early theories ignored or gave short shrift to the role of cognition in aggression, focusing instead on simple cause-and-effect mechanisms, as seen in catharsis theory (Freud, 1939) and the frustration-aggression hypothesis (Dollard *et al.*, 1939). These theories, of course, neglected many potential sources of aggression in their overly simplistic explanations; not least among these was the role of cognition. Typical early theories were automatic, viewing aggression as beyond the conscious control of the individual.

However, much of the recent theory and research in aggression stems from the conception that aggression, while usually instinctual in nature, is largely mediated by cognition (Bartholow, Sestir & Davis, 2005; Dodge, 1986). Our cognitions serve as a mediator between our aggressive instincts and their manifestation in behaviour, and, more importantly, shape our perceptions of the environment around us and the behaviours we see as appropriate responses (Huesmann, 1988).

Most modern theories of aggression that involve cognition do not exclude other psychological domains: affect, arousal, motivation and genetics often play an explicit interactive role with cognitive factors. For the purposes of this chapter, however, review of noncognitive factors will be brief in favour of a more in-depth treatment of cognitive mechanisms. In addition, there is a significant amount of overlap between the various modern theories of aggression, but there are generally some philosophical or semantic differences between even the most seemingly identical theories, and most individual research is conducted under the rubric of one specific theory. As such, research results will be discussed whenever possible within the framework of the theory from which they were hypothesised.

CURRENT THEORETICAL CONCEPTUALISATIONS

Most modern theories of aggression tend to take one of two forms: either addressing the origins of aggression within a single psychological domain, such as associative networks or media influence, or attempting to provide an omnibus model to explain all potential instances of aggressive behaviour. For simplicity's sake, this chapter will divide the discussion of relevant theories into those two categories, first discussing single-domain, then unitary models of the cognitive bases of aggression.

Single-Factor Theories

Script Theory

Script theory (Huesmann, 1988, 1998), also referred to as the social-cognitive information-processing model (not to be confused with the theory of the same name discussed later), focuses on the roles of cognitive scripts in shaping behaviour. Scripts are sequences of behaviours and their expected outcomes; an example would be a typical pattern of interaction with a waitress or cashier, which tends to have the same basic elements across time and situations. As in these everyday situations, aggressive scripts typically involve a narrow range of behaviours and are frequently enacted without conscious thought. An aggressive person typically has more aggressive scripts and these scripts are typically more accessible across a wider variety of situations, meaning that an aggressive behaviour will be more likely to be generated as an appropriate response (Huesmann & Eron, 1989; Huesmann & Reynolds, 2001).

In addition to describing the nature of cognitive scripts, script theory also seeks to establish how they are created and what predicts their use. It is posited that scripts are acquired through direct and indirect social learning processes (e.g., Bandura, 1973), that is, through reinforcement and punishment of our own behaviour, or observation of the same effects on the behaviour of others. If we see others succeed through aggression, we are likely to encode aggressive behaviours as effective responses to the perceived provocations of others.

Of course, even if a hostile script is encoded and accessible, it may not be used if it is viewed as unacceptable behaviour. This is largely shaped by normative beliefs, which are cognitive schemas about the typicality and appropriateness of a given behaviour. Normative beliefs also shape the scripts that are activated when others defy them; if we believe honking in traffic is rude, a hostile schema will most likely be activated when another does so to us (Huesmann & Guerra, 1997). If, at a formative age, we see high levels of hostility or aggression in the environment around us, we tend to view aggression as a more normal response and develop lower inhibitions toward aggressive behaviour in general (Shahinfar, Kupersmidt & Matza, 2001).

As mentioned above, the acquisition of scripts appears to primarily occur during childhood. It appears that, although a multitude of factors can cause any given instance of aggression, childhood aggression levels both remain fairly stable through adulthood and are the single biggest predictor of adult aggression (Huesmann *et al.*, 1984). Although the precise critical period for acquisition of scripts varies from person to person, recent research indicates that it lies somewhere between the ages of six and nine (Huesmann *et al.*, 1984). Huesmann and Guerra (1997), for example, found that whereas aggression-promoting beliefs were correlated with aggressive behaviour in both first- and fourth-grade students, the beliefs of first-graders did not predict later aggressive behaviour and tended to vary from year to year, whereas the beliefs of fourth-graders did predict aggressive behaviour and did not tend to vary. A similar pattern has been found for aggressive fantasies (Huesmann *et al.*, 1998). The indication, then, is that while younger children are capable of generating beliefs from their own behaviour, those beliefs do not begin to become consistent predictors of behaviour until later in childhood.

Script theory, then, provides an interesting framework for a mechanism of violent behaviour acquisition; however, from a more applied standpoint it is likely too broad and vague to facilitate successful rehabilitation. The concept of scripts is by definition an exceedingly open-ended one: virtually any conceivable behavioural sequence could be viewed as a script. Coupled with the idiosyncratic nature of each individual's repertoire of scripts and the variety of potential sources for script acquisition, as well as the theory's lack of an explicit mechanism for altering or eliminating harmful scripts, understanding and altering the script set of a specific violent offender would likely be incredibly time-consuming and highly customised. However, script theory has been incorporated into more comprehensive theories, discussed later in the chapter, in which it may prove to be more useful.

Cultivation Theory

Cultivation theory (Gerbner *et al.*, 2002; Shrum, Burroughs & Rindfleisch, 2004) is focused on media violence exposure as a cause of a subset of aggressive behaviour. According to cultivation theory, media presents an image of the world that is systematically different from the world as it actually exists. This is particularly true with regards to exciting or extreme events or individuals; movies and television depict a world of disproportionate wealth and violence, with a disproportionate number of lawyers, police officers, and physically attractive people (Lichter, Lichter & Rothman, 1994). This is, by itself, relatively meaningless from a theoretical standpoint, but cultivation theory also holds that as individuals take in media over time, they tend to internalise the characteristics of the media and apply them to the real world, developing "values, attitudes, beliefs, and perceptions that are consistent with the world as it is portrayed. . . " (Shrum, Burroughs & Rindfleisch, 2004, p. 179). In other words, we are what we consume, symbolically converting what we see depicted in the media into hypotheses about the reality in which we live.

However, cultivation theory does not hold that frequent media consumers are mere passive sponges that allow their attitudes and beliefs to be twisted and altered at the whim of whatever television show or movie they happen to be watching. Instead of the traits of media reality changing attitudes, most theory proponents believe it reinforces existing attitudes and makes them more chronically accessible (Shrum, 1999). Since aggression is a universal tendency, this affects everyone to some degree, although those already high in trait aggression will probably see the greatest change in behaviour.

Chronic accessibility implies that cultivated attitudes are more heuristically available (Shrum, 1996) and can be overridden or ignored when more elaboration takes place; that is, the attitudes reinforced by cultivation are likely to "spring to mind" automatically, but their influence can be negated by a bit of rumination if the actor has the time or motivation.

Cultivation theory can apply to virtually anything depicted in the media, including, of course, aggression. As stated above, both fictional and factual mass media tend to disproportionately focus on acts of extreme violence (Gerbner *et al.*, 1980). Over enough viewings, consumers of such media can develop what has been termed "mean world syndrome" (Gerbner *et al.*, 2002, p. 52). Mean world syndrome essentially can be deconstructed into two cognitive components. First, repeated exposure to violent media reinforces and increases the accessibility of pre-existing beliefs that the world is hostile and dangerous. Second, a perception is created that acts of violence are normal and appropriate responses to hostility or conflict. Recall from the social information processing section that this is an analogous effect to that experienced by those who repeatedly witness real-world violence; cultivation theory extends this concept to the viewing of simulated violence.

In terms of its direct relevance to the study of aggression, cultivation theory offers a relatively simplistic mechanism for the impact of the media we consume on the way we think about the world around us. Clearly, media depictions play an increasing role in the way we view the world, but much of the theoretical ground covered by cultivation theory is subsumed by more aggression-specific theories, such as social information processing and the general aggression model. The relative lack of aggression-specific studies also decreases the utility of this theory within this specific domain. In addition, even proponents of the theory admit that when basic demographic and individual differences are eliminated, cultivation effect sizes become extremely small or nonsignificant (Shrum, Burroughs & Rindfleisch, 2004). Thus, while it offers an interesting mechanism for media effects, its impact on aggression research remains relatively minor and largely untested to date.

This is, of course, its greatest flaw: while cultivation theory's lack of moderating factors has the advantage of providing an extremely parsimonious mechanism for the origins of media-based violent behaviours, in doing so it appears to hamstring its own predictive utility. Since the theory by definition could only at best explain a subset of violent behaviour, the fact that it explains little variance within that limited realm renders it of little practical use at this point.

Neuropsychological Deficits

A more atheoretical but increasingly relevant area of inquiry focuses on neuro-logical differences between violent offenders and the general populace. The key question is: can differences in neuropsychological factors go some way towards explaining aggressive behaviours? It appears there is a substantial correlation between low frontal lobe activity and an inability to inhibit impulsivity in general and aggressive behaviour specifically (Houston & Stanford, 2004; Mathias & Stanford, 1999; Stenberg, 1992). Individuals with higher levels of aggression show lowered frontal lobe responses and less efficient cognitive processing of aggressive stimuli than do normal individuals (Surguy & Bond, 2006). These findings tend to replicate across the gamut of aggressive individuals, with habitual violent offenders (Barratt *et al.*, 1997), sufferers of antisocial personality disorder (Bauer, O'Connor & Hesselbrock, 1994), teenagers (Bauer & Hesselbrock, 1999) and college students (Mathias & Stanford, 1999) who display impulsive aggressive tendencies all showing a similar pattern of lowered frontal lobe processing of aggressive stimuli.

Executive Cognitive Functioning

One school of thought (see Giancola, Mezzich & Tarter, 1998; Milner, 1995) holds that many neuropsychological deficits associated with aggression are indicative of low levels of executive cognitive functioning (ECF), defined as a "higher-order cognitive construct involved in the planning, initiation, and regulation of goal-directed behaviour" (Giancola, Mezzich & Tarter, 1998, p. 629). Executive cognitive functioning, while not restricted to the prefrontal cortex region, is believed to be the primary construct indicated by neurological activity in the area (Giancola *et al.*, 1998). Lesions to this area are associated with high levels of impulsivity and disinhibited behaviour (Price *et al.*, 1990), which in turn are associated with aggression (Raine, 1993; Houston & Stanford, 2004; however, also see Hoaken, Shaughnessy & Pihl, 2003). Alcohol consumption is also associated with lowered response in this region, and ECF proponents believe lowered executive cognitive functioning mediates the connection between alcohol use and aggression as well (Giancola, 2000a, 2000b; Hoaken, Giancola & Pihl, 1998); however, this relationship is somewhat controversial (Cherek, 2000; Lyvers, 2000; see also Chapter 12 in this volume).

Neuropsychological research is an area that has only begun to achieve the technological sophistication necessary to begin to link neurological processes and structures with behaviour and beliefs. In addition, ECF excluded, the general lack of comprehensive theoretical frameworks continues to hinder the integration of existing findings and the development of clear hypotheses for future research. However, conceptualisations such as ECF give us an intriguing explanation for the physiological bases of aggression. If one assumes that every cognition has some physiological correlate, it is clear that as research progresses, neuropsychology can be tremendously fruitful in the understanding and correction of aggressive cognitions and behaviour. For example, if it was to be discovered that in certain cases violent tendencies are linked to a chronic decrease in blood flow to a given neurological structure, drugs or therapy could be applied to correct the problem. However, it may be some time before such theoretical explanations are fully developed and researched enough to become part of treatment efforts with aggressive individuals.

Multi-Factor Theories

Cognitive Neoassociationist Aggression Model (CNA)

The CNA (Berkowitz, 1984, 1990) draws its principles from associative network models in cognitive psychology. A cognitive-associative network is essentially the idea that different memory constructs are cognitively linked to one another with bonds of varying strengths. This network functions in such a way that activating one construct will increase the accessibility of related constructs and thus the likelihood that they will be employed in information processing for the duration of the increased accessibility. The stronger the link between the originally activated construct and a related construct, the greater the increase in accessibility will be. In layman's terms, whenever we use some cognitive construct, we also become more likely to use anything we relate to that construct, due to the association between them.

The CNA takes this concept and applies it to aggression; whenever something associated with violence is activated, so too are the aggressive concepts linked with it. The stronger the linkage, the more likely the activation of the nonviolent concept is to elicit aggressive cognitions and/or behaviours. Supporting this, research has found that individuals high in trait aggression have more developed aggressive association networks and are more likely to have cognitive connections between aggressive and ambiguous words than low trait aggression individuals (Bushman, 1996). The CNA also acknowledges the strong role of affect, stressing that increased negative affect tends to increase the probability of activation of aggressive constructs across the board (Berkowitz, 1990); however, we will focus primarily on the cognitive component of the model here.

Of course, the stimuli with which aggressive constructs are associated can vary wildly from person to person (e.g., Anderson & Bushman, 2002). For example, an individual who as a child was once beaten with an extension cord while his parents' favourite Stevie Wonder album played in the background might years later experience an increase in hostile thoughts upon encountering either stimulus. However, certain constructs tend to be consistently associated with aggression across populations, and it is on those sorts of constructs that most CNA research has focused.

Most people tend to associate weapons with aggressive behaviour of some kind. This association can develop from a variety of experiences, but for many people comes simply from the frequent pairing of weapons with violent actions in the media and in everyday life. According to the CNA, exposure to weapons, or anything that activates the concept in memory, should tend to increase the accessibility of aggressive thoughts (see Anderson, Benjamin & Bartholow, 1998). In a seminal 1967 study, Berkowitz and LePage discovered that merely substituting an inconspicuous badminton racket with a rifle in a cluttered lab room could increase the length of electrical shocks delivered to a confederate; this occurred even though the gun was a relatively small part of the scenery and no attempt was made to draw attention to it. In accordance with the CNA, the mere visible presence of a stimulus associated with aggression was enough to elicit it.

However, individual differences in associations may affect the constructs that are primed for the individual. Bartholow *et al.* (2005) primed hunters and nonhunters with pictures of assault and hunting rifles, both of which could be predicted to be associated with aggressive behaviour. However, Bartholow *et al.* predicted that hunters typically have more positive and nonviolent (at least toward humans) associations linked to hunting rifles, and thus should presumably display lower accessibility of aggressive cognitions when primed with pictures of hunting weapons, compared to nonhunters. Fitting with the CNA model, when presented with pictures of hunting rifles, hunters displayed slower reaction times in classifying aggressive words than did nonhunters, indicating lower overall accessibility of aggressive thoughts. Thus, as predicted by the CNA, there is a large idiosyncratic component to the associative networks of individuals.

As alcohol consumption is often associated with lower inhibitions and increased aggression (see Giancola, 2000a; Chapter 12 of this volume), CNA would also predict that activation of the concept of alcohol would be associated with increases in the accessibility of aggressive thoughts. Alcohol is also typically associated with a number of nonaggressive concepts and activities so it is likely that the effect will be smaller than for weapons. In a recent study, Bartholow and Heinz (2006) primed participants with pictures of nature (e.g., trees), weapons, or alcoholic beverages, and tested their reaction time to recognise aggressive and nonaggressive words. Their findings replicated the "weapons effect" (i.e., quicker recognition of aggressive words following pictures of weapons) but also showed a similar, albeit smaller effect for exposure to alcohol stimuli. In a second experiment, Bartholow and Heinz asked one group of participants to look at magazine advertisements for alcohol and a different group to look at advertisements for other products, under the guise of a study on marketing practices. Later, ostensibly as part of a different study, all participants were asked to rate a story character on a number of traits, including hostility. The findings showed that participants who had been exposed to the alcohol ads rated the story character as significantly more hostile than did participants who had been exposed to the neutral ads. This effect was largest among individuals who had indicated, on a separate questionnaire, a belief that alcohol tends to increase aggressiveness. In accordance with the CNA, the mere presence of alcohol-related cues was enough in these two experiments to elicit effects associated with its consumption. This implicit association between alcohol and aggression has also been referred to as the alcohol expectancy effect.

The CNA, through its relatively simplistic design, provides an intriguing theoretical framework for understanding the bases of cognitively based aggression. This is particularly true for the issue of how chronically aggressive individuals can frequently seem to generate aggressive cognitions and responses from many ambiguous or even benign stimuli (see Copello & Tata, 1990; Dill, Anderson & Deuser, 1997; Epps & Kendall, 1995). This theory suffers from a similar problem as script theory in necessitating knowledge of each individual's idiosyncratic network but cognitive associations are likely to be somewhat more universal than scripts, as exposure to both media and real world violent content typically follows delineable patterns. A successful intervention programme based on CNA principles would likely involve instilling and developing strong associations between violently networked stimuli and more neutral or positive concepts, analogous to Bartholow *et al.*'s (2005) hunters. This could be achieved through perhaps visualisation or enactment of situations involving such positive situations, or even through subliminal priming. However, little work has been done on explicitly testing CNA's applicability in these domains; it is important to note, however, that elements of CNA are incorporated into more comprehensive models, such as social cognitive information processing, and so research on the efficacy of those models can speak indirectly to the utility of CNA.

Social Cognitive Information Processing

The social cognitive information processing model (Crick & Dodge, 1994; Dodge, 1980) views the individual as an active construer and interpreter of social information, who seeks to select the most appropriate and successful response from a limited subset of cognitively generated behaviours. The model delineates a series of steps that comprise a single instance of situational appraisal, behavioural selection and enactment. The instances are seen as cyclical and over time construals, behavioural responses, and the reactions they elicit from the environment, as well as observations of the behaviours of others, shape the latent cognitive structures that guide later cycles.

The theory breaks this process down into six discrete phases of information acquisition and behavioural response selection. In short, in a given situation, social cues are first encoded and interpreted by the actor; that is, the actor seeks out information to determine the nature of the situation. For example, assume an individual attending a crowded party has his foot stepped on by a stranger. The individual must assess what has happened ("he stepped on my foot") and interpret it ("it is crowded here, so it was probably an accident" or "he is a jerk who wasn't watching where he was going"). Based on the actor's interpretation of the scenario and past experience, he or she must decide what goal or goals are most relevant to the situation ("I'm just here to have a good time" or "No one can mess up my shoes and get away with it"). The actor then generates potential responses to the situation ("I'd like to shove that guy") and evaluates them based on potential consequences ("... but I'd get kicked out of the party") and self-efficacy ("... but I'm not much of a fighter"). If the first behavioural response considered is seen as inappropriate or likely to be unsuccessful, further responses will be considered. Lastly, the actor enacts the selected behaviour.

It is important to note that while the authors of this model believe this sequence to describe a typical scenario, under certain circumstances such as high physiological arousal or cognitive load, one or more of these steps may be skipped. For example, an intoxicated individual with a "hair-trigger" temper might simply process that his shoe has been stepped on and immediately retaliate with violence without considering goals or consequences. Also, this model is cyclical in nature, with past experiences shaping later interactions (Arsenio & Lemerise, 2004). An individual who grew up in a violent environment will typically see more situations as hostile or threatening even when removed from that environment; in addition, someone who chronically sees the world as hostile will typically select responses that will lead to increased hostility from those around him or her, thus increasing the likelihood of later hostile attributions.

Like several of the models discussed in this chapter, social information processing is a relatively new construct, so most of the research conducted within this realm could qualify as "recent". Thus we will focus only on research that is the most relevant to each step of the model, and is directly applicable to the study of aggression.

Encoding and interpretation of cues. High trait aggressive individuals are more inclined to perceive aggression or hostility in a wider variety of situations than those with more moderate levels of aggression; this has typically been linked to both exposure to a hostile environment and individual differences in aggressive tendencies (Hughes & Hasbrouck, 1996). More aggressive individuals tend to selectively attend to and recall aggressive cues from the environment (Yoon *et al.*, 2000). Aggressive individuals, as well as frequent victims of violence or aggression, are also more likely to develop a hostile attributional bias, or tendency to consistently perceive ambiguous cues as indicative of hostile intent (Shahinfar, Kupersmidt & Matza, 2001). Of course, a tendency to disproportionately perceive hostile intent will generally lead to disproportionately aggressive behaviour.

Clarification of goals. What we seek to obtain from a situation can also affect the likelihood of an aggressive response. If aggression or violence is viewed as a useful instrument for obtaining a desire, it will be more likely to be employed. Yoon *et al.* (2000) found that when comparing the cognitive tendencies of aggressive and nonaggressive children, well-adjusted children tended to generate relational goals, whereas a subset of aggressive children focused on instrumental goals centred on controlling the situation or others (the other aggressive children tended to simply act instinctively without thinking at all). In the study cited in the previous paragraph, Shahinfar *et al.* (2001) found that victims of violence also tended to develop more hostile social goals, in fitting with their perceptions of the world as a hostile place. Obviously, aggressive behaviours will be seen as more useful for obtaining instrumental goals, like dominance or manipulation, than relational goals, such as strengthening social bonds with others, and the likelihood of violence will increase.

Response access. It appears that chronically hostile individuals tend to be more likely to generate hostile or aggressive responses regardless of the situation (Bellmore *et al.*, 2005), but also are able to generate fewer potential responses overall (Lochman & Dodge, 1994). Thus, aggression-prone individuals are essentially handcuffed by their own minds; not only do they perceive the world around them as more hostile, but they generally struggle to think of nonaggressive ways to deal with it.

Response evaluation and self-efficacy. Even if an aggressive script is accessed, it will likely not be acted on if it is seen as inappropriate, unlikely to succeed, or morally wrong; this of course mirrors Huesmann's previously discussed work on script utilisation (Huesmann, 1998). Aggressive individuals, however, have tendencies that undercut each of these safeguards. Chronically aggressive people are more likely to hold norms that support violence as a legitimate response to many situations (Bellmore *et al.*, 2005; Sukhodolsky & Ruchkin, 2004), see aggressive behaviour as more likely to obtain a desired result (Toblin *et al.*, 2005; Yoon *et al.*, 2000), and believe that the victim of a violent action will suffer less than he or she actually will (Crane-Ross, Tisak & Tisak, 1998). Individuals who witness extreme violence, either in reality or in media depictions, also come to believe that violence is an appropriate and successful response to everyday situations (Hughes & Hasbrouck, 1996; Shahinfar, Kupersmidt & Matza, 2001).

Thus, at any given stage of the model, information-processing deficits can increase the likelihood of violent behaviour. Although it appears that no single deficit is more strongly predictive of aggression than another, it is clear that there is an additive effect of multiple deficits on aggression, and research has shown that many aggressive children have difficulty at each step (Yoon *et al.*, 2000), increasing the impact of violent tendencies in nearly any situation.

Social cognitive information processing theory is unique among the cited theories in this chapter, in that it was developed with an eye specifically toward developing intervention programmes for reducing or preventing violent behaviour. The typical intervention format under this rubric focuses first on examining the specific information processing deficits to which different high-risk groups may be susceptible. For example, aggressive teenage boys as a group tend to disproportionately attribute the actions of others to hostility but highly aggressive boys tend to use violence as a reaction to the perceived behaviours of others and moderately aggressive boys tend to do so proactively to reduce the expected aversive behaviours of others (Lochman & Dodge, 1994). By collecting a body of evidence as to the specific deficits of the relevant population, a more useful intervention can be devised.

Several intervention programmes have been devised with various populations of concern in mind (typically at-risk youths or adolescent violent offenders), and, while some promise has been shown, results have been somewhat mixed. In a study of 120 incarcerated adolescent offenders, Guerra and Slaby (1990) examined the effects of a 12-week social-cognitive based intervention programme on social-cognitive deficits and later aggressive behaviour. While they found substantial evidence that the programme successfully increased social problem-solving skills, decreased the endorsement of aggression-promoting beliefs, and decreased the incidence of aggressive behaviours in the facility, there was no statistically significant evidence that the intervention reduced overall recidivism subsequent to release, which is of course the key factor from a societal perspective. This may be attributable to a small sample size but it may also be an indication that the new social-cognitive perspectives instilled by the intervention may have been quickly eroded by exposure to the environment that spawned the initial unhealthy cognitive tendencies.

Greater success has been demonstrated with interventions tailored to at-risk children: multiple programmes (Muris *et al.*, 2005; Smokowski *et al.*, 2004) have found that social-cognitive oriented approaches can be successful in reducing information processing deficits and decreasing behavioural problems in children between the ages of 8 and 12. Perhaps pre-emptive intervention before a serious offence is committed may be more useful, or perhaps a younger population is more flexible in their cognitive tendencies. However, it is important to note that the set of dependent variables used by these studies does not preclude a similar problem to that reported by Guerra and Slaby. Since neither of these studies examines longer term outcomes or effects on later criminal behaviour, it may be that the social-cognitive changes observed by the researchers can be attenuated or reversed by later environmental exposure. Limited research has also demonstrated that adult violent criminal populations can also see lowered rates of recidivism when treated through a cognitive-behavioural intervention programme (Polaschek, Wilson & Townsend, 2005; see also Chapter 11 of this volume for more information regarding treatment for adult violent offenders).

In sum, while intervention programmes that focus on correcting social-cognitive deficits appear to be fairly able to do so in the short term, there is little evidence as yet that these changes can be lasting. Further study is required to make a comprehensive statement as to the efficacy of such an approach, but such evidence that exists is fairly promising.

Social Cognitive Theory

Social cognitive theory (Bandura, 1986, 2001) is a more recent expansion of the initial tenets of social learning theory (Bandura, 1977). Social learning theory focused on the acquisition and reinforcement of behaviour based on observations of others and ourselves and the positive and negative consequences of those behaviours. Social cognitive theory attempts to systematise the principles of social learning by expanding the mechanisms by which people take direct and observational experience and use them to organise and regulate behaviour. It also incorporates idiosyncratic internal events, such as cognition and affect, and environmental events into the model as working to shape psychological makeup and behavioural patterns.

A key distinction between social cognitive and social learning theory is the addition of humans' capacity for symbolisation. Social learning theory originally held that individuals would only tend to learn behaviours that were highly similar to those that were observed; it provided no explicit mechanism for the acquisition of behaviours that were only abstractly similar. For example, social cognitive theory would hold that an individual who witnessed a rewarded aggressive behaviour, such as a bully gaining lunch money by pushing a child to the ground, would become more likely to adopt other abstract behaviours, such as screaming at parents in an attempt to make them buy a toy; whereas social learning theory would only posit an increased likelihood of physical, bullying-type behaviours.

According to social-cognitive theory, there are four basic steps to the symbolic acquisition of behaviour. First, the observer must be paying attention to the actor. Second, the observer constructs a cognitive representation of the style of behaviour displayed by the actor. This is in direct contradiction to script theory (Huesmann, 1988), which holds that we acquire behavioural sequences, rather than abstract rules for behavioural strategies. If information about the behaviour is successfully restructured into symbolic behavioural rules and concepts, it becomes encoded into memory and can be translated into actual potential courses of action. Lastly, if motivation and perceived incentive is sufficient, a behaviour modelled upon the encoded rules and concepts is likely to be enacted (Bandura, 2001).

Of course, not every behaviour that is observed is encoded, and not every encoded representation manifests itself in behaviour. Research has examined the circumstances under which observed behaviour is likely to be directly or symbolically adopted, and has found various sorts of similarity to be a primary factor. Homophily, or the perception of observer/actor similarity, has been found to increase the likelihood that behaviour will be modelled (Eyal & Rubin, 2003; Hoffner & Cantor, 1991). Similarly, identification, or the feeling of sharing a perspective and experiences with an aggressive actor, has been shown to predict hostility towards others (Turner & Berkowitz, 1972) and more recently to be associated with trait hostility (Eyal & Rubin, 2003). Parasocial interaction – the sense of a perceived interactive relationship between an observer and a media character – has been found to be associated with attitude similarity (Turner, 1993), and has been shown to mediate the effects of exposure to televised content (e.g., Conway & Rubin, 1991).

Social cognitive theory provides a rich theoretical framework for correcting aggressive behaviour by delineating the paths by which aggressive behavioural rules and cognitions are acquired. This theory's most fundamental change from social learning was the addition of cognitive factors to what was previously a behavioural model. However, at least at this stage, the cognitive aspects of the model lack significant empirical support, remaining mostly in the realm of abstract theory. While some intervention programmes (e.g., Polaschek & Dixon, 2001) have been constructed around the principles of social learning, little to no work has been done with the reformulated model. As such, while it appears to be capable of generating a great deal of research and perhaps providing a significant cross-domain model of the acquisition and application of aggressive behaviours, it is difficult to say at this point how much utility the theory has.

General Aggression Model

The general aggression model (Anderson & Bushman, 2002; Anderson & Dill, 2000), or GAM, attempts to incorporate pertinent features of other, more domain-specific models of aggression under a comprehensive rubric. While less specifically delineated than more narrowly focused theories, the GAM presents a comprehensive picture of both the mechanisms of specific situations with the potential for aggression and latent, long-term knowledge structures that underlie each interaction. Figure 8.1 presents a depiction of the single episode GAM model, in which a number of key variables or "routes", including affect, arousal, and cognition, are important for predicting an aggressive action. Here, we will focus on the cognitive route to aggressive behaviour. However, this focus is not meant to imply that the other routes are less important predictors from the standpoint of the model.

The GAM starts with a foundational principle of social psychology, which is that behaviour is jointly determined by the interaction of a person, including individuating factors such as personality, temperament, and previous experiences, and the situation, conceptualised broadly as the social-contextual factors in which any given behaviour is enacted. The model posits that the characteristics of the person and situation interact to influence cognitive, affective, and arousal processes that are important for determining a behavioural response. While each stage is multiply determined by processes within these separate domains, we will focus

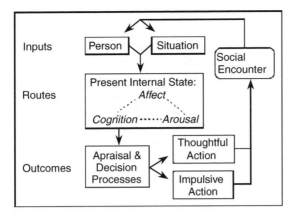

Inputs

Routes

Outcomes

Figure 8.1 Single episode general aggression model

as strictly as possible here on the cognitive aspects of the model. The cognitive "slice" of the GAM breaks a typical interaction into three discrete steps, two of which can be divided into smaller sub-categories. We will examine each in turn and discuss recent research that pertains to the relevant steps.

Person inputs. In a given person/situation interaction, the individual may bring to the interaction factors, or inputs, that may increase or decrease the likelihood of aggression; of course, the emphasis in the literature is on those factors that can be linked to an increase. These inputs may be trait-based, as when the individual has high trait aggression (Anderson, 2002), or state-based, such as when aggressive scripts are temporarily more accessible (Huesmann, 1988). Additional factors such as norms that justify aggressive response or an expectation of hostility from others can also shape the ways in which the individual interprets and responds to the terms of the situation.

Situational inputs. The situation may also include factors that promote or inhibit aggression, generally grouped under the umbrella term "aggressive cues". These can include a provocative act from another, the presence of a stimulus cognitively associated with aggression, or direct or implied social messages that condone or encourage aggression. The GAM is frequently used as a conceptual framework in studies of the effects of violent media. Such studies generally conclude that media with high violence content tend to elicit aggressive behaviour and inhibit empathy and helping behaviour in both the short term (Anderson, 1997; Anderson & Bushman, 2001; Anderson & Dill, 2000) and long term (Anderson & Dill, 2000; Bartholow, Sestir & Davis, 2005), particularly when the behaviour is unpunished or rewarded. A significant portion of the effects of violent media on behaviour is believed to be moderated by the cognitions it reinforces and makes chronically accessible; this research will be touched upon below.

Routes. Next, the interaction between individual and situation can cause a variety of cognitive responses in the individual, such as accessible violent scripts, retaliatory norms, or an expectation of successful resolution through aggression and influence behavioural response selection. Aggression-promoting "baggage" brought by the actor or situation into an interaction is more likely to lead to the generation of aggressive thoughts. In terms of situational cues, multiple studies (Carnagey & Anderson, 2005; Kirsh, Olczak & Mounts, 2005; Krahe & Moller, 2004) have demonstrated that playing violent video games, which typically present continuous aggressive cues, increases the prevalence of aggressive cognitions. In addition, Anderson *et al.* (1998) caused mild physical pain to subjects who varied in their levels of trait hostility and then had these subjects rate pairs of ambiguous and aggressive words for similarity in meaning. Within the pain condition, participants high in trait hostility rated ambiguous-aggressive and aggressive-aggressive word pairs as significantly more similar in meaning than did participants low in trait hostility or participants in the no-pain condition. These findings indicate that under situational stress, the cognitions of high trait hostility individuals took on a more aggressive tint, whereby a wide variety of words were infused with aggressive connotations when there might have been none before.

Individual cognitive associations and scripts can also shape the effect of situational cues on short-term cognition and eventual behaviour. Recall the Bartholow, Anderson *et al.* (2005) study, reviewed previously, on the cognitive responses of hunters and nonhunters to pictures of guns. Hunters generated relatively lower accessibility of aggressive cognitions when presented with pictures of hunting rifles and in a follow-up study also behaved less aggressively when primed with hunting rifles. This set of studies demonstrated how the two pre-emergent steps depicted in the GAM – person/situation interaction and aggressive cognitions – come together to determine behavioural outcomes associated with aggression. In this example, the hunters had experience with an object typically seen as aggression-related, but their experience was in activities unrelated to human-directed violence or aggression. Thus the cognitions that were activated by viewing a hunting rifle were overall less hostile than for those individuals who only associated a hunting rifle with violence (see also Berkowitz, 1993). Because of this, an aggressive response became less likely for the hunters.

Which brings us to the linkage between the second and third components of the model: an increase in aggression-promoting cognitions can both consciously and unconsciously increase the likelihood that an aggressive behaviour will be generated as an appropriate response to the situation. Of course, this is a difficult area of inquiry, as cognitions are by nature abstract and often obtained by self-report, and cannot be directly manipulated. However, in addition to the Bartholow *et al.* (2005) study mentioned previously, Joireman, Anderson and Strathman (2003) have used structural equation modelling to examine the effects of individual differences on aggressive behaviour, and found preliminary indications that the effects of trait hostility, consideration of future consequences, and sensation seeking on physical and verbal aggression is at least partially mediated by hostile cognitions. In perhaps a more telling study, Carnagey and Anderson (2005) had subjects play a video game where violence was either rewarded, punished, or impossible. While both violent conditions increased hostile affect, only the subjects who were rewarded for violence generated more aggressive cognitions and behaviour. Thus, it appears that cognitions may, at least in some scenarios, be the primary mediator between situational cues and aggressive outcomes. Still, more research needs to be conducted, to make this connection clearer.

Outcomes. Once a behaviour is selected, it can, of course, be immediately enacted, or further cognition as to the appropriateness or efficacy of the behaviour can take place. After further consideration, the original behaviour is either enacted or rejected, in which case a new behaviour is selected, which can again be enacted with or without further thought, or rejected in favour of yet another behavioural selection. In other words, we can behave instinctively or thoughtfully; if we act instinctively we cannot change the initial behaviour, if thoughtfully we may choose another behaviour or decide the original choice is the correct one. Since aggression often involves a swift, "lashing out" type effect, presumably aggression is more likely when thoughtful re-evaluation does not occur. However, there is again little to no research directly addressing this issue, likely due to the difficulty in direct manipulation and examination of thoughtful re-evaluation.

Long-term and extraneous effects. The GAM also contains considerations broader than an examination of a single generic person-situation interaction depicted in Figure 8.1. Individuals can also, due to individual differences or past experience, tend to seek out situations that are more (or less) likely to lead to aggression. Joireman, Anderson and Strathman (2003), for example, have provided preliminary evidence that high sensation seekers display this tendency. And, of course, the situations one selects or encounters over time can combine with individual differences to impact the likelihood of aggressive behaviour. Gentile *et al.* (2004) looked at the combined effects of trait hostility and chronic violent video game play on real-world aggression in children, such as physical fights and arguments with teachers, and found that although violent game play appeared to have the larger effect, the overall picture is that of an additive effect. Each individual GAM cycle leaves both the actor and the situation changed in some way: exposure to a chronically hostile environment will lead to normative beliefs about the legitimacy of aggression and expectations of hostility outside of it, and repeated aggressive behaviour will lead to more hostility in the environment around you. Each interaction can strengthen or weaken aggressive cognitive constructs, and in doing so affect the probability of aggressive behaviour at every stage of the model.

Thus, the GAM would posit, aggressive offenders may typically begin with some relatively small inclination for aggression, but rapidly become prisoners of their own past behaviour, as both the situations they find themselves in, the responses of others, and their own increasingly deeply rooted exaggerated perceptions of aggressive intent and beliefs of the legitimacy of violence steadily increase the likelihood of increasingly aggressive behaviour. Ironically, the perception of a hostile world serves to gradually create exactly such a place, at least in the offender's subjective experience, from which "escape" is a long, difficult mental climb.

The GAM is a broad, comprehensive model, and as such has yet to be fully delineated by specific research, even in the narrower "cognition-only" form detailed here. However, the considerable amount of evidence that does exist indicates strong support for the mechanisms of the model, and a strong and perhaps primary role for cognition in the generation of aggressive behaviour. The GAM does suffer from a significant issue with the open-ended nature of its mechanisms and concepts: similar to script theory, there are few conceivable situations that could not be interpreted as supporting its conceptualisations. Since a theory that can explain everything effectively explains nothing, it seems clear that the inner workings of the GAM must be more clearly elucidated by future generations of researchers before it can achieve a higher level of utility. As it stands, the model appears to be more of a guide towards conceptualising the various influences on the likelihood of aggressive behaviour, rather than a clearly falsifiable theory. On balance, however, the GAM, along with social-cognitive information processing, is the most comprehensive theory of aggression to date, and as such should eventually prove fruitful in understanding the primary roots of aggressive behaviour, and the best means by which to suppress them.

CONCLUSIONS AND FUTURE RESEARCH

Aggression is an instinct perhaps only surpassed by survival and reproduction in its centrality within human nature. As such, it permeates every domain in human psychology, from biology to affect to, of course, cognition. Acts of aggression are therefore virtually always multiply determined, and it is difficult to disentangle one specific cause from the myriad of potential sources of aggressive inclination. However, the theories and research cited here, while recognising the multifaceted nature of aggression, have provided powerful evidence that cognition may play a central role in mediating the connection between instinct and action.

As discussed above, though, many of these theories have not yet been able to successfully cross over from theory to practice, in the form of specific attempts at interventions designed to reduce future instances of aggressive behaviour. The largest exception to this general rule is social-cognitive information processing, which comes from an intervention-based background and as such has evolved intertwined with a strong applied component. Unfortunately, many of the social psychology-based models have thus far struggled to bridge the gap from theory to application; while they can provide a useful lens through which to conceptualise the origins of aggression, they are often too abstract or open-ended to lend themselves to a comprehensive programme of behavioural correction. Conversely, many intervention programmes, even when successful at reducing recidivism, lack a strong theoretical or empirical basis (Polaschek & Collie, 2004). When interventions were self-characterised as cognitive theory-based, they typically paid only lip service to their theoretical bases, and showed overall inconclusive results on recidivism rates. Other intervention programmes, while labelling themselves as "cognitive-behavioural" and attempting to incorporate elements of cognitive restructuring, had no explicitly stated or implicitly determinable theoretical background and so little can be drawn from their success or failure. Strong theoretical bases for intervention programmes do more than just generate research hypotheses: they give a conceptual framework from which more specialised, customised programmes can be developed for rarer or more extreme types of deviance. As such, it is crucially important that research be undertaken to fill in these gaps between theory and practice.

There is still a great deal of promise shown by the relatively scarce examples of heavily theory-based programmes. Speaking atheoretically, the inclusion of general cognitively based components to more behaviourally focused interventions has been found to increase their overall efficacy (Smith, Lochman & Daunic, 2005).

Work under the umbrella of social-cognitive information processing (SCIP) has also demonstrated that a carefully structured, theoretically centred intervention programme can, at least in the short term, reduce common information processing pitfalls and attenuate the effects of deficient or biased thinking on aggressive behaviour among pre-adolescents.

It is important also to note that SCIP does not exist in a conceptual vacuum: it integrates aspects of other theories discussed within this chapter, such as script theory and the cognitive-neoassociationist aggression model and overlaps conceptually with others, such as the general aggression model. Thus, the success of SCIP-based programmes speaks well to the potential of interventions designed around other theoretical frameworks. More broadly speaking, the general successes of cognitively based programmes helps to demonstrate the powerful role cognition and information processing play in the likelihood of aggressive behaviour. While much remains to be done, what exists provides strong evidence that the ideas espoused by modern aggression researchers can, in time, provide powerful tools for the reduction of the cognitive roots of aggression.

Of course, cognition does not exist in a vacuum either; how much of aggression-related cognition is determined by aggressive constructs within other psychological and physiological domains is certainly a significant question and a matter for continued scrutiny. However, it appears the cognitive domain may be the realm where aggression can be most successfully dealt with and suppressed, making it an ideal area for future investigation. Aggression may not be going anywhere, but understanding its cognitive roots can help ensure it causes the least societal damage possible.

REFERENCES

Anderson, C. A. (1997). Effects of violent movies and trait hostility on hostile feelings and aggressive thoughts. *Aggressive Behavior, 23*, 161–78.

Anderson, C. A. (2002). Violent video games and aggressive thoughts, feelings, and behaviors. In S. Calvert, A. Jordan & R. Cocking (eds). *Children in the Digital Age* (pp. 101–19). Westport, CT: Praeger.

Anderson, K. B., Anderson, C. A., Dill, K. E. & Deuser, W. E. (1998). The interactive relations between trait hostility, pain, and aggressive thoughts. *Aggressive Behavior, 24*, 161–71.

Anderson, C. A., Benjamin, A. J. Jr. & Bartholow, B. D. (1998). Does the gun pull the trigger? Automatic priming effects of weapons pictures and weapon names. *Psychological Science, 9*, 308–14.

Anderson, C. A. & Bushman, B. J. (2001). Effects of violent video games on aggressive behavior, aggressive cognition, aggressive affect, physiological arousal, and prosocial behavior: A meta-analytic review of the scientific literature. *Psychological Science, 12*, 353–9.

Anderson, C. A. & Bushman, B. J. (2002). Human aggression. *Annual Review of Psychology, 53*, 27–51.

Anderson, C. A. & Dill, K. E. (2000). Video games and aggressive thoughts, feelings, and behavior in the laboratory and in life. *Journal of Personality and Social Psychology, 78*, 772–90.

Arsenio, W. F. & Lemerise, E. A. (2004). Aggression and moral development: integrating social information processing and moral domain models. *Child Development, 75*, 987–1002.

Bandura, A. (1973). *Aggression: A Social Learning Analysis.* Englewood Cliffs, NJ: Prentice-Hall.

Bandura, A. (1977). *Social Learning Theory.* Englewood Cliffs, NJ: Prentice-Hall.

Bandura, A. (1986). *Social Foundations of Thought and Action: A Social Cognitive Theory.* Upper Saddle River, NJ: Prentice Hall.

Bandura, A. (2001). Social cognitive theory of mass communication. In J. Bryant & D. Zillman (eds). *Media effects: Advances in theory and research* (pp. 121–53). Mahwah, NJ: Erlbaum.

Barratt, E. S., Stanford, M. S., Kent, T. A. & Felthous, A. (1997). Neuropsychological and cognitive psychophysiological substrates of impulsive aggressiveness. *Biological Psychiatry,* **41,** 1045–61.

Bartholow, B. D., Anderson, C. A., Carnagey, N. L. & Benjamin, A. J. (2005a). Interactive effects of life experience and situation cues on aggression: the weapons priming effect in hunters and nonhunters. *Journal of Experimental Social Psychology,* **41,** 48–60.

Bartholow, B. D. & Heinz, A. (2006). Alcohol and aggression without consumption, alcohol cues, aggressive thoughts, and hostile perception bias. *Psychological Science,* **17,** 30–7.

Bartholow, B. D., Sestir, M. A. & Davis, E. B. (2005b). Correlates and consequences of exposure to video game violence: hostile personality, empathy, and aggressive behavior. *Personality and Social Psychology Bulletin,* **31,** 1573–86.

Bauer, L. O. & Hesselbrock, V. M. (1999). P300 decrements in teenagers with conduct problems: Implications for substance abuse risk and brain development. *Biological Psychiatry,* **46,** 263–72.

Bauer, L. O., O'Connor, S. & Hesselbrock, V. M. (1994). Frontal P300 decrements in antisocial personality disorder. *Alcoholism, Clinical and Experimental Research,* **8,** 1300–5.

Bellmore, A. D., Witkow, M. R., Graham, S. & Juvonen, J. (2005). From beliefs to behavior: The mediating role of hostile response selection in predicting aggression. *Aggressive Behavior,* **31,** 453–72.

Berkowitz, L. (1984). Some effects of thoughts on anti-social and prosocial influences of media effects: a cognitive-neoassociation analysis. *Psychological Bulletin,* **95,** 410–27.

Berkowitz, L. (1990). On the formation and regulation of anger and aggression: a cognitive-neoassociation analysis. *American Psychologist,* **45,** 494–503.

Berkowitz, L. (1993). Towards a general theory of anger and emotional aggression: implications of the cognitive-neoassociationistic perspective for the analysis of anger and other emotions. In R. S. Wyer & T. K. Srull (eds). *Perspectives on Anger and Emotion* (pp. 1–46). Hillsdale, NJ: Erlbaum.

Berkowitz, L. & LePage, A. (1967). Weapons as aggression-eliciting stimuli. *Journal of Personality and Social Psychology,* **7,** 202–7.

Bushman, B. J. (1996). Individual differences in the extent and development of aggressive cognitive-associative networks. *Personality and Social Psychological Bulletin,* **22,** 811–19.

Carnagey, N. L. & Anderson, C. A. (2005). The effects of reward and punishment in violent video games on aggressive affect, cognition, and behavior. *Psychological Science,* **16,** 882–9.

Cherek, D. (2000). Executive cognitive functioning, alcohol, and aggression: Comment on Giancola (2000*). Experimental and Clinical Psychopharmacology,* **8,** 604–6.

Conway, J. C. & Rubin, A. M. (1991). Psychological predictors of television viewing motivations. *Communications Research,* **18,** 443–63.

Copello, A. G. & Tata, P. R. (1990). Violent behavior and interpretive bias: An experimental study of the resolution of ambiguity in violent offenders. *British Journal of Clinical Psychology,* **29,** 173–81.

Crane-Ross, D., Tisak, M. S. & Tisak, J. (1998). Aggression and conventional rule violation among adolescents: social-reasoning predictors of social behavior. *Aggressive Behavior,* **24,** 347–65.

Crick, N. R. & Dodge, K. A. (1994). A review and reformulation of social information-processing mechanisms in children's social adjustment. *Psychological Bulletin,* **115,** 74–101.

Dill, K. E., Anderson, C. A. & Deuser, W. A. (1997). Effects of aggressive personality on social expectations and social perceptions. *Journal of Research in Personality,* **31,** 272–92.

Dodge, K. A. (1980). Social cognition and children's aggressive behavior. *Child Development*, **51**, 162–70.

Dodge, K. A. (1986). A social information processing model of social competence in children. In M. Perlmutter (ed.), *Minnesota Symposia on Child Psychology* (Volume 18, pp. 77–125). Hillsdale, NJ: Lawrence Erlbaum.

Dollard, J., Doob, L., Miller, N. *et al.* (1939). *Frustration and Aggression*. New Haven, CT: Yale University Press.

Epps, J. & Kendall, P. C. (1995). Hostile attributional bias in adults. *Cognitive Therapy and Research*, **19**, 159–78.

Eyal, K. & Rubin, A. M. (2003). Viewer aggression and homophily, identification, and parasocial relationships with television characters. *Journal of Broadcasting & Electronic Media*, **47**, 77–98.

Freud, S. (1939). *Civilization and its Discontents*. New York: W.W. Norton & Company.

Gentile, D. A., Lynch, P. J., Linder, J. R. & Walsh, D. A. (2004). The effects of violent video game habits on adolescent aggressive attitudes and behaviors. *Journal of Adolescence*, **27**, 5–22.

Gerbner, G., Gross, L., Morgan, M. *et al.* (2002). Growing up with television: Cultivation processes. In J. Bryant & D. Zillman (eds), *Media Effects: Advances in Theory and Research* (pp. 43–68). Mahwah, NJ: Erlbaum.

Gerbner, G., Gross, L., Morgan, M. & Signorielli, N. (1980). The "mainstreaming" of America: Violence profile no. 11. *Journal of Communication*, **30**, 10–29.

Giancola, P. R. (2000a). Executive functioning: a conceptual framework for alcohol-related aggression. *Experimental and Clinical Psychopharmacology*, **8**, 576–97.

Giancola, P. R. (2000b). Executive functioning and alcohol-related aggression: Reply to Weingartner (2000), Bates (2000), Lyvers (2000), Cherek (2000), and Berman (2000). *Experimental and Clinical Psychopharmacology*, **8**, 612–17.

Giancola, P. R., Mezzich, A. C. & Tarter, R. E. (1998). Executive cognitive functioning, temperament, and antisocial behavior in conduct-disordered adolescent females. *Journal of Abnormal Psychology*, **107**, 629–41.

Guerra, N. G. & Slaby, R. G. (1990). Cognitive mediators of aggression in adolescent offenders: 2. Intervention. *Developmental Psychology*, **26**, 269–77.

Hoaken, P. N. S., Giancola, P. R. & Pihl, R. O. (1998). Executive cognitive functions as mediators of alcohol-related aggression. *Alcohol and Alcoholism*, **33**, 47–54.

Hoaken, P. N. S., Shaughnessy, V. K. & Pihl, R. O. (2003). Executive cognitive functioning and aggression: Is it an issue of impulsivity? *Aggressive Behavior*, **29**, 15–30.

Hoffner, C. & Cantor, J. (1991). Perceiving and responding to mass media characters. In J. Bryant & D. Zillman (eds), *Responding to the Screen: Reception and Reaction Processes* (pp. 63–101). Hillsdale, NJ: Erlbaum.

Houston, R. J. & Stanford, M. S. (2004). Electrophysiological substrates of impulsiveness: Potential effects on aggressive behavior. *Progress in Neuro-Psychopharmacology and Biological Psychiatry*, **29**, 305–13.

Huesmann, L. R. (1988). An information processing model for the development of aggression. *Aggressive Behavior*, **14**, 13–24.

Huesmann, L. R. (1998). The role of social information processing and cognitive schema in the acquisition and maintenance of habitual aggressive behavior. In R. Geen & E. Donnerstein (eds), *Human Aggression: Theories, Research, and Implications for Social Policy* (pp. 73–109). New York: Academic Press.

Huesmann, L. R. & Eron, L. D. (1989). Individual differences and the trait of aggression. *European Journal of Personality*, **3**, 95–106.

Huesmann, L. R., Eron, L. D., Lefkowitz, M. M. & Walder, L. O. (1984). The stability of aggression over time and generations. *Developmental Psychology*, **20**, 1120–34.

Huesmann, L. R. & Guerra, N. G. (1997). Normative beliefs about aggression and aggressive behavior. *Aggressive Behavior*, **10**, 243–51.

Huesmann, L. R. & Reynolds, M. A. (2001). Cognitive processes and the development of aggression. In A. Bohart & D. Stipek (eds), *Constructive and Destructive Behavior:*

Implications for Family, School, and Society (pp. 249–69). Washington, DC: American Psychological Association.

Huesmann, L. R., Spindler, A., McElwain, N. & Guerra, N. G. (1998). *The roles of cognitive processes in moderating and mediating the development and prevention of childhood aggression.* Paper presented at the annual meeting of the American Psychological Association, San Francisco.

Hughes, J. N. & Hasbrouck, J. E. (1996). Television violence: implications for violence prevention. *School Psychology Review*, **25**, 134–50.

Joireman, J., Anderson, J. & Strathman, A. (2003). The aggression paradox: understanding links among aggression, sensation seeking, and the consideration of future consequences. *Journal of Personality and Social Psychology*, **84**, 1287–302.

Kirsh, S. J., Olczak, P. V. & Mounts, R. W. (2005). Violent video games induce an affect processing bias. *Media Psychology*, **7**, 239–50.

Krahe, B. & Moller, I. (2004). Playing violent electronic games, hostile attributional style, and aggression-related norms in German adolescents. *Journal of Adolescence*, **27**, 53–9.

Lichter, R. S., Lichter, L. S. & Rothman, S. (1994). *Prime Time: How TV Portrays American Culture.* Washington, DC: Regnery.

Lochman, J. E. & Dodge, K. A. (1994). Social-cognitive processes of severely violent, moderately aggressive, and nonaggressive boys. *Journal of Clinical and Consulting Psychology*, **62**, 366–74.

Lyvers, M. (2000). Cognition, emotion, and the alcohol-aggression relationship: comment on Giancola (2000). *Experimental and Clinical Psychopharmacology*, **8**, 607–8.

Mathias, C. W. & Stanford, M. S. (1999). P300 under standard and surprise conditions in self-reported impulsive aggression. *Progress in Neuro-Psychopharmalogical and Biological Psychiatry*, **23**, 1037–51.

Milner, B. (1995). Aspects of human frontal lobe function. In H. Jasper, S. Riggio & P. Goldman-Rakic (eds), *Epilepsy and the Functional Anatomy of the Frontal Lobe* (pp. 67–84). New York: Raven Press.

Muris, P., Meesters, C., Vincken, M. & Eijkelenboom, A. (2005). Reducing children's aggressive and oppositional behaviors in the schools: preliminary results on the effectiveness of a social-cognitive group intervention program. *Child & Family Behavior Therapy*, **27**, 17–32.

Polaschek, D. L. & Collie, R. M. (2004). Rehabilitating serious violent adult offenders: An empirical and theoretical stocktake. *Psychology, Crime and Law*, **10**, 323–34.

Polaschek, D. L. & Dixon, B. G. (2001). The Violence Prevention Project: the development and evaluation of a treatment programme for violent offenders. *Psychology, Crime and Law*, **7**, 1–23.

Polaschek, D. L., Wilson, N. J. & Townsend, M. R. (2005). Cognitive-behavioral rehabilitation for high-risk violent offenders: an outcome evaluation of the Violence Prevention Unit. *Journal of Interpersonal Violence*, **20**, 1611–27.

Price, B., Daffner, K., Stowe, R. & Mesulam, M. (1990). The compartmental learning disabilities of early frontal lobe damage. *Brain*, **113**, 1383–93.

Raine, A. (1993). Evoked potentials and psychopathy. *International Journal of Psychophysiology*, **8**, 1–16.

Shahinfar, A., Kupersmidt, J. B. & Matza, L. S. (2001). The relation between exposure to violence and social information processing among incarcerated adults. *Journal of Abnormal Psychology*, **110**, 136–41.

Shrum, L. J. (1996). Psychological processes underlying cultivation effects: Further tests of construct accessibility. *Human Communication Research*, **22**, 482–509.

Shrum, L. J. (1999). Television and persuasion: effects of the programs between the ads. *Media Psychology*, **1**, 3–25.

Shrum, L. J., Burroughs, J. E. & Rindfleisch, A. (2004). A process model of consumer cultivation: the role of television is a function of the type of judgment. In L. J. Shrum (ed.), *The Psychology of Entertainment Media: Blurring the Lines between Entertainment and Persuasion* (pp. 177–91). Mahwah, NJ: Lawrence Erlbaum.

Smith, S. W., Lochman, J. E. & Daunic, A. P. (2005). Managing aggression using cognitive-behavioral interventions: State of the practice and future directions. *Behavioral Disorders*, **30**, 227–40.

Smokowski, P. R., Fraser, M. W., Day, S. H. *et al.* (2004). School-based skills training to prevent aggressive behavior and peer rejection in childhood: evaluating the *Making Choices* program. *The Journal of Primary Prevention*, **23**, 233–51.

Stenberg, G. (1992). Personality and the EEG: arousal and emotional arousability. *Personality and Individual Differences*, **13**, 1097–113.

Sukhodolsky, D. G. & Ruchkin, V. V. (2004). Association of normative beliefs and anger with aggression and antisocial behavior in Russian male juvenile offenders and high school students. *Journal of Abnormal Child Psychology*, **32**, 225–36.

Surguy, S. M. & Bond, A. J. (2006). P300 to emotionally relevant stimuli as an indicator of aggression levels. *Aggressive Behavior*, **32**, 253–60.

Toblin, R. L., Schwartz, D., Gorman, A. H. & Abou-ezzeddine, T. (2005). Social-cognitive and behavioral attributes of aggressive victims of bullying. *Applied Developmental Psychology*, **26**, 329–46.

Turner, J. R. (1993). Interpersonal and psychological predictors of parasocial interaction with different television performers. *Communication Quarterly*, **41**, 443–53.

Turner, C. W. & Berkowitz, L. (1972). Identification with film aggressor (covert role taking) and reactions to film violence. *Journal of Personality and Social Psychology*, **2**, 612–16.

Yoon, J. S., Hughes, J. N., Cavell, T. A. & Thompson, B. (2000). Social cognitive differences between aggressive-rejected and aggressive-nonrejected children. *Journal of School Psychology*, **38**, 551–70.

Chapter 9

VIOLENCE-RELATED COGNITION: CURRENT RESEARCH

RACHAEL M. COLLIE, JAMES VESS AND SHARLENE MURDOCH
Victoria University of Wellington, NZ

Serious violent offenders account for a disproportionate amount of reported violent crime and cause substantial harm to others (Loeber, Farrington & Waschbusch, 1998; Moffitt *et al.*, 2002). As a consequence, they cause great concern to the general public and to the correctional agencies tasked with managing their behaviour. Professionals require a comprehensive understanding of violence and of the options available for reducing this violence and an important factor in any such understanding is the nature and role of cognition (Anderson & Bushman, 2002; Bandura, 2001; Huesmann, 1998).

Given the significance accorded to cognition in aggression theories (see Chapter 8 of this volume) and general offender rehabilitation approaches, it seems timely to review the literature on violence-related cognition in offenders. This relatively small and diverse body of research is therefore the major focus of this chapter. We begin by briefly introducing key definitional and methodological issues. We then organise the body of our review around the distinctions made in social cognitive theory between cognitive content, cognitive processing and cognitive structures. Within these three content areas research from different methodological approaches are reviewed. Where there is a complete absence of research using major cognitive methodologies with violent offenders, we review selected analogue studies with high trait aggressive students. We conclude the chapter with an integration of findings across areas and methods, and discuss the important clinical implications of these findings.

DEFINITION AND METHODOLOGY ISSUES

Distinctions have been made between cognitive content, cognitive structures and cognitive processing (for reviews see Fiske & Taylor, 1991; Hollon & Kriss, 1984;

Aggressive Offenders' Cognition: Theory, Research and Practice. Edited by T. A. Gannon, T. Ward, A. R. Beech and D. Fisher. © 2007 John Wiley & Sons, Ltd.

Huesmann, 1998; Ingram & Kendall, 1986). *Cognitive content* refers to the basic stored elements or subject matter of information in long-term memory. In the context of violent offending this is the content of what an offender actually thinks or imagines prior to, during, and following a violent incident. *Cognitive structure* refers to the architecture or form of the cognitive content and the relationship of that content to other concepts in memory. Schema and scripts are two major forms of cognitive structure. Schemas are clusters of beliefs, attitudes, and other types of cognition associated closely together in enduring networks as a result of experience and learning (Huesmann, 1998). Scripts are collections of simple event schema (Huesmann, 1998); they contain information about what events happen in the environment, how people should respond and behave during those events, and what outcomes are likely (see Chapter 8 of this volume for more detail).

In contrast, *cognitive processing* is concerned with the complex set of mechanisms that give rise to cognitive content or knowledge. In the current context, these are processes that produce violent thoughts and may result in the selection of a violent action. Cognitive processing includes acquisition, rehearsal, and retrieval of information and is the mechanism by which pre-existing knowledge structures (e.g., schema) affect subsequent understanding of the world. Cognitive processing involves a number of stages (Crick & Dodge, 1994; Dodge & Swartz, 1997; Huesman, 1998), described as: (a) perceiving and encoding situational (and internal) cues, (b) interpretation of these cues, (c) searching memory for a guide to an appropriate goal (goal formation), (d) searching memory for a guide to a behaviour that will attain that goal (response evaluation) (e) selecting one of these responses (response selection), and (f) carrying out the behaviour (response enactment) (Crick & Dodge, 1994; Dodge & Swartz, 1997). In reality, the boundaries between content, structure and process are not as discrete as the distinction implies. Cognitive processes involve a dynamic interplay between all three areas of cognition, therefore features of one area have implications for others.

Important questions centre around what violent offenders think at the various stages of committing violence, the nature of the schema that underpin this surface level thought, and the biases and deficits in information processing that promote the use of violence as a problem-solving or goal-attainment strategy. One approach to investigating these questions is to study the content or cognition process of violent offenders and compare this to nonviolent offenders or some other suitable comparison group. A major issue yet to be resolved in this comparative approach is the separation of offenders into violent and nonviolent groups. Research on violent offenders tends to show that those who commit serious violence, or at least a subset of those individuals, tend to be criminally versatile offenders who also serve sentences for nonviolent crimes (Loeber, Farrington & Waschbusch, 1998; Moffit *et al.*, 2002; Serin & Preston, 2001a, 2001b). Thus, distinguishing violent and nonviolent offenders on the basis of the index offence (current conviction) fails to account for the co-occurrence of violent and nonviolent offending within the same offender.

A second approach that bypasses classification issues is to obtain a measure of offenders' violence-related cognition and determine its relationship to a criteria of violence (e.g., self-reported aggression, past or future violent convictions). Evidence for a relationship between the cognition measure and violence criterion suggests that the measure is a valid indicator of violence-related cognition.

However, while reliance on self-reported aggression can be criticised as a weak measure of violence, reliance on official reports is also subject to a number of biases (e.g., underreporting of crimes, low rates of arrest and conviction, plea bargaining to lesser, nonviolent charges). In addition, although a predictive relationship can be established from this method, that is not equivalent to determining a causal relationship (Douglas & Skeem, 2005).

Methodologically, researchers investigating violent cognition predominantly use self-report measures. Questionnaires and interviews are used to infer the content of what offenders think about violence and in some instances aspects of their thinking during violent incidents. This surface-level cognition is then used to infer the types of schema that promote violence. From a theoretical perspective, assessed cognitions are the end *cognitive products* that arise from the dynamic interplay of cognitive content, structures, and information processing (Hollon & Kriss, 1984). Even when vignettes are used to explore how offenders interpret and respond to various social situations – a paradigm designed to measure cognitive processing – processing biases and deficits are largely determined from self-report. A major consideration when inferring cognition via self-report methods is the extent that comprehension, insightfulness, and psychological defensiveness affect the ability to self-reflect and report on internal experiences. Intentional impression management and deception may also distort self-reported responses.

Researchers also use experimental measures of nonconscious cognition (i.e., cognitive process outside conscious awareness), which bypass the requirement for self-report. Although well developed in the cognitive research field, and in the study of other forms of psychopathology (e.g., depression), there are only a few studies using these methods with violent offenders. Instead these types of studies are primarily used with high trait aggressive individuals obtained from student samples.

We use a combination of the three cognitive systems and methodological approaches outlined above to organise our review of studies pertinent to understanding the cognition of violent offenders. Specifically, we divide the chapter into the three cognitive systems (cognitive content, cognitive processing, and cognitive structure) and further divide each section into the main methodological approaches. We describe each study according to where we believe the results are most relevant. However, since all aspects of the cognitive system dynamically interact, studies are unlikely to tap only one specific area.

COGNITIVE CONTENT

Questionnaire Studies

Aggressive or Violent Attitudes

Few questionnaires exist to measure attitudes regarding general (i.e., nonsexual, nondomestic) aggression or violence in adults, and of those that do exist, very few have been used with offenders. One of the exceptions is the EXPAGG-M (Archer & Haigh, 1997a), which is a 40-item questionnaire designed to measure *instrumental* and *expressive* beliefs about aggression. Factor analysis showed the instrumental scale primarily measured a positive and instrumental view of physical aggression together with a lack of guilt and concern over harm caused to the other person, while the expressive scale measured negative feelings about physical aggression (Archer & Haigh, 1997a, 1997b).

Archer and Haigh (1997b) found British male and female prisoners' instrumental beliefs were strongly and positively correlated with self-reported physical aggression, verbal aggression, anger, and hostility ($r = 0.52$ to 0.65) on the Aggression Questionnaire (AQ; Buss & Perry, 1992). In contrast, expressive beliefs had a weak negative relationship to self-reported physical aggression and verbal aggression ($r = -0.19$ to -0.25). Thus, instrumental beliefs showed a clear relationship to self-reported aggressiveness, whilst expressive beliefs did not. Male and female prisoners had comparable instrumental belief scores but female prisoners endorsed significantly greater expressive beliefs. Comparing prisoners on the basis of their index offence showed there was no significant difference in instrumental beliefs between violent and nonviolent offenders, but violent offenders had lower expressive belief scores. Thus both groups appeared equally likely to believe violence was a positive and instrumental strategy, however, the violent offenders were also less inclined to experience negative feelings about acting aggressively, such as guilt.

Research using the EXPAGG-M with New Zealand male prisoners also found the instrumental beliefs scale (but not the expressive beliefs scale) correlated with the AQ (Nichols-Marcy, 2000). In this study there was no significant difference in either instrumental or expressive beliefs scales between violent and nonviolent offenders. Again, violent and nonviolent offenders were classified on the basis of their index offence.

In an effort to develop a measure of violence-related attitudes specifically with offenders, Polaschek, Collie, and Walkey (2004) tested a large pool of items on a sample of male New Zealand prisoners. The resulting 20-item Criminal Attitudes to Violence Scale (CAVS) comprised items that (a) most strongly correlated with self-reported physical aggression, and (b) showed little evidence of social desirability bias. The scale had high internal consistency and a single factor structure. Inspection of the items showed the content tapped into a hostile worldview where violence is an accepted and necessary element of daily life. Polaschek *et al.* found the scale differentiated between offenders with current and past convictions for violence and those with no such convictions. The scale also showed a strong positive correlation with the Instrumental scale of the EXPAGG-M ($r = 0.74$) and a measure of general criminal attitudes (i.e., the Criminal Sentiments Scale Modified, Simourd, 1997; $r = 0.65$).

Using a purpose designed 10-item questionnaire, Slaby and Guerra (1988) investigated the role of aggressive beliefs and problem-solving deficits in juvenile offenders (14 to 21 years) compared to high and low aggressive high school peers. Regarding aggressive beliefs, they found juvenile offenders endorsed significantly greater aggression-supportive beliefs than the comparison adolescents. In particular, juvenile offenders endorsed greater belief in aggression as a legitimate response to social problems, as a means to avoid a negative self-image and as a means to increase self-esteem compared to the high-aggressive high school students. In addition, they were more likely to believe that victims do not suffer compared with low aggressive students. Males across all groups had greater aggressive beliefs than females.

General Criminal Attitudes

A second avenue of research investigates whether broad criminal attitudes predict violent crime. As previously mentioned, evidence suggests incarcerated violent offenders seldom specialise exclusively in violence. Thus, general criminal attitudes may well motivate some violent crime. However, few psychometric instruments exist to assess criminal attitudes (Walters *et al.*, 2002) and few studies investigate their relationship to violence criteria. We review the exceptions below.

The Criminal Sentiments Scale Modified (CSS-M – Simourd, 1997) is a self-report questionnaire designed to measure antisocial attitudes, values, and general beliefs directly related to criminal activity. The CSS-M has five subscales. Three assess attitudes toward the law, courts, and police, respectively. Simourd and Olver (2002) found the combined scale (i.e., *Attitudes to the Law, Courts, and Police; LCP*) had good internal consistency and measured two factors, namely *General Criminal Sentiments* and *Adversarial Beliefs Towards the Law*. The other subscales measure *Criminal Subcultural Beliefs* and *Criminal Self-Concept*. The CSS-M is often used in research alongside another attitude measure, the Pride in Delinquency scale (PID) (Shields & Whitehall, 1991). The PID is a short questionnaire that assesses a respondent's degree of comfort (pride versus shame) with performing a variety of criminal behaviours. Simourd (1997) found preliminary evidence for the PID scale having a two-factor structure, namely *Attitudes Toward Offences* and *Criminal Subculture*.

In samples of Canadian federally incarcerated violent and nonviolent prisoners, Simourd (1997) found CSS-M scores did not correlate significantly with previous violent offences but PID scale scores did ($r = 0.31$). The PID Attitudes Toward Offences subscale correlated more strongly than the Criminal Subculture subscale ($r = 0.32$ and 0.24, respectively). In another study, Simourd and Van de Ven (1999) found no significant correlation between either the PID or CSS-M and future violent rearrest. In this study nonviolent offenders endorsed significantly *greater* antisocial attitudes on almost all scales (excluding the PID Criminal Subculture scale). However, violent and nonviolent groups were determined on their current conviction despite half of the nonviolent group having an official history of violence.

A third questionnaire designed, in part, to assess criminal attitudes and examined with respect to violence is the Self-Appraisal Questionnaire (SAQ) (Loza, 1996). The SAQ comprises six subscales covering the major static and dynamic risk domains and intended to provide a self-report risk assessment tool. The SAQ has been found to have acceptable psychometric properties in a range of studies (Kroner & Loza, 2001; Loza *et al.*, 2000; Loza & Loza-Fanous, 2000), although this is not uniform (Mitchell & Mackenzie, 2006). Findings regarding the Criminal Tendencies subscale and violent criteria have been mixed. For example, Loza and Loza-Fanous (2000) found the subscale significantly correlated with post-release commission of a violent offence ($r = 0.35$) in Canadian federal prisoners followed over 24 months. Other studies, however, have failed to replicate these findings (Loza *et al.*, 2000; Summers & Loza, 2004).

Another recent measure is the Measure of Criminal Attitudes and Associates questionnaire (MCAA – Mills, Kroner & Hemmati, 2004). The MCAA comprises a measure of criminal friends and four attitude scales (i.e., attitudes toward violence, sense of entitlement to act criminally, antisocial intent, and identification with criminal associates). Mills *et al.* found all four attitude scales significantly correlated with violent recidivism over a 24-month period in a Canadian federal prison sample ($r = 0.18$ to 0.30).

Interestingly, McCarthy and Stewart (1998) found evidence that violent offenders ascribe to a "deviant" value system where violence is a legitimate strategy. Using a questionnaire to measure cognitive neutralisations, their results suggested that violent offenders with a low involvement in crime distorted and rationalised their crimes in order to view their actions in accordance with the values of mainstream society. In contrast, offenders with a high involvement in crime did not distort or neutralise their violent actions suggesting they had extinguished any commitment to the dominant value system and internalised self-standards that approved of crime.

Impression Management

A major concern about the use of questionnaires and other self-report methodologies is that positive self-presentational bias will distort the results. However, Mills, Loza and Kroner (2003) found impression management had a significant negative relationship with *violent recidivism* in Canadian federal male prisoners. In essence, the greater offenders' impression management the lower was their rate of violent recidivism. Mills *et al.* proposed that the presence of impression management tendencies may result in offenders choosing more socially acceptable, less violent criminal activities to achieve their goals.

Interview Studies

We could locate few interview studies with serious violent offenders, particularly those that focused on their cognition. An early exception is research by Toch (1969, 1992) using interviews with imprisoned and paroled serious violent offenders ($n = 69$) in the United States. In this study, offenders described their histories of violence, which were then summarised. Toch proposed that two overarching approaches to interpersonal situations linked to the men's propensity for repetitive violence. The first – self-preserving strategies – involved men viewing violence as a means to bolster and enhance their image in their own and others' eyes (e.g., as self-image promoting, self-image defending, and reputation defending). The second – dehumanising others – involved individuals only valuing themselves and their own needs (e.g., exploitation and bullying).

Another small collection of studies have begun to emerge that use grounded theory methodology (Strauss & Corbin, 1998) to develop descriptive models of violent offence processes. Lopez and Emmer (2000, 2002) interviewed American adolescent male offenders ($n = 24$) to obtain their perspectives on their criminal activity, particularly how they defined, interpreted, and justified their behaviour. With regard to violent crimes, Lopez and Emmer described two primary motivations for violence. One type – belief-driven violent assaults – were characterised by extreme acts of violence and hypermasculine notions of male identity. Within

this category Lopez and Emmer included violence that was perceived as justified to (a) protect one's own or one's gang's honour from insult or threat, and (b)
avenge wrongful acts against others less fortunate or for whom there is a special
obligation (e.g., family, women, children). Lopez and Emmer argued that although
the acts were extreme, these justifications for violence reflected traditional male
gender role values and associated beliefs supportive of aggression. Adolescents
committing this type of violence described feeling positive after the violence (e.g.,
emotional satisfaction, feeling a "hero" and perceptions of enhanced peer status
and gang solidarity).

Lopez and Emmer's (2002) second type of violence – emotion-driven assaults
– involved violence committed in a reactive manner under strong negative emotional states and in the absence of adequate emotion-coping skills. Although pro-
aggression beliefs also featured for these offenders, these were emphasised less by
this group. Following acting violently the adolescents described feeling regretful
and distressed; they also minimised the extent of harm caused.

Murdoch (2006) developed an offence process model of imprisoned women's
serious violence in New Zealand ($n = 19$). In the women's backgrounds was a
common perception that violence is a normative aspect of daily life, typically
as a result of severely adverse early experiences involving systemic exposure to
violence. Murdoch described the women's normalisation of violence as having
become "inculturated" into their personal and cultural identities. Violence was
understood to be a legitimate strategy for problem solving and achieving a range
of important psychological, social and material goals. Like their male counter-
parts, the women believed willingness and ability to act violently was a personal
virtue and connected with approval and respect by peers. Violence was believed
to be a useful strategy to counter challenges to reputation, to be necessary to protect oneself from aggressive others in a dangerous world, and a normal response
to emotional distress and social pressures. However, in the immediate context of
the violent offence many women experienced a strong sense of being powerlessness and an inability to effect change in more positive ways, something that has
not emerged so far in research with men.

Similarly, Cooper (2006) – from a descriptive model of assault offences in male
and female offenders – found that offenders held beliefs in the utility of violence
to defend the self or others against psychological and physical threats in a dangerous world, to gain and defend a reputation that conferred social status and self-
respect, and to express and regulate negative affect including the punishment of
others' transgressions.

Cognitive Content Summary

As can be seen from our review, a small and diverse body of research has investigated the content of violence-relevant cognition. A number of themes are evident, although described in various terminologies. One theme is that many violent
offenders believe the world is a hostile place in which violence is both normal
and necessary for survival. Violence also appears to be viewed as a positive strategy for obtaining goals such as self-esteem, social esteem and status, showing

commitment to antisocial allegiances, exerting dominance, and obtaining pecu-niary gains from other crimes. This endorsement in the legitimacy of violence is complimented by an absence of concern about the harmful consequences of violence, either for the victims or the perpetrators themselves. However, this latter finding may be less so for female than male violent offenders.

The role of general criminal attitudes in violence propensity is less clear. Some studies show a moderate association between general criminal attitudes and vio-lence, while other studies do not. Further clarification is required. Also, the re-search to date has been too static, focused either on generalised descriptions of beliefs and attitudes or post-offence cognition. Thus, the challenge for researchers is to try to capture the dynamic nature of offenders' cognition.

COGNITIVE PROCESSING

Questionnaire Studies

Self-report questionnaires that ask respondents to reflect upon and describe their own thinking style are one means of assessing information processing charac-teristics (e.g., the Psychological Inventory of Criminal Thinking Styles, PICTS – Walters, 1995). The PICTS is an 80-item self-report measure designed to sample the process and content of thinking hypothesised to promote and maintain a criminal lifestyle. The PICTS has been subject to a series of factor analyses by its author (Walters, 1995, 2002, 2005) and other independent researchers (Egan *et al.*, 2000; Palmer & Hollin, 2003) with various structures purported to fit data with different samples. Walters (2002, 2005) proposed that a four-factor solution containing two major factors and two minor factors is the best model. The two major factors are Reactive Criminal Thinking, which reflects avoidance of thinking about the nega-tive aspects of committing crime, and Proactive Criminal Thinking which reflects a sense of privilege, a view of oneself as the "nice guy" despite criminal actions, attributions of blame toward others and perceptions of oneself as the victim. The two minor factors were Interpersonal Hostility and Denial of Harm.

In a sample of American maximum security prison inmates, Walters (2005) found the Reactive Criminal Thinking factor (but not the Proactive Criminal Thinking factor) predicted subsequent total, aggressive and nonaggressive disciplinary in-fractions. Walters (2006) found the cutoff subscale of the Reactive Thinking factor predicted total, aggressive, and nonaggressive disciplinary infractions in a sample of male prisoners over a 24-month period. Elevations on the cutoff scale indicate high levels of impulsivity, irresponsibility and anger (Walters, 2006).

The Hostile Interpretations Questionnaire (HIQ) (Mamuza & Simourd, 1997; Simourd & Mamuza, 2000) is a self-report inventory designed to assess respondents' hostile attributional biases using vignettes representing various social situations. The HIQ produces measures of the sources of hostility and vari-ous cognitive distortions leading to hostility. Simourd and Mamuza found the HIQ total score and all subscales had acceptable internal consistency in a sample of Canadian male violent prisoners. The HIQ total score was moderately correlated with self-reported physical aggression on the AQ ($r = 0.38$). Cognitive distortions that remained significant once impression management was controlled for were hostile reaction and external blame ($r = 0.28$ and 0.23, respectively).

Hosser and Bosold (2006) compared juvenile sexual offenders to juvenile nonsexual violent offenders on the HIQ among other measures. They found no significant differences in hostility between juvenile sexual and nonsexual violent offenders. There were also no differences on the measures of impulsivity or empathy but the violent offenders reported higher self-esteem and general self-efficacy.

Experimental Studies

A number of studies have investigated hostile attributional biases using vignettes studies with aggressive adolescent and juvenile offender samples (e.g., Dodge *et al.*, 1990; Guerra, Huesmann & Zelli, 1993; Slaby & Guerra, 1988). For example, as previously discussed, Slaby and Guerra investigated the role of problem solving deficits and aggressive beliefs in juvenile offenders (14 to 21 years) compared to high and low aggressive high school peers. Regarding problem solving deficits, juvenile offenders construed more social problems as hostile, generated fewer facts, solutions, and consequences, and chose less effective best and second best solutions compared to high aggressive students. In addition, juvenile offenders were more likely to choose a hostile goal compared to low aggressive students. Males displayed less extensive social problem-solving skills than females across all three groups. Slaby and Guerra's study is one of the few to characterise problem-solving deficits at all stages of cognitive processing (i.e., encoding, interpretation, goal formation, response evaluation, and response enactment). Overall, they found the combination of problem-solving skills and aggressive beliefs measures best discriminated between the three groups of adolescents.

Copello and Tata (1990) investigated hostile attributional bias in adult male offenders using a sentence-recognition task. The sample consisted of a violent offender group (i.e., forensic inpatients who had committed interpersonal violence), a nonviolent offender group (i.e., offenders on probation for nonviolent offences), and a nonoffender control group (i.e., hospital workers). The sentence-recognition task involved ambiguous sentences that could be interpreted in a violent threatening manner, in a social anxiety-threatening manner, or in a neutral manner. Copello and Tata found violent and nonviolent offenders were more likely to infer threat from ambiguous violent sentences than the nonoffender control group. In contrast, the groups did not differ on inferences of social anxiety threat showing that social anxiety was not the mechanism driving the misinterpretation of ambiguous stimuli. This finding partially supported the hypothesis that violent offenders demonstrate hostile attributional bias when presented ambiguous information. As Copello and Tata note, it may be that both groups have similar levels of hostile attribution bias but nonviolent offenders have greater self-control (i.e., they evaluate a violent solution less favourably than the violent offenders).

In an effort to use cognitive methods with offenders, Seager (2005; James & Seager, 2006) used two paradigms to investigate the relationship between hostility and violence. In the first study, Seager (2005) used a binocular rivalry task to measure the perception and encoding of hostile visual cues. In brief, the binocular rivalry task involved the simultaneous presentation of two distinct images to each eye (one containing a violent cue, the other absent of the violent cue) and the participant reporting all objects seen in either eye. However, rather than seeing both images or a blend of the two, in this paradigm typically one image is registered at a time due to binocular predominance (i.e., the images are not fused due to dissimilar overlapping retinal information – Seager, 2005). Seager argued that because individuals are more likely to recognise scenes with personal valance or meaning, individuals holding hostile schema ought to show a bias to immediately perceive and encode scenes with violent cues. Using Canadian prisoners, Seager found the binocular rivalry measure correlated significantly and moderately with a measure of violence based on official records (i.e., convictions, charges, and infractions; $r = 0.44$), as did a vignette measure of attributional bias ($r = 0.46$) and self-reported impulsivity ($r = 0.51$; I-7; Eysenck et al., 1985). The binocular rivalry and vignette measures of hostile bias were moderately correlated ($r = 0.37$), thus suggesting they measured somewhat overlapping constructs (Seager, 2005). Both the binocular rivalry and vignette measures of hostile bias also correlated strongly and significantly with the Psychopathy Checklist Revised (PCL-R; Hare, 1991) ($r = 0.58$ and 0.66, respectively), and impulsivity ($r = 0.48$ and 0.50, respectively). Seager contended that these findings were consistent with psychopaths' propensity for violence being largely due to a combination of hostile schema about the world and impulsivity problems (Serin & Kuriychuk, 1994).

In the second study, James and Seager (2006) used a dichotomous listening paradigm that involved presenting participants simultaneous but different auditory stimuli to each ear while being required to repeat aloud (shadow) only one of the messages. In a sample of Canadian prisoners, the dichotomous listening measure of hostility (i.e., shadowing interference) was strongly correlated with offenders' violence rating based on official records ($r = 0.65$). Thus, offenders with greater histories of violence were more prone to attend to and encode hostile stimuli. In contrast, the vignette measure of hostility was moderately correlated with violence rating ($r = 0.31$), as was impulsivity ($r = 0.30$). Surprisingly, no significant correlation among any of the three independent measures (dichotomous listening, vignette, or impulsivity) emerged. However, this is potentially consistent with each measure tapping into a different stage or defect in the cognitive processing chain.

With the exception of the three studies just described, use of cognitive paradigms to understand directly the characteristics of cognitive processing associated with violence has occurred with high trait aggressive student samples. Two significant examples of this research are reviewed here. Zelli, Huesmann and Cervone (1995) studied spontaneous trait inferences of hostility in ambiguous situations using a cued recall paradigm. Participants were instructed to memorise a list of sentences describing social encounters for later recall. Zelli Huesmann and Cervone (1995) found high-aggressive individuals recalled more information when provided with hostile cue words during sentence recall than when provided with semantically related cue words. Aided recall using hostile cues indicated that the social encounter had been initially encoded in a hostile manner. Zelli et al. concluded that these findings indicated aggressive individuals' highly accessible knowledge structures (e.g., schemata) caused their hostile social inferences at the point of encoding. Zelli *et al.* also included a deliberate inference condition in which participants were instructed to memorise the list of sentences for later recall *and* consider the reasons for the subject's actions. High and low aggressive individuals' recall did not differ as a function of the cue type in the deliberate recall condition. Zelli *et al.* argued that this showed spontaneous inference paradigms were more effective at finding individual differences in hostile bias than deliberate processing paradigms (such as those that use vignettes).

Tiedens (2001) built on Zelli *et al.*'s research by investigating the role of anger on hostile inferences using a similar cued recall method, but with the addition of a mood induction procedure. Tiedens found the angry high trait aggressive participants' recall benefited more from hostile cue words than the high trait aggressive students who underwent other mood induction conditions. The angry high trait aggressive participants also made more hostile inferences than angry low trait aggressive individuals. Thus, anger facilitated spontaneous hostile inferences in high trait but not low trait aggressive individuals.

Although most cognitive processing research has focused on hostile inferential or attributional biases, a different approach taken by US researchers investigated the effect of a "culture of honour" schema on information processing. Specifically, Nisbett and colleagues (Cohen *et al.*, 1996; Nisbett, 1993) argued that differential homicide rates between Southern and Northern states in the US reflected Southerners' belief that personal affronts are best dealt with using violence (i.e., their "culture of honour"). In a series of experiments, Cohen *et al.* assessed the impact of an insult to white male students classified by their Southern and Northern residential status. Cohen *et al.* found Southerners were more angered in response to the insult than the Northerners, were more likely to write a violent ending to an honour-based vignette but were not more likely to write a violent ending to a hospital-based vignette (suggesting violent scripts for honour-based transgressions) and had higher cortisol and testosterone levels (indicators of aggressiveness).

Cognitive Processing Summary

Taken together, research on violent offender cognitive processing has generally shown that violent offenders more readily perceive threat and hostility in ambiguous situations than less violent individuals. Studies using cognitive paradigms with offenders and high aggressive students indicate that for highly aggressive individuals hostile inferences are made automatically and without awareness early in the cognitive processing sequence. Factors that increase such spontaneous inferences such as anger further facilitate aggressive individuals' hostile inferences. An important finding to emerge is that cognitive experimental paradigms appear to be a more sensitive and specific measure of hostile bias than self-report (vignette) measures. This signals a need for greater incorporation of these cognitive methods in research with offenders.

Few studies have investigated social problem-solving skills deficits that occur further in the cognitive processing chain. Slaby and Guerra's (1988) research with juvenile offenders suggested deficits occurred at all stages, but additional studies are required. An avenue that also requires further investigation is the combined effect of violent supportive beliefs and cognitive processing deficits on violence propensity. For example, research into culture of honour schema suggests that for some individuals hostile biases are not the problem but rather it is at the goal formation and response selection stages that violence evolves. Finally, this review highlights that insufficient attention has been given to the cognitive processing characteristics of violent women.

COGNITIVE STRUCTURES: SCHEMA

Cognitive structures are not directly accessible from self-report (or cognitive products) to the same degree that cognitive content and information processing are. Instead their existence and form (e.g., content and relationship to other schema) have to be inferred from self-report and cognitive paradigms. One approach to advance the conceptualisation of offenders' schema from self-report studies is the application of grounded theory methodology. This methodology involves inductively inferring schema by grouping related content from various sources together (Polaschek & Gannon, 2004; Polaschek & Ward, 2002; Ward & Keenan, 1999). Applying this framework to serious violent offender cognition, Polaschek, Calvert and Gannon (in press) analysed serious violent offenders' offence narratives to identify violence-relevant statements. Five schema variants emerged that captured the dominant themes in offenders' violence cognition. First, a *normalisation of violence* schema contained beliefs and attitudes about violence being a normal occurrence and means for achieving a number of valued personal and social goals. Such goals included gaining respect, resolving disputes, persuading others on a course of action, and having fun. Another aspect of the schema was beliefs that minimised the criminality and harmfulness of violence. Polaschek *et al.*, found that the normalisation of violence schema was so prevalent in the violent offenders sampled that it was best conceptualised as a background assumption that underlies other violence schema.

Another schema to emerge was called *beat or be beaten*, which contained beliefs that focused on the world as a hostile place in which violence is necessary to (a) protect oneself against others (i.e., self-preservation subtype) and (b) achieve social status or power (i.e., self-enhancement subtype). An *I am the law* schema contained beliefs and attitudes that some people are superior to others, which entitles or even obliges them to use violence in the service of protecting others (e.g., family, friends, or society). Finally, an *I get out of control* schema contained beliefs and attitudes that the offender could not regulate his affect and behaviour without assistance. Polaschek *et al.*, (in press) concluded that against the highly prevalent backdrop of normalised violence, violent offenders' schema promoted violence as a means of achieving three types of social influence: self-enhancement, self-preservation and the protection of others. The remaining schema related to deficient self-regulation.

Experimental methods to study the structure of violent offenders' cognition are rare. An exception is the Implicit Association Test (IAT) (Greenwald, McGhee & Schwartz, 1998), a methodology designed to examine the strength of association between concepts in memory. Gray *et al.* (2003) compared IAT performance between psychopathic and nonpsychopathic murderers. Participants were required to classify words rapidly into one of two complex categories. In the response congruent condition, words were categorised into *unpleasant and violent words* or *pleasant and peaceful words*. In the response incongruent condition, the categories were switched to *unpleasant and peaceful* or *pleasant and violent*. The congruent condition is typically easier and faster to perform accurately than the latter condition since well-established associations exist between unpleasant and violent words compared with pleasant and violent words (Gray *et al.*, 2003). Gray *et al.* found the psychopathic murderers showed less of a performance difference on the congruent and incongruent conditions than the nonpsychopathic murderers. In other words, the psychopathic murderers' cognitive networks more closely associated violent words with positive evaluations suggesting they hold positive schema about violence.

Experimental methods to study cognitive structure are far more common with student samples. In this area, Bushman (1995) and Bushman and Geen (1990) tested the hypotheses that viewing media violence was more likely to elicit aggressive affect in high-trait aggressive rather than low-trait aggressive individuals. In brief, Bushman's (1995) participants were randomly allocated to view a 15-minute video clip of either a violent movie or a nonviolent movie (controlled for excitement level). High trait aggressive individuals reported greater hostile affect than low trait aggressive individuals after watching the violent movie. The effect was not present when high trait aggressive individuals watched the nonviolent movie. Further, in a second study, Bushman extended these findings by showing that viewing violent media was also more likely to lead to aggressive behaviour in high versus low trait aggressiveness individuals. Such findings suggest that high trait aggressive individuals have more extensive cognitive-associative networks for aggression that are more readily primed (activated) by violent stimuli. In addition, these networks appear to contain both aggressive affect and aggressive behavioural tendencies.

A major limitation of the above studies is that they provide only indirect support for aggressive cognitive structures (Bushman, 1998). Therefore, Bushman directly investigated the aggressive cognitive associative networks of high versus low aggressive individuals using a word pair evaluation task. High and low trait aggressive participants rated the similarity between pairs of words that contained combinations of aggressive words (e.g., fight, kill) and ambiguous words (e.g., alley, stick) chosen as such from an earlier study. Bushman found that the high trait aggressive individuals rated the aggressive-ambiguous word pairs as more similar to the aggressive-aggressive word pairs than the low trait aggressive individuals. This result suggested the high trait aggressive individuals had stronger associations between ambiguous and aggressive words than the low trait aggressive individuals. Network analysis to depict these associations graphically showed that the high trait aggressive individuals were more likely to associate ambiguous words with aggressive words than the low trait aggressive individuals (e.g., alley with fight versus alley with night, respectively). The high trait- and low trait-aggressive individuals did not differ in the extent that they associated the aggressive words with each other. Bushman concluded that these results were consistent with characteristically aggressive individuals having more developed and extensive cognitive-associative networks.

Cognitive Structure Summary

The studies reviewed demonstrate different approaches to determining violence related cognitive structures. The thematic approach focuses on schema identification by paying careful attention to the content of offenders' self-report and others' experience with violent offenders and drawing out similarities across studies. There is room, however, for considerably more research into both the content of schemas and the relationship between various schemas.

Experimental approaches investigating the structure of violent offenders' cognition are virtually nonexistent. Gray *et al.* (2003) is the one exception. Instead research in this area is conducted with high and low trait aggressive student samples. We reviewed two key research studies here, one involving the use of a priming paradigm and the other a modelling design. Both conclude that high aggressive individuals have better developed aggressive cognitive networks, however, the findings need to be replicated with aggressive samples other than students, and ultimately with violent offenders. Knowing the characteristics of violent offenders' networks will increase our understanding of the nature of violent offender cognition.

SUMMARY AND CLINICAL IMPLICATIONS

Looking across the various research areas and methodologies related to cognition and violent offending, several consistent findings emerge. One is that violent individuals maintain beliefs and attitudes about the world as a hostile place in which violence is a normal and necessary part of daily life. Violence is seen as an effective instrumental means to a number of desirable goals. It can be used to solve problems, to defend and enhance one's self-esteem, to promote status within one's social hierarchy, and to provide a sense of personal safety and personal effectiveness. There is also a corresponding absence of beliefs that violence has particularly harmful consequences for one's self or victims.

Violent individuals also more readily perceive and encode threat and hostility in others, related to beliefs and schemas about a hostile dangerous world. This hostile bias occurs automatically. Violent individuals are also more likely to be impulsive and reactive in their thinking increasing their propensity to infer hostility in the environment around them. In the absence of potentially more accurate neutral attributions and interpretations, and without the capacity to develop more varied and potentially more effective nonviolent solutions, violent individuals characteristically resort to violence to deal with their environment. And instead of experiencing the negative cognitions and associated affects that might inhibit subsequent episodes of violence, they tend to make more positive appraisals of their violent behaviour, thereby reinforcing the associated cognitive process and increasing the likelihood of future violent displays.

According to social cognitive theory these beliefs and attitudes and the information-processing biases and deficits that arise from them primarily develop during childhood and are organised in memory as schema (Huesmann, 1998). These schemas are thought to exert an enduring influence throughout an individual's life and be resistant to change (Anderson & Bushman, 2002). Research with violent offenders on the content of cognition at the schema level is only beginning to emerge. Schemas are identified as the appropriate focus for treatment and management in the sex offender area, rather than the individual beliefs and attitudes that they generate (Mann & Shingler, 2006; Ward, 2000). This appears equally relevant for (nonsexual) violent offenders.

A few measures have been developed to assess cognitive content and information processing and these can serve as a starting point in the design of treatment interventions. However, in the absence of clear typologies reflecting the causal relationships between cognition and violence, treatment planning appears to require an individualised understanding of each unique offender. Therefore an individualised assessment, one that carefully explores the sequence of thoughts and behaviours associated with violence, is essential in developing the most effectively targeted treatments. Although questionnaires can be a useful aid to assessment, it is likely that careful attention to the offender's here-and-now interactions with the therapist and with others will yield important information about the offender's underlying schema. Violent offenders will inevitably bring their own attitudes, beliefs, and information processing style into interpersonal encounters with prison and clinical staff such that schema associated with aggression and violence will in some fashion be displayed.

A similarly important factor to bear in mind is that offenders' violence-related cognition will also come into therapeutic encounters. It follows then that treatment programmes should target violence-related cognition from a treatment *process* as well as treatment *content* focus. From this perspective, interventions that emerge directly from interactions where violence-related schema are displayed are likely to provide more powerful corrective experiences than rigidly didactic, manualised treatment activities, as these may provide little room for the emergence of current, immediate experiences of the cognitions associated with violent offending. A promising finding to emerge from cognitive processing research is that the *deliberate* processing of information can negate spontaneous hostile inferences in aggressive individuals (Zelli, Huesmann & Cervone, 1995). Thus a starting point for process-related therapeutic interventions appears to involve careful structuring of sessions and discussion of the process of thinking to help offenders consciously process and reflect upon therapeutic interactions and thereby minimise incorrect hostile inferences.

What appears to be needed is a balance between sufficiently well defined treatment procedures that will allow for programme integrity and evaluation, and a dynamic process that allows for and attends to current cognitive and related affective experiences. This will require treatment staff to not only be familiar with the cognitive features of violent individuals but to recognise and respond effectively to the display of these features in the context of the therapeutic process.

CONCLUDING COMMENTS

A small body of research relevant to the content, processes and structure of violent offenders' cognition is beginning to emerge. As expected, this research shows violent offenders hold hostile schema and make hostile attributional biases. However, this research also highlights that violent offenders hold a number of other attitudes, beliefs and schema that motivate violence for a range of other goals. To some extent, this criminally oriented and versatile view of violence is likely to be specific to offenders and less readily accessed from studies with mainstream populations. Not surprisingly, their interpersonally aggressive characteristics and treatment resistance has led violent offenders as a group to be characterised as difficult to treat and less desirable to engage with than other offenders (Serin & Preston, 2001b; Wormith & Olver, 2002). However, given the significant harm caused by their violence and the scarcity of demonstrated effective programmes for these offenders, it is imperative that further research is undertaken to enable a more thorough understanding of their treatment needs and to inspire clinical innovation.

REFERENCES

Anderson, C. A. & Bushman, B. J. (2002). Human aggression. *Annual Review of Psychology*, **53**, 27–51.

Archer, J. & Haigh, A. (1997a). Beliefs about aggression among male and female prisoners. *Aggressive Behavior*, **23**, 405–15.

Archer, J. & Haigh, A. (1997b). Do beliefs about aggressive feelings and actions predict reported levels of aggression. *British Journal of Social Psychology*, **36**, 83–105.

Bandura, A. (2001). Social cognitive theory: an agentic perspective. *Annual Review of Psychology*, **52**, 1–26.

Bushman, B. J. (1995). Moderating role of trait aggressiveness in the effects of violent media on aggression. *Journal of Personality and Social Psychology*, **69**, 950–60.

Bushman, B. J. (1998). Priming effects of media violence on the accessibility of aggressive constructs in memory. *Personality and Social Psychology Bulletin*, **24**, 537–45.

Bushman, B. J. & Geen, R. G. (1990). Role of cognitive-emotional mediators and individual differences in the effects on media violence on aggression. *Journal of Personality and Social Psychology*, **58**, 156–63.

Buss, A. H. & Perry, M. (1992). The Aggression Questionnaire. *Journal of Personality and Social Psychology*, **63**, 452–59.

Cohen, D., Nisbett, R. E., Bowdle, B. F. & Schwarz, N. (1996). Insult, aggression, and the Southern culture of honor: an "experimental ethnography". *Journal of Personality and Social Psychology*, **70**, 945–60.

Cooper, J. (2006). *The violence situation: a descriptive model of the offence process of assault for male and female offenders*. Unpublished doctorate thesis, University of Melbourne, Australia.

Copello, A. G. & Tata, P. R. (1990). Violent behaviour and interpretative bias: An experimental study of the resolution of ambiguity in violent offenders. *British Journal of Clinical Psychology*, **29**, 417–28.

Crick, N. R. & Dodge, K. A. (1994). A review and reformulation of social information-processing mechanisms in children's social adjustment. *Psychological Bulletin*, **115**, 74–101.

Dodge, K. A., Price, J. M., Bachorowski, H. & Newman, J. P. (1990). Hostile attributional biases in severely aggressive adolescents. *Journal of Abnormal Psychology*, **99**, 385–92.

Dodge, K. A. & Schwartz, D. (1997). Social information processing mechanisms in aggressive behavior. In D. M. Stoff, J. Breiling & J. D. Maser (eds), *Handbook of Antisocial Behavior* (pp. 171–80). New York: Wiley.

Douglas, K. S., & Skeem, J. L. (2005). Violence risk assessment: Getting specific about being dynamic. *Psychology, Public Policy & Law*, **11**, 347–83.

Egan, V., McMurran, M., Richardson, C. & Blair, M. (2000). Criminal cognitions and personality: what does the PICTS really measure? *Criminal Behaviour and Mental Health*, **10**, 170–84.

Eysenck, B.G., Pearson, P.R., Easting, G. & Allsop, J.F. (1985). Age norms for impulsiveness, venturesomeness and empathy in adults. *Personality and Individual Differences*, **6**, 613–19.

Fiske, S. T. & Taylor, S. E. (1991). *Social Cognition* (2nd edn). New York: McGraw-Hill.

Gray, N. S., MacCulloch, M. J., Smith, J. *et al.* (2003). Violence viewed by psychopathic murderers: adapting a revealing test may expose those psychopaths who are most likely to kill. *Nature*, **423**, 497–8.

Greenwald, A. G., McGhee, D. E. & Schwartz, J. L. K. (1998). Measuring individual differences in implicit cognition: the implicit association test. *Journal of Personality and Social Psychology*, **74**, 1464–80.

Guerra, N. G., Huesmann, L. R. & Zelli, A. (1993). Attributions for social failure and adolescent aggression. *Aggressive Behavior*, **19**, 421–34.

Hare, R. D. (1991). *Hare Psychopathy Checklist-Revised (PCL-R): Technical Manual*. New York: Multi-Health Systems.

Hollon, S. D. & Kriss, M. R. (1984). Cognitive factors in clinical research and practice. *Clinical Psychology Review*, **4**, 35–76.

Hosser, D. & Bosold, C. (2006). Comparison of sexual and violent offenders in a German youth prison. *Howard Journal of Criminal Justice*, **45**, 159–70.

Huesmann, L. R. (1998). The role of social information processing and cognitive schema in the acquisition and maintenance of habitual aggressive behavior. In R. G. Geen & E. Donnerstein (eds), *Human Aggression: Theories, Research, and Implications for Social Policy* (pp. 73–109). San Diego, CA: Academic Press.

Ingram, R. E. & Kendall, P. C. (1986). Cognitive clinical psychology: Implications of an information processing perspective. In R. E. Ingram (ed.), *Information Processing Approaches to Clinical Psychology* (pp. 3–21). Orlando, FL: Academic Press.

James, M. & Seager, J. A. (2006). Impulsivity and schemas for a hostile world. *International Journal of Offender Therapy & Comparative Criminology*, **50**, 47–56.

Kroner, D. G. & Loza, W. (2001). Evidence for the efficacy of self-report in predicting non-violent and violent criminal recidivism. *Journal of Interpersonal Violence*, **16**, 168–77.

Loeber, R., Farrington, D. P. & Waschbusch, D. A. (1998). Serious and violent juvenile offenders. In R. Loeber & D. P. Farrington (eds), *Serious and Violent Juvenile Offenders: Risk Factors and Successful Interventions*. Newbury Park, CA: Sage.

Lopez, V. A. & Emmer, E. T. (2000). Adolescent male offenders: a grounded theory study of cognition, emotion, and delinquent crime contexts. *Criminal Justice and Behavior*, **27**, 292–311.

Lopez, V. & Emmer, E. (2002). Influences of beliefs and values on male adolescents' decision to commit violent offenses. *Psychology of Men and Masculinity*, **3**, 28–40.

Loza, W. (1996). *Self-Appraisal Questionnaire (SAQ): A Measure for Assessing Violent and Non-violent Recidivism*. Unpublished manuscript.

Loza, W., Dhaliwal, G., Kroner, D. & Loza-Fanous, A. (2000). Reliability, construct, and concurrent validities of the Self-Appraisal Questionnaire: a tool for assessing violent and non-violent recidivism. *Criminal Justice and Behavior*, **27**, 356–74.

Loza, W. & Loza-Fanous, A. (2000). Predictive validity of the Self-Appraisal Questionnaire (SAQ): a tool for assessing violent and non-violent release failures. *Journal of Interpersonal Violence*, **15**, 1183–91.

Mamuza, J. & Simourd, D. J. (1997). The Hostile Interpretations Questionnaire: Psychometric properties and construct validity. *Criminal Justice and Behavior*, **27**, 645–63.

Mann, R. E. & Shingler, J. (2006). Schema-driven cognition in sexual offenders: Theory, assessment and treatment. In W. L. Marshall, Y. M. Fernandez, L. E. Marshall &

G. A. Serran (Eds.), *Sexual Offender Treatment: Controversial Issues* (pp. 173–85). Chichester: Wiley.

McCarthy, J. G. & Stewart, A. L. (1998). Neutralisation as a process of graduated desensitisation: moral values of offenders. *International Journal of Offender Therapy and Comparative Criminology*, **42**, 278–90.

Mills, J. F., Kroner, D. G. & Hemmati, T. (2004). The Measures of Criminal Attitudes and Associates (MCAA): the prediction of general and violent recidivism. *Criminal Justice and Behavior*, **31**, 717–33.

Mills, J. F., Loza, W. & Kroner, D. G. (2003). Predictive validity despite social desirability: Evidence for the robustness of self-report among offenders. *Criminal Behaviour and Mental Health*, **13**, 140–50.

Mitchell, O. & Mackenzie, D. L. (2006). Disconfirmation of the predictive validity of the Self-Appraisal Questionnaire in a sample of high-risk drug offenders. *Criminal Justice and Behavior*, **33**, 449–66.

Moffitt, T., Caspi, A., Harrington, H. & Milne, B. J. (2002). Males on the life-course-persistent and adolescence-limited antisocial pathways: follow-up at age 26 years. *Development and Psychopathology*, **14**, 179–207.

Murdoch, S. (2006). *Preliminary descriptive model of the offence process of violent women offenders.* Doctor of Philosophy thesis, Victoria University of Wellington, New Zealand.

Nichols-Marcy, T. (2000). *Beliefs about aggression: a trial of the Revised EXPAGG and the Aggression Questionnaire with New Zealand student and offender population.* Unpublished Masters' Thesis, Victoria University of Wellington, New Zealand.

Nisbett, R. E. (1993). Violence and U. S. regional culture. *American Psychologist*, **48**, 441–9.

Palmer, E. J. & Hollin, C. R. (2003). Using the Psychological Inventory of Criminal Thinking Styles with English prisoners. *Legal and Criminological Psychology*, **8**, 175–87.

Polaschek, D. L. L., Calvert, S. & Gannon, T. A. Linking violent thinking: implicit theory based research with violent offenders. *Journal of Interpersonal Violence* (in press).

Polaschek, D. L. L., Collie, R. M. & Walkey, F. H. (2004). Criminal attitudes to violence: development and preliminary validation of a scale for prisoners. *Aggressive Behavior*, **30**, 484–503.

Polaschek, D. L. L. & Gannon, T. A. (2004). The implicit theories of rapists: what convicted offenders tell us. *Sexual Abuse: Journal of Research and Treatment*, **16**, 299–314.

Polaschek, D. L. L. & Ward, T. (2002). The implicit theories of potential rapists: What our questionnaires tell us. *Aggression and Violent Behavior*, **7**, 385–406.

Seager, J. A. (2005). Violent men: the importance of impulsivity and cognitive schema. *Criminal Justice and Behavior*, **32**, 26–49.

Serin, R. C. & Kuriychuk, M. (1994). Social and cognitive processing deficits in violent offenders: Implications for treatment. *International Journal of Law and Psychiatry*, **17**, 431–41.

Serin, R. C. & Preston, D. L. (2001a). Managing and treating violent offenders. In J. B. Ashford, B. D. Sales & W. H. Reid (eds), *Treating Adult and Juvenile Offenders with Special Needs.* Washington D.C.: American Psychological Association.

Serin, R. C. & Preston, D. L. (2001b). Designing, implementing and managing treatment programs for violent offenders. In G. A. Bernfeld, D. P. Farrington & A. W. Leschied (eds), *Offender Rehabilitation in Practice: Implementing and Evaluating Effective Programs* (pp 205–26). Chichester: Wiley.

Shields, I. W. & Whitehall, G. C., (1991, December). *The Pride in Delinquency Scale.* Paper presented at the eastern Ontario correctional psychologists' winter conference, Burrits Rapids, Canada.

Simourd, D. J. (1997). The Criminal Sentiments Scale – Modified and Pride in Delinquency Scale: Psychometric properties and construct validity of two measures of criminal attitudes. *Criminal Justice and Behavior*, **24**, 52–70.

Simourd, D. J. & Mamuza, J. M. (2000). The Hostile Interpretations Questionnaire: psychometric properties and construct validity. *Criminal Justice and Behavior*, **27**, 645–63.

Simourd, D. J. & Olver, M. E. (2002). The future of criminal attitudes research and practice. *Criminal Justice and Behavior*, **29**, 427–46.

Simourd, D. J. & Van De Ven, J. (1999). Assessment of criminal attitudes: criterion-related validity of the Criminal Sentiments Scale-Modified and Pride in Delinquency Scale. *Criminal Justice and Behavior*, **26**, 90–106.

Slaby, R. G. & Guerra, N. G. (1988). Cognitive mediators of aggression in adolescent offenders: 1. Assessment. *Developmental Psychology*, **34**, 580–8.

Strauss, A. & Corbin, J. (1998). *Basics of Qualitative Research: Techniques and Procedures for Developing Grounded Theory* (2nd edn). Thousand Oaks, CA: Sage.

Summers, R. & Loza, W. (2004). Cross-validation of the Self-Appraisal Questionnaire (SAQ): a tool for assessing violent and non-violent recidivism in Australian offenders. *Psychiatry, Psychology, and Law*, **11**, 254–62.

Tiedens, L. Z. (2001). The effect of anger on the hostile inferences of aggressive and non-aggressive people: specific emotions, cognitive processing, and chronic accessibility. *Motivation and Emotion*, **25**, 233–51.

Toch, H. (1969, 1992). *Violent Men*. Chicago: Aldine Press.

Walters, G. (1995). The Psychological Inventory of Criminal Thinking Styles: I. Reliability and preliminary validity. *Criminal Justice and Behavior*, **22**, 307–25.

Walters, G. (2002). The Psychological Inventory of Criminal Thinking Styles (PICTS): A review and meta-analysis. *Assessment*, **9**, 278–91.

Walters, G. (2005). How many factors are there on the PICTS? Criminal *Behaviour and Mental Health*, **15**, 237–83.

Walters, G. (2006). Use of the Psychological Inventory of Criminal Thinking Styles to predict disciplinary adjustment in male inmate program participants. *International Journal of Offender Therapy and Comparative Criminology*, **50**, 166–73.

Walters, G., Trgovac, M., Rychlec, M. *et al.* (2002). Assessing change with the Psychological Inventory of Criminal Thinking Styles: a controlled analysis and multisite cross-validation. *Criminal Justice and Behavior*, **29**, 308–31.

Ward, T. (2000). Sexual offenders' cognitive distortions as implicit theories. *Aggression and Violent Behaviour*, **5**, 491–507.

Ward, T. & Keenan, T. (1999). Child molesters' implicit theories. *Journal of Interpersonal Violence*, **14**, 821–38.

Wormith, J. S. & Olver, M. E. (2002). Offender treatment attrition and its relationship with risk, responsivity and recidivism. *Criminal Justice and Behavior. Special Issue: Risk and assessment in contemporary corrections*, **29**, 447–71.

Zelli, A., Huesmann, C. R. & Cervone, D. (1995). Social inference and individual differences in aggression: Evidence for spontaneous judgments of hostility. *Aggressive Behavior*, **21**, 405–17.

Chapter 10

MORAL COGNITION AND AGGRESSION

EMMA J. PALMER

University of Leicester, UK

One area in which there has been much interest with respect to aggression and violence is moral cognition. Often referred to as "moral reasoning" or "judgment", this relates to how people reason about and justify their actions. Within the psychological literature moral reasoning is conceptualised within a cognitive-developmental framework, based on Piaget's (1932) work examining how children understand the world around them. This work was refined into a full theory of moral reasoning development by Lawrence Kohlberg (1969, 1984) and has since been applied to a range of behaviours; including antisocial, aggressive, violent, and offending behaviour (for recent reviews, see Palmer, 2003a, 2003b, 2005).

This chapter, therefore, aims to cover four main areas. First, it will briefly describe and evaluate cognitive-developmental theories of moral reasoning. Second, methods of assessing moral reasoning, including some of the common standardised tools will be outlined. The relationship between moral reasoning and aggression will be examined in the third section. Finally, interventions that target the moral reasoning of violent individuals will be considered, along with some evidence as to their effectiveness.

THEORIES OF MORAL REASONING

Piaget's Theory of Moral Reasoning

The study of moral reasoning in psychology using a cognitive-developmental approach dates back to Piaget's (1932) work on children's intelligence. Unlike other contemporary researchers, Piaget was interested in examining the development of children's understanding of the world around them in terms of its cognitive structures and processes, rather than its content. For example, Piaget was interested in the different sorts of wrong answers that children provided in response

Aggressive Offenders' Cognition: Theory, Research and Practice. Edited by T. A. Gannon, T. Ward, A. R. Beech and D. Fisher. © 2007 John Wiley & Sons, Ltd.

to questions on IQ tests, and how these could be classified *structurally*. From his research Piaget (1952) proposed four stages of logical reasoning that children progress through: the *sensorimotor* stage, the *preoperational* stage, the *concrete operational* stage, and the *formal operational* stage.

Piaget (1932) proposed that children's moral reasoning developed in line with their ability to reason logically. Thus, in contrast to prevailing views of morality at that time (i.e., internalisation of societal norms; Durkheim, 1925/1961), Piaget conceptualised morality as a developmental process that was actively constructed from an individual's social experiences.

Piaget (1932) found two broad conceptions of justice existed among children in his research: "reciprocity as a fact" and "reciprocity as an ideal". Young children showed a limited understanding of justice and reciprocity, such as "if I do something for you, you will do something for me". However, as they matured this was replaced by recognition that people should behave towards others as they would wish to be treated themselves. In this more mature view of justice, psychological intentions and motives for behaviours are also given consideration.

As his research showed children's conception of justice to often vary, Piaget (1932) proposed two overlapping "phases" of moral reasoning: heteronomous and autonomous moral reasoning.

- *Hetereonomous moral reasoning* – rules are perceived as fixed and set by authority figures. Emphasis is placed on tit-for-tat exchanges.
- *Autonomous moral reasoning* – rules are perceived as resulting from consensus and co-operation between individuals. Fairness and justice are the main principles determining interactions between people.

Piaget proposed that his logical reasoning stages act as preconditions for the moral reasoning phases. Autonomous moral reasoning could not be reached prior to the individual attaining the formal operational stage of logical reasoning. However, although formal operational logical reasoning was proposed to be a necessary condition for autonomous moral reasoning, it was not seen to be a sufficient condition.

Kohlberg's Theory of Moral Reasoning

Piaget's research was expanded upon by Kohlberg (1969, 1984) in his theory of the development of moral reasoning. In this theory, Kohlberg considered morality in the context of social and nonsocial cognitive development. The theory takes a formal approach to morality, since it focuses on the structure and process of moral reasoning (i.e., why an action is right or wrong in terms of cognitive justification), in contrast to substantive approaches to morality which are concerned with the content of moral beliefs (i.e., whether a behaviour is morally right or wrong). There is an assumption in the cognitive-developmental approach that there is a generalised motivation for morality based on competence, acceptance, self-esteem or self-realisation (Kohlberg, 1984). This is in contrast to motivations based on biological needs (cf. psychoanalytic approaches to morality) or seeking/avoiding punishment (cf. socialisation and social learning approaches to morality).

Table 10.1 Kohlberg's stages of moral reasoning

Level 1: Preconventional reasoning

Stage 1: Moral reasoning is based on avoiding punishment and obeying authority figures.

Stage 2: Moral reasoning is egocentric, and based on the perceived balance of rewards and punishment.

Level 2: Conventional reasoning

Stage 3: Moral reasoning is determined by other people's needs, with personal relationships of greatest importance.

Stage 4: Moral reasoning is based on keeping society's rules and laws in order to maintain society.

Level 3: Postconventional reasoning

Stage 5: Moral reasoning is underpinned by an understanding that society's laws are a contract between the individual and society. However, under certain circumstances these laws can be broken.

Stage 6: Moral reasoning is determined by self-chosen ethical principles that are consistent over time and situations. If these come into conflict with society's laws, behaviour is determined by the self-chosen principles.

Kohlberg's theory outlined six stages of moral reasoning, with reasoning becoming more complex and abstract at the higher stages. These moral stages are defined with reference to the structure of interactions between the self and other people, rather than the internalisation of rules or norms. The six stages are split into three levels: pre-conventional reasoning, conventional reasoning, and post-conventional reasoning (see Table 10.1) (Kohlberg, 1984). At the pre-conventional level, reasoning is determined by selfish considerations and shows little or no understanding of social norms or rules. Reasoning at the conventional level incorporates a comprehension of societal conventions and the importance of maintaining them. Individuals reasoning at the post-conventional level are able to differentiate between the expectations and rules that govern society and their own self-chosen moral and ethical principles. Where conflict occurs between these two, it is the individual's own personal moral and ethical principles that take precedence.

Progression through the stages is proposed to be sequential (i.e., no reversals), with individuals reasoning mainly at one stage at a given point in time (Kohlberg, 1969). Although Kohlberg's own longitudinal research mainly supported these assertions (Colby *et al.*, 1983), it has been argued that this could have been a result of the scoring methods in this study (Krebs *et al.*, 1991). Indeed, as noted by Gibbs (2003), more recent measures that may be less open to these biases show that most individuals reason across a number of stages, depending on the situation and moral domain.

Following Piaget (1932), Kohlberg viewed moral reasoning development to be linked to general cognitive development (Kohlberg, 1969). He also proposed that an individual's social perspective-taking ability was closely linked to level of moral development, with specific reference to Selman's (1976, 1980) six-stage theory of social perspective-taking. This theory describes how social perspective-taking

Table 10.2   Selman's stages of social perspective taking

Level 1: Preconventional Reasoning – concrete individual perspective

Stage 1:   The individual has a self-centred view of the world, with little recognition of other people's perspectives.

Stage 2:   The individual begins to appreciate that other people have their own views of the world, but their own personal view remains of most importance.

Level 2: Conventional Reasoning – member-of-society perspective

Stage 3:   The individual takes account of the perspective of people they have relationships with (e.g., family and friends).

Stage 4:   The individual is able distinguish between the societal point of view and the views of people within society.

Level 3: Postconventional Reasoning – prior-to-society perspective

Stage 5:   The individual takes a perspective that acknowledges that people have rights that exist regardless of social contracts (i.e., are prior to society). Differing perspectives are combined in a rational way, although there is recognition that this may not always be possible.

Stage 6:   The individual takes a perspective derived from holding his/her own set of consistent moral principles.

develops, taking account of how other people and their thoughts and feelings are perceived, as well as the individual's role in the wider world. The six stages of Selman's theory of the development of social perspective-taking parallel those of Kohlberg's theory of the development of moral reasoning (see Table 10.2).

The mirroring of the stages of social perspective-taking within Kohlberg's six stages of moral reasoning development shows how progress through the moral reasoning stages represents a restructuring of modes of role-taking. Therefore, the social perspective-taking stages form a pre-condition for the development of the parallel moral reasoning stages in Kohlberg's theory. However, it is important to note that while the social perspective-taking stages are a necessary pre-condition for the equivalent moral reasoning stage, they are not a sufficient requirement.

Although Kohlberg placed an emphasis on the role of social perspective-taking in moral reasoning, he made a clear distinction between the two concepts. Drawing on moral philosophy, Kohlberg (1969) identified four types of reasons or "orientations" used in moral decision-making: normative order, utility consequences, ideal-self, and justice or fairness.

- *Normative order orientation* – the main principle of moral reasoning is respect for rules, drawing on the work of Kant, Durkheim, and Piaget.
- *Utility consequences orientation* – the main principles of moral reasoning is the positive and negative consequences for oneself or others in terms of their welfare. This view draws on the work of Mill and Dewey.
- *Ideal self-orientation* – moral reasoning is based on a view of the self as being "good", having a conscience, and being relatively independent of other's approval. This view is informed by philosopher such as Bradley, Royce, and Baldwin.
- *Justice or fairness orientation* – an emphasis is placed on the concepts of equality, reciprocity, liberty, and contract between people in moral reasoning. The work of Kohlberg and Rawls is central to this approach.

While Kohlberg acknowledged that individuals use all of these orientations in their moral reasoning, he argued that the justice orientation is the most important in morality. He based this view on the argument that moral situations all involve conflicts between different interests, and he believed that the concepts of justice and fairness offered the best resolutions to these conflicts. Therefore, despite the role he saw for social perspective-taking in moral reasoning, Kohlberg saw the justice orientation as being the key distinction between the two concepts and as providing the over-arching orientation in moral reasoning. The domain-specificity of Kohlberg's theory with respect to the justice and fairness orientation is also seen in the fact that the final stage of moral reasoning (Stage 6) represents "pure" justice reasoning, with the other five stages progressively leading up to this stage. As a result, Kohlberg often referred to his theory as a *theory of justice moral reasoning* (Kohlberg, 1981).

Gibbs' Theory of Sociomoral Reasoning

More recently, Kohlberg's theory has been revised by Gibbs (1993, 2003) to give a theory of "sociomoral" reasoning (see Table 10.3).

This theory divides the development of morality into two overlapping phases: standard and existential. Standard moral development incorporates two overlapping levels of reasoning, each comprising two stages. As such, Gibbs' theory of-

Table 10.3   Gibbs' stages of sociomoral reasoning

Standard development

A. Immature moral reasoning

Stage 1:   Unilateral and physicalistic
Reasoning makes reference to powerful authority figures (e.g. parents) and the physical consequences of behaviour. Individuals show little or no perspective-taking.

Stage 2:   Exchanging and instrumental
Reasoning shows a basic understanding of social interaction. However, this typically reflects cost/benefit deals, with the benefits to the individual being given greatest importance.

B. Mature moral reasoning

Stage 3:   Mutual and prosocial
Reasoning illustrates an understanding of interpersonal relationships and the norms associated with these. Social perspective-taking is apparent, along with appeals to one's own conscience.

Stage 4:   Systemic and standard
Reasoning reflects an understanding of complex social systems, with appeals to societal requirements, basic rights and values, and character/integrity.

Existential development

Reasoning involves hypothetical contemplation, meta-ethical thinking, forming of own moral principles, and ontological inspiration. Meta-ethical reflections move from a relativistic perspective to a postsceptical one. Results of such thinking can lead to the production of "natural" philosophies.

fers some response to criticisms of Kohlberg's assertion that an individual's moral reasoning performance is consistent across all situations (see Krebs *et al.*, 1991).

Stages 1 and 2 are termed "immature" moral reasoning and reflect superficial and egocentric reasoning. At these stages morality is conflated with physical and financial outcomes, pragmatics, and egocentric motivations for behaviour. In contrast, Stages 3 and 4 are labelled "mature" reasoning and reflect an understanding of interpersonal relationships (Stage 3) and societal needs (Stage 4).

Existential development reflects "qualitative changes no longer characterisable as an invariant stage sequence." (Gibbs, 2003, p. 75), and is not attained by all individuals, even in adulthood. The evolution of existential development is seen to result from contemplation and hypothetical reflection, as well as sudden insights that may occur during existentially profound events (e.g., meditation, life-threatening circumstances). Therefore, Gibbs proposes that existential development is not "constructed" in the same way as a Piagetian or Kohlbergian stage, but is a product of "hypothetical reflection on normative ethics, stemming from the morality of one of another of the basic moral judgment stages." (Gibbs, 2003, p. 77).

Gibbs (1993, 2003) also considers the role of emotion within the development of moral reasoning, noting that the development of social perspective-taking abilities will lead to emotions, such as empathy, sympathy, and benevolence, that may motivate decisions about moral judgments and behaviour (Hoffman, 2000). Gibbs emphasises the need to have acquired these affective processing abilities before the mature stages of moral reasoning can be attained. Gibbs' revised theory also has a greater element of relativism to it, with mature moral reasoning reflecting "the cognitive-structural norm for any culture" (Gibbs, Potter & Goldstein, 1995, p. 44), such as formal laws and informal values of a society or culture.

ASSESSING MORAL REASONING

The assessment of moral reasoning has a history dating back to the development of Kohlberg's theory, with the first measure being devised by Kohlberg during his PhD research. There is now a small group of measures in this area, which fall into two categories: production measures and recognition measures (for a full review of a range of measures, see Palmer, 2003b). Production measures use moral dilemmas to elicit formal moral justifications that represent reasoning processes from respondents, whereas recognition measures present respondents with a list of statements relating to formal moral reasoning, which they are required to rank in order of preference to a question.

Production Measures

There are three main production measures of moral reasoning that are regularly used in this area: the Moral Judgment Interview (MJI) (Colby & Kohlberg, 1987), the Sociomoral Reflection Measure (SRM) (Gibbs & Widaman, 1982), and the Sociomoral Reflection Measure-Short Form (SRM-SF) (Gibbs, Basinger & Fuller, 1992).

Moral Judgment Interview

The MJI is the assessment tool that was developed out of Kohlberg's work examining moral reasoning, and has undergone a number of refinements over the years (Colby & Kohlberg, 1987). It presents respondents with a moral dilemma – that is, a situation in which there is a conflict between two moral issues and there is no clear right course of action – in order to elicit moral justifications. One of the most well known moral dilemmas from the MJI is the Heinz dilemma, in which Heinz's wife is very sick and the only way to cure her is with a new drug. However, this drug is very expensive and Heinz cannot afford the cost. The dilemma then sets up a scenario between Heinz stealing the drug to cure his wife and not stealing it to avoid breaking the law. Thus, a conflict is created between the moral values of saving life and respecting others' property rights.

Respondents are first asked to state what they think Heinz should do (i.e., steal the drug or not). Questions are then posed to get respondents to evaluate the moral values in the dilemma (i.e., life and property). Finally, respondents are asked questions to elicit moral justifications to support their decision about Heinz's behaviour and their evaluation of the moral values. It is these justifications that are then scored in terms of Kohlberg's stages, rather than the moral decision *per se*. The standardised version of the MJI comprises three moral dilemmas, each of which involves two moral issues in conflict: life versus property, conscience versus punishment, and contract versus authority.

The MJI has been used extensively in research and has been showed to have high levels of reliability and validity (Colby & Kohlberg, 1987; Colby *et al.*, 1983). One issue that has remained contentious is its degree of construct validity, or whether it is actually measuring moral reasoning development. As noted by Colby (1978) and Kohlberg (1981), a true assessment of any measure of moral reasoning needs to consider it in terms of the theoretical tenets of Kohlberg's theory. Thus, a valid measure needs to confirm the invariant sequence of the moral stages and show that respondents are consistent in their moral reasoning. However, this gives rise to a tautology, in that the MJI and its scoring system were designed to provide a psychometric tool for the assessment of Kohlberg's theory of moral reasoning. It is also difficult to use moral action as an index of validity, with Kohlberg himself noting that the relationship between his theory of moral reasoning and moral action was an area that had not been addressed theoretically or empirically.

In practice the MJI is time-consuming to use; it requires individual administration with interviews being tape-recorded for scoring and the scoring system is complex.

Sociomoral Reflection Measure

As a result of both the practical problems associated with the MJI and his revision of Kohlberg's theory, Gibbs developed the Sociomoral Reflection Measure (SRM) (Gibbs & Widaman, 1982) as an alternative to this measure. The SRM retains moral dilemmas but has standardised probe questions for each one rather than relying on the interviewers themselves. There are two moral dilemmas within the SRM, involving eight values: affiliation (marriage and friendship), life, law and property, legal justice, conscience, family affiliation, contract, and property.

Psychometric validation of the SRM has shown it to have good reliability and validity, with figures that are comparable to the MJI (Gibbs & Widaman, 1982). Correlations between scores on the MJI and SRM are also high. As with the MJI, there remain questions about the construct validity of the SRM. However, the SRM has proved to be more practical to use than the MJI, with it being feasible to administer to groups. The scoring system is also less complex and extensive self-training materials have been prepared. However, scoring the questionnaires still proved to be time-consuming, leading to the development of a shortened form of the SRM.

Sociomoral Reflection Measure-Short Form

The SRM-SF is essentially very similar to the SRM in that it retains the production nature of the longer measure while reducing administration, training, and scoring times (Gibbs et al., 1992). Rather than using moral dilemmas to elicit moral justifications, the SRM-SF poses a series of short vignettes to set the context of moral issues. For example, asking respondents to "Think about when you have made a promise to a friend of yours" to get them thinking about the importance of keeping promises to friends. This statement is followed by a question about whether the moral issue (i.e., keeping a promise to a friend) is important, and finally, respondents are asked to provide reasons for their evaluation of the moral issue. Overall, the SRM-SF consists of 11 items that cover the five moral issues of contract (keeping promises and telling the truth), affiliation (helping people), life, property and law, and legal justice.

Again, the SRM-SF has been shown to have good psychometric properties, even when used by self-trained raters (Gibbs et al., 1992). Self-training to score the SRM-SF takes around 30 hours, and it is much quicker and easier to use and score than previous production measures of moral reasoning.

Recognition Measures

Defining Issues Test

The main recognition measure that is used to assess moral reasoning is the Defining Issues Test (Rest, 1975). The DIT was developed to provide a shorter alternative to the MJI, and moved away from using an inferential scoring system (i.e., a system whereby moral reasoning is assessed from respondents' moral justifications). In contrast, the DIT uses a multiple-choice format of responses to moral dilemmas, with twelve statements presented for each one. These statements reflect reasoning across the six stages of Kohlberg's theory, plus a number of filler responses to identify tendencies to choose complex but nonsense reasons. The pattern of responses across the dilemmas is then used to identify the respondent's level of moral reasoning.

Examination of the reliability and validity of the DIT have shown it to have good psychometric properties. However, low to moderate correlations between scores on the MJI and DIT suggest that the two tests are not necessarily equivalent, with respondents typically scoring higher on the DIT. This has led to a consideration of whether people are able to spontaneously produce moral justifications at the same level at which they can recognise them.

Other recognition measures have been developed by Gibbs and his colleagues as parallel measures to the Sociomoral Reflection Measure and Sociomoral Reflection Measure-Short Form. These are the Sociomoral Reflection Objective Measure (Gibbs *et al.*, 1984) and the Sociomoral Reflection Objective Measure-Short Form (Basinger & Gibbs, 1987). However, these two recognition measures have limited reliability and validity and so their use is not recommended.

Overall, while production and recognition measures of moral reasoning both have advantages and disadvantages, it appears that recognition measures such as the DIT cannot provide an equivalent substitute to production measures. This lack of equivalence makes it difficult to draw any conclusions as to which type of measure provides the best measure of moral reasoning development. All of these measures also suffer from the same difficulties surrounding their construct validity. On a more general level, these measures are all grounded in the cognitive-developmental approach to moral development, meaning that assessment is based solely on the structure of moral judgements, rather than other aspects of morality such as motives and character. In response to this is the point that as measures of Kohlberg's moral development stages, these measures do not set out to assess these aspects of morality.

MORAL REASONING AND AGGRESSION

There is now an established literature on the relationship between moral reasoning and criminal behaviour in general (e.g., Palmer, 2003a, 2003b) and aggression specifically (see Palmer, 2005). Early research focused on examining the differences between offenders and nonoffenders. By applying Kohlberg/Gibbs' moral reasoning theory to antisocial behaviour and offending it appeared that these behaviours can be morally justified at each of the moral stages:

- Stage 1 – offending is morally justified if punishment can be avoided.
- Stage 2 – offending is morally justified if the benefits outweigh the risks.
- Stage 3 – offending is morally justified if it maintains personal relationships.
- Stage 4 – offending is morally justified if it maintains society or is sanctioned by a social institution.

However, research has demonstrated that offending and other antisocial behaviours are typically associated with reasoning at the *less mature* moral stages (for reviews, see Blasi, 1980; Nelson, Smith & Dodd, 1990; Palmer, 2003b), although most studies have examined official offending behaviour in adolescent samples (e.g., Gregg, Gibbs & Basinger, 1994; Palmer & Hollin, 1998, 2000).

Two studies with young offenders and nonoffenders have examined the issue of whether this moral immaturity holds across a range of values, or just those related to offending behaviour (Gregg *et al.*, 1994; Palmer & Hollin, 1998). These studies both used the Sociomoral Reflection Measure-Short Form to compare the moral reasoning of young offenders and nonoffenders on the five values of contract and truth, affiliation, life, property and law, and legal justice. Both of the studies showed offenders to have less mature moral reasoning on all five of the values, although this difference was greater for property and law and legal justice. Furthermore,

Palmer and Hollin (1998) reported that the young offenders had significantly more mature reasoning on the life value than on the other four values. It is possible, however, that this finding reflected the predominance of property offences within the offender sample in this study.

More recently, however, attention has shifted to considering the psychological mechanisms that may explain the relationship between moral reasoning and the development of a range of antisocial behaviours, including aggression, juvenile delinquency, and offending. As a result, the interaction of moral reasoning with other factors, such as cognitive distortions, social information-processing and early socialisation experiences, has been examined in order to provide a greater understanding of the development of aggressive and antisocial behaviour.

Gibbs (2003) considers the role that cognitive distortions play in the relationship between moral reasoning and offending. The primary offence-supporting cognition identified by Gibbs was that of egocentric bias. An egocentric bias and limited social perspective-taking appears characteristic of immature moral reasoning, with the individual's own wishes being placed ahead of those of other people. Egocentricity is also a common feature of the thinking styles of aggressive individuals and offenders (Antonowicz & Ross, 2005; Ross & Fabiano, 1985).

Egocentricity is proposed to be supported by a raft of secondary cognitions that contribute to antisocial behaviour (Gibbs, 2003). First, assumption of the worst, or having a hostile attributional bias, refers to interpreting ambiguous events as having a hostile intent. Second, blaming others or external factors (e.g., being drunk), rather than oneself, for behaviour that harms others. Finally, minimising consequences/mislabelling one's own behaviour to reduce feelings of regret and guilt, which in turn can lessen inhibitions to indulge in antisocial behaviour.

There are a number of studies that show these secondary cognitive distortions are used by antisocial and aggressive adolescents (Barriga & Gibbs, 1996; Liau, Barriga & Gibbs, 1998; Palmer & Hollin, 2000; Slaby & Guerra, 1988). Thus, aggressive behaviour can be conceptualised as resulting from moral (or sociomoral) developmental delay beyond childhood that is accompanied by an egocentric bias. This type of reasoning allows individuals to disengage from self-evaluation of their own behaviour on a moral level (Bandura, 1991).

Development of Social Cognition

A useful model for considering the development of the wider social cognitive patterns implicated in the association between moral reasoning and aggressive behaviour is Crick and Dodge's (1994) six-step model of social information processing. This model outlines how individuals perceive and interpret their social world, and the influence of previous experiences and emotion on these processes (Lemerise & Arsenio, 2000). The six steps in this model are:

1. Encoding of social cues;
2. Interpretation and mental representation of the situation;
3. Clarification of goals and outcomes for the situation;
4. Response access or construction;

5. Response choice;
6. Enactment of behavioural response.

A large body of research has shown that as compared to their nonaggressive peers, aggressive children and adolescents have distinct patterns of social information-processing across the six steps (for reviews see Palmer, 2003b, 2005). As these patterns concern the interpretation of social information and goals and motivations in social situations, they impact on the quality of information available in making moral judgments and the development of social perspective-taking and associated emotions implicated in moral reasoning development.

The available research exploring the development of social information-processing patterns and associated cognitions (e.g., schema, social scripts) has shown that these patterns become established at quite a young age – with many of the studies being conducted with primary school children (from 5 years). It would seem, therefore, that early socialisation experiences play an important role in this development, with parents likely to be the main agents. Research examining the relationship between parenting, social information-processing, and behaviour in school-aged children has confirmed this suggestion. Dodge *et al.* (1995) found that harsh parental disciplinary practices were associated with a hostile attributional bias among children. Harsh maternal discipline has also been shown to be associated with high levels of aggression in young children (Strassberg *et al.*, 1994; Weiss *et al.*, 1992). Maternal endorsement and use of aggression has also been shown to be related to children's beliefs about and use of aggression (Hart, Ladd & Burleson, 1990; Pettit, Dodge & Brown, 1988).

It is clear, then, that there is a constellation of parenting variables implicated in the development of offence supporting cognitions. Many of these parenting factors are also associated with the development of aggressive behaviour among children, juvenile delinquency, and adult criminality (for reviews, see Farrington, 2005; Haapasalo & Pokelo, 1999; Patterson, Reid & Dishion, 1992). Furthermore, the cognitions proposed by Gibbs (2003) as mediating the relationship between moral developmental delay and aggressive behaviour map closely onto those among aggressive young children and adolescent in the social information-processing literature. The presence of these cognitions and the associated social information-processing styles appear to show that, among aggressive individuals, immature moral reasoning can lead to aggressive behaviour. As suggested by Palmer (2000, 2003b, 2005) it seems that children who experience harsh and neglectful parenting are at risk of developing offence supporting cognitions and hostile schema relating to interpersonal relationship, and moral developmental delay. Subsequently, new situations are interpreted through these schema and distortions, which can be magnified in emotionally arousing situations. As a result of this tendency to interpret situations in a hostile way and their negative beliefs about the world, aggressive and antisocial behaviour become more likely.

INTERVENTIONS TO IMPROVE MORAL REASONING OF AGGRESSIVE INDIVIDUALS

As a factor that plays a role in aggressive behaviour, moral reasoning provides a target for interventions that aim to reduce aggression. There are two such programmes that explicitly do this, both of which are for young people. The two interventions are Aggression Replacement Training (ART) (see also Chapter 11 of this volume) and Equipping Youth to Help One Another (EQUIP).

Aggression Replacement Training (ART) (Goldstein, Glick & Gibbs, 1998) was developed for working with aggressive youths in North America. Based on a social learning theory of aggression it consists of three components that are delivered concurrently: skillstreaming, anger control training, and moral reasoning training. Skillstreaming forms the behavioural component of ART, and aims to address the social skill deficits associated with aggression by teaching participants prosocial skills. This is achieved through the use of techniques such as modelling, role-play, and provision of feedback by tutors. The ART programme covers 50 skills, although the skills delivered in each group are based upon a needs assessment of participants prior to commencing the programme.

Anger control training seeks to address the affective aspect of aggression and is based on the work of Novaco (Novaco & Welsh, 1989) and Meichenbaum (1977) on reducing anger. Through six steps, this aspect aims to help participants increase their self-control and manage their anger, and thus reduce the likelihood of aggression.

The third component is moral reasoning training, and aims to address moral developmental delay and the associated offence supporting cognitions outlined by Gibbs (2003). Theoretical moral dilemmas in which a youth has a problem that has been caused by another person's selfishness (i.e. egocentricity) are discussed in group sessions. The tutor then presents alternative actions for the youth, in order to stimulate a discussion that examines and challenges the secondary distortions outlined by Gibbs (2003) and immature moral reasoning they support.

There is no prescribed length for the ART programme, although Goldstein *et al.* (1998) outline an example 10-week programme, with three sessions (i.e. one per component) delivered each week. The intervention has been delivered in a range of settings, including schools, residential institutions, and family settings, and in a number of countries, including the United States, Canada, the United Kingdom, Holland, and Scandinavia (see Goldstein *et al.*, 2004). It has also recently been adapted for use with adult populations in a community setting in England and Wales (McGuire & Clark, 2004).

There is a growing body of research evaluating the effectiveness of ART, although most studies have small samples (for reviews, see Goldstein *et al.*, 1998; Goldstein, Glick & Gibbs, 2004). For example, Goldstein *et al.* (1986) compared a group of young offenders receiving ART with an instruction treatment and no treatment control group in Annsville Youth Centre, United States. Compared to the other two groups, the ART group improved significantly on 4 out of 10 skills in the skillstreaming component and were rated by staff as having better behaviour. Furthermore, parole officers rated ART participants as having better functioning with their family, peers, and the legal system at a one-year follow-up than participants in the other two groups, although there was no difference with respect to work or school settings. Similar results were reported in a replication study with young males in a maximum security institution (Goldstein *et al.*, 1986).

Equipping Peers to Help Another (EQUIP) (Gibbs, Potter & Goldstein, 1995) takes the ART curriculum and delivers it within a peer group therapy setting. By placing the responsibility for group management and behaviour onto the group participants, it is hoped that the EQUIP will create a "climate for change" in which participants will be motivated and help each other change.

EQUIP is delivered in two types of sessions: mutual-help meetings and "equipment" meetings. Mutual-help meetings involve group discussions relating to how problem behaviours and offence-supporting cognitions relate to the problems they encounter in their own lives. The ART curriculum is then delivered as normal in the "equipment" meetings.

There are few published evaluations of the EQUIP programme. One such study with 57 incarcerated young male offenders was reported by Leeman, Gibbs and Fuller (1993). Offenders who had received EQUIP showed improved institutional behaviour after completion of the programme as compared to two comparison groups (motivation group and no treatment control group). The recidivism rate of the EQUIP group was also lower than that of the comparison groups at 6- and 12-month followup, although this was only significant at 12 months. A review of some recent small-scale evaluations of EQUIP with young offenders in New Zealand can be found in Polaschek (2006).

A major limitation of the evaluations of these two interventions is that none have attempted to dismantle the effects of the various components within the programmes. There is, therefore, no way of knowing the relative impact of each component or whether the moral reasoning component brings additional value to such interventions. Clearly this is an important issue and one that should be taken into account in the design of future evaluations.

CONCLUSION

To conclude, this chapter has shown how moral reasoning can contribute to aggressive behaviour, through its interaction with a range of other social cognitive processes. An attempt has also been made to consider the developmental antecedents to these variables, including socialisation experiences provided by parents and peers. Together, this literature suggests that moral reasoning and other social cognitive variables act as a mediating factor between socialisation experiences (particularly early parenting styles) and aggressive behaviour. Further research examining the interaction of these variables is now needed to extend our understanding in this area. The results from this research can then be used to inform future developments in treating aggression that focus on moral reasoning and social cognition.

REFERENCES

Antonowicz, D. H. & Ross, R. R. (2005). Social problem solving deficits in offenders. In M. McMurran & J. McGuire (eds), *Social Problem Solving and Offending: Evidence, Evaluation and Evolution* (pp. 91–102). Chichester: John Wiley & Sons.

Bandura, A. (1991). Social cognitive theory of moral thought and action. In W. M. Kurtines & J. L. Gewirtz (eds), *Handbook of Moral Behavior and Development. Vol. 1. Theory* (pp. 45–103). Hillsdale, NJ: Erlbaum.

Barriga, A. Q. & Gibbs, J. C. (1996). Measuring cognitive distortion in antisocial youth: Development and preliminary validation of the "How I Think" questionnaire. *Aggressive Behavior*, **22**, 333–43.

Basinger, K. S. & Gibbs, J. C. (1987). Validation of the Sociomoral Reflection Objective Measure-Short Form. *Psychological Reports*, **61**, 139–46.

Blasi, A. (1980). Bridging moral cognition and moral action: a critical review of the literature. *Psychological Bulletin*, **88**, 1–45.

Colby, A. (1978). Evolution of a moral-developmental theory. In W. Damon (ed.), *Moral Development* (pp. 89–104). San Francisco: Jossey-Bass.

Colby, A. & Kohlberg, L. (1987). *The Measurement of Moral Judgment: Theoretical Foundations and Research Validation.* (Vol. 1). New York: Cambridge University Press.

Colby, A., Kohlberg, L., Gibbs, J. C. & Lieberman, M. (1983). A longitudinal study of moral judgment. *Monographs of the Society for Research in Child Development*, **48** (1–2, Serial No. 200).

Crick, N. R. & Dodge, K. A. (1994). A review and reformulation of social information-processing mechanisms in children's social adjustment. *Psychological Bulletin*, **115**, 74–101.

Dodge, K. A., Pettit, G. S., Bates, J. E. & Valente, E. (1995). Social information processing patterns partially mediate the effect of early physical abuse on later conduct problems. *Journal of Abnormal Psychology*, **104**, 632–43.

Durkheim, E. (1925/1961). *Moral Education: A Study in the Theory and Application of the Sociology of Moral Education.* (E. K. Wilson & H. Schnurer, trans.). New York: Free Press. (Original work published in 1925).

Farrington, D. P. (2005). Childhood origins of antisocial behavior. *Clinical Psychology and Psychotherapy*, **12**, 177–90.

Gibbs, J. C. (1993). Moral-cognitive interventions. In A. P. Goldstein & C. R. Huff (eds), *The Gang Intervention Handbook* (pp. 159–85). Champaign, IL: Research Press.

Gibbs, J. C. (2003). *Moral Development and Reality: Beyond the Theories of Kohlberg and Hoffman.* Thousand Oaks, CA: Sage Publications.

Gibbs, J. C., Arnold, K. D., Morgan, R. L. *et al.* (1984). Construction and validation of a multiple-choice measure of moral reasoning. *Child Development*, **55**, 527–36.

Gibbs, J. C., Basinger, K. S. & Fuller, D. (1992). *Moral Maturity: Measuring the Development of Sociomoral Reflection.* Hillsdale, NJ: Lawrence Erlbaum Associates.

Gibbs, J. C., Potter, G. B. & Goldstein, A. P. (1995). *The EQUIP program: Teaching youth to think and act responsibly through a peer-helping approach.* Champaign, IL: Research Press.

Gibbs, J. C. & Widaman, K. F. (1982). *Social Intelligence: Measuring the Development of Sociomoral Reflection.* Englewood Cliffs, NJ: Lawrence Erlbaum Associates.

Goldstein, A. P., Glick, B. & Gibbs, J. C. (1998). *Aggression Replacement Training* (2nd edn). Champaign, IL: Research Press.

Goldstein, A. P., Glick, B., Reiner, S. *et al.* (1986). *Aggression Replacement Training.* Champaign, IL: Research Press.

Goldstein, A. P., Nensén, R., Daleflod, B. & Kalt, M. (eds). (2004). *New Perspectives on Aggression Replacement Training: Practice, Research, and Application.* Chichester: John Wiley & Sons.

Gregg, V. R., Gibbs, J. C. & Basinger, K. S. (1994). Patterns of developmental delay in moral judgment by male and female delinquents. *Merrill-Palmer Quarterly*, **40**, 538–53.

Haapasalo, J. & Pokelo, E. (1999). Child-rearing and child abuse antecedents of criminality. *Aggression and Violent Behavior*, **4**, 107–27.

Hart, C. H., Ladd, G. W. & Burleson, B. R. (1990). Children's expectations of the outcomes of social strategies: relations with sociometric status and maternal disciplinary styles. *Chid Development*, **61**, 127–37.

Hoffman, M. L. (2000). *Empathy and Moral Development: Implications for Caring and Justice.* Cambridge: Cambridge University Press.

Kohlberg, L. (1969). Stage and sequence: the cognitive-developmental approach to socialization. In D. A. Goslin (ed.), *Handbook of Socialization Theory and Research* (pp. 347–480). Chicago: Rand McNally.

Kohlberg, L. (1981). *Essays on Moral Development: The Philosophy of Moral Development*. San Francisco, CA: Harper & Row.

Kohlberg, L. (1984). *Essays on Moral Development: The Psychology of Moral Development*. San Francisco, CA: Harper & Row.

Krebs, D., Vermuelen, S. C. A., Carpendale, J. I. & Denton, K. (1991). Structural and situational influences on moral judgment: an interaction between stage and dilemma. In W. M. Kurtines & J. L. Gewirtz (eds), *Handbook of Moral Behavior and Development: Volume 2. Research* (pp. 139–70). Hillsdale, NJ: Lawrence Erlbaum.

Leeman, L. W., Gibbs, J. C. & Fuller, D. (1993). Evaluation of a multicomponent group treatment program for juvenile delinquents. *Aggressive Behavior*, **19**, 281–92.

Lemerise, E. A. & Arsenio, W. E. (2000). An integrated model of emotion processes and cognition in social information processing. *Child Development*, **71**, 107–18.

Liau, A. K., Barriga, A. Q. & Gibbs, J. C. (1998). Relations between self-serving cognitive distortions and overt vs. covert antisocial behavior in adolescents. *Aggressive Behavior*, **24**, 335–46.

McGuire, J. & Clark, D. (2004). A national dissemination program. In A. P. Goldstein, R. Nensén, B. Daleflod & M. Kalt (eds), *New Perspectives on Aggression Replacement Training* (pp. 139–50). Chichester: John Wiley & Sons.

Meichenbaum, D. H. (1975). *Stress Inoculation Training*. New York: Pergamon.

Nelson, J. R., Smith, D. J. & Dodd, J. (1990). The moral reasoning of juvenile delinquents: A meta-analysis. *Journal of Abnormal Child Psychology*, **18**, 231–9.

Novaco, R. W. & Welsh, W. N. (1989). Anger disturbances: cognitive mediation and clinical prescriptions. In K. Howells & C. R. Hollin (eds), *Clinical Approaches to Violence* (pp. 39–60). Chichester: John Wiley & Sons.

Palmer, E. J. (2000). Perceptions of parenting, social cognition and delinquency. *Clinical Psychology and Psychotherapy*, **7**, 303–9.

Palmer, E. J. (2003a). An overview of the relationship between moral reasoning and offending. *Australian Psychologist*, **38**, 165–74.

Palmer, E. J. (2003b). *Offending Behaviour: Moral Reasoning, Criminal Conduct and the Rehabilitation of Offenders*. Cullompton: Willan Publishing.

Palmer, E. J. (2005). The relationship between moral reasoning and aggression, and the implications for practice. *Psychology, Crime & Law*, **11**, 353–61.

Palmer, E. J. & Hollin, C. R. (1998). A comparison of patterns of moral development in young offenders and nonoffenders. *Legal and Criminological Psychology*, **3**, 225–35.

Palmer, E. J. & Hollin, C. R. (2000). The inter-relations of sociomoral reasoning, perceptions of own parenting, and attribution of intent with self-reported delinquency. *Legal and Criminological Psychology*, **5**, 201–18.

Patterson, G. R., Reid, J. B. & Dishion, T. (1992). *Antisocial Boys*. Eugene, OR: Castalia.

Pettit, G. S., Dodge, K. A. & Brown, M. M. (1988). Early family experience, social problem solving patterns and children's social competence. *Child Development*, **59**, 107–20.

Piaget, J. (1932). *The Moral Judgment of the Child*. London: Routledge & Kegan Paul.

Piaget, J. (1952). *The Origins of Intelligence in Children*. New York: International Universities Press.

Polaschek, D. L. L. (2006). Violent offender programmes: concept, theory, and practice. In C. R. Hollin & E. J. Palmer (eds), *Offending Behaviour Programmes: Development, Application, and Controversies* (pp. 113–54). Chichester: John Wiley & Sons.

Rest, J. R. (1975). Longitudinal study of the Defining Issues Test of moral judgment: a strategy for analysing developmental change. *Developmental Psychology*, **11**, 738–48.

Ross, R. R. & Fabiano, E. A. (1985). *Time to Think: A Cognitive Model of Delinquency Prevention and Offender Rehabilitation*. Johnson City, TN: Institute of Social Sciences and Arts.

Selman, R. L. (1976). Social-cognitive understanding: A guide to educational and clinical practice. In T. Lickona (ed.), *Moral Development and Moral Behaviour* (pp. 299–316). New York: Holt, Rinehart & Winston.

Selman, R. L. (1980). *The Growth of Interpersonal Understanding*. New York: Academic Press.

Slaby, R. G. & Guerra, N. G. (1988). Cognitive mediators of aggression in adolescent offenders: Part 1. Assessment. *Development Psychology*, **24**, 580–8.

Strassberg, Z., Dodge, K. A., Bates, J. E. & Pettit, G. S. (1994). Spanking in the home and children's subsequent aggression towards kindergarten peers. *Development and Psychopathology*, **6**, 445–61.

Weiss, B., Dodge, K. A., Bates, J. E. & Pettit, G. S. (1992). Some consequences of early harsh discipline: chid aggression and a maladaptive social information processing system. *Child Development*, **63**, 1321–35.

Chapter 11

TREATMENTS FOR ANGRY AGGRESSION

CLIVE R. HOLLIN AND CLAIRE A. J. BLOXSOM

University of Leicester, UK

Violence assumes many forms, causing widespread distress and harm: indeed, a World Health Organisation (WHO) report refers to violence as a "global public health problem" (Krug *et al.*, 2002). The WHO report describes four manifestations of violence, namely "physical", "sexual", "psychological", and "deprivation and neglect", which in turn may be "self-directed", "interpersonal", or "collective" in nature. Self-directed violence includes self-harm and suicide, interpersonal violence includes physical and sexual assault, and collective violence includes acts such as genocide. In WHO terms, the focus here lies in the broad domain of interpersonal violence, specifically where physical harm is the outcome. Within acts of interpersonal violence the distinction can be drawn between violent acts that are either reactive or proactive in nature. Reactive violent acts are typically impulsive and characterised by the aggressor's state of negative affect; proactive acts are premeditated and serve to attain the aggressor's personal goal. Notwithstanding the debate about the conceptual neatness of this reactive-proactive distinction (Bushman & Anderson, 2001), it is certainly the case that some acts of interpersonal violence occur when the aggressor is in an angry state. It is this very specific form of interpersonal violence, violence associated with anger, which is of concern in this chapter.

Raymond Novaco's conceptualisation of anger, within a general cognitive-behavioural framework, is perhaps the current predominant model of anger, widely used by both researchers and practitioners to inform interventions (Novaco, 1976, 1994; Robins & Novaco, 1999). This model therefore provides a good starting point for understanding and working with the angry violent offender.

NOVACO'S MODEL OF ANGER

Anger may be understood to be a subjectively experienced, adaptive, and complex emotion that may have both functional and dysfunctional effects for the individual.

Aggressive Offenders' Cognition: Theory, Research and Practice. Edited by T. A. Gannon, T. Ward, A. R. Beech and D. Fisher. © 2007 John Wiley & Sons, Ltd.

Within Novaco's model, anger is understood to be an emotion with interacting physiological and cognitive components, typically triggered by an environmental cue. Thus, an individual becomes angry when an environmental cue provokes physiological and cognitive arousal which, in turn, interact so leading to a subjective emotional experience that is labelled "anger". This subjective experience is then associated with a behavioural expression of anger which may be a violent act against another person. The exact way that anger-related behaviour is expressed may depend on a range of individual factors, including the perception of a provocation, cognitive processing, and one's ability to cope with the perceived provocation.

Figure 11.1 illustrates Novaco's model schematically, highlighting the interacting nature of the environmental, physiological, cognitive, affective, and behavioural components. The model suggests that the relationship between the components is interactive and dynamic, as changes in one element bring about reciprocal changes elsewhere.

The *physiological* arousal associated with anger may be manifested in increases in cardiovascular activity, body temperature, and muscular tension. The cognitive arousal is associated with the effects of the *cognitive labelling* of anger and the activation of individual *schemas* (Novaco & Welsh, 1989). *Cognitive labelling* of anger results from an appraisal of one's subjective state in terms of "anger" (or a semantically related term such as "irritation", "annoyance", or "rage"). Robins and Novaco (1999) describe *schemas* as psychological representations of an environment-behaviour relationship, the content and functioning of which are

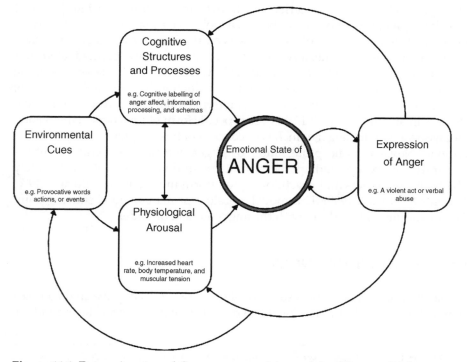

Figure 11.1 Determinants and Consequences of Anger (after Novaco, 1994)

typically based on previous experience. Schemas enable fast and efficient (although not necessarily accurate) responding to external stimuli in that they contain procedural rules that automatically manage interactions and situations. Within Novaco's model, *anger schemas* predispose an individual, given the appropriate environmental cues, to activate selectively a subjective negative perception of "anger", then to express this anger in line with their set expectations (Novaco, 2007; Novaco & Welsh, 1989). For some individuals their anger schemas will increase the likelihood of antisocial behaviour.

Schemas are allied to social information processing, which allows the individual to evaluate, store, and retrieve information relevant to their perceived social environment (Crick & Dodge, 1994, 1996; Huesmann, 1988). Therefore, whether an environmental event is seen to have a provocative or threatening value, and its subsequent relationship with physiological and cognitive activity, depends on the individual's subjective appraisal of the event. It is assumed that individuals' past experiences will influence their present social appraisal (Nisbitt & Ross, 1980). The active process of appraisal may be affected by schemas which influence judgement, minimise the impact of contextual factors, and intensify the initial (and sustained) impact of individual expectations and beliefs (Lazarus, 1966).

The experience of anger can have positive, adapting, self-mobilising, energising, and protective qualities, all of which are functional to both individual and group survival (Novaco, 1994). However, anger can become *dysfunctional* when the experience and expression of anger have a predominantly *negative* effect.

Dysfunctional Anger

The negative effects of anger may be felt by the individual experiencing the anger, as with physiological problems and ill health; or felt by others who are recipients or victims of the individual's "angry behaviour". Anger may become dysfunctional when it is not appropriately *regulated*. In essence, anger regulation refers to an individual's capacity to stay calm in the face of perceived provocation, which necessarily involves the cognitive processes by which anger is managed or controlled (Novaco, 2003). An individual's functional level of control of their anger may depend on several of the variables contained within Novaco's model. Thus, the cognitive label given to one's internal state – from irritation, through anger, to rage – may influence one's degree of control. The content and efficiency of the individual's anger schemas, and the degree to which these are influenced by cognitive biases, perceptions of justification, physiological activity and environmental factors, may also play a role with regard to level of control.

There are several types of cognitive processing that are associated with dysfunctional anger. *Selective attention* to environmental and, social cues, may act to maintain awareness of certain cues in preference to others: this cue selection may, in turn, be important in the individual's subjective appraisal of provocation. Selectively cued attention to provoking stimuli may activate anger schemas, depending on other environmental and psychological factors. As noted above, schemas may be useful shortcuts in information processing but they may also introduce "bias" with a subsequent increase in anger (Dodge & Newman, 1981).

Novaco and Welsh (1989) identified five types of information processing biases characteristic of individuals who frequently exhibit dysfunctional anger and who express this anger with violence. These information-processing biases are seen in both *cognitive operations* and *cognitive propositions*: cognitive operations refer to the way information in memory is encoded, stored, and retrieved; cognitive propositions are the content of cognitive structures. The two cognitive operations viewed by Novaco and Welsh (1989) as associated with dysfunctional anger are *attentional cueing* and *perceptual matching*.

Attentional cueing is a preoccupation with and continued rumination about a provoking cue, such as an event or another person's actions, which is perceived to be threatening. The consequences of preoccupation and rumination may be sustained feelings of provocation and continued irritation, serving to maintain angry arousal for some time after the event or interaction has occurred (Novaco, 1986). Perceptual matching takes place when emotions associated with the appraisal of a previous provoking experience are "mapped" onto the current situation. A characteristic of perceptual matching is that the more an individual has been exposed to situations that involve anger, the more likely they are to perceive matches between the past and present, and so the easier it is to become aroused by perceived provocation. The cumulative process of perceptual mapping occurs through the development of associative networks and schemas, allowing faster retrieval in response to related cues (see Novaco & Welsh, 1989). Studies with violent offenders have, indeed, shown that previous exposure to violence increases the likelihood of a fast recall of a "violence schema" (Shelley & Toch, 1968).

The three cognitive propositions that may promote a negative use of anger are *fundamental attribution errors, false consensus,* and *anchoring effects*. A fundamental attribution error refers to "A pervasive tendency to underestimate the importance of external situational pressures and to overestimate the importance of internal motives and dispositions in interpreting the behaviour of others" (Colman, 2003, p. 293). Attribution errors can lead to anger through a misunderstanding which may escalate when there is a conflict of opinion between those involved. Attribution error as a factor in dysfunctional anger and aggression has been thoroughly documented (Allred, 2000; Dyck & Rule, 1978; Zillmann, 1979). A false consensus occurs when individuals overestimate the degree to which other people hold the same beliefs and opinions. A false consensus effect has been related to a lack of perspective-taking, leading to heightened tension, increased sensitivity to provocation, and subsequent anger (Russell & Arms, 1995). Anchoring effects refer to the tendency to adhere to one's first impression of another person or a situation, regardless of later contradictory or mitigating evidence. In addition, *proximity bias* occurs when the source of the provocation to anger is misperceived to be a proximal event rather than the current situation (Novaco, 1993).

Consequences of Dysfunctional Anger

Dysfunctional anger has been associated with various problematic consequences (Eckhardt & Deffenbacher, 1995; Miller *et al.*, 1996). In terms of physical health, these negative consequences include cardiovascular pathology, such as hypertension, coronary heart disease and carotid and coronary atherosclerosis (Engebretson, Matthews & Scheer, 1989; Julkunen *et al.*, 1994; Ketterer, 1996; Kubzansky *et al.*, 2006). With respect to behavioural and mental disturbance, the Diagnostic and Statistical Manual of Mental Disorders (DSM-IV-TR; American Psychiatric Association, 2000) notes dysfunctional anger as a clinical symptom of oppositional defiant disorder, conduct disorder, borderline personality disorder, major depressive disorder, antisocial personality disorder, and some types of schizophrenia. Dysfunctional anger has also been associated with suicide (Kotler *et al.*, 1993) and attention deficit hyperactivity disorder (Brown, 2002). However, perhaps the closest association between dysfunctional anger and behavioural disturbance is seen with intermittent explosive disorder, where anger is manifested in outbursts of "aggressive behaviour" or violent acts (American Psychiatric Association, 2000). Of course, anger has also been consistently associated with interpersonal violence (Blackburn, 1993; Howells *et al.*, 1997; Levey & Howells, 1990; Monahan *et al.*, 2001; Zamble & Quinsey, 1997), sometimes concurrent with a corresponding psychiatric diagnosis (Craig, 1982; Monahan *et al.*, 2001; Novaco, 1994).

ANGER, AGGRESSION, AND VIOLENCE

The term *aggression* is notoriously difficult to define, as seen from different theoretical perspectives over time (Bandura, 1973; Berkowitz, 1962, 1990; Dollard *et al.*, 1939; Freud, 1961; Lorenz, 1966), and is sometimes used interchangeably with "violence" (Siann, 1985). The most typical definition views aggression in terms of an intention to either hurt or gain advantage over another person: for example, Bushman and Anderson (2001) view human aggression as "any behaviour directed toward another individual that is carried out with the proximate (immediate) intent to cause harm" (p. 274). However, "harm" can take many forms, ranging from emotional and psychological harm to extreme physical injury or death. In offender populations it is likely that the majority of offenders who have harmed others will have committed an act that caused physical harm to the other person. Thus, we use the term "violence" rather than "aggression" to refer to behaviours that involve the use of injurious physical force against another person. The term "criminal violence" specifically refers to violent behaviour that is forbidden in law. It is the case that not all violence is associated with anger and similarly not all anger leads to violence: however, there is plentiful evidence to suggest that there is sometimes a close relationship between anger and (criminal) violent behaviour (Berkowitz, 1986; Blackburn, 1993; Craig, 1982; Howells *et al.*, 1997; Monahan *et al.*, 2001; Novaco, 1994; Novaco & Taylor, 2004; Zamble & Quinsey, 1997).

The increasing theoretical sophistication of models of anger and the associated evidence base has led to the development of interventions to help people manage and control their anger. As well as violent offenders, anger management has been offered to a range of client groups, including Vietnam veterans (Reilly *et al.*, 1994), people with learning difficulties (Taylor & Novaco, 2005), adolescents (Feindler, 1995), police officers (Novaco, 1977), and undergraduate students (Deffenbacher *et al.*, 1990). The next section looks at the technique of anger management and, in particular, its use with violent offenders.

ANGER MANAGEMENT

Assessment

There is a range of assessments appropriate for anger management that can be used with violent offenders for both practical and research purposes. These assessments include *self-report questionnaires* such as the State-Trait Anger Expression Inventory (STAXI; Spielberger, 1999) and the Novaco Anger Scale (NAS; Novaco, 2003); *self-monitoring* through either structured or informal diary entries; and *behavioural observation* as when routinely recorded within an institution. The use of a range of methods of assessment allows a full picture of the nature and degree of anger to emerge, together with its role in acts of violence.

Pre-Intervention

It is important to note that the aim of anger management is, indeed, precisely that: to manage, *not* to eliminate anger. As Novaco (2007) makes clear, anger management is not so much concerned with how to cope with being angry; rather it is about managing the contingencies that lead to anger. This is an important point for practice: the aim of anger management is not *eliminative*, in that it seeks to take something away from the person, rather it is a *constructive* approach that aims to build the person's capacity to control and regulate their anger.

While there have been some refinements to the practice of anger management since Novaco's original formulation of the approach, one of the most important developments has concentrated upon the offender's engagement with treatment. In the wider therapeutic field the notion of treatment motivation has attracted increasing attention, with particular emphasis upon ideas such as motivation and stages of change (Prochaska & DiClemente, 1982). However, it has become apparent that there are conceptual difficulties with the notion of treatment motivation generally (Drieschner, Lammers & Van der Staak, 2004), and when applied to offender populations specifically (Casey, Day & Howells, 2005). A more satisfactory concept than the ambiguous "motivation" might lie in "readiness for change" (Serin, 1998). The notion of readiness to change encompasses motivation to change in addition to the individual and situational factors that can influence engagement in the process of behaviour change (Howells & Day, 2002; Ward *et al.*, 2004). With violent offenders specifically, attention to the affective antecedents to an offender's engagement with an intervention may be fundamental to initiating and maintaining change (Howells & Day, 2006). It is clear that strategies to increase participation and engagement in the process of behaviour change are becoming increasingly important in work with offenders. For example, the technique of motivational interviewing (Rollnick & Miller, 1995) has been incorporated into treatment programmes for offenders, including domestic violence offenders (Murphy & Baxter, 1997; see also Chapter 13 for information regarding domestic violence treatment programmes).

Intervention

Novaco's (1975, 1977) stress inoculation therapy for anger control is perhaps the classic psychological intervention for anger problems. In its original form anger management contained three distinct stages. The first stage is *cognitive preparation* where the aims are to establish the rationale for intervention, to educate about the function of anger, and to identify and assess the individual's patterns of angry arousal and experience of anger and its consequences. Indeed, Feindler and Ecton (1986) suggest that the primary goal at this stage is to encourage individuals to become experts in recognising their own personal patterns of anger. Eventually, they will be able to identify the positive and negative consequences of their reactions to provoking cues. Necessarily, this stage requires the individual to develop self-monitoring skills, becoming aware of their internal state and its relationship with environmental events (Kassinove & Tafrate, 2002).

The second stage of the intervention is *skills acquisition and rehearsal*, during which individuals learn to identify, cope with, and manage the cognitive, affective and behavioural aspects of their anger. Feindler (1995) suggests that anger management programmes should initially focus upon teaching the recognition of physiological arousal – increased heart rate, muscle tension and so on – and how accurately to label and manage arousal when provoked. At this stage techniques from relaxation training, such as deep breathing, may be introduced to aid control of physiological arousal. Deffenbacher *et al.* (1988) reported that participants in anger management containing a relaxation component were both less resistant in initial sessions and more accepting when the cognitive components were introduced. Deffenbacher *et al.* (1990) assessed the effectiveness of a cognitive, relaxation and behavioural coping skills package for reducing general anger: they found the type of programme that combined different techniques was generally effective in impacting upon anger.

The development of emotional control and regulation requires individuals to develop their use of internal dialogue to aid self-monitoring and self-instruction. The techniques of self-instructional training and thought-stopping can be used to guide learning of how to generate new and different verbal commands to control arousal and prompt appropriate social behaviour (Feindler, 1995). McDougall *et al.* (1990) suggested that self-instruction can be facilitated by considering the individual's self-statements associated with the angry episode and generating new, positive, self-statements as replacements.

The third stage is the *application phase*, which is the period during which the individual practises, in role-play then in real life, the skills developed in the previous stage. The progression from the security of role-play to the uncertainty of real life should be managed in a graduated way, introducing different levels of anger-provoking situations that allow the application of the newly acquired anger management skills. The behavioural and social skills training element may be concerned with behaviours that are appropriate to co-operation, assertion, responsibility, empathy, and self-control. These social skills are usually developed through the use of instruction, modelling, role-play, and performance feedback. The goal of this final stage is to expose the individual to anger-provoking situations of graded intensity in order to provide the opportunity to practise the newly acquired anger management skills (Feindler & Ecton, 1986). The successful application of newly acquired skills and reinforcement of their use in real life concludes the anger management programme.

Thus, the overall aim of anger management is to identify and modulate the cognitive, physiological, and behavioural responses to provocation (real or imagined) to anger. A variety of treatment techniques may be used – including physiological monitoring, relaxation training, assertiveness training, cognitive restructuring of appraisals and distortions, and self-instructional training – to target the different dimensions of anger (Edmondson & Conger, 1996). The finer clinical details of anger treatment with violent offenders have been described in a range of case studies, research reports, and literature reviews (e.g., Browne & Howells, 1996; Howells, 1989; Levey & Howells, 1990). In a survey of the general anger treatment literature Beck and Fernandez (1998) reported that most anger treatment studies have utilised a cognitive-behavioural approach. While the meta-analytic reviews indicate that cognitive-behavioural approaches are effective for anger reduction (Beck & Fennandez, 1998; DiGiuseppe & Tafrate, 2003), it cannot be assumed that the findings from clinical populations will necessarily generalise to offender populations.

Effectiveness of Anger Management with Offenders

Hughes (1993) reported one of the first controlled outcome studies of anger management, undertaken with prisoners in the Canadian Correctional Service. Although Hughes reported a reduction in violent reoffending in prisoners taking part in anger management, compared with a no treatment control, the magnitude of the difference fell short of statistical significance. Marquis *et al.* (1996) evaluated a prison-based anger management programme and reported that violent offenders who completed the programme had a significantly lower rate of recidivism than violent offenders in the control group. In this study, Marquis *et al.* combined behaviour change techniques, blending the anger management programme with relapse prevention. Dowden, Blanchette and Serin (1999) also reported an outcome evaluation of an anger management programme with Canadian prisoners. They showed that the anger management programme had significant impact in reducing the recidivism of the violent offenders as assessed over a three-year period. However, in a study of violent prisoners, Watt and Howells (1999) found no post-treatment differences in measures of anger, such as anger experience and levels of aggressive behaviour, between anger treatment and control groups. These studies have therefore provided some support for the effectiveness of anger management with general offender populations.

Anger can also be associated with violence in mentally disordered offender populations (Novaco, 1994; Skeem *et al.*, 2006) and several studies have examined the effectiveness of anger management with this specific population. Some studies have reported successful anger treatment using a single-case approach with small numbers of forensic patients. Bornstein, Weisser and Balleweg (1985) used an anger-management approach, based upon Novaco's stress inoculation model, with three forensic patients held in secure conditions. The patients had extensive histories of violence, including sexual offences, domestic violence, and assaults on hospital staff. Bornstein *et al.* used a multiple-baseline design and recorded significant treatment gains as seen with lower levels of self-reported anger, a reduction in the frequency aggressive incidents, and improvements in interpersonal style. McMurran *et al.* (2001) described the progress of four male personality disordered offenders, detained in a medium secure psychiatric unit, who took part in a 15-session structured, cognitive-behavioural anger management programme. McMurran *et al.* reported that three of the patients had improved over the course of the programme as assessed by self-report and ward behaviour rating scales. Other studies with mentally disordered offenders have used traditional group comparisons designs. Stermac (1986) evaluated a short, six-session anger management programme with male personality disordered offenders in a forensic inpatient facility. Stermac reported significant positive changes in anger, impulsivity, and coping-strategies in the anger treatment group compared with a control group. There is a continued positive trend in the evaluative literature based on small-scale studies for anger management programmes (Howells, 1989; Renwick *et al.*, 1997). Jones and Hollin (2004) described the development and implementation of a 36-week anger management programme designed for mentally disordered offenders in a high security hospital. The programme was based on Novaco's methods, delivered in a group setting but with accompanying individual sessions, and blended with motivational work. The programme laid emphasis on the importance of establishing a therapeutic alliance with patients in order to maintain their motivation and reduce the likelihood that they would drop out of the programme (DiGiuseppe, Tafrate & Eckhardt, 1994). Eight male personality disordered patients, all with an anger problem and who had displayed aggressive behaviour within the hospital, participated in the programme. Alongside a low dropout rate, repeated measures showed positive changes in the frequency and intensity of anger-related incidents both during the programme and at a short follow-up. Jones and Hollin suggest that the preliminary findings from this pilot study are encouraging in that they indicate that the programme is able both to keep patients in treatment and bring about appropriate change.

ANGER MANAGEMENT IN A MULTIMODAL CONTEXT

One of the main points to emerge from the "What Works?" research on effective practice with offenders to reduce reoffending was that interventions should be "multimodal" (Hollin, 1993, 1994). In other words, interventions to change complex behaviours such as violent conduct must reflect that complexity in the way they seek to address and change multiple aspects of the individual's functioning. The development of offending behaviour programmes was a direct consequence of the need to move towards more complex and effective ways of working with offenders generally (Hollin & Palmer, 2006) and with violent offenders specifically (Bush, 1995; Polaschek, 2006). The multimodal programme *Aggression Replacement Training* provides an excellent example of the integration of anger management into a wider programme context.

Aggression Replacement Training

The ideas underpinning *Aggression Replacement Training* (ART) were developed during the 1980s, culminating in the 1987 text *Aggression Replacement Training:*

A Comprehensive Intervention for Adolescent Youth by Arnold Goldstein and Barry Glick. The original text has been substantially revised and the programme refined across the three components that together constitute ART (Goldstein, Glick & Gibbs, 1998). The three components of ART, delivered sequentially, are *Skillstreaming, Anger Control Training,* and *Moral Reasoning Training,* all with a clear basis in cognitive-behavioural theory and practice (Hollin, 2004).

Skillstreaming serves to develop the skills that displace out of control destructive, violent behaviours with constructive, social behaviours. The skills element of ART teaches social skills using step-by-step instructions to manage aggression provoking social situations. Aggression Replacement Training is concerned with a range of social skills, spanning social perception, social cognition, and social performance. Thus, ART attends to the individual's ability to perceive and understand both verbal and nonverbal social cues. Aggression Replacement Training also attends to social cognition in the sense of social information processing and problem solving, and to social performance as seen in verbal and nonverbal actions. The socially competent, nonviolent, individual will be able to use all aspects of their social skills to function effectively in their interactions with other people. However, the effective use of skills may, at times, mean that strong emotions have to be controlled. Aggression Replacement Training therefore encompasses *Anger Control Training,* in a similar way to Novaco's work, to determine triggers for anger, to enhance self-awareness of internal angry thoughts and reactions, and to teach coping strategies, self-instruction, and social problem solving.

The third component of ART is *Moral Reasoning Training,* which seeks to address the values placed on both the behaviour of the self and others. Through self-instructional training, social problem solving skills training, and guided peer group social decision making, this phase of ART seeks to develop offenders' moral reasoning skills and broaden their social perspective taking. Importantly, as Gibbs (1993) notes, moral reasoning should be seen in the context of other aspects of social cognition, particularly social information processing. Gibbs (1993, 1996) describes the interaction between moral reasoning and social information processing in the form of "cognitive distortions". Such cognitive distortions are taken to be the attitudes or beliefs regarding one's social behaviour and, as such, they serve to support and rationalise antisocial behaviour. These powerful types of distorted thinking and their associated behaviour may be socially reinforced by the offender's peer group.

As the practice and evidence base grows there have been further refinements of ART (Goldstein *et al.,* 2004) and its use has spread to other client groups (Hornsveld, Nijman & De Ruiter, 2005). The outcome evidence suggests that ART is an effective method by which to reduce aggressive behaviour (Goldstein, 2004).

CONCLUSION

Violent behaviour is a complex behaviour, any explanation for which demands the integration of a wide range of factors, from the individual, to the immediate social environment, and to wider cultural mores. For example, the association between alcohol and drug use and violent behaviour is firmly established (Hollin & Palmer,

2003; Roberts, Roberts & Leonard, 1999); with further evidence to support an association between substance use, dysfunctional anger, and aggression (Parrott & Giancola, 2004). In working with violent offenders it would therefore be prudent to screen for alcohol use and, where alcohol use is present, to incorporate this factor into the treatment plan. As described by McMurran (2006), there is a range of programmes available for work with offenders who have substance use problems. It follows that attempts to reduce levels of violence must reflect this complexity. It would be a grave mistake to assume that individually-based interventions with offenders who display angry aggression will solve the problem of violence and its consequences. However, as part of a wider approach, the evidence to date indicates that interventions aimed at modifying angry aggression may well have a role to play in at least reducing levels of victimisation to violence.

REFERENCES

Allred, K. G. (2000). Anger and retaliation in conflict. In T. M. Deutsch & P. T. Coleman (eds). *The Handbook of Conflict Resolution: Theory and Practice* (pp. 236–55). San Francisco, CA: Jossey-Bass.

American Psychiatric Association, (2000). *Diagnostic and Statistical Manual of Mental Disorders* (4th edn, Text revision). Washington, DC: APA.

Bandura, A. (1973). *Aggression: A Social Learning Analysis*. Englewood Cliffs, NY: Prentice-Hall.

Beck, R. & Fernandez, E. (1998). Cognitive-behavioral therapy in the treatment of anger: A meta-analysis. *Cognitive Therapy and Research*, **22**, 63–74.

Berkowitz, L. (1962). *Aggression: A Social Psychological Analysis*. New York: McGraw Hill.

Berkowitz, L. (1986). Some varieties of human aggression: criminal violence as coercion, rule-following, impression-management and impulsive behaviour. In A. Campbell & J. J. Gibbs (eds), *Violent Transactions* (pp. 87–103). Oxford: Basil Blackwell.

Berkowitz, L. (1990). On the formation and regulation of anger and aggression - a cognitive-neoassociationistic analysis. *American Psychologist*, **45**, 494–503.

Blackburn, R. (1993). *The Psychology of Criminal Conduct: Theory, Research and Practice*. Chichester: John Wiley & Sons.

Bornstein, P. H., Weisser, C. E. & Balleweg, B. J. (1985). Anger and violent behavior. In M. Hersen & A. S. Bellack (eds), *Handbook of Clinical Behavior Therapy with Adults* (pp. 603–29). New York: Plenum Press.

Brown, T. (2002). DSM-IV: ADHD and executive function impairments. *Advanced Studies in Medicine*, **25**, 910–14.

Browne, K. & Howells, K. (1996). Violent offenders. In C. R. Hollin (ed.), *Working with Offenders* (pp. 188–210). Chichester: John Wiley & Sons.

Bush, J. (1995). Teaching self-risk management to violent offenders. In J. McGuire (ed.), *What Works: Reducing Reoffending* (pp. 139–54). Chichester: John Wiley & Sons.

Bushman, B. J. & Anderson, C. A. (2001). Is it time to pull the plug on the hostile versus instrumental aggression dichotomy? *Psychological Review*, **108**, 273–9.

Casey, S., Day, A. & Howells, K. (2005). The application of the transtheoretical model to offender populations: Some critical issues. *Legal and Criminological Psychology*, **10**, 151–71.

Colman, A. M. (2003). *A Dictionary of Psychology*. Oxford: Oxford University Press.

Craig, T. J. (1982). An epidemiological study of problems associated with violence among psychiatric patients. *American Journal of Psychiatry*, **139**, 1262–6.

Crick, N. R. & Dodge, K. A. (1994). A review and reformulation of social information-processing mechanisms in children's social adjustment. *Psychological Bulletin*, **115**, 74–101.

Crick, N. R. & Dodge, K. A. (1996). Social information-processing mechanisms in reactive and proactive aggression. *Child Development*, **67**, 993–1002.

Deffenbacher, J. L., McNamara, K., Stark, R. S. & Sabadell, P. M. (1990). A comparison of cognitive-behavioral and process-oriented group counseling for general anger reduction. *Journal of Counseling and Development*, **69**, 167–72.

Deffenbacher, J. L., Story, D. A., Brandon, A. D. *et al.* (1988). Cognitive and cognitive-relaxation treatments of anger. *Cognitive Therapy and Research*, **12**, 167–84.

DiGiuseppe, R. & Tafrate, R. (2003). Anger treatment for adults: a meta-analytic review. *Clinical Psychology: Science and Practice*, **10**, 70–84.

DiGiuseppe, R., Tafrate, R. & Eckhardt, C. (1994). Critical issues in the treatment of anger. *Cognitive and Behavioral Practice*, **1**, 111–32.

Dodge, K. A. & Newman, J. P. (1981). Biased decision making processes in aggressive boys. *Journal of Abnormal Psychology*, **90**, 375–9.

Dollard, J., Doob, L., Miller, N. *et al.* (1939). *Frustration and Aggression*. New Haven, CT: Yale University Press.

Dowden, C., Blanchette, K. & Serin, R. (1999). *Anger Management Programming for Federal Male Inmates: an Effective Intervention*. Research Report R82e. Ottawa: Correctional Service of Canada.

Drieschner, K. H., Lammers, S. M. M. & van der Staak, C. P. F. (2004). Treatment motivation: an attempt for clarification of an ambiguous concept. *Clinical Psychology Review*, **23**, 1115–37.

Dyck, R. J. & Rule, B. G. (1978). Effect on retaliation of causal attributions concerning attack. *Journal of Personality and Social Psychology*, **36**, 521–9.

Eckhardt, C. I. & Deffenbacher, J. L. (1995). Diagnoses of anger disorders. In H. Kassinove (ed.), *Anger Disorders: Definitions, Diagnosis, and Treatment* (pp. 27–47). Washington, DC: Taylor & Francis.

Edmondson, C. B. & Conger, J. C. (1996). A review of treatment efficacy for individuals with anger problems: conceptual, assessment, and methodological issues. *Clinical Psychology Review*, **16**, 251–75.

Engebretson, T. D., Matthews, K. A. & Scheer, M. F. (1989). Relations between anger expression and cardiovascular reactivity: Reconciling inconsistent findings through a matching hypothesis. *Journal of Personality and Social Psychology*, **57**, 513–521.

Feindler, E. L. (1995). Ideal treatment package for children and adolescents with anger disorders. In H. Kassinove (ed.), *Anger Disorders: Definition, Diagnosis and Treatment* (pp. 173–96). Washington, DC: Taylor & Francis.

Feindler, E. L. & Ecton, R. B. (1986). *Adolescent Anger Control: Cognitive-behavioral Techniques*. New York: Pergamon Press.

Freud, S. (1961). The ego and the id. In J. Strachey (ed.), *The Standard Edition of the Complete Psychological Works of Sigmund Freud* (Vol. 19, pp. 1–59). London: Hogarth Press.

Gibbs, J. C. (1993). Moral-cognitive interventions. In A. P. Goldstein & C. R. Huff (eds), *The Gang Intervention Handbook* (pp. 159–85). Champaign, IL: Research Press.

Gibbs, J. C. (1996). Sociomoral group treatment for young offenders. In C. R. Hollin & K. Howells (eds), *Clinical Approaches to Working with Young Offenders* (pp. 129–49). Chichester: Wiley.

Goldstein, A. P. (2004). Evaluations of effectiveness. In A. P. Goldstein, R. Nensen, B. Daleflod & M. Kalt (eds), *New Perspectives on Aggression Replacement Training* (pp. 230–44). Chichester: Wiley.

Goldstein, A. P. & Glick, B. (1987). *Aggression Replacement Training: A Comprehensive Intervention for Adolescent Youth*. Champaign, IL: Research Press.

Goldstein, A. P., Glick, B. & Gibbs, J. C. (1998). *Aggression Replacement Training* (revised edn). Champaign, IL: Research Press.

Goldstein, A. P., Nensen, R., Daleflod, B. & Kalt, M. (eds). (2004). *New Perspectives on Aggression Replacement Training*. Chichester, UK: John Wiley & Sons.

Hollin, C. R. (1993). Advances in the psychological treatment of criminal behaviour. *Criminal Behaviour and Mental Health*, **3**, 42–57.

Hollin, C. R. (1994). Designing effective rehabilitation programmes for young offenders. *Psychology, Crime and Law*, **1**, 193–9.

Hollin, C. R. (2004). Aggression replacement training: the cognitive-behavioral context. In A. P. Goldstein, R. Nensen, B. Daleflod & M. Kalt (eds), *New Perspectives on Aggression Replacement Training* (pp. 3–19). Chichester: John Wiley & Sons.

Hollin, C. R. & Palmer, E. J. (2003). Level of Service Inventory-Revised profiles of violent and non violent prisoners. *Journal of Interpersonal Violence*, **18**, 1075–86.

Hollin, C. R. & Palmer, E. J. (2006). Offending behaviour programmes: history and development. In C. R. Hollin & E. J. Palmer (eds), *Offending Behaviour Programmes: Development, Application, and Controversies* (pp. 1–32). Chichester: John Wiley & Sons.

Hornsveld, R., Nijman, H. & De Ruiter, C. (eds). (2005). Working with aggression and violence. *Psychology, Crime and Law: Special Issue*, **11**, 343–495.

Howells, K. (1989). Anger-management methods in relation to the prevention of violent behaviour. In J. Archer & K. Browne (eds), *Human Aggression: Naturalistic Approaches* (pp. 153–81). London: Routledge.

Howells, K. & Day, A. (2002). Readiness for anger management: clinical and theoretical issues. *Clinical Psychology Review*, **23**, 319–37.

Howells, K. & Day, A. (2006). Affective determinants of treatment engagement in violent offenders. *International Journal of Offender Therapy and Comparative Criminology*, **50**, 174–86.

Howells, K., Watt, B., Hall, G. & Baldwin, S. (1997). Developing programmes for violent offenders. *Legal and Criminological Psychology*, **2**, 117–28.

Huesmann, L. R. (1988). An information-processing model for the development of aggression. *Aggressive Behavior*, **14**, 13–24.

Hughes, G. V. (1993). Anger management program outcomes. *Forum on Corrections Research*, **5**, 3–5.

Jones, D. & Hollin, C. R. (2004). Managing problematic anger: the development of a treatment programme for personality disordered patients in high security. *International Journal of Forensic Mental Health*, **3**, 197–210.

Julkunen, J., Salonen, R., Kaplan, G. A. *et al.* (1994). Hostility and the progression of carotid atherosclerosis. *Psychosomatic Medicine*, **56**, 519–25.

Kassinove, H. & Tafrate, R. C. (2002). *Anger Management: The Complete Treatment Guidebook for Practitioners*. Atascadero, CA: Impact.

Ketterer, M. W. (1996). Anger and myocardial infarction. *Circulation*, **94**, 1788–9.

Kotler, M., Finkelstein, G., Molcho, A. *et al.* (1993). Correlates of suicide and violence risk in an inpatient population: coping styles and social support. *Psychiatry Research*, **47**, 281–90.

Krug, E. G., Dahlberg, L. L., Mercy, J. A. *et al.* (eds). (2002). *World Report on Violence and Health*. Geneva: World Health Organisation.

Kubzansky, L. D., Cole, S. R., Kawachi, I. *et al.* (2006). Shared and unique contributions of anger, anxiety, and depression to coronary heart disease: a prospective study in the normative aging study. *Annals of Behavioral Medicine*, **31**, 21–9.

Lazarus, R. S. (1966). *Psychological Stress and the Coping Process*. New York: McGraw-Hill.

Levey, S. & Howells, K. (1990). Anger and its management. *Journal of Forensic Psychiatry*, **1**, 305–27.

Lorenz, K. (1966). *On Aggression*. London: Methuen.

Marquis, H.A., Bourgon, G. A., Armstrong, B. & Pfaff, J. (1996). Reducing recidivism through institutional treatment programs. *Forum on Corrections Research*, **8**, 3–5.

McDougall, C., Boddis, S., Dawson. K. & Hayes, R. (1990). Developments in anger control training. In M. McMurran (ed.), Applying psychology to imprisonment: young offenders. *Issues in Criminological and Legal Psychology*, **15**. Leicester: The British Psychological Society.

McMurran, M. (2006). Drug and alcohol programmes: concept, theory, and practice. In C. R. Hollin & E. J. Palmer (eds), *Offending Behaviour Programmes: Development, Application, and Controversies* (pp. 179–207). Chichester: John Wiley & Sons.

McMurran, M., Charlesworth, P., Duggan, C. & McCarthy, L. (2001). Controlling angry aggression: A pilot group intervention with personality disordered offenders. *Behavioral and Cognitive Psychotherapy*, **29**, 473–85.

Miller, T. Q., Smith, T. W., Turner, C. W. *et al.* (1996). A meta-analytic review of research on hostility and physical health. *Psychological Bulletin*, **119**, 322–48.

Monahan, J., Steadman, H. J., Silver, E. *et al.* (2001). *Rethinking Risk Assessment: The MacArthur Study of Mental Disorder and Violence*. Oxford: Oxford University Press.

Murphy, C. M. & Baxter, V. A. (1997). Motivating batterers to change in the treatment context. *Journal of Interpersonal Violence*, **12**, 607–19.

Nisbitt, R. & Ross, L. (1980). *Human Inference: Strategies and Shortcomings of Social Judgement*. Englewood Cliffs, NJ: Prentice-Hall.

Novaco, R. W. (1975). *Anger Control: The Development and Evaluation of an Experimental Treatment*. Lexington, MA: D. C. Heath.

Novaco, R. W. (1976). The functions and regulation of the arousal of anger. *American Journal of Psychiatry*, **133**, 1124–8.

Novaco, R. W. (1977). A stress inoculation approach to anger management in the training of law enforcement officers. *American Journal of Community Psychology*, **5**, 327–46.

Novaco, R. W. (1986). Anger as a clinical and social problem. In R. Blanchard & C. Blanchard (eds), *Advances in the Study of Aggression* (Vol. 2, pp. 131–69). New York: Academic Press.

Novaco, R. W. (1993). Clinicians ought to view anger contextually. *Behaviour Change*, **10**, 208–18.

Novaco, R. W. (1994). Anger as a risk factor for violence among the mentally disordered. In J. Monahan & H. J. Steadman (eds), *Violence and Mental Disorder: Developments in Risk Assessment* (pp. 21–59). Chicago, IL: University of Chicago Press.

Novaco, R. W. (2003). *The Novaco Anger Scale and Provocation Inventory Manual (NAS-PI)*. Los Angeles: Western Psychological Services.

Novaco, R. W. (2007). Anger dysregulation: its assessment and treatment. In T. A. Cavell & K. T. Malcom (eds), *Anger, Aggression and Interventions for Interpersonal Violence* (pp. 3–54). Mahwah, NJ: Erlbaum.

Novaco, R. W. & Taylor, J. L. (2004). Assessment of anger and aggression among male offenders with developmental disabilities. *Psychological Assessment*, **16**, 42–50.

Novaco, R. W. & Welsh, W. N. (1989). Anger disturbances: Cognitive mediation and clinical prescriptions. In K. Howells & C. R. Hollin (eds), *Clinical Approaches to Violence* (pp. 39–60). Chichester: John Wiley & Sons.

Parrott, D. J. & Giancola, P. R. (2004). A further examination of the relation between trait anger and alcohol-related aggression: the role of anger control. *Alcoholism: Clinical and Experimental Research*, **28**, 855–64.

Polaschek, D. (2006). Violent offender programmes: concept, theory, and practice. In C. R. Hollin & E. J. Palmer (eds), *Offending Behaviour Programmes: Development, Application, and Controversies* (pp. 113–54). Chichester: John Wiley & Sons.

Prochaska, J. O. & DiClemente, C. C. (1982). Transtheoretical therapy: toward a more integrative model of change. *Psychotherapy: Theory, Research and Practice*, **19**, 276–88.

Reilly, P. M., Clark, H. W., Shopshire, M. *et al.* (1994). Anger management and temper control: Critical components of post-traumatic stress disorder and substance abuse treatment. *Journal of Psychoactive Drugs*, **20**, 401–7.

Renwick, S. J., Black, L., Ramm, M. & Novaco, R. W. (1997). Anger treatment with forensic hospital patients. *Legal and Criminological Psychology*, **2**, 103–16.

Roberts, L. J., Roberts, C. F. & Leonard, K. E. (1999). Alcohol, drugs, and interpersonal violence. In V. B. Van Hasselt & M. Hersen (eds), *Handbook of Psychological Approaches with Violent Offenders: Contemporary Strategies and Issues* (pp. 493–519). New York: Kluwer Academic/Plenum Publishers.

Robins, S. & Novaco, R. W. (1999). A systems conceptualization and treatment of anger. *Journal of Clinical Psychology*, **55**, 325–37.

Rollnick, S. & Miller, W. M. (1995). What is motivational interviewing? *Behavioral and Cognitive Psychotherapy*, **12**, 325–34.

Russell, G. W. & Arms, R. L. (1995). False consensus effect, physical aggression, anger, and a willingness to escalate a disturbance. *Aggressive Behavior*, **21**, 381–6.

Serin, R. C. (1998). Treatment responsivity, intervention and reintegration: A conceptual model. *Forum on Corrections Research*, **10**, 29–32.

Shelley, E. L. V. & Toch, H. H. (1968). The perception of violence as an indicator of adjustment in institutionalized offenders. In H. Toch & H. C. Smith (eds), *Social Perception: The Development of Interpersonal Impressions. An Enduring Problem in Psychology* (pp. 198–208). Princeton, NJ: D. Van Nostrand.

Siann, G. (1985). *Accounting for Aggression: Perspectives on Aggression and Violence*. London: Allen & Unwin.

Skeem, J. L., Schubert, C., Odgers, C. *et al.* (2006). Psychiatric symptoms and community violence among high-risk patients: a test of the relationship at a weekly level. *Journal of Consulting and Clinical Psychology*, **74**, 967–79.

Speilberger, C. D. (1999). *State-Trait Anger Expression Inventory-2 (STAXI-2)*. Odessa, FL: Psychological Assessment Resources.

Stermac, L. (1986). Anger control treatment for forensic patients. *Journal of Interpersonal Violence*, **1**, 446–57.

Taylor, J. L. & Novaco, R. W. (2005). *Anger Treatment for People with Developmental Disabilities: A Theory, Evidence, and Manual Based Approach*. Chichester: John Wiley & Sons.

Ward, T., Day, A., Howells, K. & Birgden, A. (2004). The multifactor offender readiness model. *Aggression and Violent Behavior*, **9**, 645–73.

Watt, B. D. & Howells, K. (1999). Skills training for aggression control: evaluation of an anger management programme for violent offenders. *Legal and Criminological Psychology*, **4**, 285–300.

Zamble, E. & Quinsey, V. L. (1997). *The Criminal Recidivism Process*. Cambridge: Cambridge University Press.

Zillmann, D. (1979). *Hostility and Aggression*. Hillsdale, NJ: Lawrence Erlbaum.

Chapter 12

ALCOHOL AND AGGRESSIVE COGNITION

MARY MCMURRAN

University of Nottingham, UK

Violence has been acknowledged by the World Health Organisation (2002) as a significant public health problem and the role of alcohol as a contributor to youth violence, child abuse, domestic violence, sexual violence, and self-directed violence has been highlighted. In this chapter, the focus is on what is sometimes called "street violence" – the reactive violence perpetrated usually by young men on each other in social situations. In some cultures, alcohol and aggression, even to the point of violence, go together like Jekyll and Hyde. There is plenty evidence to support this from a variety of types of study: epidemiological research, cross-sectional studies of offenders, longitudinal studies of birth cohorts, and experimental studies. In this chapter, I will give some examples of research from each of these domains but the purpose here is not to provide a comprehensive overview of the alcohol and violence literature. Rather, the purpose is to look more closely at the mechanisms, particularly cognitive mechanisms, whereby alcohol increases the likelihood of aggression. The main part of the chapter will be devoted to this. If cognitions have a part to play, then attention needs to be paid to how these might be addressed in interventions to reduce the likelihood of alcohol-related aggression and violence. This will be the focus in the last part of the chapter.

ALCOHOL AND AGGRESSION

At a population level, as sales of alcohol increase, so does the incidence of violent crime, although the strength of the association varies between countries and within countries across time (Room & Rossow, 2001). In epidemiological data, the figures for drinking and violence are independent yet the connection between the two can be estimated by calculating the "attributable fraction". This refers to the proportion of cases of violence that may be attributed to the risk factor of alcohol. The attributable fraction varies according to the type of violence measured

---

Aggressive Offenders' Cognition: Theory, Research and Practice. Edited by T. A. Gannon, T. Ward, A. R. Beech and D. Fisher. © 2007 John Wiley & Sons, Ltd.

and where and when the data were collected. In short, those countries in which the relationship is stronger are typically those where drinking to intoxication is part of the prevailing pattern (Room & Rossow, 2001).

Surveys of offender populations show large proportions of both males and females to be heavy drinkers. In a large-scale survey of substance misuse among 3,563 prisoners in England and Wales, Singleton, Farrell and Meltzer (1999) used the Alcohol Use Disorders Identification Test (AUDIT) (Babor *et al.*, 2001), a 10-item screening tool for alcohol abuse. They identified 63 % hazardous drinkers (i.e., a score of 8 or more) among sentenced men, 58 % hazardous drinkers in remanded men, 39 % among sentenced women, and 36 % among remanded women. Furthermore, among male prisoners, the heaviest drinkers, compared with less problematic drinkers, were those more likely to be held for a violent offence (Singleton, Farrell & Meltzer, 1999). In a study of male prisoners with convictions for violence, the mean AUDIT score of those who were drunk at the time of their violent offence – the majority of the sample – was significantly higher than that for those not drunk at the time of their offence. This appears to show that offenders who are violent when intoxicated are more problematic drinkers than those who are violent when they are not intoxicated (McMurran, 2006).

In a study of 1,595 perpetrators of homicide over a three-year period in England and Wales, Shaw *et al.* (2006) estimated that 45 % of offences were alcohol-related. Haggård-Grann, Hallqvist, Långström and Möller (2006) used a case-crossover design with violent offenders to examine the effects of drinking on violence. The hazard period was defined as the 24 hours prior to the violent offence and drinking during this hazard period was compared with usual drinking during the whole of the previous year. There was a 13-fold increase in the risk of committing violence in those who had been drinking alcohol in the 24 hours before the event.

Using data from a longitudinal study of a birth cohort in New Zealand, Fergusson and colleagues (Fergusson & Horwood, 2000; Fergusson, Lynskey & Horwood, 1996) have shown that a substantial amount of the relationship between alcohol use and crime is related to shared factors, such as social disadvantage and deviant peer affiliations. Nevertheless, when these confounding variables are controlled, a significant relationship remains between alcohol misuse and crime, particularly violent crime, with heavy drinkers being three times more likely to be violent than light drinkers. The suggestion is that alcohol misuse and violent offending arise via a similar route – the antecedent risk factors are highly similar – but that there is also a direct cause and effect between alcohol misuse and violent offending.

Exum (2006) reviewed and integrated findings from seven meta-analyses of experimental studies of alcohol on aggression. Experimental studies typically ask participants to administer an electric shock as punishment to an unseen competitor, who is, in fact, not there at all. The type of task can be varied to simulate levels of provocation and the dependent variable is the level or duration of the shock administered. Alcohol consumption is one variable that can be manipulated, varying amounts and types. Also, the pharmacological versus the expected effects of alcohol can be separated using the balanced placebo design. Typically, in this kind of study there are four conditions:

1. Participants are told they will receive alcohol and are given alcohol (alcohol condition).
2. Participants are told they will not receive alcohol and are given a nonalcoholic drink (control).
3. Participants are told they will receive alcohol are given a nonalcoholic drink (placebo).
4. Participants are told they will not receive alcohol are given alcohol (anti-placebo).

Looking at the pharmacological effect of alcohol, overall, these meta-analyses reported effect sizes of around 0.50. An effect size is a standardised index of the magnitude of the observed effects, and a value of 0.50 indicates that alcohol exerts a medium effect (i.e., accounts for 25 % of the total variance) on aggressive behaviour. This effect is more pronounced for spirits, at high doses of alcohol, and when there are no nonaggressive options. Alcohol mainly increases aggression at low levels of provocation. At high levels of provocation aggression is likely regardless of alcohol. When it comes to an expectancy effect (i.e., the effect observed when people think they have been given alcohol but have not), the evidence for this was weak.

Most experimental research has been conducted with men. Women do respond aggressively in laboratory tasks and alcohol does increase their aggression, yet this effect is not as pronounced as it is for men. Evidence suggests that women respond aggressively to certain types of provocation, and that the effect of alcohol is not especially important in this relationship (Hoaken & Pihl, 2000).

Evidence from all these studies and others like them indicates a substantial relationship between alcohol and aggression or violence, however, drinking alcohol is neither necessary nor sufficient in explaining violence. This individual variation is what engages the psychologist. If alcohol is a risk factor, but at an individual level is not sufficient in explaining violence after drinking, what then are the conditional factors that may increase and decrease risk? What is it about the person who is drinking (i.e., traits, behavioural style, and beliefs)? What is it about the circumstances in which that person is drinking (i.e., when, where, and with whom)? What is it about the person's drinking style (i.e., beverage, speed, and amount)? What is it about all these things that could increase the likelihood that the drinker will perpetrate an act of aggression or violence upon a partner, a family member, an acquaintance, or a complete stranger?

HOW DOES ALCOHOL INCREASE AGGRESSIVENESS?

One way to answer the list of questions posed at the end of the previous section is to take a developmental risk factor perspective on an individual's potential for alcohol-related aggression and violence (McMurran, 1996, 2002). In this, reciprocal interactions between the individual and the social environment (i.e., parents, school and peers) serve either to exacerbate or to ameliorate the likelihood of violent crime, heavy drinking and alcohol-related violence across the life span.

Early impulsivity, hyperactivity, and aggression are associated both with later aggressive offending and problem drinking (e.g., af Klinteberg et al., 1993). These early characteristics, particularly if allowed to flourish into conduct disorder, are strong predictors of later serious violence and alcohol problems. First, these characteristics may be directly associated with deficits in executive cognitive functioning, this being a term used to cover diverse higher-order cerebral activities such as attention, abstracting relevant information, reasoning, problem solving, planning, and self-regulation (White *et al.*, 1994). These cognitive abilities are needed to control and plan one's behaviour to achieve the best outcomes in any situation. Poor executive cognitive functioning is associated with aggressiveness, impulsive violent crime and with antisocial personality disorder (Giancola *et al.*, 1996; Golden *et al.*, 1996). Second, difficult characteristics may impact upon the child's carers, leading to family management practices that increase risk. These are characterised by unclear expectations for behaviour, lax supervision, little in the way of rewards for positive behaviour, harsh punishment for unwanted behaviour and inconsistency in the application of rewards and punishments (Farrington & Hawkins, 1991; Hawkins, Catalano & Miller, 1992). Under these circumstances, the child is less likely to learn to behave appropriately and is less likely to develop those cognitive skills relevant to behavioural self-control (Bennett, Farrington & Huesmann, 2005).

The child whose behaviour is undercontrolled is not normally a successful student and school may well be an unpleasant experience, which some children may escape through truancy. Low commitment to school is strongly related to persistence in crime into early adulthood, perhaps because poor performance at school is predictive of job instability (Farrington & Hawkins, 1991; Le Blanc, 1994). In life so far, the difficult child may have experienced repeated chastisement from parents and teachers, as well as unpopularity with pro-social peers. The experience of harshness and unpopularity may lead to the acquisition of hostile attributional biases; that is, these children see the world as antagonistic and unfriendly towards them. Hostile attributional biases have been shown to correlate with anger and aggression in children and adolescents (Dodge *et al.*, 1990; Matthys & Lochman, 2005; Slaby & Guerra, 1988).

Once drinking begins, its effects become evident. There are four main ways that alcohol acts on the brain to increase the likelihood of violence (Pihl & Hoaken, 2002). First, alcohol activates the *cue for reward system*, which means that, as alcohol is associated with positive outcomes, it increases psychomotor activity, which increases an organism's approach behaviour. In the course of this increased activity, particularly in certain contexts, the likelihood of provoking aggression is increased. Second, alcohol affects the *cue for punishment system* in that its pharmacological effect is to reduce anxiety and, as anxiety protects against punishment by inhibiting behaviour in the presence of novel or threatening stimuli, alcohol increases the likelihood of risk-taking behaviour, including aggression. Third, alcohol also affects the *pain system*. At low doses pain sensitivity is increased, which may serve to increase the significance of threat and may lead to pre-emptive action to remove the threat. At high doses pain sensitivity decreases, which may serve to increase risk-taking or may be a condition actively sought by those who intend violence. Finally, alcohol also interferes with the *cognitive control system* (Pihl & Hoaken, 1997). Most relevant to this chapter is that the acute effect of alcohol is to disrupt executive cognitive functioning. As we have already seen, poor executive cognitive functioning is related to aggression and violence and so further impairment by means of alcohol intoxication is likely to heighten risk of violence.

When they are of a legal age to drink in bars, people then begin to drink more in social settings – pubs, clubs, and parties. Violence is more likely to happen where people are grouped together, particularly if others are also drunk and of an aggressive disposition. Violence most commonly occurs in and around city centre licensed premises and entertainment venues, especially where young men gather and drink heavily on weekend nights (Lang *et al.*, 1995). Not only is the assailant likely to be intoxicated,but so is the victim of violence (Lindqvist, 1991). In social drinking venues, where the probability of both the assailant and the victim being intoxicated is high, it is likely that the probability of aggression would be elevated, regardless of the occurrence of drinking (Lang & Sibrel, 1989). While this may be true, the co-occurrence of drinking and violence is an important consideration. Repeated experiences of an association between drinking and violence leads to the formation of the expectancy that where there is alcohol there is also aggression or violence (McMurran *et al.*, 2006).

Finally, while most people grow out of substance use and delinquency as they acquire responsibilities relating to work, accommodation, partners and children, some people will continue to drink heavily and will remain involved in crime. In fact, both heavy drinking and a criminal record may present obstacles to a conventional lifestyle and substance use and crime become a way of life (Walters, 1998).

Lifestyles of substance use and crime lead people into social contexts that reinforce these behaviours, make relationships difficult to sustain and make job prospects diminish, until eventually the person seems trapped in an antisocial lifestyle. Like the rest of us, offenders rationalise their behaviour, developing and strengthening beliefs that hard drinking, antisocial behaviour and crime are acceptable, or at least are unavoidable given their circumstances. These antisocial attitudes militate against change (Walters, 1998).

This brief overview of the developmental risk factor model of alcohol-related aggression and violence indicates that risk factors lie in number of domains: individual, social, pharmacological, situational, and cognitive. Most relevant to this chapter are cognitive risk factors. General cognitive risk factors for aggression and violence include hostile attributional biases and antisocial beliefs and attitudes. Although these may be exacerbated by alcohol and in drinking contexts, these will not be covered in this chapter (see Chapter 9 of this volume for information on the hostile attribution bias). Two specific cognitive themes that warrant further elaboration in relation to alcohol use are:

- executive cognitive functioning; and
- alcohol-aggression outcome expectancies.

ALCOHOL AND AGGRESSIVE COGNITION

Executive Cognitive Functioning

Executive cognitive functioning is the term used for a range of higher order cognitive abilities, which include attention, abstracting relevant information, reasoning, problem-solving, planning, and self-regulation (White *et al.*, 1994).

Reviewers of executive cognitive functioning and its relationship with aggression conclude that violent offenders and men with antisocial personality disorder have poorer executive cognitive functioning than nonviolent offenders and nonoffenders (Giancola, 2000; Hoaken, Shaughnnessy & Pihl, 2003). However, the range of functions subsumed within the term executive cognitive functioning is wide, and the connection between executive cognitive functioning and aggression needs to be clarified.

One hypothesis is that poor executive cognitive functioning is related to aggression through impulsivity: people with poor executive cognitive functioning are less able to inhibit behaviour, including aggression. In a laboratory study of executive cognitive functioning and aggression, Hoaken, Shaughnessy and Pihl (2003) found that participants with low executive cognitive functioning responded more aggressively to provocation than did those with high executive cognitive functioning, and that this effect was more pronounced for men than women. However, in identifying the mechanism by which low executive cognitive functioning led to increased aggression, poor behavioural inhibition was not the main contender, as was expected. Compared to those with high executive cognitive functioning, those with low executive cognitive functioning made more errors of commission on a Go/No Go task (i.e., where a participant is asked to withhold a response to a stimulus previously paired with a reward). Although this finding was not statistically significant, Hoaken, Shaughnessy and Pihl (2003) took it as supportive of the impulsivity hypothesis. However, compared to those with high executive cognitive functioning, participants with low executive cognitive functioning took significantly *longer* to select the intensity of shock that would putatively be delivered to their opponent in a competitive reaction time task, which argues against the impulsivity hypothesis. Hoaken, Shaughnessy and Pihl (2003) interpreted these results as indicating the importance of a social component: people with low executive cognitive functioning make poor social decisions in that they are aggressive but they make these decisions slowly. People with low executive cognitive functioning are more aggressive because they are unable to cope with the number of response options, fail to access socially appropriate responses, and make default aggressive responses when provoked. That is, they are poor at social problem solving.

Social problem solving is the ability to recognise, define and solve problems in the interpersonal domain – skills that require higher order cognitive abilities. In fact, Zelazo *et al.* (1997) hold that the construct of executive cognitive functioning is inadequately characterised and that it may be better construed as a family of processes within a problem-solving framework. How is social problem solving related to and affected by drinking?

In studies of the relationships among impulsiveness, social problem solving, aggression, and alcohol use, McMurran and colleagues (McMurran, Blair & Egan, 2002; Ramadan & McMurran, 2005) found that impulsivity and aggression were related via the mediator of social problem solving in both men and women. That is, impulsivity leads to poor social problem solving which, in turn, leads to aggression. Impulsivity was related to hazardous drinking, as measured by the AUDIT, also via the mediator of poor social problem solving, but only in men. In this student sample there was no relationship between hazardous drinking and aggression. Given the evidence for a relationship between alcohol and aggression generally, this suggests the possibility that good social problem solving skills, as one would expect to find in a student sample, may protect against alcohol-related aggression. Indeed, in a longitudinal study of young men, many of whom were delinquent, Welte and Wieczorek (1999) found that both drinking and IQ predicted violence, with a combination of heavy drinking and low verbal IQ being the strongest predictor of all. They concluded that, if alcohol causes violence by reducing intellectual functioning and promoting misunderstandings, then those with low IQ, particularly low verbal IQ, are more vulnerable to the negative consequences of alcohol.

Over the developmental pathway, low intelligence, especially verbal intelligence, may militate against the acquisition of good social problem solving skills. Furthermore, Howard (2006) suggests that youngsters with early disinhibitory psychopathology who drink heavily during adolescence cause permanent impairment to frontal lobe functioning that, in view of their personality traits, increases the likelihood of antisocial behaviour, including aggression, throughout adulthood. Alcohol intoxication also increases the risk of head injury, through fighting and accidental blows, which may further impair brain functioning (Solomon & Molloy, 1992).

Alcohol intoxication impairs problem solving in the moment. "Alcohol myopia" (Steele & Josephs, 1990) is the term used for the way alcohol restricts the range of cues that a person can perceive and attend to in any situation. The more intoxicated a person becomes the more that person's attention will reduce until he or she can focus only on salient and immediate cues. If these salient and immediate cues are threatening, focusing attention on these will result in increased anxiety and also few resources will be left to access cognitive strategies that could help defend against stressors in the environment (Josephs & Steele, 1990). Put another way, the intoxicated person attends to the immediate events around him or her and is more affected by instigatory situational cues (e.g., an insult), is less affected by distal inhibitory cues (e.g., the consequences of punching the insulting person), and is less able to figure out alternatives to aggression.

It is clear from the above research that social problem solving is likely to be one useful aspect of any intervention to reduce alcohol-related aggression and violence.

Alcohol-Aggression Outcome Expectancies

Alcohol outcome expectancies are the effects one expects to experience as a result of drinking (Goldman, Del Boca & Darkes, 1999). Expectancies develop from early on in life through observation of how people relate and respond to alcohol. The behaviour of family members, depictions of drinking on television and the cultural context as it pertains to alcohol all have relevance here. Young people are also given information and instruction with regard to alcohol and its effects, which will contribute still further to their expectancies. Hence, expectancies exist before a person has even sipped a drink, and develop further with drinking experience. Expectancies may be positive, such as alcohol enhancing social and sexual functioning, or negative, such as alcohol leading to loss of self-control or feelings of depression (Jones, Corbin & Fromme, 2001; Leigh & Stacy, 2004).

Put simply, expectancies may be construed as cognitive representations of an "if-then" relationship: "If I drink, then I will ... " How this proposition is completed depends upon a range of factors that depend upon the individual's drinking experience in relation to culture, family, and peers, and individual differences such as age, gender, and personality characteristics. Outcome expectancies also vary according to the time of day, the day of the week, drinking venue and with whom one is drinking. One critical question is 'do alcohol expectancies predict future behaviour?'

Greater endorsement of positive alcohol outcome expectancies is significantly associated with higher levels of alcohol consumption and greater endorsement of negative alcohol outcome expectancies is significantly associated with lower levels of alcohol consumption (Brown, Goldman & Christiansen, 1985; Fromme, Stroot & Kaplan, 1993; Leigh & Stacy, 2004).

In her meta-analysis of experimental work on the influence of alcohol on aggression, Exum (2006) did not find much support for the placebo effect: participants who thought they were drinking alcohol but were not mostly behaved similarly to the control group. However, Giancola, Godlaski and Parrott (2005) point out that experimental studies test the belief that alcohol has been consumed, not the prevailing belief that alcohol causes aggression.

Quigley, Corbett and Tedeschi (2002) investigated 339 New York State male and female students around 18 years of age using the five aggression-related items of a general alcohol expectancy questionnaire (Leigh, 1987). Self-reported fighting and alcohol consumption in the previous year were assessed, and a scale measuring desire for power was administered. Heavy drinking was associated with violence in men but not women. The belief that alcohol leads to aggression personally was associated with alcohol-related violence, and this was moderated by the desire to convey an image of power. This study indicates the importance of alcohol-aggression outcome expectancies on outcomes of violence, at least for young male students.

As part of a longitudinal study of substance use and delinquency, Zhang, Welte and Wieczorek (2002) studied 405 young men in New York State, aged 16 to 19 years, who had been aggressive or violent in the previous year. The measures taken were aggression-related alcohol expectancies, again assessed using the five aggression-related items from Leigh's (1987) general alcohol expectancy questionnaire, self-reported drinking, and self-reported drinking before violent offending. Heavy drinkers were more likely to have been drinking prior to acts of violence and this was particularly true for those who held high aggression-related alcohol expectancies; that is, aggression-related alcohol expectancies moderated the effect of heavy drinking on violence. Aggression-related alcohol expectancies were associated with increased drinking prior to offending, suggesting that offenders may drink to give them courage for violence or to excuse their violence after the event.

Experimental evidence comes from studies using competitive reaction time tasks. In one study, male students were divided into those who expect alcohol to increase aggression and those who expect alcohol to decrease aggression, based upon their responses to the three-item aggression scale of the Effects of Drinking

Questionnaire (EDQ) (George, Dermen & Mochajski, 1989). Participants in each group were then assigned to receive alcohol or a placebo prior to the experimental task. The results indicated that, whereas the pharmacological effects of alcohol are probably more potent than expectancies, at high doses of alcohol consumption those who think alcohol makes them aggressive are more extreme in their aggression when provoked (Chermack & Taylor, 1995). Dispositional aggressiveness was not measured in this study.

Giancola (2006) tested the alcohol-aggression outcome expectancy using a competitive reaction time task, but in his research he controlled for dispositional aggressiveness. Alcohol-aggression expectancies, measured by five relevant items drawn from a number of questionnaires, significantly predicted aggression for men but not women, however this relationship disappeared when dispositional aggressiveness was controlled for in the analysis. Giancola (2006) concluded that intoxicated aggression, at least in men, is mainly the result of the pharmacological properties of alcohol in conjunction with an aggressive disposition.

Giancola's (2006) work clearly points to the need to reduce intoxication if there is to be a reduction in alcohol-related aggression, particularly in dispositionally aggressive men. However, the role of alcohol-aggression outcome expectancies cannot yet be dismissed. First, the way alcohol-aggression outcome expectancies are measured in experimental work seems currently to be of dubious adequacy. Using a mere five items drawn from a test not specifically designed for the purpose may not be a sensitive and or comprehensive way of measuring alcohol-aggression expectancies, hence the conclusions may be founded on studies using poor measures. To address this issue, a 28-item scale that incorporates alcohol-aggression outcome expectancies, personality dimensions, and drinking styles, called the Alcohol-Related Aggression Questionnaire (ARAQ), has been designed, and this may be of use in experimental work (McMurran et al., 2006). Also, while it is important to minimise alcohol intoxication, there remains the strong possibility that aggressive men will nevertheless become intoxicated. Based on Giancola's (2006) pharmacological perspective, to protect against aggression in these circumstances, it is the aggressive disposition that needs to be targeted. Whether interventions can change personality is a topic of some contention, but it might be considered reasonable that if interventions target a person's thoughts, feelings, and behaviour, then they are, to some extent, targeting personality. In this case, targeting alcohol-related aggression outcome expectancies may be useful as one component in interventions to tackle alcohol-related aggression in dispositionally aggressive men.

Expectancies of Confidence and Social Facilitation

Alcohol-related aggression expectancies are not the only expectancies associated with aggression. McMurran (1997) reported a study of 85 literate male young offenders who were given the Alcohol Expectancies Questionnaire – Adolescent Form (AEQ-A) (Goldman, Christiansen & Brown, 1987). The AEQ-A has seven subscales, but for this sample a three factor solution best fitted the AEQ-A data: (1) global positive change, (2) change in cognitive and motor abilities, and (3) change in social behaviour. Alcohol-related violence was associated with expecting changes in social behaviour after drinking.

In a study of the routes through which alcohol-related aggression proneness, as measured by the Alcohol-Related Aggression Questionnaire (ARAQ) (McMurran et al., 2006), leads to alcohol-related aggression, McMurran (2007) examined 98 UK male prisoners of whom 21 were serving sentences for violent offences that were not alcohol-related and 77 were serving sentences for violent offences that were alcohol-related. The hypothesised model was that alcohol expectancies and hazardous drinking (as assessed by the AUDIT) would mediate the relationship between proneness to alcohol-related aggression and alcohol-related violence. Additionally, expectancies would predict drinking.

The relationship between proneness to alcohol-related aggression, as measured by the ARAQ, and alcohol-related violence was mediated by alcohol outcome expectancies, as measured by the Drinking Expectancy Questionnaire (DEQ) (Young & Oei, 1996), particularly the increased confidence scale of the DEQ. Alcohol outcome expectancies overall predicted hazardous drinking in this group, with *negative* outcome expectancies being the strongest predictor. This scale includes items such as alcohol increasing tension, irritability, and aggressiveness, suggesting that some members of this sample may view these as *positive* rather than negative consequences. Consistent with Zhang et al.'s (2002) findings, some offenders may drink heavily before violent offending either to give them courage or to excuse their behaviour.

Among violent offenders, those who are more prone to alcohol-related aggression, as measured by the ARAQ, are more likely to be perpetrators of alcohol-related violence if they expect alcohol to increase their confidence. The Increased Confidence scale of the DEQ contains items about alcohol enabling the expression of feelings, increasing friendliness, and promoting a "who cares" attitude. This confirms McMurran's (1997) findings, where expectancies of positive social change after drinking were associated with alcohol-related violence in young offenders. The DEQ-Increased Confidence scale also predicts hazardous drinking, as measured by the AUDIT, a relationship also identified by Connor et al. (2000) for male students. Thus, drinking to increase confidence in social situations appears to be an important facet of young men's drinking, and one that is associated with violence.

How may drinking to increase social confidence be associated with aggression and violence? Those who drink to increase their social confidence are likely to be drawn to social drinking venues where confidence is relevant, for instance, to fare well in sexual competition (Egan & Hamilton, 2006). These may be the bars and clubs where other young people drink for the same reasons and it is in these social drinking venues where aggression and violence are more likely (Lang et al., 1995). The increased likelihood of violence may be explained by intoxicated, confident (perhaps overconfident), young men meeting others who are drinking for the same reasons in noisy, crowded drinking venues, which may well lead to clashes where aggression and violence result.

To integrate the information on alcohol-related expectancies and aggression from a developmental perspective, it is likely that young people who drink alcohol experience increased confidence and form a positive outcome expectancy that becomes a predictor of heavy drinking. For dispositionally aggressive males, drinking and increased confidence are associated with an increased likelihood of aggression and violence. The repeated association between drinking and aggression appears to contribute to the development of an alcohol-aggression outcome expectancy that may precipitate alcohol-related aggression and violence.

Thus, interventions for offenders whose violence is alcohol-related should address drinking to increase confidence, the alcohol-aggression outcome expectancy, and also the risks inherent in drinking in certain venues.

TREATMENT

The above research has identified various targets that are relevant in treatment for alcohol-related aggression and violence. Before describing a comprehensive treatment programme, it must be acknowledged that the research pertains largely to men belonging to cultures where drinking to intoxication is common, particularly in the United States and United Kingdom, so these findings may not generalise to women or to men in dissimilar cultures. Nevertheless, this research gives direction to the development of alcohol-related aggression treatment programmes for male offenders in cultures where alcohol-related violence is a problem. Programmes may be best targeted at young male offenders, amongst whom alcohol-related violence is strongly associated with binge drinking and public violence (Lang et al., 1995; Richardson & Budd, 2003). Few treatment programmes specifically for alcohol-related violence exist, although there is an acknowledged need for interventions that "not only employ standard treatment techniques (e.g., anger management), but also use knowledge of the effects of alcohol and the process of aggression in treating violent individuals" (Graham et al., 1998, p. 670).

Control of Violence for Angry Impulsive Drinkers (COVAID)

A treatment programme for alcohol-related violence informed by the evidence presented in this chapter has been developed and is under evaluation (McMurran & Cusens, 2003). Control of Violence for Angry Impulsive Drinkers (COVAID) is a structured, cognitive-behavioural treatment programme for people who have been repeatedly aggressive or violent when intoxicated. Central to COVAID is the systems approach to angry aggression described by Robins and Novaco (1999), where anger provocations are appraised in the light of hostile beliefs, which leads to physiological arousal that is readily labelled anger, and hence to aggression or violence, which are overlearned behaviours. Consideration is then given to this system when alcohol enters the equation (see Figure 12.1), for example being intoxicated in certain drinking contexts inflates the likelihood of experiencing and causing provocations to anger; provocations are processed through a cognitive system that is not operating effectively, in which threat is salient, and which is influenced by aggression-related outcome expectancies; the anxiolytic and analgesic effects of alcohol erode violence inhibitions; and more complex alternatives to aggression as a response to provocation are less accessible. The

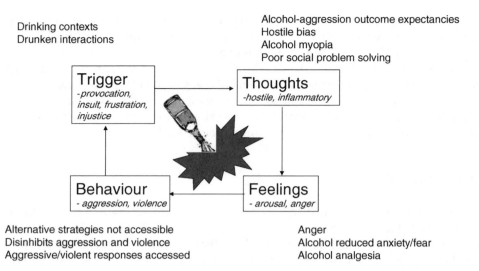

Figure 12.1 The Control of Violence for Angry Impulsive Drinkers (COVAID) model

intervention teaches participants to address all parts of the system, as well as moderating their drinking, especially drinking to intoxication, to reduce the likelihood of aggression and violence.

Over 10-sessions, COVAID covers the following components:

- Explaining drunken aggression.
- Crime harm reduction.
- Managing stress and arousal.
- Modifying drinking.
- Altering triggers.
- Weakening beliefs about the effects of alcohol.
- Identifying and coping with high-risk situations.
- Enhancing problem-solving skills.
- Lifestyle change.

Emphasis is placed upon participants becoming their own "personal scientist" (Mahoney & Thoresen, 1974), so that they learn the skills for analysing problem behaviours and experimenting with change. Based upon the premise that participants often drink without becoming aggressive, self-efficacy is enhanced throughout by identifying the methods participants already use to control alcohol-related aggression.

Clearly, any intervention needs to target multiple areas, not just cognitions, but cognitions are specifically relevant to this chapter. Outcome expectancies are defined and the potential effect of the specific "alcohol makes me violent" expectancy is explored. The expectancy of positive social change is addressed by challenging negative views about abstainers and moderate drinkers since challenging alcohol outcome expectancies can reduce alcohol consumption (Darkes & Goldman, 1993). Methods of escaping or avoiding confrontation without losing face are also taught for use when threat is perceived. Social problem solving is taught through a brief version of a *Stop & Think!* programme, which invites participants to cue into problems, set goals, generate potential solutions, think through the consequences of each solution, select actions that are likely to be maximally effective, and formulate a means-end action plan (Huband *et al.*, 2007; McMurran, Egan & Duggan, 2005).

A pilot study of six COVAID completers, all men aged between 21 and 31 who were on probation orders or licence from prison, indicated that COVAID was having the desired effect (McMurran & Cusens, 2003). Overall improvements were noted on psychometric measures of the treatment targets, namely anger, impulsiveness, and alcohol-related aggression. Self-reported incidents of aggression were rare and no participants were convicted of any violent offence during COVAID. Six COVAID completers were compared with 10 referred but untreated or noncompleters four months after referral. Without COVAID, the chances of reconviction were just over twice as high compared with those who participated in COVAID. Changes in alcohol consumption were variable: of the six participants, two improved, three stayed much the same, and one got worse. However, this was a measure of overall alcohol consumption, rather than instances of intoxication, and so may not have been directly relevant to alcohol-related aggression. Overall, the indicators are that COVAID may have promise as an intervention for offenders whose violence is alcohol-related. Work continues to develop and evaluate the COVAID programme, and this may be of use in the development of services for offenders with alcohol-related problems.

CONCLUSIONS

Lipton *et al.* (2002a,b) reported a meta-analysis of 68 methodologically acceptable behavioural and cognitive-behavioural programmes with over 10,000 participants as part of their Correctional Drug Abuse Treatment Effectiveness (CDATE) project. Overall, there was a positive mean effect size of 0.12, with separate analyses revealing that the 23 evaluations of behavioural programmes (i.e., without the cognitive element) produced a mean effect size of 0.07, and that the 44 cognitive-behavioural programmes was 0.14. Although these effect sizes are only modest, what is clear is that focusing on cognitions enhances the effectiveness of interventions.

In this chapter, a case has been made for targeting social problem solving skills, alcohol-aggression outcome expectancies, and expectancies of social facilitation and confidence. With regard to confidence, one specific area for study might be where alcohol is used deliberately to give confidence for violence. As ever, the need for further research is evident, and there should be emphasis upon devising and evaluating treatments for alcohol-related aggression that focus on cognitions.

REFERENCES

Af Klinteberg, B. A., Andersson, T., Magnusson, D. & Stattin, H. (1993). Hyperactive behavior in childhood as related to subsequent alcohol problems and violent offending: A longitudinal study of male subjects. *Personality and Individual Differences*, **15**, 381–38.

Babor, T. F., Higgins-Biddle, J. C., Saunders, J. B. & Monteiro, M. G. (2001). *AUDIT: The Alcohol Use Disorders Identification Test*. Geneva: World Health Organisation.

Bennett, S., Farrington, D. P. & Huesmann, L. R. (2005). Explaining gender differences in crime and violence: The importance of social cognitive skills. *Aggression and Violent Behavior*, **10**, 263–88.

Brown, S. A., Goldman, M. S. & Christiansen, B. A. (1985). Do alcohol expectancies mediate drinking patterns of adults? *Journal of Consulting and Clinical Psychology*, **53**, 512–19.

Chermack, S. T. & Taylor, S. P. (1995). Alcohol and human physical aggression: Pharmacological versus expectancy effects. *Journal of Studies on Alcohol*, **56**, 449–56.

Connor, J. P., Young, R. McD., Williams, R. J. & Ricciardelli, L. A. (2000). Drinking restraint versus alcohol expectancies: which is the better indicator of alcohol problems? *Journal of Studies on Alcohol*, **61**, 352–9.

Darkes, J. & Goldman, M. S. (1993). Expectancy challenge and drinking reduction. *Journal of Consulting and Clinical Psychology*, **61**, 344–53.

Dodge, K. A., Price, J. M., Bachorowski, J., and Newman, J. P. (1990). Hostile attributional bias in severely aggressive adolescents. *Journal of Abnormal Psychology*, **99**, 385–92.

Egan, V. & Hamilton, E. (2006). Personality, mating effort, and alcohol-related violence expectancies. Manuscript under review.

Exum, M. L. (2006). Alcohol and aggression: an integration of findings from experimental studies. *Journal of Criminal Justice*, **34**, 131–45.

Farrington, D. P. & Hawkins, J. D. (1991). Predicting participation, early onset, and later persistence in officially recorded offending. *Criminal Behaviour and Mental Health*, **1**, 1–33.

Fergusson, D. M. & Horwood, L. J. (2000). Alcohol abuse and crime: a fixed-effects regression analysis. *Addiction*, **95**, 1525–36.

Fergusson, D. M., Lynskey, M. T. & Horwood, L. J. (1996). Alcohol misuse and juvenile offending in adolescence. *Addiction*, **91**, 483–94.

Fromme, K., Stroot, E. & Kaplan, D. (1993). Comprehensive effects of alcohol: Development and psychometric assessment of a new expectancy questionnaire. *Psychological Assessment*, **5**, 19–26.

George, W. H., Dermen, K. H. & Nochajski, T. H. (1989). Expectancy set, self-reported expectancies and predispositional traits: Predicting interest in violence and erotica. *Journal of Studies on Alcohol*, **50**, 541–51.

Giancola, P. R. (2000). Executive functioning: A conceptual framework for alcohol-related aggression. *Experimental and Clinical Psychopharmacology*, **8**, 576–97.

Giancola, P. R. (2006). Influence of subjective intoxication, breath alcohol concentration, and expectancies on the alcohol-aggression relationship. *Alcoholism: Clinical and Experimental Research*, **30**, 844–50.

Giancola, P. R., Godlaski, A. J. & Parrott, D. J. (2005). "So I can't blame the booze?" Dispositional aggressivity negates the moderating effects of expectancies on alcohol-related aggression. *Journal of Studies on Alcohol*, **66**, 815–24.

Giancola, P. R., Martin, C. S., Tarter, R. E. *et al.* (1996). Executive cognitive functioning and aggressive behaviour in preadolescent boys at high risk for substance abuse/dependence. *Journal of Studies on Alcohol*, **57**, 352–9.

Golden, C. J., Jackson, M. L., Peterson-Rohne, A. & Gontkovsky, S. T. (1996). Neuropsychological correlates of violence and aggression: A review of the clinical literature. *Aggression and Violent Behaviour*, **1**, 3–25.

Goldman, M. S., Christiansen, B. A. & Brown, S. A. (1987). *Alcohol Expectancy Questionnaire – Adolescent Form*. Odessa, FL: Psychological Assessment Resources, Inc.

Goldman M. S., Del Boca, F. K. & Darkes, J. (1999). Alcohol expectancy theory: The application of cognitive neuroscience. In K. E. Leonard & H. T. Blane (eds), *Psychological Theories of Drinking and Alcoholism* (2nd edn, pp. 203–46). New York: Guilford.

Graham, K., Leonard, K. E., Room, R. *et al.* (1998). Current directions in research on understanding and preventing intoxicated aggression. *Addiction*, **93**, 659–76.

Haggård-Grann, U., Hallqvist, J., Långström, N. & Möller, J. (2006). The role of alcohol and drugs in triggering criminal violence: a case cross-over study. *Addiction*, **101**, 100–8.

Hawkins, J. D., Catalano, R. F. & Miller, J. Y. (1992). Risk and protective factors for alcohol and other drug problems in adolescence and early adulthood: Implications for substance abuse prevention. *Psychological Bulletin*, **112**, 64–105.

Hoaken, P. N. S. & Pihl, R. O. (2000). The effects of alcohol intoxication on aggressive responses in men and women. *Alcohol and Alcoholism*, **35**, 471–7.

Hoaken, P. N. S., Shaughnessy, V. K. & Pihl, R. O. (2003). Executive cognitive function and aggression: is it an issue of impulsivity?*Aggressive Behavior*, **29**, 15–30.

Howard, R. (2006). How is personality disorder linked to dangerousness? A putative role for early-onset alcohol abuse. *Medical Hypotheses*, **67**, 702–708.

Huband, N., McMurran, M., Evans, C., & Duggan, C. (2007). Social problem solving plus psychoeducation for adults with personality disorder: a pragmatic randomised clinical trial. *British Journal of Psychiatry*, **190**, 307–13.

Josephs, R. A. & Steele, C. M. (1990). The two faces of alcohol myopia: attentional mediation of psychological stress. *Journal of Abnormal Psychology*, **99**, 115–26.

Jones, B. T., Corbin, W. & Fromme, K. (2001). A review of expectancy theory and alcohol consumption. *Addiction*, **96**, 57–72.

Lang, A.E. & Sibrel, P.A. (1989). Psychological perspectives on alcohol consumption and interpersonal aggression. *Criminal Justice and Behavior*, **16**, 299–324.

Lang, E., Stockwell, T., Rydon, P. & Lockwood, A. (1995). Drinking settings and problems of intoxication. *Addiction Research*, **3**, 141–9.

Le Blanc, M. (1994). Family, school, delinquency, and criminality: The predictive power of an elaborated social control theory for males. *Criminal Behaviour and Mental Health*, **4**, 101–17.

Leigh, B. C. (1987). Beliefs about the effects of alcohol on self and others. *Journal of Studies on Alcohol*, **48**, 467–75.

Leigh, B. C. & Stacy, A. W. (2004). Alcohol expectancies and drinking in different age groups. *Addiction*, **99**, 215–27.

Lindqvist, P. (1991). Homicides committed by abusers of alcohol and illicit drugs. *British Journal of Addiction*, **86**, 321–6.

Lipton, D. S., Pearson, F. S., Cleland, C. M. & Yee, D. (2002a). The effects of therapeutic communities and milieu therapy on recidivism. In J. McGuire (ed.), *Offender Rehabilitation and Treatment: Effective Programmes and Policies to Reduce Re-offending* (pp. 39–77). Chichester: John Wiley & Sons.

Lipton, D. S., Pearson, F. S., Cleland, C. M. & Yee, D. (2002b). The effectiveness of cognitive-behavioural treatment methods on offender recidivism. In J. McGuire (ed), *Offender Rehabilitation and Treatment: Effective Programmes and Policies to Reduce Re-offending* (pp. 79–112). Chichester: John Wiley & Sons.

Mahoney, M.J. & Thoresen, C.E. (1974). *Self-control: Power to the Person*. Monterey, CA: Brookes/Cole.

Matthys, W. & Lochman, J.E. (2005). Social problem solving in aggressive children. In M. McMurran & J. McGuire (eds), *Social Problem Solving and Offending: Evidence, Evaluation, and Evolution* (pp. 51–66). Chichester: John Wiley & Sons.

McMurran, M. (1996). Substance use and delinquency. In C. R. Hollin & K. Howells (eds), *Clinical Approaches to Working with Young Offenders* (pp. 209–35). Chichester: John Wiley & Sons.

McMurran, M. (1997). Outcome expectancies: an important link between substance use and crime? In S. Redondo, V. Garrido, J. Pérez & R. Barbaret (eds), *Advances in Psychology and Law* (pp. 312–21). Berlin: De Gruyter.

McMurran, M. (2002). Alcohol, aggression, and violence. In J. McGuire (ed.), *Offender Rehabilitation and Treatment: Effective Programmes and Policies to Reduce Reoffending* (pp. 221–43). Chichester: John Wiley & Sons.

McMurran, M. (2006). Drinking, violence, and prisoners' health. *International Journal of Prisoner Health*, **1**, 25–9.

McMurran, M. (2007). The relationships between alcohol-aggression proneness, general alcohol expectancies, drinking, and alcohol-related violence in adult male prisoners. *Psychology, Crime and Law*, **13**, 275–284.

McMurran, M., Blair, M. & Egan, V. (2002). An investigation of the correlations between aggression, impulsiveness, social problem-solving, and alcohol use. *Aggressive Behavior*, **28**, 439–45.

McMurran, M. & Cusens, B. (2003). Controlling alcohol-related violence: a treatment programme. *Criminal Behaviour and Mental Health*, **13**, 59–76.

McMurran, M., Egan, V., Cusens, B. *et al.* (2006). The Alcohol-Related Aggression Questionnaire. *Addiction Research and Theory*, **14**, 323–43.

McMurran, M., Egan, V. & Duggan, C. (2005). Stop & Think! Social problem- solving therapy with personality disordered offenders. In M. McMurran & J. McGuire (eds), *Social Problem Solving and Offending: Evidence, Evaluation, and Evolution* (pp. 207–21). Chichester: John Wiley & Sons.

Pihl, R. O. & Hoaken, P. N. S. (1997). Clinical correlates and predictors of violence in patients with substance use disorders. *Psychiatric Annals*, **27**, 735–40.

Pihl, R. O. & Hoaken, P. N. S. (2002). Biological bases of addiction and aggression in close relationships. In C. Wekerle & A.-M. Wall (eds). *The Violence and Addiction Equation* (pp. 25–43). New York: Brunner-Routledge.

Quigley, B. M., Corbett, A. B. & Tedeschi, J. T. (2002). Desired image of power, alcohol expectancies, and alcohol-related aggression. *Psychology of Addictive Behavior*, **16**, 318–24.

Ramadan, R. & McMurran, M. (2005). Alcohol and aggression: gender differences in their relationships with impulsiveness, sensation seeking and social problem solving. *Journal of Substance Use*, **10**, 215–24.

Richardson, A. & Budd, T. (2003). Young adults, alcohol, crime, and disorder. *Criminal Behaviourand Mental Health*, **13**, 5–17.

Robins, S. & Novaco, R. (1999). Systems conceptualization and treatment of anger. *Journal of Clinical Psychology*, **55**, 325–37.

Room, R. & Rossow, I. (2001). The share of violence attributable to drinking. *Journal of Substance Use*, **4**, 218–28.

Shaw, J., Hunt, I. M., Flynn, S. *et al.* (2006). The role of alcohol and drugs in homicides in England and Wales. *Addiction*, **101**, 1117–24.

Singleton, N., Farrell. M. & Meltzer, H. (1999). *Substance Misuse among Prisoners in England & Wales*. London: Office for National Statistics.

Slaby, R. G. & Guerra, N. G. (1988). Cognitive mediators of aggression in adolescent offenders: 1. Assessment. *Developmental Psychology*, **24**, 580–8.

Solomon, D. A. & Molloy, P. F. (1992). Alcohol, head injury, and neuropsychological function. *Neuropsychological Review*, **3**, 249–80.

Steele, C. M. & Josephs, R. A. (1990). Alcohol myopia: its prized and dangerous effects. *American Psychologist*, **45**, 921–33.

Walters, G. D. (1998). *Changing Lives of Crime and Drugs*. Chichester: John Wiley & Sons.

Welte, J. W. & Wieczorek, W. F. (1999). Alcohol, intelligence, and violent crime in young males. *Journal of Substance Abuse*, **10**, 309–19.

White, J. L., Moffitt, T. E., Caspi, A. *et al.* (1994). Measuring impulsivity and examining its relationship to delinquency. *Journal of Abnormal Psychology*, **103**, 192–205.

World Health Organisation (2002). *World Report on Violence and Health*. Geneva: WHO.

Young, R. McD. & Oei, T. P. S. (1996). *Drinking Expectancy Profile: Test Manual*. Brisbane, Australia: The University of Queensland.

Zelazo, P. D., Carter, A., Reznick, J. S. & Frye, D. (1997). Early development of executive function: A problem-solving framework. *Review of General Psychology*, **1**, 198–226.

Zhang, L., Welte, J.W. & Wieczorek, W.W. (2002). The role of aggression-related alcohol expectancies in explaining the link between alcohol and violent behavior. *Substance Use and Misuse*, **37**, 457–71.

Chapter 13

THE COGNITION OF DOMESTIC ABUSERS: EXPLANATIONS, EVIDENCE AND TREATMENT

ELIZABETH GILCHRIST

University of Kent, UK

The study of specific cognitive deficits in domestic violence offenders has not received a great deal of attention, possibly due to the lack of a specific offence of domestic violence and because of debates around definitions (Gilchrist & Kebbell, 2004) but also due to the interests, level of explanation and beliefs of those centrally involved in studying this area. Following early focus on battered women, feminist researchers and victim advocates tended to approach the area from the perspective that any behaviour that was so common could not be considered to be abnormal and thus studying individual differences was inappropriate. It was considered that general societal structures, and patriarchal attitudes and concepts of masculinity across the whole of Western society were the more appropriate foci. The thinking here was that general beliefs of male entitlement and differential power between males and females both caused and maintained male violence against women.

However, it may be unhelpful to ignore differences at an individual level because across all societies the risk of abuse differs greatly from one individual to another and this needs to be explained. Further, whilst there have been debates as to whether domestic violence is a gendered concept and should only be seen as male on female violence or whether it should allow for other patterns of violence or abuse to be included, there is one helpful way of resolving this conflict. Johnson (1995) suggested a binary definition separating "common couple" violence (i.e., physical violence by either gender to resolve conflict), and "patriarchal terrorism" (i.e., a range of abusive behaviours, including, but not restricted to physical violence, primarily perpetrated by a male on an intimate female partner which reinforce male power and control).

In this chapter the term "domestic violence" will be used to encompass a range of abuses as included in the broad definitions adopted by both professionals in the United States (e.g., the power and control wheel of the Duluth model of

Aggressive Offenders' Cognition: Theory, Research and Practice. Edited by T. A. Gannon, T. Ward, A. R. Beech and D. Fisher. © 2007 John Wiley & Sons, Ltd.

intervention – Pence & Paymar, 1993) and in the United Kingdom (as identified in the "constellation of abuses" – Dobash & Dobash, 1980). The focus will be on exploring whether there are identifiable differences in cognition that distinguish domestically abusive men from nonabusive men and which might add to our understanding of why certain men are of greater risk of perpetrating domestic violence than others. The implications for intervention with domestic violence perpetrators and for future research are also briefly considered. The chapter reviews the general and cognitive correlates of domestic violence, typologies of domestic violence offenders (and potential relevance for cognitive research), attitudinal and qualitative studies of domestic violence offenders' cognition, relationship specific beliefs, experimental studies of cognition and domestic abuse, social competence and domestic abuse. Finally, implications for further study and practice are considered.

WHAT COGNITIVE FEATURES ARE IMPLICATED IN DOMESTIC ABUSE?

Whilst there has been little work conducted on cognitive processes and domestic violence specifically, a good deal of work has been conducted identifying cognitive correlates of domestic violence. Prior to reviewing this material it is important to clarify the range of cognitive features that might be implicated in domestic violence. As identified in previous work in this area (Eckhardt & Dye, 2000) cognition can be split into two different but interrelated areas: *cognitive content and structure*, the semantic content and structure of thoughts within an individual. This material can be seen as being the product of initial cognitive processing of encoding and storing. The second area of cognition is *cognitive processing*, which can be seen as encompassing the various operations by which cognitive material is learned, stored, accessed and replicated. Processing can be seen as including the initial steps of attending to information, encoding data and storing this as meaningful representations, and the later processes of response search and response enactment (Dodge & Crick, 1990). It is clear that these two phenomena are not independent of each other and indeed are highly interrelated. For example, cognitive content (and its structure) must be the outcome of early cognitive processes and later cognitive processes of response search and enactment must rely on cognitive content. However, it is of some benefit conceptually and perhaps methodologically, to maintain these distinctions.

One very important issue identified by Dye and Eckhardt (2000) is the distinction between conscious and automatic aspects of cognition. Dye and Eckhardt identified that the majority of research has focused on conscious and accessible aspects of cognition, via general attitude questionnaires. They suggest that this method is deficient in two ways:

- there is an assumption that general attitudes affect thinking concurrent with (abusive) behaviour; and
- there is little study of the more automatic aspects of cognition.

The study of cognitive processing under conditions as near as possible to the abusive or violent event, which might access more automatic features, may be one innovative way of developing knowledge as to how the links between cognition and domestic abuse operate (Eckhardt & Dye, 2000).

GENERAL DOMESTIC VIOLENCE RESEARCH AND INFERRED COGNITION

Various reviews of domestic abusers have identified certain features in early experience, social attitudes and previous behaviour that are associated with a higher likelihood of perpetrating domestic violence in certain individuals (Cunningham et al., 1998). Very early research tended to portray domestic abusers as being "ordinary men" with higher anger and impulse control problems. Poor impulse control, generally pro-offending attitudes, poor response to stress, violent backgrounds and previous antisocial behaviour have also been identified as differentiating these groups (Dutton & Painter, 1993; Sonkin, Martin & Walker, 1985). Studies have also identified proximal factors, which were more closely temporally linked to when the violence was likely to occur, for example, use of alcohol (Makepeace, 1981), stress (Riggs, O'Leary & Breslin, 1990), sexual jealousy and anger (Dutton et al., 1994; Holtzworth-Munroe, Stuart & Hutchinson, 1997). It has been suggested that men may use physical violence against a partner to defend themselves against feelings of frustration, or when they feel vulnerable or under attack (Jasinski, William & Brewster, 2004). There is also evidence to suggest that abusing men are more insecure (Kane, Staiger & Ricciardelli, 2000), hold more anxieties about inferiority, inadequacy, and abandonment (Gilchrist & Kebbell, 2004), have lower self-esteem, and greater alcohol and drug use than nonabusers. Further, some studies have found more social skills deficits for domestic abusers (e.g., poorer problem solving – Browne & Herbert, 1997).

From these studies one might infer that the cognitive content of domestic abusers might differ from nonabusers, perhaps similarly to general offenders or violent offenders, but also that the performance of social behaviours, i.e. the fifth stage of a social information processing model of aggression, response enactment, might be less skilled (Dodge & Crick, 1990).

Specific offence-supportive beliefs that have been proposed are that domestically violent men expect partners to meet a wider range of needs than others, regularly externalise blame for their anger and violence (e.g., alcohol), and lack empathy (Browne & Herbert, 1997). They may also show more displaced anger, although this is related to a lack of social control within a domestic setting as much as specific beliefs. Beliefs about control within the family are also identified as important. It has been suggested that, in families where the abuser has less control, the violence is due to frustration at powerlessness; in families where the abuser has control violence is used to maintain power; and in families where the abusers perceive a loss of control, they use violence to reassert power (Babcock et al., 1993; Prince & Arias, 1994).

The "intergenerational transmission of violence" is an often cited concept in the area of domestic violence. Broadly this suggests that boys who witness violence in their homes learn that violence is acceptable and integral to relationships (Riggs & O'Leary, 1996) Such co-occurrence of beliefs mirror those described in generally violent men (see Chapter 9 of the current volume) and may help to facilitate abusive behaviour towards intimate partners.

Additionally, those raised in violent families, do not appear to learn appropriate social competence and skills and lack the personal resources to develop positive intimate relationships (Dutton, 1998). However not all men who witness domestic violence in their family of origin go on to perpetrate domestic violence, and exposure to violence in family of origin does not always distinguish between abusive and nonabusive men (Stets & Pirog-Good, 1987). For example, researchers have suggested that many factors may not directly impact on risk of later abusiveness, but rather have an indirect effect, via attitudinal variables, on domestic violence (Silverman & Williamson, 1997).

It is important to note that recent research has identified a great deal of heterogeneity within domestic abusers. This must be incorporated into any study of domestic abusers' cognition as it is highly likely that abusive behaviours and violence in different offender subgroups are driven by different needs and serve different functions and thus have differing underpinning cognitions and processing characteristics. For example, when violence is split into instrumental and hostile/reactive aggressive acts, it is clear that the underlying thoughts and emotions are likely to vary. Instrumental aggressors are driven by goals rather than emotions whilst hostile and reactive aggressors react to provocation and hostile arousal (Cornell *et al.*, 1996). Thus some domestic abusers may differ from nonabusers only in terms of the antisocial nature of their goals whereas for others the differences might lie in biased processing following emotional arousal.

TYPOLOGIES OF DOMESTIC ABUSER: IMPLICATIONS FOR COGNITION

Many single factor theories of domestic violence have been criticised as being incomplete for various reasons, either being based on small clinical samples or being overly reductionistic and seeking to explain abuse at inappropriately low levels of analysis (Dutton, 1995). Dutton additionally criticised many of the original theories of domestic violence as being unable to explain cycles of abuse, abuse within same-sex relationships and the heterogeneity of attitudes to women within patriarchal societies. He suggested instead that a theory that incorporated aspects of early parental rejection, insecure attachment and shaming arising from poor parental discipline, leading to intimacy anger, might be more helpful in explaining the behaviours of at least the "borderline/emotionally volatile" type of domestic abuser (Dutton, 1995).

Other researchers have also argued that there is more than one type of domestic abuser with different proximal and distal features and personal characteristics. For example, Hamberger and Hastings (1986) proposed a three-group typology including an antisocial/narcissistic group, a schizoid/borderline group and a dependent/compulsive group. Later, Holtzworth-Munroe and Anglin (1991) identified a three- (then four-) subgroup typology including a generally violent/antisocial group, (a low-level antisocial was identified later – see Holtzworth-Munroe, 2000), a dysphoric/borderline passive group and a dependent (family only) group (see also Saunders, 1992 or Tweed & Dutton, 1998 for other three-group typologies). Gilchrist *et al.* (2003), in a study which incorporated the perspective of the partner, suggested a two group typology identifying an antisocial/narcissistic group, and an emotionally volatile group.

In summary, all the typologies outlined above included an antisocial or generally violent group for whom abuse is held to be more instrumental and a more emotionally volatile group whose abuse appeared to be more associated with negative emotion and impulsivity.

Whilst the above typology research has not expanded into a specific exploration of the cognitions underlying abusiveness, the general attitudes displayed appear to indicate cognitions themed by *hostility, selfishness, entitlement and narcissism* in the generally violent/antisocial abuser and *fear, dependence, anger, external blaming and jealousy* in the emotionally volatile group. Thus, such groups might differ from nonabusing men and from one another in terms of cognitive content and structure. At the very least the identification of types of domestic abuser suggests a need to be alert to potential different clusters of cognition underpinning the behaviours of different types of abuser.

DO ABUSIVE MEN HOLD ATTITUDES THAT DIFFERENTIATE THEM FROM OTHERS? WHAT DO QUESTIONNAIRES SHOW?

One area which has been the subject of a reasonable number of studies is the extent to which domestic abusers hold general attitudes about themselves, their partner's violence and gender roles in comparison to nonabusers. The research has focused on attitudes and thoughts at a variety of levels, from broad beliefs or schema to more specific and focused statements.

Given the feminist influence in the area of domestic violence, beliefs about gender have been hypothesised to be highly influential in domestic abuse. What is the evidence? A meta-analysis of research into the role of patriarchal attitudes conducted by Sugarman and Frankel (1996) did not find overwhelming support for the hypothesis that differences in patriarchal attitudes were central to understanding domestic abuse, finding instead that whilst there was evidence to suggest that domestic abusers held beliefs endorsing violence within their relationship, there was little evidence that patriarchal attitudes in themselves were influential.

Later work has also addressed the role of patriarchal attitudes with similar results. Moore and Stuart (2001) operationalised masculinity in four separate ways to explore different ways in which "masculinity" might link to domestic violence: (a) traditional masculine orientation were proposed to be more closely linked to domestic violence; (b) masculinity was viewed as a set of normative beliefs about how men and women should think; (c) masculinity was hypothesised to be related to stress of gender role conflict; and (d) a final operationalisation of masculinity was a more indirect link looking at concepts of approval of violence and need for power and control which might be indicative of higher adherence to patriarchal values. Following their review, Moore and Stuart (2001) argued that there was little utility in focusing on masculinity as a trait. They found some evidence that men's beliefs about appropriate male behaviour – but not female behaviour – may be predictive of domestic violence; moderate support for an association between gender role stress and domestic violence, and strong support that approval of marital violence and pro-violence beliefs was positively linked with domestic violence. Moore and Stuart concluded that masculinity does have a role in predicting domestic violence but this is less about how men see themselves, and more about how men *think* men *ought to behave*, the stress men feel when faced with conflict situations that challenge these beliefs, and male beliefs about appropriate power sharing within a relationship. This suggests that domestic violence might be underpinned by cognitions linked to beliefs about appropriate male behaviour and generally pro-violence beliefs but also perhaps deficits in responses available and selected by the men concerned.

Date and Ronan (2000) also studied patriarchal attitudes, more general pro-violence attitudes, social problem-solving beliefs and response selection and response enactment skills using The Bakker Assertiveness-Aggressiveness Inventory (Bakker, Bakker-Rabdau & Breit, 1978) and the Problem Solving Inventory (Heppner & Petersen, 1982). They explored the thinking in three groups derived from a larger prison sample: men convicted of a domestic assault, men who were violence to other men, and nonviolent offenders. They found that "sexist" attitudes and values, such as dominance, the distribution of financial resources, and the location of power within the relationship did not discriminate amongst their three groups but that there were differences in *assertiveness, problem solving* and *anger* between the two violent and the nonviolent group. As they identified general deficits linked to violence, rather than any specifically domestic violence differences, they suggest that focusing on antifeminist attitudes in domestic violence offenders is unhelpful. Date and Ronan also recommended that focusing on style of violence (instrumental or expressive), rather than the direction of the violence (i.e., towards a partner, or more general), might be more helpful. This work implies that domestic violence offenders should share the cognitive content and processing features of generally violent offenders (see Chapter 9 of the present volume).

However, given the specificity of some abusers' assaultative behaviour, it is suggested that further exploration of relationship specific beliefs, might be of benefit in pulling out specific features of domestic abusers. Murphy, Meyer and O'Leary (1994) compared domestically violent men with maritally discordant nonviolent and maritally satisfied nonviolent men and found that those who were violent in their relationship reported higher interpersonal dependency, higher spouse-specific dependency and lower self-esteem, but not higher levels of jealousy. Murphy, Meyer and O'Leary proposed that there were two constructs underlying these results, *perceived personal inadequacy* and *emotional investment in the relationship*. Domestically violent men were high on both whereas the nonviolent dissatisfied men were moderate on perceived personal inadequacy and low on investment. Further, the happily married men were low on perceived inadequacy and high on investment. Murphy *et al.* queried whether emotional disengagement might allow some men to deal with marital problems but that because maritally violent men continued to invest in difficult relationships they were unable to disengage and instead resorted to coercive control tactics.

An alternative interpretation of the above research might be that it is the co-existence of pro-violence beliefs, in addition to high relationship investment and perceived personal inadequacy that results in domestic abuse. Williamson and Silverman (2001) identified that beliefs about relationships, in particular *mutual responsiveness* within relationships, in addition to association with peers who verbally endorsed pro intimate abuse beliefs and behaved abusively, were predictive of violence against female partners. Similarly, O'Hearn and Margolin (2000) found that there was an interaction between attitudes and history of exposure to violence in family of origin. They found a strong relationship between early exposure to domestic violence and later domestic violence for those who held *attitudes condoning physical aggression* but no relationship between witnessed behaviour and later behaviour if there was no endorsement of violence. They emphasised the importance of the interaction between variables and suggest that, in particular, attitudinal variables such as condoning violence, which may develop from various sources including pro-violence peers, has a significant role in mediating the impact of social and interpersonal experiences.

HOW DO DOMESTICALLY ABUSIVE MEN TALK ABOUT THEIR ABUSE? WHAT CAN THIS TELL US?

This section will review some of the recent work that has been undertaken specifically on cognition and abuse within relationships, highlighting the important messages and also the limits of the work, both methodologically and theoretically. Additionally, some studies on cognition relating to conflict within relationships are also reviewed since expanding this work may shed some light on the role of these conflict-related cognitions in domestic violence.

Much of the research reviewed above looked at general attitudes and beliefs and how they varied between domestically violent and nonviolent men rather than focusing on specific types of cognitions. One approach to assessing specific types of cognition in domestic violence offenders has been the exploration of men's self-reports of their behaviours. These studies have identified key themes on which further experimental work could be based. Anderson and Umberson (2001) reviewed accounts of 33 domestically violent men, who were recruited from a domestic violence programme on a voluntary basis. Anderson and Umberson concluded that men used their accounts as texts to deny responsibility for violence and to present nonviolent identities. They suggested that in the accounts the men presented they used concepts of "masculinity" in describing their use of and response to violence, and they *minimised, denied and blamed* gender concepts in order to do this. That is, the men made recourse to culturally accepted negative stereotypes of women and culturally acceptable concepts around parenting and masculinity, being critical of their partners' parenting and interaction styles and claiming to feel emasculated by their partners' behaviour.

Reitz (1999) conducted a similar study exploring themes within men's accounts of their domestic violence. They analysed interviews of nine domestic violence men, again volunteers from a batterer programme, using a phenomenological approach and conducting open-ended interviews. Reitz found that the men reported that their abuse occurred when they thought that their partner was "doing something bad or wrong" (p. 153). She also suggested that men framed their abuse within oppositional interactions or identities, and she identified themes of *winning and losing, being good or bad, big or little, weak or strong, adult or child, controlled or controlling and getting and giving*. Reitz suggested that, rather than focusing on managing tension within a relationship, it might be more important to explore how to reduce the conflict between oppositional labels and examine "the context of identity-in-relationship from which violence is inexorably reproduced" (p. 163).

Wood (2004) reviewed the domestic violence accounts of 22 incarcerated domestic violent men and identified four themes: *justifications, dissociations, remorse*, and *failure to identify with the abuser*. For example, lack of respect was used to justify abuse *"You ain't going to smart ass K, not if you're my woman" and "I really didn't like her tone of voice. . . I felt that I has been disrespected"* (p. 562). Some saw their violence as being limited and so they dissociated from abusers who would not limit their abuse. Others regretted their acts and stated so. Wood argued that masculinity and femininity and related concepts of entitlement enabled men to have a language to explain away their abuse and present themselves as nonviolent.

It is clear from the above studies that certain consistent themes can be identified in the accounts of abusive men and these studies provide a rich source of information as to common thinking patterns in abusive men. What is not clear is how far the cognitions reflected by these accounts, for example, that violence is normal and justifiable, responsibility should be shared, and abuse is relative, differ from that which would be given by nonabusive men if they too had to provide accounts of shameful behaviour (see Chapter 6 of the present volume for a discussion of this issue in relation to child abusers). The small samples and the lack of comparison groups makes it difficult to establish whether these cognitions are criminogenic and functional in the development or maintenance of domestic abuse.

DO RELATIONSHIP-SPECIFIC BELIEFS VARY BETWEEN ABUSIVE AND NONABUSIVE MEN?

There has been little questionnaire-based work, which has sought to explore *specific* beliefs about relationships and their role in abuse. However, there has been work looking more broadly at conflict in relationships and broader beliefs. Field, Caetano and Nelson (2004) undertook a large-scale study with a sample of over 1,000 respondents in an attempt to identify the role of "cognitive risk factors" in intimate partner violence. They conducted face-to-face interviews using standardised measures to assess physically violent behaviours, (using a modified version of the conflict tactics scale) and beliefs (i.e., approval of marital aggression, alcohol as an excuse, expectation of violence following alcohol use, and impulsivity) to look at the association between cognitive factors and perpetration of intimate partner violence, whilst accounting for impulsivity. Field *et al.* found that while all of the cognitive risk factors were more common in those who perpetrated domestic violence, strong *expectation of aggressive behaviour following alcohol consumption* was the best predictor of later perpetration of intimate partner violence. Respondents who endorsed this view were over three times more likely to perpetrate intimate partner violence.

Hamamci (2005) reviewed attitudinal data from 182 married men looking at their relationship beliefs and marital conflict using responses on the Interpersonal Cognitive Distortions Scale (ICDS). Hamamci identified a number of pertinent themes in the resulting data which appeared to increase the likelihood of marital conflict: *arbitrary inference* (drawing conclusions without evidence), *over generalisation* (e.g., being in a relationship always causes trouble) and *unrealistic expectations* (e.g., people should always be positive about me). *Mindreading* (e.g., knowing what a partner thinks without being told) had a negative correlation with frequency of conflict.

Exploring cognitive difference at a slightly different level, also in conflictual, but not abusive relationships, Sanford (2006) used observational techniques to study expectancy of partner behaviour within relationships and explored how this affected behaviour within the relationship. Using a sample of 72 recently married couples recruited on a self-selection basis from the community, Sanford examined the effect of expectancy of partner understanding, expectancy of negative communication and attributions in communication style on behaviour and outcome in conflict situations. Expectancies of partner behaviour reported prior to the interactions were good predictors of the respondents' own behaviour in conflictual situations and also of outcome.

One potentially interesting question to ask is whether differences exist between those in nonabusive but conflictual relationships, and those in abusive relationships? Holtzworth-Munroe and Stuart (1994) conducted a study comparing maritally violent, maritally distressed but nonviolent and maritally satisfied men. They used the Relationships Beliefs Inventory (RBI) (Eidelson & Epstein, 1982) and the Inventory of Specific Relationship Standards (ISRS) (Baucom *et al.*, 1996) to explore the beliefs held and sought to identify whether abusive men held different beliefs about the nature of relationships and how a relationship ought to work. They found that although there were differences between the nondistressed group and the distressed and abusive groups, relationship beliefs did not distinguish between the abusive and nonabusive groups.

Eckhardt and Dye (2000) identified a number of studies of general beliefs and relationship violence but also suggested that methodological flaws undermined the conclusions of many of these studies. For example they reported a study by Lohr, Hamberger and Bonge (1988) who analysed the general beliefs of domestically abusive men using the Irrational Beliefs Test (IBT) (Jones, 1968). However they did not include any comparison group and so it is again unclear how far these beliefs would differentiate the abusive men from other groups (Eckhardt & Dye, 2000). Further work that has sought to address these shortcomings (see Eckhardt, Barbour & Davidson, 1998; Eckhardt & Dye, 2000) has failed to find differences to distinguish abusive from nonabusive groups in these beliefs.

It is clear that there is further work to be done in this area, firstly to explore whether the themes identified as common to abusive men from qualitative interview studies can distinguish them from nonabusive men and secondly to explore whether other aspects of beliefs about relationships are better at differentiating conflictual from abusive men than the measures currently used. The further work should also address the methodological limitations with much of the work reported. Many of the studies are based on small samples and self-report data, and the lack of comparison groups does make interpretation of the data limited. So, can experimental studies tell us anything about the difference between domestic abusers' and nonabusers' cognition?

EXPERIMENTAL STUDIES OF COGNITION IN DOMESTIC ABUSERS

There is a body of relatively recent research that has attempted to address the methodological and theoretical limitations of the broad attitudinal studies. This work has broadened the comparison groups used and made use of more experimental techniques to explore the cognitive content and processing of abusive as opposed to nonabusive men. This research is starting to address some key issues in this area; one of the key challenges being that identified by Eckhardt and Dye (2000) of extending "investigation to the more basic question of how the maritally violent man arrives at a given cognition and how this cognitive process may relate to observable patterns of emotion and behavior" (Eckhardt & Dye, 2000, p. 143).

Attribution is one area where there has been research exploring how differential processing of material by abusive and nonabusive men might give access to latent cognitive content and illuminate how these content differences affect behaviour (Eckhardt & Dye, 2000). Holtzworth-Munroe and Hutchinson (1993) explored the attributions of maritally violent, maritally distressed nonviolent and happily married nonviolent control groups in terms of responsibility (intention, motivation and blame) and causality (locus, stability and globality). They asked the men to imagine nine vignettes related to relationship difficulties and then report (1) how far they attributed negative intent and selfish motivation to their partner and how much their partner deserved to be blamed and (2) whether the behaviour fitted with five different negative intentions, (e.g., to hurt them, make them angry etc.). They found some support for their hypotheses in that violent men attributed more negative intent to the vignettes, identifying *more selfish motivation for the reported behaviours* and also attributed more responsibility to the actors within the vignettes seeing the reported behaviour *as blameworthy*. The assessment of negative motivation and responsibility was more severe in situations of *jealousy, rejection* and *public embarrassment*, perhaps indicating that cognitions linked to being rejected or humiliated might be of paramount importance in the context of domestic violence. Holtzworth-Munroe and Hutchinson argued that further exploration of the links between attribution and behaviour was needed and also that future research should incorporate an element of emotional arousal to fully access the thinking extant concurrent to abuse.

Eckhardt, Barbour and Davidson (1998) applied a method of using articulated thoughts and simulated situations to incorporate the element of arousal and measure more effectively the cognition present in violent incidents within relationships. They used the Survey of Personal Beliefs (SPB) (Demaria, Kassinove & Dill, 1989) as a standard attitudinal measure and also a measure of articulated thoughts to explore the cognition of domestic abusers, distressed nonabusive, and nondistressed nonabusive men. All men were asked to articulate their thoughts in anger arousing and nonanger-arousing audiotaped marital conflict scenarios. Findings showed that the groups did not differ on paper-and-pencil tasks but they did vary on the thoughts articulated. When aroused, those in the maritally violent group articulated thoughts that evidenced more global irrational beliefs, specifically they *demeaned* others' value or worth, evidenced high levels of *demandingness* (i.e., absolutist demands that others act appropriately) and *magnified* the importance of the situation. They also demonstrated *dichotomous thinking* (i.e., categorising situations into one of two extremes), drew a*rbitrary conclusions* (i.e., reaching conclusions without evidence), made *hostile attributions*, and also evidenced *fewer anger controlling* statements. Dye and Eckhardt (2000) found similar results with abusive dating partners.

Moore, Eisler and Franchina (2000) studied the effect of female provocation on attribution and affective response in a sample of over 100 verbally abusive and nonabusive college males. They asked participants to listen to tapes of hypothetical dating situations which varied by level of provocation. They utilised the Conflict Tactics Scale (CTS) (Straus, 1979) to assess abusive behaviour and the Responsibility Attribution Questionnaire (RAQ) (Fincham & Bradbury, 1992) to assess how culpability was assigned generally in conflict situations. The Negative Intentions Questionnaire (NIQ) (Holtzworth-Munroe & Hutchinson, 1993) was used to assess partner specific attributions. Moore, Eisler and Franchina found that abusive males reported more *negative attribution, feelings of jealousy, rejection* and *abandonment* in medium provocation conditions. The attribution of both negative intent and responsibility was higher for abusive males in the conditions of moderate and high partner provocation, but greater under moderate partner provocation conditions. This does not appear to be explained by any ambiguity of the stimuli as both the moderate and the high provocation situations would be open to interpretation as to the meaning behind the behaviour. Additionally, they found that attribution of negative intent and responsibility increased by level of partner provocation for both groups. Under highly provocative situations both groups made negative attributions about intent and responsibility. Moore *et al.* suggested that abusive men misinterpreted the woman's intent whereas nonabusive males could make a more realistic appraisal but that under intense provocation both groups attribute responsibility and blame to the partners.

From the work of Eckhardt and colleagues and the work of Holtzworth-Munroe and colleagues, it does appear that what distinguishes abusive men from nonabusive men is their specific processing of cues in relationship conflict rather than their general attitudes. It seems perhaps that abusive men are biased in their interpretation of relationship issues and have lower thresholds with respect to these biased and blaming cognitions.

However, Moore, Eisler and Franchina (2000) suggested that the differences between abusive and nonabusive males were perhaps not focused on attribution and interpretation but rather around coping with perceived negative behaviour. They identified similarities between their findings and those of McFall (1982) who had proposed that, applying a social information processing model, attributions should affect coping responses. The work also fits with previous studies of coping in domestic violence men, for example specific studies of competence of coping found abusive men to evidence less competent coping strategies (Holtzworth-Munroe & Anglin, 1991). Thus, future research is needed to explore interaction effects between attribution and social skills.

DO ABUSIVE MEN AND NONABUSIVE MEN VARY MORE ON RESPONSE DECISION AND ENACTMENT THAN ATTITUDE AND ATTRIBUTION?

Skuja and Halford (2004) compared a sample of 30 young males who had witnessed domestic violence with a group of 30 who had not been exposed to domestic violence, to explore their communication style in a conflict situation. These groups were recorded discussing a conflictual topic with their female dating partners and on a number of relevant measures, including conflict resolution and relationship satisfaction. Conflict management was derived from observation of 10 minute discussions of conflictual topic and coded using the Rapid-KPI (Halford, Sanders & Behrens, 2000). The "video mediated recall procedure" which involved short burst video replays of the previous discussions with interruptions for cognition to be recalled and recorded and later blind coded, was used to assess participant cognition (Skuja & Halford, 2004). Skuja and Halford found that there was more abuse within the dating relationships reported by those in the group who had witnessed domestic violence in their family of origin both male to female and female to male, but that only family of origin violence in the males predicted later poor conflict management. Additionally, they discovered that the exposed men and women reported higher relationship aggression, and demonstrated more *negative communication*, were more *domineering* and displayed more *negative affect* during the study. However they found no difference in reported cognitions. Skuja and Halford suggested that, rather than being a difference between either cognitive content or structure, it was in maladaptive conflict management that the differences existed.

Feldman and Ridley (2000) conducted a study that specifically explored conflict management and communication. They recruited over 200 participants to take part in a study on conflict and resolution from both health and abuse intervention settings. They set out to explore the relationship between styles of interaction during relationship conflict, the outcome of conflicts and abuse within relationships. They used the abusive behaviour inventory (ABI) (Shepherd & Campbell, 1992) to explore previous abuse, the Communications Patterns Questionnaire (CPQ) (Christensen, 1988) to explore interaction style and the Marital Opinion Questionnaire (MOQ) (Huston & Vangelesti, 1991) to assess relationship satisfaction. They found that violent men used more *negative verbal strategies* (blame, accusation, criticisms and so on); *less mutual problem solving* behaviours (mutual discussion, compromise and expression of feeling) and *more avoidance, demanding* and *nagging* tactics, than nonviolent men. Also, the outcomes were poorer with violent men reporting more often that following the conflict at least one partner felt the issue had not been resolved and that neither felt understood. Feldman and Ridley (2000) concluded that not only do domestic violence men appraise situations differently they also respond less effectively.

Also exploring the effectiveness of the responses of abusive men, Anglin and Holtzworth-Munroe (1997) compared groups of domestic abusers, distressed nonviolent, and nondistressed, nonviolent men in their responses to conflict situations. They found that abusive men provided less competent responses. They suggested that skills at all stages of the social information processing model need to be addressed before men can change and perhaps communication and problem solving skills might be useful foci for interventions

Anglin and Holtzworth–Munroe raised some very interesting questions concerning further foci for research. Do domestically abusive men hold different goals from nonabusive men? Is getting what they want more important for abusive men whilst for nonabusive men preserving the relationship is more important? It might be that the differences in goals reflect different core beliefs so abusive behaviour is adaptive and goal congruent, even if undesirable. A further difference that might be hypothesised is that abusive men have different outcome expectancies in the sense that they believe aggression will be successful more than nonabusive men or perhaps they believe that nonabusive tactics will be less successful? Thus abusive men would be making rational decisions in the light of their expectancies and select abusive behaviour as being the better response. This would fit with the fourth and fifth stages of a social information processing model of aggressive behaviour (Dodge & Crick, 1990) such that responses that are accessible are evaluated in terms of how desirable the likely outcome following a response would be and in terms of how well the selected response could be performed. This decision making might not be conscious and thus it might be of benefit to attempt to apply techniques borrowed from the cognitive field to address these questions. In summary, both of these questions would be areas worthy of further study.

Additional to the direct problem solving skill of abusive versus nonabusive groups, Holtzworth-Munroe et al. (1997) explored wider social support behaviour in groups of domestically violent compared to distressed, but nonviolent and nondistressed, nonviolent men. They observed couples during a discussion of a personal problem of the wives and found that the domestic violence men were less positive, more belligerent and domineering, more contemptuous, disgusted and more upset by their wives' problem; they also showed more anger and were more critical. Holtzworth-Munroe and colleagues suggested that this implied that domestic violence offenders suffer from skills deficits across a number of relationship related domains. The researchers argued that, given this breadth of deficit, it is difficult to identify which aspect of the social information processing model would explain this.

IMPLICATIONS FOR INTERVENTIONS

Similarly to the review undertaken by Eckhardt and Dye in 2000, I have found that abusive men do appear to have a hostile attribution bias in relation to their relationship conflicts. They blame their partners for any problems, they hold attitudes that support the use of violence either to solve conflict and within relationships and they do evidence more negative thinking and poorer conflict-resolution skills when under conditions that replicate some aspects of an actual conflict. However, broad attitudinal differences have not been proved to separate the abusive from the nonabusive and it is unclear how the above mentioned specific cognitions link to a higher risk of abuse.

The very early responses to domestic violence involved the application of anger management programmes and techniques to address this behaviour. With these types of intervention there was a focus on increasing self-awareness and self-monitoring to avoid angry outcomes. The techniques used challenged "hot thoughts" and schema and provided alternative strategies to avoid thinking leading to anger arousal and set out to increase the individual's ability to inhibit angry physiological response (for example using competing relaxation techniques to inhibit arousal). This fell out of favour with the increase in awareness of the possibility that some or all of the offending might not simply reflect high anger and poor impulse control but rather might be controlling and controlled. This work was even seen as dangerous as, if the abuse has been misconceptualised as linking to angry thoughts when in fact it reflected a pattern of purposeful controlling behaviours, this would be dangerous for the victims as it is likely to increase skill in control rather than challenge offence-related cognitions and emotions.

More recent work, based on broadly feminist informed theory, sought to address domestic abuse by challenging biases in cognitive content, which are seen as being linked to broad and culturally supported patriarchal beliefs. One of the most influential programmes, the Duluth model (Pence & Paymar, 1993) proposes that domestic violence has at its core two complementary beliefs, linked to masculinity and patriarchy; those of entitlement and power.

Indeed, many of the cognitive-behavioural programmes developing from the Duluth model, focus on the thoughts linked to both general domestic violence and individual offending behaviour (Scourfield & Dobash, 1999) assuming that altering these beliefs will reduce the abuse. For example within an intervention of this type, the entitlement of any man to control his partner, or to have his needs served by his partner are explored and challenged, the "truth" of rigid sex role beliefs are evaluated and alternative views proposed; the cultural specificity of the views are acknowledged and the role of societal learning in the development and maintenance of these views discussed. Furthermore, for individual offenders the thoughts they held about themselves and their partners generally, and the specific thoughts and interpretations of their offending situations and their partner's behaviours and expectations around both are made explicit and explored. Many of programmes in the UK incorporate a component of addressing general beliefs and values and some also address more specific abuse-related thoughts.

Scourfield and Dobash (1999) identified a range of interventions in the UK, most of which were broadly psycho-educational interventions based on the Duluth model, but some of which were more psychodynamic in their approach. Bowen, Brown and Gilchrist (2002) also identified a range of approaches in the intervention for domestic violence in the UK but pointed out that the distinction between the cognitive behavioural groups and the feminist informed programmes may be less important in practice than previously suggested. That is, both types of programmes utilised concepts derived from feminist theories of domestic violence and techniques of anger management and behavioural change suggested by cognitive behavioural therapy (CBT).

These programmes generally hold that men are led into offending through concepts of male entitlement and appropriate gender role behaviour and that, having offended, men minimise and justify their behaviour through common techniques of neutralisation (Sykes & Matza, 1957). Men are described as making external and exculpatory attributions of blame, blaming their partners or factors such as alcohol or drugs and situational stress to avoid taking responsibility for their behaviour. Thus even with interventions which hold that cultural beliefs and societal structures are key features in domestic violence offending, there is some assumption that the thoughts of intimate abusers are relevant to their offending. The offence-supportive beliefs are held to reflect male entitlement and traditional views of masculinity and femininity. Within tools designed to address domestic violence risk two items related to cognition have been identified: "Extreme minimisation or denial or spousal assault history" and "Attitudes that support or condone spousal assault". These cognitions are linked to higher likelihood of further domestic abuse (Spousal Assault Risk Assessment – Kropp *et al.*, 1999).

In terms of the effectiveness of individual programmes, Edleson (1995) reported that success rates varied from between 53 % to 85 % and Gondolf (1997) identified that dropouts from such programmes were approximately 13 % more likely to have reassaulted their partners, thus implying some limited success for those who complete the programmes. The actual effectiveness of domestic violence offender programmes remains unclear. As has been stated elsewhere, the majority of evaluations have at best employed a quasi – experimental design (Dobash *et al.*, 1999). Also, the majority of participants in domestic violence offender programmes have been court referred and therefore represent a skewed sample and additionally face alternative sanctions if they do not complete the programme (Fagan, 1996). There is typically no random allocation of participants to treatment and no treatment conditions as it has been considered that this would be unethical and few true experiments have been conducted so the true impact of any programme is hard to judge. Overall the effect sizes calculated in terms of impact varied from between 0.02 and 0.54. The effect sizes of quasi- and true experimental evaluations were moderate when police reports of reoffending were used ($d = 0.32$), but smaller when partner report was used within a true experimental design ($d = 0.11$). (According to Cohen, 1988, an effect size of $r = 0.10$ is small, $r = 0.30$ is medium, and $r = 0.50$ is large). These results provide some evidence of the success of treatment, perhaps not as much as one would like, but these studies also emphasise the importance of appropriate research designs, comparison groups and measurements (Babcock & LaTaillard, 2000). Additionally, the work that has considered the content of the programmes as well as competing or not completing a treatment, can find no difference between feminist, CBT and other therapies in terms of outcome.

It is clear that we should not be complacent about current interventions. However it is also clear that there is limited information on which to build change. A review of characteristics of domestically violent men in the UK concluded by suggesting that the presence of "sexist" attitudes, problematic attachment styles, alcohol and mental health issues and anger suggested that attitudinal components might be appropriate targets for intervention but that abusers with particular profiles, suggesting more emotionally driven offending might also benefit from anger intervention (Gilchrist *et al.*, 2003). However, in the light of the material reviewed here, it is suggested that these proposals might be mistaken. This study shared methodological limitations of many of the reviewed studies in that it did not have a comparison group and as such the foci identified for intervention merely reflected the cognitions present within the group without evidence that these would separate them from nonabusive men and without evidence directly relating these cognitions to their abusive behaviours.

SUMMARY AND FUTURE DIRECTIONS FOR RESEARCH

From the review of current literature and research in this area, it appears few key cognitive features of domestic violence offenders have been unequivocally established. However, many further methodological and conceptual issues have been raised as issues to be addressed. Qualitative data suggests that abusive men tend to justify and minimise their behaviours and make reference to culturally available beliefs about masculinity and femininity to do this. Cognitions or the access to cognitions may alter under arousal conditions and in response to perceived provocation it is suggested that we need to employ more sophisticated methodologies to tap into these more temporally and emotionally relevant cognitions. Such methods have already been used in the areas of general violence and sexual offending, and so it is important that the domestic violence literature makes use of these methodologies. For example, the implicit association test (Greenwald, McGhee & Schwartz, 1998) could be used to identify structural features of domestic abusers' cognitions and interpretation tasks could be used to establish whether domestic abusers actually perceive and encode women's actions and communications differentially. Also, it may not just be the content of the cognition that differs but as suggested by McFall (1982) it may be at the enactment stage of processing that there are differences. It may be that we should look for differences in communication skills, conflict resolution skills, and support behaviours. Such aspects could be tested in more sophisticated ways using the "online processing" techniques as discussed previously (see review of Eckhardt and Dye's work on articulated thoughts, above) but focusing on the step after the conflict and the arousal, or perhaps looking at behavioural responses to even nonrelationship specific problem solving or communication tasks following the exposure to a relationship conflict situation.

Some key questions remain. For example, do abusive men develop a set of overarching beliefs, which then mediate their responses to novel situations in a top-down way? Do they learn a series of scripts which more directly link to previously encountered situations and then re-enact them when exposed to the same situation, or generalise them to novel but similar situations? Or, do they develop a set of idiosyncratically linked concepts which if one is activated, then the others are too, leading to increased accessibility of certain cognitions in preference to others and an increased likelihood of abusive behaviours? How far would any distortions in these areas differentiate abusive from conflictual men?

A further question raised by previous researchers in this area (Eckhardt & Dye, 2000) is whether and to what extent are any of these processes under conscious control and to what extent any differences reflect unconscious or automatic processes which are more immediate, less open to conscious control, and less easy to access both for research purposes and intervention?

As Eckhardt and Dye (2000) suggested, it will be of real benefit when well designed and theoretically informed cognitive studies are finally applied to domestic abuse. This will ensure that we can start to move beyond the question of whether there are differences in the cognition of abusers and nonabusers to start to explore how differences between unhappy but nonabusive men and unhappy and abusive men develop. It will also enable us to explore how different aspects and levels of cognition interact and finally and most importantly, the mechanism through which cognition affects domestic abuse.

REFERENCES

Anderson, K. L. & Umberson, D. (2001). Gendering violence: masculine and power in men's accounts of domestic violence. *Gender and Society*, **15**, 358–80.

Anglin, K. & Holtzworth–Munroe, A. (1997). Comparing responses of maritally violent and nonviolent spouses to problematic marital and nonmarital situations: Are the skill deficits of physically aggressive husbands and wives global? *Journal of Family Psychology*, **11**, 301–13.

Babcock, J. C. & LaTaillade, J. J. (2000). Evaluating interventions for men who batter. In J. P. Vincent & E. N. Jouriles (eds), *Domestic Violence: Guidelines for Research Informed Practice*. London: Jessica Kingsley.

Babcock, J. C., Waltz, J., Jacobson, N. S. & Gottman, J. M. (1993). Power and violence: the relation between communication patterns, power discrepancies, and domestic violence. *Journal of Consulting and Clinical Psychology*, **61**, 40–50.

Bakker, C. B., Bakker-Rabdau, M. K. & Breit, S. (1978). The measurement of assertiveness and aggressiveness. *Journal of Personality Assessment*, **42**, 277–84.

Baucom, D. H., Epstein, N., Rankin, L. A. & Burnett, C. K. (1996). Assessing relationship standards: the Inventory of Specific Relationship Standards. *Journal of Family Psychology*, **10**, 72–88.

Bowen, E., Brown, L. & Gilchrist, E. (2002). Evaluating probation based offender programmes for domestic violence perpetrators: a pro-feminist approach. *The Howard Journal of Criminal Justice*, **41**, 221–36.

Browne, K. & Herbert, M. (1997). *Preventing Family Violence*. New York: John Wiley & Sons.

Christensen, A. (1988). Dysfunctional interaction patterns in couples. In P. Noller & M. A. Fitzpatrick (eds), *Perspectives on Marital Interactions* (pp. 31–52). Philadelphia: Multilingual Matters.

Cohen, J. (1988). *Statistical Power Analysis for Behavioural Sciences* (2nd edn). New York: Academic Press.

Cornell, D. G., Warren, J., Hawk, G. *et al.* (1996). Psychopathy of instrumental and reactive violent offenders. *Journal of Consulting and Clinical Psychology*, **64**, 783–90.

Cunningham, A., Jaffe, P., Baker, L. *et al.* (1998). *Theory Derived Explanations for Male Violence Against Female Partners: Literature Review and Related Implications for Treatment and Evaluation*. London: London Family Court Clinic.

Date, A. & Ronan, G. (2000). An examination of attitudes and behaviors presumed to mediate partner abuse: A rural incarcerated sample. *Journal of Interpersonal Violence*, **15**, 1140–55.

Demaria, T. P., Kassinove, H. & Dill, C. A. (1989). Psychometric properties of the Survey of Personal Beliefs: A rational-emotive measure of irrational thinking. *Journal of Personality Assessment*, **53**, 329–41.

Dobash, R. E. & Dobash, R. P. (1980). *Violence Against Wives: A Case Against the Patriarchy*. London: Open Books.

Dobash, R. P., Dobash, R. E., Cavanagh, K. & Lewis, R. (1999). A research evaluation of British programmes for violent men. *Journal of Social Policy*, **28**, 205–33.

Dodge, K. & Crick, N. (1990). Social information-processing bases of aggressive behavior in children. *Personality and Social Psychology Bulletin*, **16**, 8–22.

Dutton, D. G. (1995). *The Domestic Assault of Women*. Vancouver: UBC Press.

Dutton, D. G. (1998). *The Abusive Personality*. New York: Guilford Press.

Dutton, D. & Painter, S. (1993). Emotional attachment in abusive relationships: a test of traumatic bonding theory. *Violence and Victims*, **8**, 105–20.

Dutton, D. G., Saunders, K., Starzomski, A. & Bartholomew, K. (1994). Intimacy-anger and insecure attachment as precursors of abuse in intimate relationships. *Journal of Applied Social Psychology*, **24**, 1367–86.

Dye, M. L. & Eckhardt, C. I. (2000). Anger, irrational beliefs, and dysfunctional attitudes in violent dating relationships. *Violence and Victims*, **15**, 337–50.

Eckhardt, C., Barbour, K. A. & Davidson, G. C. (1998). Articulated thoughts of maritally violent and nonviolent men during anger arousal. *Journal of Consulting and Clinical Psychology*, **66**, 259–69.

Eckhardt, C. & Dye, M. (2000). The cognitive characteristics of maritally violent men: theory and evidence. *Cognitive Therapy and Research*, **24**, 139–58.

Edleson, J. L. (1995). *Do Batterer's Programs Work?* Minnesota: Minnesota Center Against Violence and Abuse. University of Minnesota and Domestic Abuse Project Inc.

Eidelson, R. J. & Epstein, N. (1982). Cognition and relationship maladjustment development of a measure of dysfunctional relationship. *Journal of Consulting and Clinical Psychology*, **50**, 715–20.

Fagan, J. (1996). *The Criminalization of Domestic Violence: Promises and Limits*. Washington: US Department of Justice, Office of Justice Programs.

Feldman, C. M. & Ridley C. A. (2000). The role of conflict based communication responses. *Journal of Personal and Social Relationships*, **17**, 552–73.

Field, C. A., Caetano, R. & Nelson, S. (2004). Alcohol and violence related cognitive risk factors associated with the perpetration of intimate partner violence. *Journal of Family Violence*, **19**, 249–53.

Fincham, F. D. & Bradbury, T. N. (1992). Assessing attributions in marriage: the relationship attribution measure. *Journal of Personality and Social Psychology*, **62**, 457–68.

Gilchrist, E., Johnson, R., Takriti, R. *et al.* (2003). Domestic violence offenders: Characteristics and offending related needs. *Findings No. 217*, London: Home Office.

Gilchrist, E. & Kebbell, M. (2004). Domestic violence: current issues in definitions and intervention. In J Adler (ed.), *Forensic Psychology: Debates, Concepts, Practice* (pp. 219–45). Uffculme: Willan.

Gondolf, E. W. (1997). Batterer programs: what we know and need to know. *Journal of Interpersonal Violence*, **12**, 83–98.

Greenwald, A. G., McGhee, J. L. & Schwartz, J. L. (1998). Measuring individual difference in implicit cognition: The Implicit Association Test. *Journal of Personality and Social Psychology*, **74**, 1464–80.

Halford, W. K., Sanders, M. R. & Behrens, B. C. (2000). Repeating the errors of our parents? Family-of-origin spouse violence and observed conflict management in engaged couples. *Family Process*, **39**, 219–235.

Hamamci, Z. (2005). Dysfunctional relationship beliefs in marital conflict. *Journal of Rational-Emotive and Cognitive Behavioural Therapy*, **23**, 245–61.

Hamberger, L. K. & Hastings, J. E. (1986). Personality correlates of men who abuse their partners: A cross-validation study. *Journal of Family Violence*, **4**, 323–41.

Heppner, P. P. & Petersen, C. H. (1982). The development and implications of a personal problem solving inventory. *Journal of Counseling Psychology*, **29**, 66–75.

Holtzworth-Munroe, A. (2000). A typology of men who are violent towards their female partner: Making sense of the heterogeneity in husband violence. *Current Direction in Psychological Science*, **9**, 140–3.

Holtzworth-Munroe, A. & Anglin, K. (1991). The competency of responses given by maritally violent men versus nonviolent men to problematic situations. *Violence and Victims*, **6**, 257–68.

Holtzworth-Munroe, A. & Hutchinson, G. (1993). Attributing negative intent to wife behaviour: the attributions of maritally violent versus non-violent men. *Journal of Abnormal Behaviour*, **102**, 206–11.

Holtzworth-Munroe, A. & Stuart G. L. (1994). The relationship standards and assumptions of violent versus nonviolent husbands. *Cognitive Therapy and Research*, **18**, 87–103.

Holtzworth-Munroe, A., Stuart, G. L. & Hutchinson, G. (1997). Violent versus nonviolent husbands: Differences in attachment patterns, dependency, and jealousy. *Journal of Family Psychology*, **11**, 314–31.

Huston, T. L. & Vangelisti, A. L. (1991). Socioemotional behavior and satisfaction in marital relationships: A longitudinal study. *Journal of Personality and Social Psychology*, **61**, 721–33.

Jasinski, J., Williams, L. & Brewster, A. (2004). *Dynamics of Partner Violence and Types of Abuse and Abusers in Partner Violence: A 20-year Review and Synthesis*. Durham, NH: Family Research Laboratory, University of New Hampshire NFER.

Johnson, M. P. (1995). Patriarchal terrorism and common couple violence: two forms of violence against women. *Journal of Marriage and the Family*, **57**, 283–94.

Jones, R. (1968). *A Factorial Measure of Ellis' Irrational Beliefs System*. Unpublished doctoral thesis, Texas Technical College.

Kane, T. A., Staiger, P. K. & Ricciardelli, L. A. (2000). Male domestic violence, attitudes, aggression, and interpersonal dependency. *Journal of Interpersonal Violence*, **15**, 16–29.

Kropp, P. R., Hart, S. D., Webster, C. D. & Eaves, D. (1999). *Spousal Assault Risk Assessment: User's Guide*. Toronto (ON): Multi-Health Systems.

Lohr, J. M., Hamberger, L. K. & Bonge, D. (1988).The nature of irrational beliefs in different personality clusters of spouse abusers. *Journal of Rational-Emotive & Cognitive-Behavior Therapy*, **6**, 273–85.

Makepeace, J. M. (1981). Courtship violence among college students. *Family Relations*, **30**, 97–102.

McFall, R. N. (1982). A review and reformulation of the concept of social skills. *Behavioural Assessment*, **4**, 1–33.

Moore, T. M., Eisler, R. & Franchina, J. J. (2000). Causal attributions and affective responses to provocative female partner behaviour by abusive and nonabusive males. *Journal of Family Violence*, **15**, 69–80.

Moore, T. M. & Stuart, G. L. (2001). A review of the literature on masculinity and partner violence. *Psychology of Men & Masculinity*, **6**, 46–61.

Murphy, C. M., Meyer, S. L. & O'Leary, K. D. (1994). Dependency characteristics of partner assaultive men. *Journal of Abnormal Psychology*, **103**, 729–35.

O'Hearn, H. G. & Margolin, G. (2000). Men's attitudes condoning marital aggression: A moderator between family of origin abuse and aggression against female partners. *Cognitive Therapy and Research*, **24**, 159–74.

Pence, E. & Paymar, M. (1993). *Education Groups for Men Who Batter: The Duluth Model*. New York: Springer Publishing Company.

Prince, E. & Arias, I. (1994). The role of perceived control and the desirability of control among abusive and nonabusive husbands. *American Journal of Family Therapy*, **22**, 126–34.

Reitz, R. R. (1999). Batterers' experiences of being violent. *Psychology of Women Quarterly*, **23**, 143–65.

Riggs, D. S. & O'Leary, K. D. (1996). Aggression between heterosexual dating partners: an examination of a causal model of courtship aggression. *Journal of Interpersonal Violence*, **11**, 519–40.

Riggs, D. S., O'Leary, K. D. & Breslin, F. C. (1990). Multiple correlates of physical aggression in dating couples. *Journal of Interpersonal Violence*, **5**, 61–73.

Sanford, K. (2006). Communication during marital conflict: when couples alter their appraisal, they change their behaviour. *Journal of Family Psychology*, **20**, 256–65.

Saunders, D. G. (1992). A typology of men who batter: three types derived from cluster analysis. *American Journal of Orthopsychiatry*, **62**, 264–75.

Scourfield, J. B. & Dobash, R. P. (1999). Programmes for violent men: recent developments in the UK. *The Howard Journal of Criminal Justice*, **38**, 128–43.

Shepard, M. F. & Campbell, J. A. (1992). The Abusive Behaviour Inventory: a measure of psychological and physical abuse. *Journal of Interpersonal Violence*, **7**, 291–305.

Silverman, J. & Williamson, G. (1997). Social ecology and entitlements involved in battering by heterosexual college males: Contributions of family and peers. *Violence and Victims*, **12**, 147–64.

Skuja, K. & Halford, W. K. (2004). Repeating the errors of our parents? Parental conflict in men's family of origin and conflict management in dating couples. *Journal of Interpersonal Violence*, **19**, 623–38.

Sonkin, D. J., Martin, D. & Walker, L. (1985). *The Male Batterer: A Treatment Approach*, New York: Springer.

Stets, J. E. & Pirog-Good, M. A. (1987). Violence in dating relationships. *Social Psychology Quarterly*, **50**, 237–46.

Straus, M. (1979). Measuring intrafamily conflict and violence: the conflict tactics (CT) scale. *Journal of Marriage and the Family*, **41**, 75–88.

Sugarman, D. B. & Frankel, S. L. (1996). Patriarchal ideology and wife-assault: a meta-analytic review. *Journal of Family Violence*, **11**, 13–40.

Sykes, G. M. & Matza, D. (1957). Techniques of neutralization: A theory of delinquency. *American Sociological Review*, **22**, 664–70.

Tweed, R. G. & Dutton, D. G. (1998). A comparison of impulsive and instrumental subgroups of batterers. *Violence and Victims*, **13**, 215–30.

Williamson, G. & Silverman, J. (2001). Violence against female partners: Direct and interactive effects of family history, communal orientation and peer-related variables. *Journal of Social and Personal Relationships*, **18**, 535–49.

Wood, J. (2004). Monsters and victims: Male felons' accounts of intimate partner violence. *Journal of Social and Personal Relationships*, **21**, 555–76.

INDEX